Tragedy

Tragedy

Edited and Introduced by

JOHN DRAKAKIS
and
NAOMI CONN LIEBLER

LONGMAN
LONDON AND NEW YORK

Addison Wesley Longman
Edinburgh Gate
Harlow
Essex CM20 2JE
England
and Associated Companies throughout the world.

Published in the United States of America
by Addison Wesley Longman Inc., New York.

© Addison Wesley Longman Limited 1998

First published 1998

ISBN 0 582 20998 6 CSD
ISBN 0 582 20997 8 PPR

British Library Cataloguing-in-Publication Data

A catalogue record of this book is available
from the British Library

Library of Congress Cataloging-in-Publication Data

Tragedy / edited and introduced by John Drakakis and Naomi Conn
Liebler.
    p. cm. — (Longman critical readers)
    Includes bibliographical references and index.
    ISBN 0-582-20998-6. — ISBN 0-582-20997-8 (pbk.)
    1. Tragedy—History and criticism. 2. Tragic, The. I. Drakakis,
John. II. Liebler, Naomi Conn, 1944- . III. Series.
PN1892.T65 1998b
809.2'512—DC21   97-43677
                                                         CIP

Set by 35 in 9/11.5 pt Palatino
Produced by Longman Singapore Publishers (Pte) Ltd.
Printed in Singapore

Contents

Contents

General Editors' Preface

The outlines of contemporary critical theory are now often taught as a standard feature of a degree in literary studies. The development of particular theories has seen a thorough transformation of literary criticism. For example, Marxist and Foucauldian theories have revolutionised Shakespeare studies, and 'deconstruction' has led to a complete reassessment of Romantic poetry. Feminist criticism has left scarcely any period of literature unaffected by its searching critiques. Teachers of literary studies can no longer fall back on a standardised, received, methodology.

Lecturers and teachers are now urgently looking for guidance in a rapidly changing critical environment. They need help in understanding the latest revisions in literary theory, and especially in grasping the practical effects of the new theories in the form of theoretically sensitised new readings. A number of volumes in the series anthologise important essays on particular theories. However, in order to grasp the full implications and possible uses of particular theories it is essential to see them put to work. This series provides substantial volumes of new readings, presented in an accessible form and with a significant amount of editorial guidance.

Each volume includes a substantial introduction which explores the theoretical issues and conflicts embodied in the essays selected and locates areas of disagreement between positions. The pluralism of theories has to be put on the agenda of literary studies. We can no longer pretend that we all tacitly accept the same practices in literary studies. Neither is a *laissez-faire* attitude any longer tenable. Literature departments need to go beyond the mere toleration of theoretical differences: it is not enough merely to agree to differ; they need actually to 'stage' the differences openly. The volumes in this series all attempt to dramatise the differences, not necessarily with a view to resolving them but in order to foreground the choices presented by different theories or to argue for a particular route through the impasses the differences present.

General Editors' Preface

The theory 'revolution' has had real effects. It has loosened the grip of traditional empiricist and romantic assumptions about language and literature. It is not always clear what is being proposed as the new agenda for literature studies, and indeed the very notion of 'literature' is questioned by the post-structuralist strain in theory. However, the uncertainties and obscurities of contemporary theories appear much less worrying when we see what the best critics have been able to do with them in practice. This series aims to disseminate the best of recent criticism and to show that it is possible to re-read the canonical texts of literature in new and challenging ways.

RAMAN SELDEN AND STAN SMITH

The Publishers and fellow Series Editor regret to record that Raman Selden died after a short illness in May 1991 at the age of fifty-three. Ray Selden was a fine scholar and a lovely man. All those he has worked with will remember him with much affection and respect.

Acknowledgements

We are grateful to the following for permission to reproduce copyright material:

Allyn & Bacon, Paramount Publishing Group, for 'The Great Dramatic Forms: The Tragic Rhythm' from *Feeling and Form* by Susanne K. Langer Copyright © by Allyn and Bacon; The Athlone Press and The University of Chicago Press for Ch. 11 from *Dissemination* by Jacques Derrida, trans. by Barbara Johnson (University of Chicago Press 1981); Cambridge University Press and the translator for the essay 'Towards a Psycho-analytic Reading of Tragedy' from *The Tragic Effect* by André Green, trans. by Alan Sheridan; Cambridge University Press and the author for the essay 'Morality and aesthetics in the ritual archetype' from *Myth, Literature and the African World* by Wole Soyinka (1976); Chatto & Windus for 'Tragedy and Contemporary Ideas' and 'Tragedy and Revolution' from 'Part One: Tragic Ideas' in *Modern Tragedy* by Raymond Williams (1966); Doubleday, a division of Bantam Doubleday Dell Publishing Group, Inc. for an extract from *The Birth of Tragedy and the Genealogy of Morals* by Friedrich Nietzsche, trans. by Francis Golffing, Copyright © 1956 by Doubleday, a division of Bantam, Doubleday, Dell Publishing Group Inc.; Harvard University Press for the essay 'The Rope and the Sword' from *Tragic Ways of Killing a Woman* by Nicole Loraux, Copyright © 1987 by the President and Fellows of Harvard College; The Johns Hopkins University Press for the essay 'The Sacrificial Crisis' from *Violence and the Sacred* by René Girard, trans. by Patrick Gregory, pp. 39–58. English translation copyright © 1977 by The Johns Hopkins University Press; the author, Jan K. Kott for 'The Eating of the Gods, or The Bacchae' from *The Eating of the Gods: An Interpretation of Greek Tragedy*, trans. Boleslaw and Czerwinski (Random House, 1973); Methuen and Hill and Wang, a division of Farrar, Straus & Giroux, Inc. for the essay 'A Short Organum for the Theatre' from *Brecht on Theatre* edited and trans. by John Willett. Translation copyright © 1964 renewed © 1992 by John Willett; Pantheon Books, a division of

Acknowledgements

Random House Inc. for Ch. IV 'Images of Women in the Literature of Classical Athens' from *Goddesses, Whores, Wives and Slaves* by Sarah B. Pomeroy Copyright © 1975 by Sarah B. Pomeroy; the authors' agents on behalf of Henry & Anne Paolucci for extracts from 'Tragedy as a Dramatic Art' from *Hegel on Tragedy* (ed) Anne and Henry Paolucci (Harper Torchbooks, Harper & Row Publishers); Pluto Press for extracts from *Theatre of the Oppressed* by Augusto Boal, translated from the Spanish by Charles A. & Maria-Odilia Leal McBride; Routledge and Editions Gallimard for extracts from Ch. IV 'The Tragic Vision: Man' and Ch. V 'World Visions and Social Classes' from *The Hidden God* by Lucien Goldmann, trans. from the French by Philip Thody; Routledge and W. W. Norton & Company for 'The Splendour of Antigone' from *The Ethics of Psychoanalysis 1959–1960: The Seminar of Jacques Lacan Book VII* (ed) Jacques-Alain Miller, trans. by Dennis Porter Copyright © 1986 by Les Editions du Seuil. English Translation Copyright © 1992 by W. W. Norton, Inc.; George Borchardt, Inc. for the author, for Ch. 1 from *The Death of Tragedy* by George Steiner. Copyright © 1968 by George Steiner; Verso, The Imprint of New Left Books Ltd., for an extract from *The Origin of German Tragic Drama* by Walter Benjamin, trans. by John Osborne, pp. 102–120.

We have unfortunately been unable to contact the author, Augusto Boal, of *Theatre of the Oppressed* (Pluto Press) and would appreciate any information which would enable us to do so.

We also wish to record our thanks to the Carnegie Trust for the Universities of Scotland, for a grant which made possible the initial stages of the collaboration for this project.

1 Introduction

ANDREA: Unhappy the land that has no heroes!
[. . .]
GALILEO: No. Unhappy the land where heroes are needed.

Bertold Brecht, *Life of Galileo*

'The search for a definition of tragedy', as the Shakespearean critic
Stephen Booth astutely observes, 'has been the most persistent and
widespread of all nonreligious quests for definition.'[1] It is a search
that takes us back to Aristotle, and from there forward, through the
Renaissance, to nineteenth-century European philosophers such as
Marx, Nietzsche, Hegel and Kierkegaard, thence into the political
science of Althusser and Goldmann, the stage theory of Augusto Boal
and Antonin Artaud, the psychoanalytical theories of Freud and his
successors, especially Jacques Lacan and André Green, and the social
anthropology of Victor Turner and René Girard. Literary and cultural
critics such as George Steiner and Raymond Williams have also joined
the search, as indeed have linguistic philosophers such as Jacques
Derrida and theologians such as Reinhold Niebuhr, while playwrights
such as Bertold Brecht (himself as much a political theorist as he was
a dramatist), Arthur Miller and Wole Soyinka have all offered major
pronouncements on this the most ubiquitous of Western dramatic forms.
Some feminist writers, such as Eva Figes or Linda Bamber, have found
the genre difficult to engage with on the grounds that it privileges a
masculine ethos either by victimising women or by relegating them
to the allegedly more hospitable form, comedy, which is presumed
to afford women more positive role models. More radical forms of
feminism, however, have suggested that tragedy implicates 'woman' in
a hierarchy of discourses, the unravelling of which discloses, among
other things, the constitutive features of gendered subjectivity itself.
Indeed, as Nicole Loraux has provocatively argued, in the ancient
world, tragedy was preeminently the genre that, 'as a civic institution,
delighted in blurring the formal frontier between masculine and

feminine and freed women's deaths from the banalities to which they were restricted by private mourning'. In classical tragedy death is always violent, and it is Loraux's contention that 'men suffered from this convention no less than women. So for a while at least, a balance was reestablished between the sexes'.[2] Thus a central issue for modern critical theory involves the construction of the tragic subject as 'hero', and its definition within a range of social, political, sexual, moral, ethical, philosophical, cultural and aesthetic discourses.

Historically, tragedy is thought to have originated in a choral performance to celebrate the Greek god Dionysos, but it has evolved as the dramatic form which stages the relationship between suffering and joy in a universe which is often perceived as at best inimical, or at worst radical in its hostility to human life. It deals, above all, with the relationship between harmony and discord, which may be interpreted *inter alia* in positive terms, as Nietzsche has done when he argues that: 'The delight created by tragic myth has the same origin as the delight dissonance in music creates. That primal Dionysiac delight, experienced even in the presence of pain, is the source common to both music and tragic myth',[3] or in negative terms as the pain and anguish attendant upon an assertion of will in the face of metaphysical despair. Instances of the latter might be the claim made by I. A. Richards that 'Tragedy is only possible to a mind which is for the moment agnostic or Manichean',[4] or A. C. Bradley's neo-Hegelian dialectical account of how 'order' generates its antithesis:

> The whole or order against which the individual part shows itself powerless seems to be animated by a passion for perfection: we cannot otherwise explain its behaviour towards evil. Yet it appears to engender this evil within itself, and in its effort to overcome and expel it, it is agonized with pain, and driven to mutilate its own substance and to lose not only evil but priceless good.[5]

For Bradley tragedy is a 'painful mystery',[6] an experience articulated through the plight of the hero, which in the final instance resists analysis. That painful mystery is tied up with what it is to be 'human', a process which simultaneously recognises fatalism and elicits human fortitude in the face of irresolvable difficulty. That difficulty invariably involves suffering, which Adorno defined as 'objectivity that weighs upon the subject'.[7] It involves also an interiorising of the dynamic forces which contribute to the psychology of the human subject, and, paradoxically, an assertion of dignity set against irreparable loss. This is not the 'absolute tragedy' which George Steiner, following Schopenhauer, has recently described as the ethos in which 'it is the crime of man that he is, that he exists', but rather a 'negative ontology'[8] with some qualifications. Steiner goes on to observe:

in the theatre, more probably than in any other representational
mode, likeness, credibility, the underlying gravitational force of the
reality principle, are persistent. As they are in the Homeric epics,
which are the font of drama. Niobe has seen her ten children slain.
Her grief makes stones weep. But as it ebbs, she takes nourishment.
Homer insists on this. It is an interposition of daylit truth cardinal
also to Shakespeare. The organic is tragi-comic in its very essence.
The absolutely tragic is, therefore, not only insupportable to human
sensibility: it is false to life.[9]

It is not difficult to locate in this notion of 'nourishment' an *essential*
humanity which inevitable suffering is alleged to disclose, but which
tragedy is alleged to compensate for. It is with this inevitability of
suffering, and with the compensatory creation of the figure of the
'tragic' hero that Brecht's Galileo takes issue, implying that heroism is,
in fact, the result of a clash of determinate social forces rather than the
metaphysically inaugurated means by which the human essence reveals
its potential. At one level the 'human' is made to define itself against
those transcendental forces from which it seeks liberation, but at another
level, the challenge is to the liberal humanist notion that suffering is
itself formative. However, even this conclusion can be problematical:
as Morris Weitz has observed, no 'true, real definition' of tragedy is
possible, since the form is ever open to new historical possibilities.
Weitz insists that 'It is simply a historical fact that the concept, as we
know and use it, has continuously accommodated new cases of tragedy,
and, more important, the new properties of these new cases.'[10]
    The force of Weitz's historical argument notwithstanding, the formal
Aristotelian categories used to describe tragedy have, for the most part,
remained current although their discursive force has been transformed
over time. However we interpret the concept of *mimesis* – and the
current shift from the emphasis upon imitation to representation offers
us a case in point – the view that 'A tragedy, then, is the imitation of
an action', which is both 'serious' and has 'magnitude', and which is
'complete in itself', continues to provide the core of the representation
of tragic action. Moreover, the tragic action consists of a series of related
'incidents' which are formally organised into elements of plot involving
such processes as *peripeteia* (reversal) and *anagnorisis* (recognition).
Through these processes tragedy arouses 'pity and fear, wherewith to
accomplish its catharsis of such emotions'.[11] The overall effect is the
production of *catharsis*, which has traditionally been translated as the
'purgation' of the specific emotions of pity and fear:[12]

> The true tragic fear becomes an almost impersonal emotion, attaching
> itself not so much to this or that particular incident, as to the general
> course of the action which is . . . an image of human destiny. . . .

The spectator who is brought face to face with grander sufferings than his own experiences a sympathetic ecstasy, or lifting out of himself. It is precisely in this transport of feeling, which carries a man beyond his individual self, that the distinctive tragic pleasure resides. Pity and fear are purged of the impure element which clings to them in life. In the glow of tragic excitement these feelings are so transformed that the net result is a noble emotional satisfaction.[13]

Much controversy surrounds the concept of *catharsis* and the Aristotelian claim that tragedy is a liberating form. Clearly the 'purgation' of pity and fear and the return to some sort of psychic equilibrium may be read as a cautionary device. In this sense tragedy can be said to liberate its audience through a recognition and an articulation of those very forces which conspire to undermine civic identity. In this respect 'liberation' is perhaps a misleading term to use insofar as the freedom which it promises turns out to be a very positive recognition of human limitation, an acknowledgement and an acceptance of boundaries beyond which the heroic representative of humanity transgresses at his or her peril.

This ideological formulation of liberation, which offers the spectator the freedom to conform, is to be distinguished from Antonin Artaud's much more modern recognition of the theatre as a space which offers the *possibility* of liberation from the dead hand of romantic and early-twentieth-century reiterative social complacencies. In tragedy, when the ordered relations of a community are disrupted, the hero draws to herself or himself all of the ambiguity and crisis present in the community, in the same way that an organism fighting a disease localises antibodies at the site of infection. This is the operation of Artaud's influential analogy of theatre and plague. Artaud's argument for what he calls a 'Theater of Cruelty' springs from his objections to the vacuity of Western theatre during the first half of the twentieth century. This theatre, he believed, had long since lost touch with the momentous theatre of the ancients which was still available, in some exempla, to audiences in Jacobean England but by the twentieth century had all but disappeared in the West, supplanted by a vitiated theatre for dilettantes. He calls for a regeneration of the kind of theatre that, as he puts it, exercises a profound cruelty, not that of dismembered bodies and brutal human behaviour but one that reenacts the cruelty of the universe. Such a theatre encompasses the foundational rituals of its producing culture within the frame of the narratives that it performs. This emphasis is represented in this volume in a number of ways, from Nietzsche's account of the birth of tragedy through social anthropological accounts of the dramatisation of ritual in Northrop Frye's *The Anatomy of*

Criticism,[14] in the work of Kott, Girard and Soyinka, and the critique of those foundations to be found in Derrida.

Restraining evil and disease is as much the aim of ritual in tragedy as it is in traditional cultures. As Mary Douglas explains in *Purity and Danger*, defilement, dirt, is 'matter out of place. . . . It implies two conditions: a set of ordered relations and a contravention of that order'; 'Uncleanness or dirt is that which must not be included if a pattern is to be maintained. . . . It involves us in no clear-cut distinction between sacred and secular'.[15] But as Antonin Artaud observed, in his *The Theater and Its Double*, no communal structure has permanent immunity from such danger: 'We are not free. And the sky can still fall on our heads and the theater has been created to teach us that first of all'.[16] In so saying, Artaud aims to return Western theatre not to specific narratives of ancient Greek tragedy but to the kind of impact upon modern audiences that Greek tragedy undoubtedly had upon its own patrons. Artaud believed it was still possible to restore the mystery and the terror that Greek tragedy originally brought into the theatre, and like Kott and Brecht he found exemplary models for that drama in the gestural performances of the Eastern world.

Artaud begins from a position which, initially, appears to echo a number of nineteenth-century philosophers of tragedy. Schopenhauer, for example, had spoken about how 'In tragedy the terrible side of human life is presented to us, the wail of humanity, the reign of chance and error, the fall of the just, the triumph of the wicked; thus the aspect of the world which directly strives against our will is brought before our eyes.'[17] His perception of what was positive in tragedy is cast in the form of a negative humanism:

> At this sight we feel ourselves challenged to turn away our will
> from life, no longer to will it or love it. But just in this way we
> become conscious that then there still remains something over to us,
> which we absolutely cannot know positively, but only negatively, as
> that which does not will life. As the chord of the seventh demands
> the fundamental chord; as the colour red demands green, and even
> produces it in the eye; so every tragedy demands an entirely different
> kind of existence, another world, the knowledge of which can only be
> given us indirectly just as here by such a demand. In the moment of
> the tragic catastrophe the conviction becomes more distinct to us than
> ever that life is a bad dream from which we have to awake. So far
> the effect of the tragedy is analogous to that of the dynamical
> sublime, for like this it lifts us above the will and its interests, and
> puts us in such a good mood that we find pleasure in the sight of
> what tends directly against it.[18]

For Artaud, the delight in tragedy is generated from another source, the danger of enslavement coming not from the gods but from the cultural and psychological constructions with which modern Western humanity has deluded itself. Those constructions have their anchoring point in a structure of representations which extends right back to the Aristotelian concept of *mimesis*. In his commentary on Artaud's 'Theater of Cruelty' Derrida identifies the theological power invested in a theatre 'dominated by speech, by a will to speech, by the layout of a primary logos which does not belong to the theatrical site and governs it from a distance'. Such a theatre, whose structure is one 'in which each agency is linked to all others by representation, in which the irrepresentability of the living present is dissimulated or dissolved, suppressed or deported within the infinite chain of representations',[19] promotes in its audience an ethos of consumerism, and makes of theatre what Wole Soyinka has similarly rejected as 'a form of esoteric enterprise spied upon by fee-paying strangers'.[20] For Artaud, Derrida argues, the theatre of cruelty conducts a struggle with a tradition of logocentrism in order to return to its origins, which we may observe bears a striking resemblance to the operations of tragedy itself: 'The origin of theater, such as it must be restored, is the hand lifted against the abusive wielder of the logos, against the father, against the God of a stage subjugated to the power of speech and text'.[21] Indeed, Artaud himself argues that 'the theater is a formidable call to the forces that impel the mind by example to the source of its conflicts'.[22]

This is, however, a far cry from Schopenhauer's 'sublime', extending a tradition which effectively begins with Nietzsche, and which finds its way in different forms into a variety of twentieth-century materialist reimaginings and rewritings of tragic theory. It is also a far cry from the Aristotelian notion of *catharsis*, since the issue is not now the purgation of emotion, but rather the mobilisation of a radical energy against what Adorno identified as 'objectivity'. Thus Artaud may align with Brecht in referring the conflicts enacted in tragedy back to the human subject itself, enmeshed in webs of social, political, economic and psychological life. And yet, as Eva Figes has concluded, if in the past, 'the tragic pattern has been a way of justifying the ways of God to man', the substitution of an explicitly 'political' tradition would mean 'the development of a philosophy whereby the ends were seen to justify the means, a path with obvious pitfalls'.[23]

The difficulty which Eva Figes pinpoints is that the traditional notion of tragedy is dependent upon the concept of hierarchy which guarantees the essentially *public* nature of suffering consequent upon the act of transgression. Detached from that hierarchy suffering becomes private, having no meaning beyond the individual life of the sufferer. It is this notion of hierarchy which also guarantees the hubris of the transgressor, and a larger critical valuation of any action which is perceived as a violation of its imperatives.

The *public/private* binary has to a very considerable extent dominated much modern thinking about tragedy. In the public world the protagonist is engaged in a metaphysical struggle with some transcendent force. These are the gods, or Fate, of classical tragedy, and the struggle they initiate postulates the human as 'other', alienated from divinity, seeking constantly to wrest control for itself. At a public and political level it is not difficult to see how this dialectic might serve a variety of positions: for Nietzsche the Dionysiac eruption of energy into the sphere of Appollonian rational control is something to be celebrated; for Hegel, the self-division of the Absolute Spirit is less a matter of celebration but more a struggle in which there is both gain and loss; for Bakhtin and Brecht the radical energy which tragedy releases signals the irrepressibility of the human; while for commentators such as Jan Kott, René Girard, Victor Turner or Wole Soyinka, the process is a ritualistic cleansing of the community from those energies which threaten to undermine its social practices. In each case the protagonist is pro-active, and, with only a few exceptions, gendered as male. But in almost every case, the tragic action is initiated as a result of a crisis of authority, one which in a very real sense draws attention to the behaviour of the protagonist. It is, in short, an action which has 'magnitude', to use Aristotle's terminology. But the struggle in the *public* arena is also accompanied by a *private* struggle in the inner life of the protagonist. We may perceive this as a psychic struggle, a failure to adjust to the demands imposed by the metaphysical order itself, or by an order which stands in its place, and which imposes its own demands upon the protagonist. Or, we may perceive this as a crisis of 'character', emanating from a deficiency or 'flaw' in the psychological makeup of the tragic hero which causes such exceptional behaviour. Bakhtin perceived the discomfort emanating from this kind of division arising from modern man's uncertainty of his own actions; in his *Toward a Philosophy of the Act* he observed that:

> Contemporary man feels sure of himself, feels well-off and clear-headed, when he is himself essentially and fundamentally not present in the autonomous world of a domain of culture and its immanent law of creation. But he feels unsure of himself, feels destitute and deficient in understanding, where he has to do with himself, where he is the center from which answerable acts or deeds issue, in actual and once-occurrent life. That is, we *act* confidently only when we do so not as ourselves, but as those possessed by the immanent necessity of the meaning of some domain of culture.[24]

In tragedy generally the protagonist acts in ignorance of the larger context of his actions, and this lack of awareness is frequently folded back into psychological motivation. Acting in ignorance becomes the external manifestation of a deficiency within the character of the protagonist, thus betraying what is often labelled a 'flaw' in his inner life, his psychological makeup which effectively *causes* the tragedy. In Bakhtinian terms the tragic hero is and is not the centre of his actions, and the gulf between his ignorance and the knowledge which an audience possesses marks out the space of tragic irony. But we need also to remember that for Aristotle *action* and not 'character' is the dominant feature of tragedy.

The concept of 'tragic flaw' returns us to another Aristotelian term, one whose domestication has been a cause of some confusion: *hamartia*. We may begin here by glossing Bakhtin's phrase 'the immanent necessity of the meaning of some domain of culture' as the context of action provided by the larger phenomenon of community. If this is so, then the vilification of the tragic protagonist on account of some deficiency which he possesses, must be something other than an aversion to a strictly personal trait. We suggest that what is misrecognised as a flaw of 'character' is, in fact, a projection of something which has its roots, not in the inner psychological life of the protagonist, but in the larger domain of culture, and even in communal fear or desire. The term *hamartia* is properly glossed as 'missing the mark',[25] a phrase which answers more directly than the concept of a tragic flaw the Aristotelian insistence that *hamartia* is an action, something protagonists do and not something inherent in their 'characters'. It is possible that the transference of *hamartia* from the domain of action to that of character has something to do with a modern/postmodern insistence on domination and/or self-determination, neither of which figured very prominently in classical or early modern culture. 'Missing the mark' therefore redirects our attention away from modern modes of subjectivity and towards the issue of positionality; on the medieval and Renaissance stages, for example, *positions* were inscribed, as Robert Weimann has convincingly shown, as *figurenposition*,[26] the formal identification of a particular dramatic character with 'the actor's position on the stage, and the speech, action, and degree of stylization associated with that position'. This focuses the actor's position in relation to the audience, and points to a capability for breaking dramatic illusion, or for the more general violations of what Weimann calls 'spatial and sometimes moral positions'.[27]

This adjustment of the relation between actor and audience is of crucial significance when it comes to the question of *hamartia* since it is what the protagonist shares with the audience which is of primary importance, as opposed to the audience's submerging of its own identity in the subjectivity of the protagonist. Here what we might read as the autonomy of the tragic subject is, in fact, primarily a *relation* between the action of a protagonist and the cultural milieu of an audience. To insist that *hamartia* refers primarily to the subjectivity of the tragic protagonist is to elevate the audience to a position of moral and ethical superiority, and to miss the complex transaction which is taking place between culturally over-determined spectator and stage representation.

Equally important in this regard is the relation of *hamartia* to another central idea in Aristotle's treatise, that of *dilemma*, the positioning of protagonist, represented community and audience alike between two choices of equal value both politically and morally. If one choice is seen to be clearly better than another, if one is 'right' and the other manifestly 'wrong' in the represented circumstances, then the drama takes on the shape of simple melodrama, pitting forces clearly identifiable as 'good' and 'evil' respectively against each other, and not tragedy. The centrality of the operation of dilemma to the shape of tragedy requires that the choices a protagonist makes must be difficult ones between options equally 'right'; thus *hamartia*, 'missing the mark', is understood not as an optional and avoidable 'error' resulting from some inadequacy or 'flaw' in the 'character' of the protagonist but as something that *happens* in consequence of the complex situation represented in the drama. It is this situation and the impossible or paradoxical nature of dilemma to which the audience responds, and which precludes any 'morally superior' judgement it might otherwise make.

This means that tragedy is not of itself satirical. It may involve elements of satire, but the information which the spectator posesses renders the protagonist's *situation* ironical, and it is with this, rather than with character, that spectators may identify. What, according to Aristotle, has the greatest impact on the spectators, are events which 'appear to have a background of design',[28] and which derive a larger meaning therefrom. The ironies generated by particular situations are frequently the result of the representation of divisions within the social formation itself, and raise crucial questions of epistemology which achieve some measure of clarification only at the moment of extreme suffering or death. Thus, Oedipus's quest for knowledge, initially concerned with the plight of Thebes and his responsibilities as king, turns into a quest for individual identity and implicates his actions in a larger, supernatural design over which he manages to gain, at best, only illusory control. As the action unfolds, both protagonist and spectator are implicated in patterns of discrepant knowledge, fissures in a hitherto integrated design, which discloses the conditions of its formation. In this context irony is disclosed at that moment when the social contradictions, which it is the business of ideology to smoothe over, show through.

Repeated affirmation and celebration of the limits defined by social, political and religious domains are, in large part, the business of ritual, but these limits are only ever put into question when the ideologies which underpin ritual cease to function effectively. In one of the earliest Marxist accounts of tragedy, George Thomson shows, for example, how in the development of the formal properties of ancient Greek tragedy, what is at stake is a historic evolution from 'the mimetic rite of the primitive totemic clan' towards a secular hierarchical society. This hierarchy is a condition of the definition of tragedy for George Steiner; the form declines, he claims, when, with the rise of the urban middle class, tragedy loses its purchase on the 'public' world, and through the emergence of the novel, develops 'a literary form exactly appropriate to the fragmented audience of modern urban culture'.[29] It is to this essentially aristocratic view of tragedy that Arthur Miller's own play, *The Death of A Salesman*, and his essays 'Tragedy and the Common Man' and 'The Nature of Tragedy', as well as Raymond Williams's more extensive analysis of modern tragic form in *Modern Tragedy*, pose a challenge.

Clearly, discussion of tragedy oscillates between questions of form and content. If, as Susanne Langer observed, 'tragedy is a cadential form', a form which 'reflects the basic structure of personal life, and therewith of feeling when life is viewed as a whole', then what she calls the 'crisis' of tragic action is 'always the turn towards an absolute close' (p. 323). That absolute close is death itself, although accompanying the passage to death is what Langer identifies as a mental, emotional or moral growth of the protagonist, a growth demanded by the action. Whereas in Hegel the self-restitution of divided spirit is achieved through sublation, in A. C. Bradley's re-reading of Hegel that sublation is, through the conflicted experience of tragedy, never complete. What Langer perceives to be, among other things, the *moral* growth of the protagonist in adversity, Steiner resists in his emphasis on the non-Judaic reading of tragic catastrophe: that in classical tragedy it is manifestly *not* 'a specific moral fault or failure of understanding' (p. 145), and that the forces which determine human life 'lie outside the governance of reason or justice' (p. 145). In another version of this, Walter Benjamin notes that in tragedy 'pagan man realizes that he is better than his gods, but this realization strikes him dumb, and it remains unarticulated' (p. 112). Benjamin resists the notion that at the end of tragedy there is some restitution of the moral order, though he holds on to the notion that man is inherently moral: 'it is the attempt of moral man, still dumb, still inarticulate – as such he bears the name of hero – to raise himself up amid the agitation of that painful world' (p. 112).

We said a moment ago that discussion of tragedy oscillates between a perception of the relation between form and content. But that is only one side of the coin, albeit one which a number of commentators have chosen to emphasise. However, in focusing on the plight of the protagonist, we risk glossing over the possible response of an audience to the spectacle of suffering. For Brecht, as Raymond Williams has argued, this possible response juxtaposed suffering and affirmation:

> We have to see not only that suffering is avoidable, but that it is not avoided. And not only that suffering breaks us, but that it need not break us. . . . 'The sufferings of this man appal me, because they are unnecessary.' . . . Against the fear of a general death, and against the loss of connection, a sense of life is affirmed, learned as closely in suffering as ever in joy, once the connections are made.[30]

More recently, A. D. Nuttall has argued that, 'In the tragic theatre suffering and death are perceived as matter for grief and fear, after which it seems that grief and fear become in their turn matter for enjoyment.'[31] What it is that tragedy imitates (Aristotle's *mimesis*), and the attitude of the spectator towards that representation, are of crucial importance in this discussion, and they are not matters that admit of an easy resolution. Aristotelian *mimesis*, as Nuttall suggests, deals not in actualities but in probabilities.[32]

Georg Lukács, in his essay 'The Metaphysics of Tragedy', puts the matter a little differently when he says that 'Real life is always unreal, always impossible, in the midst of empirical life'.[33] However, Lukács goes on to suggest that tragedy is 'the becoming real of the concrete, essential nature of man'.[34] This is some way from Nuttall's insistence that tragic poetry is *made*,[35] in that its concern is not with a representation of empirical reality so much as a bringing into being 'the concrete, essential nature of man'. Lukács's concern in his essay is not so much with the probable events of the tragic action, but rather with the *essence* which tragedy discloses. In a manner which eschews a materialist reading, Lukács insists that 'Realism is bound to destroy all the form-creating and life-maintaining values of tragic drama'.[36] By contrast, Brecht insists that what the theatre represents is not essences but 'the structure of society' (p. 97). Even in classical Greek tragedy, as, for example, explicitly in the *Oresteia* and implicitly in Sophocles's Oedipus trilogy, the protagonists' offences, first and foremost, are against society. Divine power is not in these plays, as it clearly is for Lukács, an essential reality, but rather the objectified form which social prohibition takes. George Thomson, in his study *Aeschylus and Athens* (1941) offers an extended analysis of the social conditions which produced ancient Greek tragedy, and fleshes out historically Brecht's

insistence upon the social origins of all drama. Walter Benjamin's
The Origins of German Tragic Drama, by slight contrast, offers both a
historical account, which would align it to some extent with Thomson's
method, but at another level, anticipates, as Terry Eagleton has shown,[37]
certain developments in post-structuralist thinking concerning the
materiality of the signifier. Eagleton contends that Benjamin identifies
the German *Trauerspiel* as being free from what he calls 'that fetishism of
the "organic" which haunts an Eliot or Leavis'.[38] Rather, his concern is
with an ontological division between what Eagleton calls 'an expressive
ecstasy at odds with that fateful enslavement to meaning which the
language of allegory entails'.[39] Benjamin's emphasis on the 'ostentation'
of performance is coupled with a dialectical account of the history which
these plays enact: 'Bound to the court, it yet remains a travelling theatre;
metaphorically its boards represent the earth as the setting created for
the enactment of history' (p. 120). It is this gulf between tragic, and
possibly all, meaning and the material world, between the representation
in Greek tragedy of the stage as 'a cosmic topos' and the stage as 'a
space which belongs to an inner world of feeling and bears no relation
to the cosmos', that draws attention to the materiality of the signifier
and to a phenomenon which Derrida was later to explore more fully,
that of 'writing' itself.

Traditional accounts of tragedy have sought to understand its
operations as being crucial to the definition of what it is to be 'human'.
The result has been to reaffirm confidence in an indestructible human
'essence' which is thought to emerge in the face of extreme suffering.
Alain Robbe-Grillet was one of a number of writers to challenge this
'humanist' foundation of tragedy,[40] while Lucien Goldmann, remaining
within the purview of a materialist account of tragedy, but at the same
time following certain of Hegel's arguments, perceives the tragic
moment to come at precisely the historical moment when the
transcendent guarantor of structural harmony (God) ceases to inspire
confidence: 'worldly existence changes into tragedy and into the
universe of the hidden God, who is at one and the same time both
absent and present; and, as an inevitable result of this change, tragic
man ceases to be able to understand the life that he led before his
moment of conversion, and sees that all his earlier values have been
overthrown' (p. 70). It is Goldmann's contention, however, that 'facts
concerning man always present themselves in a significant pattern, and
this pattern can be understood only by explaining how it came into
being' (p. 72). This emphasis upon scientific factuality is a product
of Enlightenment rationalism, and concentrates on the question of the
formative significance of structure. Its end-point in this collection is
Augusto Boal's trenchant critique of Aristotelian tragic theory, in which
the purging of emotion (*catharsis*) is perceived as a form of political

management. To be sure, Brecht had already begun to move along this trajectory, but Boal locates the theory of tragedy much more tersely within the purview of a dialectical materialist account of theatre. At one level this debate is played out in the opposition in this selection between George Steiner's *The Death of Tragedy* and Raymond Williams's *Modern Tragedy*, the one seeking to hold on to universalist categories, while at the same time articulating an ambivalence about the nihilistic force of tragic experience, and the other seeking to situate the philosophy of tragedy historically and thereby undermining its claims to an abstract universality.

The resituation of tragedy within the purview of the social, associated in the first instance with the tradition of Marxist thought, has however taken on a different guise through an association with that line of thought which takes its cue from Nietzschean anti-rationalism. At one level, Nietzsche's quest to illuminate *The Birth of Tragedy* is a search for origins which has an obvious affinity with social and anthropological accounts. However, its celebration of a radical Dionysiac spirit does much to pave the way for an equally radical attack on the structures of representation *per se* which are to be found in feminist, deconstructive and psychoanalytic accounts of tragic experience. Nietzschean anti-rationalism, in addition to providing a philosophical basis for post-structuralist thought, directs attention to the *conditions* under which certain categories are constructed. What is frequently taken to be the Derridean undermining of the metaphysical foundations of Western thought is, in fact, a critical attempt to demonstrate precisely how those foundations are authorised and receive their validation in the first place; it is emphatically *not* an attempt to dispense with them altogether. In Derrida's case, it has to be said, however, that all forms of foundationalist thinking are subjected to critical analysis.

While it would be quite misleading to generalise, it would seem that endemic to each of these different positions is a certain structural similarity: tragedy occurs when two antagonistic forms of energy encounter each other's force in such a way that the hierarchies which hold them in place undergo radical disturbance. However, despite these appearances of similarity, there are significant differences of interpretation of the relation between these elements of tragic conflict. For example, Hegel's self-division of the absolute spirit generates a dialectical narrative whose ultimate objective is to resolve conflict. For a critic such as A. C. Bradley, Hegelian sublation is accompanied by a consciousness of irreparable loss, and it is this sense of loss, allied to a renewal of the recognition of human dignity – not so much a poetic justice but rather an attenuated recognition of the operations of justice *per se* – that has sustained traditional notions of tragedy. For Bradley, this consciousness of loss reformulates the very irrationality which the

Nietzschean celebration of Dionysiac energies foregrounds so positively. Although Nietzsche eschews a dialectical account of tragic form, the opposition between 'Apollonian' and 'Dionysiac' seems to contain all the elements of a dialectical encounter. If we transpose this structure of constitutive oppositions into another dimension, one which recognises a productive tension between the conscious and the unconscious, then we are able to bring both Freudian and post-Freudian accounts of tragedy into a clearer focus.

The Freudian unconscious is emphatically not the Dionysiac energy which Nietzsche celebrated, though the challenge to the organising principle of the ego from the anarchic libidinal force of the id appears at first glance to be similar. For A. D. Nuttall, the Freudian descent into the libidinal depths is a descent into an 'unchanging psychic world . . . like Orpheus, like Aeneas finding the way to his dead father, to the dark place under our feet'.[41] What psychoanalysis brings to the surface is an archetypal triangulated Oedipal desire, a structure which determines the lineaments of both authority and gender identity. But what Nuttall also observes, shrewdly, is that the pleasure which the formal control of tragedy affords may also be offset by something much darker, and baffling, that something 'in us which actively *desires* death and violence'.[42] The question of pleasure is one that we need constantly to keep before us, and it goes without saying that different inflections of the meaning of tragedy entail different pleasures to be derived from its operation. For Nietzsche, for example, the pleasure derived from the revelation of Dionysian energy was contingent upon the celebration of its irresistible emergence, a pleasure different from that to be derived from the Hegelian notion of aesthetic harmony consequent upon the restitution of the self-divided spirit. One suspects that tragedy could afford no pleasure for Brecht, except insofar as it could disclose to a critical spectator the historical conditions of its own construction in a manner which Brecht himself sets out to uncover in a play such as *St Joan of the Stockyards*.

Nuttall's quest is for the more difficult terrain of the pleasure we take, and continue to take, in tragedy. Psychoanalytical accounts, and those dealing more specifically with questions of gender, especially in the wake of the Lacanian re-reading of Freud, have been more inclined to view tragedy as *expressive* of particular definitions of the human, definitions which eschew generalisation for more particularised accounts of the operations of the unconscious, and/or of the engendering of the tragic subject. Lacan is concerned with 'the dialectic of desire' (p. 191), and he uses the tragedy of *Antigone* to explicate its operations. It is important not to overlook this use of classical tragedy. Elsewhere in *The Ethics of Psychoanalysis*, Lacan admits that the ecstatic praise for Dionysus involves his devotees in an activity in which they do not

'really know what they are doing', and he asks pointedly, 'Aren't Hades
and Dionysos one and the same thing?'.[43] At issue is the request for
happiness which, according to Lacan, the patient makes to the analyst,
but the latter is in the position of denying this as a possibility: 'Not
only doesn't he [the analyst] have that Sovereign Good that is asked of
him, but he also knows there isn't any. To have carried an analysis
through to its end is no more nor less than to have encountered that
limit in which the problematic of desire is raised'.[44] Lacan's concern
generally is with the signifying power of the phallus and its place in the
dialectic of desire. His distinction between comedy and tragedy hinges
on comic violations of the Law of the Father, a realisation that 'life slips
away, runs off, escapes all those barriers that oppose it, including
precisely those that are most essential, those that are constituted by
the agency of the signifier'.[45] By contrast, tragedy raises fundamentally
the question of *judgement*, and hence a recognition of limits; Lacan
continues, 'And it is because we know better than those who went
before how to recognize the nature of desire, which is at the heart of
this experience, that a reconsideration of ethics is possible, that a form
of ethical judgement is possible, of a kind that gives this question the
force of a Last Judgement: Have you acted in conformity with the
desire that is in you?'[46] For Lacan, and for André Green, tragedy *enacts*
that psychic drama, insofar as the dramatic 'scene' itself figures forth,
represents, and is a projection of, what Green calls 'that "other scene"
the unconscious' (p. 206).

It is out of that drama that the gendered human subject emerges.
If traditional accounts of tragedy have an investment in the definition
of what it is to be human, then discourses such as feminism seek to
dismantle that universalist account in the interests of reinstating an
occluded narrative. For Lacan hegemony is phallogocentric, that is to
say, power is fundamentally patriarchal in its validating structures,
deriving its authority from the phallus as signifier. However, certain
feminist re-readings, such as that of Elizabeth Bronfen, attempt to
displace the phallus from its supreme position as the legitimating source
of signification.[47] Deprived of its controlling signification, its power must
therefore be annulled. Moreover, as Sarah Pomeroy has argued, to apply
the insights of psychoanalysis to classical texts is to illuminate the
'myths of the past' using 'the critical tools of the present' (p. 216). In
resuscitating those ancient myths, she argues, Greek tragedy called into
question the traditional social values and valences exemplified in such
myths, especially where those principles govern gendered behaviour, as
in the traditions of feminine submission to masculine hierarchy, social
isolation, and a willingness to commit suicide. Nicole Loraux is
specifically concerned with the kind of death Greek tragedy requires of
its characters: death by sword or knife-wound is masculine; death by

hanging or suffocation – the closure of the voice and preservation of the intact body – 'is a woman's way of death'. The ways in which Greek tragedy represents not only such gendered codes of dying but also what occurs when these codes are violated, call into question the social constructs that inform the tragic drama of ancient Greece. Thus tragedy, even at its beginnings in Western culture, served both to reinforce and to challenge the structural principles of its producing culture.

As we noted earlier, tragedy's origins have been located historically in performances associated with ancient Dionysian ritual. For the last group of selections in this volume, tragedy remains in important ways inseparable from the concerns of ritual that constitute its foundation. Jan Kott's essay examines the vestiges in Greek tragedy of the rites of *sparagmos* and *omophagia*, the tearing and eating of the raw flesh of the sacrificial surrogate for the divine, and finds in these vestigial representations the pattern of death-and-rebirth not only of the represented god-head but, by extension, of social structure as well. René Girard retracts that extension; for him, the sacrificial surrogate substitutes not for the divine but for his own human community, whose conflicts and anxieties regarding the collapse of necessary social structures, which Girard calls the 'sacrificial crisis', are crystallised in the victim. Girard distinguishes 'sacred' or 'pure' violence – the sacrifice of such a victim – from 'impure' violence which is merely slaughter; thus the death or removal of the surrogate temporarily purges the community of violence which would otherwise destroy it. As tragedy represents this 'sacrificial crisis', the seeds of structural collapse and its redressive violence always remain immanent in the social and continually threaten to recur. Writing from the perspective of an African culture that, in his view, retains its 'belief in culture as defined within man's knowledge of fundamental, unchanging relationships between himself and society and within the larger context of the observable universe',[48] the Nigerian playwright Wole Soyinka examines the relation between tragic drama and the traditional values, both present and lost, that attend on its production in post-colonial Africa as well as in the West, and asks whether it is possible to preserve, and to perform, a drama inextricably bound to such traditional foundations in societies dominated and driven by economic concerns. Aside from the commercialisation of such performance, Soyinka objects vigorously to interpretive and theoretical interventions that have made of this experiential form a matter for debate and for academic study, and have thereby depleted tragedy of its once-powerful spiritual and emotional impact. Departing from specifically ritualistic concerns but still anchoring discussion to a representation of natural order that Soyinka fears losing, Susanne Langer, in a different but related way, reminds us that

16

tragedy's focus is always on the human within the natural community: 'man' is the subject of his own literary structures.

And yet, the issue of man's essential humanity is one which recent critical theory has done much to bring into question. The Saussurean emphasis upon linguistic process as the model for different forms of knowledge, has served to draw our attention to questions of *difference* rather than issues of identity. The resultant emphasis on discontinuity serves, in the case of Jonathan Dollimore, to point up the lineaments of a social and political realism which disclose the relationship between the internal dissonances of literature and their connection with 'social process, actual historical struggle and ideological contradiction'.[49] The difference between this position, and that of, say, Lucien Goldmann, is that the latter invests considerable energy in a totalising account of structures, which, in the wake of post-structuralism, and especially the writings of Michel Foucault, have been brought seriously into question. That radical questioning is represented in this volume in the final excerpt, from Jacques Derrida's long essay 'Plato's Pharmacy'. Here Derrida takes up the ritual elements that Artaud, Kott and Soyinka identify as crucial to tragic experience, but he aligns the question of ritual with the debate in Plato about the beneficial and harmful effects of writing itself. For Derrida, and for Plato, the *pharmakon* is an ambivalent phenomenon, simultaneously beneficial and harmful. It is this ambivalence that constitutes 'the movement, the locus, and the play: (the production of) difference. It is the difference of difference' (p. 484). As in Sophocles's *Oedipus*, or in Shakespeare's *Hamlet* or *King Lear*, the community becomes a 'body' which defines its own values through a form of violent exclusion of 'the representative of an external threat or aggression'. What Derrida calls 'the ceremony of the *pharmakos*' is therefore 'played out on the boundary line between inside and outside, which it has as its function ceaselessly to trace and retrace' (p. 488). Derrida's concern here is not so much with the *content* of this ritual activity – arguably the preoccupation of Girard, Kott, and Soyinka – but the *form* of the struggle, and what it discloses about precisely how boundaries are constructed and prohibitions articulated. We may, of course, argue that this is part of a larger Derridean project, the challenge to the exclusive efficacy of Enlightenment rationalism as the dominant mode of perception. It would also be misleading simply to emphasise the 'play' of language to which Derrida refers. Isolated from these other considerations, it becomes nothing more than a quest for an indeterminacy which is itself a domestication of a radical potential. To this extent deconstruction as a strategy designed to expose the strategic investments of all strategies, may be said to continually re-open the question of closure to which tragedy seems always impelled.

The selection which follows begins with excerpts from the writings of philosophers such as Hegel and Nietzsche, both of whom have been instrumental in shaping modern thinking. It then proceeds to take a path through materialist accounts which locate tragic experience in the social formation itself, and from thence to critiques of the role of the signifier in strategies for the demystification of the experience of the tragic. The question of whether in a secular world tragedy is at all possible is raised in the section headed 'Tradition and Innovation' by the discussion conducted between Raymond Williams and George Steiner. With the advent of Structuralism, and with the renewed interest in Freudian psychoanalytical method, the emphasis upon what we have called the materiality of the signifier has become more pronounced. The focus on tragic subjectivity constitutes a different emphasis upon material practice, and the re-articulation of the coordinates of triangulated Oedipal desire raises questions which are taken up in the section on 'Feminism and Tragedy'.

However, far from disintegrating the concept of tragedy these radical strategies serve to refocus our attention on the *ritual* basis of tragic experience. The question here is whether we are justified in perceiving tragedy as part of a larger rhythm of natural life, as the excerpt from Susanne K. Langer suggests, or whether the definitions of ritual serve, as we saw in Benjamin's discussion of the German *Trauerspiel*, to demystify the form itself. In concluding with Derrida, we raise the question of deconstruction more directly, and suggest that the concept of ritual, which has been present in all definitions of tragedy from its historical origins to the present, may itself be a 'writing', which when investigated further inscribes a radical *difference* at its core which discloses the material conditions of its own construction. We do not mean to suggest that such an account succeeds in distintegrating tragic form *per se*, rather that there are ways of locating and defining what many commentators have thought is an essentially religious, and therefore mysterious, experience. The Brecht epigraph with which we began this introduction confronts directly the question of the *need* for tragic heroism, and posits the question of whether human beings can ever feel sufficiently empowered to take control of or overcome the historical contingencies, sometimes represented as transcendent forces, in which they are enmeshed. So long as those contingencies remain beyond our grasp, then there will be a need to represent the resultant complexity in that agonistic form which we know as tragedy.

Notes

1. STEPHEN BOOTH, *King Lear, Macbeth, Indefinition, and Tragedy* (New Haven, 1983), p. 81.
2. NICOLE LORAUX, *Tragic Ways of Killing a Woman*, trans. Anthony Forster (Cambridge, Mass., 1987), p. 3.
3. FRIEDRICH NIETZSCHE, *The Birth of Tragedy*, trans. Francis Golffing (New York, 1956), p. 143.
4. I. A. RICHARDS, *Principles of Literary Criticism* (London, 1934), p. 246.
5. A. C. BRADLEY, *Shakespearean Tragedy* (London, 1904), p. 37.
6. Ibid., p. 38.
7. THEODOR W. ADORNO, *Negative Dialectics*, trans. E. B. Ashton (London, 1973), p. 18.
8. GEORGE STEINER, 'A Note on Absolute Tragedy', *Literature and Theology*, 4 (2) (July 1990), pp. 147–56.
9. Ibid.
10. MORRIS WEITZ, 'Tragedy', in *The Encyclopedia of Philosophy*, ed. Paul Edwards, 8 vols (New York, 1967; rpt. 1972), vol. 8, p. 160.
11. Ibid., p. 155.
12. Ibid.
13. S. BUTCHER, ed., *Aristotle: The Poetics* (New York, 1951), pp. 262 and 267.
14. NORTHROP FRYE, 'The Mythos of Autumn', *The Anatomy of Criticism: Four Essays* (Princeton, 1957).
15. MARY DOUGLAS, *Purity and Danger* (London, 1966), pp. 35, 40.
16. ANTONIN ARTAUD, *The Theater and Its Double*, trans. Mary Caroline Richards (New York, 1958), p. 79.
17. ARTHUR SCHOPENHAUER, *The World as Will and Idea*, trans. R. B. Haldane (London, 1883), vol. 3, p. 213.
18. Ibid.
19. JACQUES DERRIDA, 'The Theater of Cruelty and the Closure of Representation', in *Writing and Difference*, trans. Alan Bass (London, 1978), p. 235.
20. WOLE SOYINKA, *Myth, Literature and the African World* (Cambridge, 1976), p. 38.
21. DERRIDA, 'The Theater of Cruelty and the Closure of Representation', p. 239.
22. ARTAUD, 'The Theater of Cruelty', in *The Theater and Its Double*, p. 30.
23. EVA FIGES, *Tragedy and Social Evolution* (New York, 1976), p. 163.
24. M. M. BAKHTIN, *Toward a Philosophy of the Act*, ed. Vadim Liapunov and Michael Holquist (Austin, Tex., 1993), pp. 20–1.
25. Cf. NAOMI CONN LIEBLER, *Shakespeare's Festive Tragedy: The Ritual Foundations of Genre* (New York and London, 1995), pp. 42–3.
26. ROBERT WEIMANN, *Shakespeare and the Popular Tradition in the Theater*, trans. Robert Schwartz (Baltimore and London, 1978), pp. 224 ff.
27. Ibid., p. 233. See also BRECHT's discussion of the performer's relation to the audience in 'Alienation Effects in Chinese Acting', *Brecht on Theatre: The Development of an Aesthetic*, trans. John Willett (New York, 1966), pp. 91 ff., and ANTONIN ARTAUD, 'On the Balinese Theater', in *The Theater and Its Double*, pp. 53 ff.
28. BUTCHER, ed., *Aristotle: The Poetics*, p. 19.
29. GEORGE THOMPSON, *Aeschylus and Athens: A Study in the Social Origins of Drama*, 4th edition (London, 1980), pp. 165–84.
30. RAYMOND WILLIAMS, *Modern Tragedy* (London and Stanford, 1966), pp. 202–3.
31. A. D. NUTTALL, *Why Does Tragedy Give Pleasure?* (Oxford, 1996), p. 1.

32. Ibid., p. 18.
33. GEORG LUKÁCS, 'The Metaphysics of Tragedy', *Soul and Form*, trans. Anna Bostock (London, 1974), p. 153.
34. Ibid., p. 18.
35. NUTTALL, op cit., p. 24.
36. LUKÁCS, op. cit., p. 159.
37. TERRY EAGLETON, *Walter Benjamin or Towards a Revolutionary Criticism* (London, 1981), pp. 6–19.
38. Ibid., p. 7.
39. Ibid., p. 5.
40. ALAIN ROBBE-GRILLET, 'Nature, Humanism and Tragedy', *Snapshots and Towards a New Novel*, trans. Brabara Wright (London, 1965), pp. 75–95.
41. NUTTALL, op. cit., p. 49.
42. Ibid., p. 54.
43. JACQUES LACAN, *The Ethics of Psychoanalysis 1959–1960*, ed. Jacques Alain-Miller and trans. Dennis Porter (London, 1992), p. 299.
44. Ibid., p. 300.
45. Ibid., p. 314.
46. Ibid.
47. ELIZABETH BRONFEN, 'From Omphalos to Phallus: Cultural Representations of Femininity and Death', *Women: A Cultural Review*, 3 (2) (Oxford, 1992), pp. 144–58.
48. SOYINKA, *Myth, Literature and the African World*, p. 38.
49. See JOHN DRAKAKIS, ed., *Shakespearean Tragedy* (London, 1994), pp. 24 ff.

2 The Philosophy of Tragedy

Of all the dramatic genres, tragedy is thought to be the most closely aligned with the discipline of philosophy. Its concern is with the production of knowledge and the human limits to its acquisition, and also with questions of politics, ethics and spirituality. In *The Philosophy of Fine Art*, Hegel perceived drama generally as having 'to exhibit situations and the spiritual atmosphere that belongs to them as definitely motivated by the individual character, who is charged with specific aims, and which makes these an effective part of the practical content of its volitional self-identity'. In his affirmation that 'the true theme of primitive tragedy is godlike', Hegel is concerned to emphasise the *ethical* content of tragic form. He goes on to insist that the godlike or divine here does not simply mean 'religious consciousness' as such, but the substance which informs ethical life: 'the divine in its secular or world realization, the substantive as such, the particular no less than the essential features of which supply the changing content of truly human actions, and in such action itself render this essence explicit and actual' (p. 26). In his essay 'Hegel's Theory of Tragedy', A. C. Bradley offers a partial interpretation of this position, which problematises the issue of identity articulated dialectically in Hegel. Where Hegel sees in the denouement of tragedy 'a feeling of *reconciliation*' (p. 29), a restitution of identity through the process of dialectics, Bradley is more sceptical, preferring to insist on the mystery of tragedy, while at the same time invoking the moral categories of good and evil and resisting the suggestion that tragedy is moral. The philosophical context of Hegel's theory is Enlightenment thought, which privileges rationality, the very movement which Nietzsche's own anti-rationalism challenged. *The Birth of Tragedy*, by contrast, aims to offer an alternative history of the emergence of the form, and in focusing upon the celebration of the cult of Dionysus, paves the way for those agonistic accounts of tragedy concerned much less with *identity* than with *difference*. Nietzsche locates tragedy in the ritual of celebration of the cult of the Greek god Dionysus, but a secular version of the energy to which he points in *The Birth of Tragedy* has been of enormous influence within the sphere of post-structuralism generally, and particularly in relation to radical accounts of the subversive potential of tragedy. Hegel is the philosopher of harmony in this respect, while Nietzsche celebrates that energy which would undermine rationality altogether. By partial contrast, a philosopher such as Søren Kierkegaard re-reads Aristotle from the perspective of a 'modern' despair, where, as in Strindberg's famous *Preface to Miss Julie* (1888), forces such as Fate are replaced by the guilt which the hero feels as a consequence of his actions: 'the hero suffers his total guilt, is transparent to himself in his suffering of his guilt' (*Either/Or*, Part 1, p. 148). This important distinction between 'ancient' and 'modern' tragedy is that in the modern age the loss of 'substantial categories' such as 'the family, state, kindred' 'must turn the individual over to himself completely in such a way that, strictly speaking, he becomes his own creator' (Kierkegaard, p. 149). Kierkegaard chooses to focus on the tragic heroine Antigone, and to illuminate the profound nature of the tragic conflict in which she is involved, although he anticipates George Steiner in his suggestion that in the modern world 'suffering tragedy in the stricter sense has essentially lost its tragic interest, for the power that is the source of the suffering has lost its meaning' (ibid.). The question is whether there can be such a genre as 'modern tragedy' is taken up later in the section entitled 'Tradition and Innovation'.

Tragedy as a Dramatic Art*

G. W. F. HEGEL

Types of dramatic poetry and the chief phases of their historical development

Viewing for a moment the course of our present inquiry in retrospect, it will be seen that we have, *first*, established the principle of dramatic poetry in its widest and more specific characteristics, and, further, in its relation to the general public. *Secondly*, we deduced from the fact of the drama's presenting an action distinct and independent in its actually visible development the conclusion that a fully complete sensuous reproduction is also essential, such as is for the first time possible under artistic conditions in the theatrical performance. In order that the action, however, may adapt itself to an external realization of this kind, it is necessary that both in poetic conception and detailed execution it should be absolutely definite and complete. This is only effected, our *third* point, by resolving dramatic poetry into *particular types*, receiving their typical character, which is in part one of opposition and also one of mediatory relation to such opposition, from the distinction, in which not only the end but also the characters, as also the conflict and entire result of the action, are manifested. The most important aspects emerging from this distinction, and carrying it into a many-sided historical development, are the tragic and the comic, as well as the counter-balancing of both modes of comprehension, which, in dramatic poetry, become for the first time so essentially important that they form the basis of classification of the different types.

In considering more closely the nature of these distinctions we shall do well to discuss their subject-matter in the following order:

First, we must define the general principle of tragedy, comedy, and the so-called drama.

* Reprinted from *Hegel on Tragedy*, ed. with an introduction by ANNE and HENRY PAOLUCCI (New York and London: Harper Torchbooks, 1975).

Secondly, we must indicate the character of ancient and modern dramatic poetry, to the contrast between which the distinctive relation of the above-named types is referable in their historical development.

Thirdly, we will attempt, in conclusion, to examine the concrete modes, which these types, though mainly comedy and tragedy, are able to exhibit within the boundary of this opposition.

The Principle of Tragedy, Comedy, and the Drama, or Social Play

The essential basis of differentiation among the types of epic poetry is to be found in the distinction whether the essentially substantive displayed in the epic manner is expressed in its universality, or is communicated in the form of objective characters, exploits, and events. In contrast to this, the classification of lyric poetry, in its series of varied modes of expression, is dependent upon the degree and specific form in which the content is assimilated in more or less stable consistency with subjective experience, as its inwardness reveals itself. And, finally, dramatic poetry, which accepts as its centre of significance the collision of aims and characters, as also the necessary resolution of such a conflict, cannot do otherwise than deduce the principle of its separate types from the relation in which *individual persons* are placed relatively to their purpose and its content. The definition of this relation is, in short, the decisive factor in the determination of the particular mode of dramatic schism and the issue therefrom, and consequently presents the essential type of the entire process in its animated and artistic display. The fundamental points we have to examine in this connection are, speaking broadly, those phases or features in the process, the mediation of which constitutes the essential purport of every true action. Such are from one point of view the substantively sound and great, the fundamental stratum of the realized divine nature in the world, regarded here as the genuine and essentially eternal content of individual character and end. And, on its other side, we have the *personal conscious life* simply as such in its unhampered power of self-determination and freedom. Without doubt, essential and explicit truth is asserted in dramatic poetry; it matters not in what form it may be manifested from time to time in human action. The specific type, however, within which this activity is made visible receives a distinct or, rather, actually opposed configuration, according as the aspect of substantive worth or in its opposition thereto, that of individual caprice, folly, and perversity is retained as the distinctive *modus* of operation either in individuals, actions, or conflicts.

We have therefore to consider the principle in its distinctive relation to the following types:

First, as associated with tragedy in its substantive and primitive form.

Secondly, in its relation to comedy, in which the life of the individual soul as such in volition and action, as well as the external factor of contingency, are predominant over all relations and ends.

Thirdly, in that to the drama, the theatrical piece in the more restricted use of the term, regarding such as the middle term between the two first-mentioned types.

(1) With respect to *tragedy*, I will here confine myself to a consideration of only the most general and essential characteristics, the more concrete differentiation of which can only be made clear by a review of the distinctive features implied in the stages of its historical process.

(a) The genuine content of tragic action subject to the *aims* which arrest tragic characters is supplied by the world of those forces which carry in themselves their own justification, and are realized substantively in the volitional activity of mankind. Such are the love of husband and wife, of parents, children, and kinsfolk. Such are, further, the life of communities, the patriotism of citizens, the will of those in supreme power. Such are the life of churches, not, however, if regarded as a piety which submits to act with resignation, or as a divine judicial declaration in the heart of mankind over what is good or the reverse in action; but, on the contrary, conceived as the active engagement with and demand for veritable interests and relations. It is of a soundness and thoroughness consonant with these that the really tragical *characters* consist. They are throughout that which the essential notion of their character enables them and compels them to be. They are not merely a varied totality laid out in the series of views of it proper to the epic manner; they are, while no doubt remaining also essentially vital and individual, still only the one power of the particular character in question, the force in which such a character, in virtue of his essential personality, has made himself inseparably coalesce with some particular aspect of the capital and substantive life-content we have indicated above, and deliberately commits himself to that. It is at some such elevation, where the mere accidents of unmediated individuality vanish altogether, that we find the tragic heroes of dramatic art, whether they be the living representatives of such spheres of concrete life or in any other way already so derive their greatness and stability from their own free self-reliance that they stand forth as works of sculpture, and thus the lofty tragic characters of the Greeks also interpret the essentially more abstract statues and figures of gods more completely than is possible for any other kind of elucidation or commentary.

Broadly speaking, we may, therefore, affirm that the true theme of primitive tragedy is the godlike. But by godlike we do not mean the Divine, as implied in the content of the religious consciousness simply as such, but rather as it enters into the world, into individual action, and enters in such a way that it does not forfeit its substantive character under this mode of realization, nor find itself converted into the contradiction of its own substance. In this form the spiritual substance of volition and accomplishment is ethical life. For what is ethical, if we grasp it, in its direct consistency – that is to say, not exclusively from the standpoint of personal reflection as formal morality – is the divine in its secular or world realization, the substantive as such, the particular no less than the essential features of which supply the changing content of truly human actions, and in such action itself render this their essence explicit and actual.

(b) These ethical forces, as also the characters of the action, are *distinctively defined* in respect to their content and their individual personality, in virtue of the principle of differentiation to which everything is subject, which forms part of the objective world of things. If, then, these particular forces, in the way presupposed by dramatic poetry, are attached to the external expression of human activity, and are realized as the determinate aim of a human pathos which passes into action, their concordancy is cancelled, and they are asserted *in contrast* to each other in interchangeable succession. Individual action will then, under given conditions, realize an object or character, which, under such a presupposed state, inevitably stimulates the presence of a pathos opposed to itself, because it occupies a position of unique isolation in virtue of its independently fixed definition, and, by doing so, brings in its train unavoidable conflicts. Primitive tragedy, then, consists in this, that within a collision of this kind both sides of the contradiction, if taken by themselves, are *justified*; yet, from a further point of view, they tend to carry into effect the true and positive content of their end and specific characterization merely as the negation and *violation* of the other equally legitimate power, and consequently in their ethical purport and relatively to this so far fall under *condemnation*.

I have already adverted to the general ground of the necessity of this conflict. The substance of ethical condition is, when viewed as concrete unity, a totality of *different* relations and forces, which, however, only under the inactive condition of the gods in their blessedness achieve the works of the Spirit in enjoyment of an undisturbed life. In contrast to this, however, there is no less certainly implied in the notion of this totality itself an impulse to move from its, in the first instance, still abstract ideality, and transplant itself in the real actuality of the phenomenal world. On account of the nature of this primitive obsession, it comes about that mere difference, if conceived on the basis of definite conditions of individual personalities, must inevitably associate with contradiction and collision. Only such a view can pretend to deal

26

seriously with those gods which, though they endure in their tranquil repose and unity in the Olympus and heaven of imagination and religious conception, yet, in so far as they are actual, viewed at least as the energic in the definite pathos of a human personality, participate in concrete life, all other claims notwithstanding, and, in virtue of their specific singularity and their mutual opposition, render both blame and wrong inevitable.

(c) As a result of this, however, an unmediated contradiction is posited, which no doubt may assert itself in the Real, but, for all that, is unable to maintain itself as that which is wholly substantive and verily real therein; which rather discovers, and only discovers, its essential justification in the fact that it is able to *annul* itself as such contradiction. In other words, whatever may be the claim of the tragic final purpose and personality, whatever may be the necessity of the tragic collision, it is, as a consequence of our present view, no less a claim that is asserted – this is our *third* and last point – by the tragic resolution of this division. It is through *this* latter result that Eternal Justice is operative in such aims and individuals under a mode whereby it restores the ethical substance and unity in and along with the downfall of the individuality which disturbs its repose. For, despite the fact that individual characters propose that which is itself essentially valid, yet they are only able to carry it out under the tragic demand in a manner that implies contradiction and with a one-sidedness which is injurious. What, however, is substantive in truth, and the function of which is to secure realization, is not the battle of particular unities, however much such a conflict is essentially involved in the notion of a real world and human action; rather it is the reconciliation in which definite ends and individuals unite in harmonious action without mutual violation and contradiction. That which is abrogated in the tragic issue is merely the *one-sided* particularity which was unable to accommodate itself to this harmony, and consequently in the tragic course of its action, through inability to disengage itself from itself and its designs, either is committed in its entire totality to destruction or at least finds itself compelled to fall back upon a state of resignation in the execution of its aim in so far as it can carry this out. We are reminded of the famous dictum of Aristotle that the true effect of tragedy is to excite and purify *fear* and *pity*. By this statement Aristotle did not mean merely the concordant or discordant feeling with anybody's private experience, a feeling simply of pleasure or the reverse, an attraction or a repulsion, that most superficial of all psychological states, which only in recent times theorists have sought to identify with the principle of assent or dissent as ordinarily expressed. For in a work of art the matter of exclusive importance should be the display of that which is conformable with the reason and truth of Spirit; and to discover the principle of this

27

we have to direct our attention to wholly different points of view. And consequently we are not justified in restricting the application of this dictum of Aristotle merely to the emotion of fear and pity, but should relate it to the principle of the *content*, the appropriately artistic display of which ought to purify such feelings. Man may, on the one hand, entertain fear when confronted with that which is outside him and finite; but he may likewise shrink before the power of that which is the essential and absolute subsistency of social phenomena. That which mankind has therefore in truth to fear is not the external power and its oppression, but the ethical might which is self-defined in its own free rationality, and partakes further of the eternal and inviolable, the power a man summons against his own being when he turns his back upon it. And just as fear may have two objectives, so also may compassion. The first is just the ordinary sensibility – in other words, a sympathy with the misfortunes and sufferings of another, and one which is experienced as something finite and negative. Your countrified cousin is ready enough with compassion of this order. The man of nobility and greatness, however, has no wish to be smothered with this sort of pity. For just to the extent that it is merely the nugatory aspect, the negative of misfortune which is asserted, a real depreciation of misfortune is implied. True sympathy, on the contrary, is an accordant feeling with the ethical claim at the same time associated with the sufferer – that is, with what is necessarily implied in his condition as affirmative and substantive. Such a pity as this is not, of course, excited by ragamuffins and vagabonds. If the tragic character, therefore, just as he aroused our fear when contemplating the might of violated morality, is to awake a tragic sympathy in his misfortune, he must himself essentially possess real capacity and downright character. It is only that which has a genuine content which strikes the heart of a man of noble feeling, and rings through its depths. Consequently we ought by no means to identify our interest in the tragic *dénouement* with the simple satisfaction that a sad story, a misfortune merely as misfortune, should have a claim upon our sympathy. Feelings of lament of this type may well enough assail men on occasions of wholly external contingency and related circumstance, to which the individual does not contribute, nor for which he is responsible, such cases as illness, loss of property, death, and the like. The only real and absorbing interest in such cases ought to be an eager desire to afford immediate assistance. If this is impossible, such pictures of lamentation and misery merely rack the feelings. A veritable tragic suffering, on the contrary, is suspended over active characters entirely as the consequence of their own act, which as such not only asserts its claim upon us, but becomes subject to blame through the collision it involves, and in which such individuals identify themselves heart and soul.

Over and above mere fear and tragic sympathy we have therefore the feeling of *reconciliation*, which tragedy affords in virtue of its vision of eternal justice, a justice which exercises a paramount force of absolute constringency on account of the relative claim of all merely contracted aims and passions; and it can do this for the reason that it is unable to tolerate the victorious issue and continuance in the truth of the objective world of such a conflict with and opposition to those ethical powers which are fundamentally and essentially concordant. Inasmuch as then, in conformity with this principle, all that pertains to tragedy pre-eminently rests upon the contemplation of such a conflict and its resolution, dramatic poetry is – and its entire mode of presentation offers a proof of the fact – alone able to make and completely adapt the tragic, throughout its entire course and compass, to the principle of the art product. And this is the reason why I have only now found occasion to discuss the tragic mode of presentation, although it extends an effective force, if no doubt one of subordinate degree, in many ways over the other arts.

(2) In tragedy then that which is eternally substantive is triumphantly vindicated under the mode of reconciliation. It simply removes from the contentions of personality the false one-sidedness, and exhibits instead that which is the object of its volition, namely, positive reality, no longer under an asserted mediation of opposed factors, but as the real support of consistency. And in contrast to this in *comedy* it is the purely *personal experience*, which retains the mastery in its character of infinite self-assuredness. And it is only these two fundamental aspects of human action which occupy a position of contrast in the classification of dramatic poetry into its several types. In tragedy individuals are thrown into confusion in virtue of the abstract nature of their sterling volition and character, or they are forced to accept that with resignation, to which they have been themselves essentially opposed. In comedy we have a vision of the victory of intrinsically self-assured subjectivity, the laughter of which resolves everything through the medium and into the medium of such individuality.

(a) The general basis of comedy is therefore a world in which man has made himself, in his conscious activity, complete master of all that otherwise passes as the essential content of his knowledge and achievement; a world whose ends are consequently thrown awry on account of their own lack of substance. A democratic folk, with egotistic citizens, litigious, frivolous, conceited, without faith or knowledge, always intent on gossip, boasting and vanity – such a folk is past praying for; it can only dissolve in its folly. But it would be a mistake to think that any action that is without genuine content is therefore comic because it is void of substance. People only too often in this respect confound the merely *ridiculous* with the true comic. Every

contrast between what is essential and its appearance, the object and
its instrument, may be ridiculous, a contradiction in virtue of which
the appearance is absolutely cancelled, and the end is stultified in its
realization. A profounder significance is, however, implied in the comic.
There is, for instance, nothing comic in human crime. The satire affords
a proof of this, to the point of extreme aridity, no matter how emphatic
may be the colours in which it depicts the condition of the actual world
in its contrast to all that the man of virtue ought to be. There is nothing
in mere folly, stupidity, or nonsense, which in itself necessarily partakes
of the comic, though we all of us are ready enough to laugh at it. And
as a rule it is extraordinary what a variety of wholly different things
excite human laughter. Matters of the dullest description and in the
worst possible taste will move men in this way; and their laughter
may be excited quite as much by things of the profoundest importance,
if only they happen to notice some entirely unimportant feature,
which may conflict with habit and ordinary experience. Laughter is
consequently little more than an expression of self-satisfied shrewdness;
a sign that they have sufficient wit to recognize such a contrast and
are aware of the fact. In the same way we have the laughter of
mockery, of disdain, of desperation and the like. What on the other
hand is inseparable from the comic is an infinite geniality and
confidence capable of rising superior to its own contradiction, and
experiencing therein no taint of bitterness or sense of misfortune
whatever. It is the happy frame of mind, a hale condition of soul,
which, fully aware of itself, can suffer the dissolution of its aims and
realization. The unexpansive type of intelligence is on the contrary least
master of itself where it is in its behaviour most laughable to others.

(b) In considering with more detail the kind of content which
characterizes and educes the object of comic action, I propose to
limit myself to the following points of general interest.

On the *one* hand there are human ends and characters essentially
devoid of substantive content and contradictory. They are therefore
unable to achieve the former or give effect to the latter. Avarice, for
example, not only in reference to its aim, but also in respect to the petty
means which it employs, is clearly from the first and fundamentally a
vain shadow. It accepts what is the dead abstraction of wealth, money
simply as such, as the *summum bonum*, the reality beyond which it
refuses to budge; and it endeavours to master this frigid means of
enjoyment by denying itself every other concrete satisfaction, despite the
fact too that, in the impotency of its end no less than the means of its
achievement, it is helpless when confronted with cunning and treachery,
and the like. In such a case then, if anyone identifies *seriously* his
personal life with a content so essentially false, to the extent of a man
confining the embrace of his existence to that exclusively, and in the

result, if the same is swept away as his foot-hold, the more he strives to retain that former foot-hold, the more the life collapses in unhappiness – in such a picture as this what is most vital to the comic situation fails, as it does in every case where the predominant factors are simply on the one side the painfulness of the actual conditions, and on the other scorn and pleasure in such misfortune. There is therefore more of the true comic in the case where, it is true, aims intrinsically mean and empty are meant to be achieved with an appearance of earnest solemnity and every kind of preparation, but where the individual himself, when he falls short of this, does not experience any real loss because he is conscious that what he strove after was really of no great importance, and is therefore able to rise superior with spontaneous amusement above the failure.

A situation which is the reverse of this occurs where people vaguely grasp at aims and a personal impression of real substance, but in their own individuality, as instruments to achieve this, are in absolute conflict with such a result. In such a case what substance there is only exists in the individual's imagination, becomes a mere appearance to himself or others, which no doubt offers the show and virtue of what is thus of material import, but for this very reason involves end and personality, action and character in a contradiction, by reason of which the attainment of the imaged end or characterization is itself rendered impossible. An example of this is the 'Ecclesiazusae' of Aristophanes, where the women who seek to advise and found a new political constitution, retain all the temperament and passions of women as before.

We may add to the above two divisions of classification, as a distinct basis for yet *another*, the use made of external accident, by means of the varied and extraordinary development of which situations are placed before us in which the objects desired and their achievement, the personal character and its external conditions are thrown into a comic contrast, and lead to an equally comic resolution.

(c) But inasmuch as the comic element wholly and from the first depends upon contradictory contrasts, not only of ends themselves on their own account, but also of their content as opposed to the contingency of the personal life and external condition, the action of comedy requires a *resolution* with even more stringency than the tragic drama. In other words, in the action of comedy the contradiction between that which is essentially true and its specific realization is more fundamentally asserted.

That which, however, is abrogated in this resolution is not by any means either the *substantive* being or the *personal* life as such.

And the reason of this is that comedy too, viewed as genuine art, has not the task set before it to display through its presentation what is essentially rational as that which is intrinsically perverse and comes to naught, but on the contrary as that which neither bestows the victory, nor ultimately allows any standing ground to folly and absurdity, that is to say the false contradictions and oppositions which also form part of reality. The masculine art of Aristophanes, for instance, does not turn into ridicule what is truly of ethical significance in the social life of Athens, namely genuine philosophy, true religious faith, but rather the spurious growth of the democracy, in which the ancient faith and the former morality have disappeared, such as the sophistry, the whining and querulousness of tragedy, the inconstant gossip, the love of litigation and so forth; in other words, it is those elements directly opposed to a genuine condition of political life, religion, and art, which he places before us in their suicidal folly. Only in more modern times do we find in such a writer as Kotzebue the baseness possible which throws over moral excellence, and spares and strives to maintain that which only exists under a condition of sufferance. To as little extent, however, ought the individual's private life suffer substantial injury in comedy. Or to put it otherwise, if it is merely the appearance and imagined presence of what is substantive, or if it is the essentially perverse and petty which is asserted, yet in the essential self-stability of individual character the more exalted principle remains, which in its freedom reaches over and beyond the overthrow of all that such finite life comprises, and continues itself in its character of self-security and self-blessedness. This subjective life that we above all identify with comic personality has thus become master of all the phenomenal presence of the real. The mode of actual appearance adequate to what is, so to speak, substantive, has vanished out of it; and, if what is essentially without fundamental subsistence comes to naught with its mere pretence of being that which it is not, the individual asserts himself as master over such a dissolution, and remains at bottom unbroken and in good heart to the end.

(3) Midway between tragedy and comedy we have furthermore a *third* fundamental type of dramatic poetry, which is, however, of less distinctive importance, despite the fact that in it the essential difference between what is tragic and comic makes an effort to construct a bridge of mediation, or at least to effect some coalescence of both sides in a concrete whole without leaving either the one or the other in opposed isolation.

(a) To this class we may, for example, refer the *Satyric* drama of the ancients, in which the principal action itself at least remains of a serious if not wholly tragic type, while the chorus of its Satyrs is in contrast to this treated in the comic manner. We may also include in such a class the tragic-comedy. Plautus gives an example of this in his 'Amphitryo',

and indeed in the prologue, through verses given to Mercury, asserts
this fact; the declamation runs as follows:

Quid contraxistis frontem? Quia Tragoediam
Dixi futuram hanc? Deus sum: commutavero
Eamdem hanc, si voltis: faciam, ex Tragoedia
Comoedia ut sit, omnibus eisdem versibus.
Faciam ut conmista sit Tragicocomoedia.

He offers us as a reason for this intermixture the fact, that while
gods and kings are represented among the *dramatis personae*, we have
also in comic contrast to this the figure of the slave Sofia. With yet
more frequency in modern dramatic poetry we have the interplay of
tragic and comic situation; and this is naturally so, because here, even
in tragedy, the principle of subjectivity which is asserted by comedy in
all its freedom, from the first has been predominant, forcing into the
background the substantive character of the content of ethical forces.

(b) The profounder mediation, however, of tragic and comic
composition in a new whole does not consist in the juxtaposition
or alteration of these contradictory points of view, but in a mutual
accommodation, which blunts the force of such opposition. The element
of subjectivity, instead of being exercised with all the perversity of the
comic drama, is steeped in the seriousness of genuine social conditions
and substantial characters, while the tragic steadfastness of volition and
the depth of collisions is so far weakened and reduced that it becomes
compatible with a reconciliation of interests and a harmonious union
of ends and individuals. It is under such a mode of conception that
in particular the modern play and drama arise. The profound aspect
of this principle, in this view of the playwright, consists in the fact
that, despite the differences and conflicts of interests, passions, and
characters, an essentially harmonious reality none the less results from
human action. Even the ancient world possesses tragedies which accept
an issue of this character. Individuals are not sacrificed, but maintained
without serious catastrophe. In the 'Eumenides' of Aeschylus, for
example, both parties there brought to judgment before the Areopagus,
namely Apollo and the avenging Furies, have their claims to honourable
consideration vindicated. Also in the 'Philoctetes' the conflict between
Neoptolemos and Philoctetes is disposed of through the divine
interposition of Hercules and the advice he gives. They depart
reconciled for Troy. In this case, however, the accommodation is
due to a *deus ex machina*, and the actual source of such is not traceable
to the personal attitude of the parties themselves. In the modern play,
however, it is the individual characters alone who find themselves

induced by the course of their own action to such an abandonment
of the strife, and to a reciprocal reconciliation of their aims and
personalities. From this point of view the 'Iphigenia' of Goethe is
a genuine model of a play of this kind, and it is more so than his
'Tasso', in which in the first place the reconciliation with Antonio is
rather an affair of temperament and personal acknowledgment that
Antonio possesses the genuine knowledge of life, which is absent from
the character of Tasso, and along with this that the claim of ideal life,
which Tasso had rigidly adhered to in its conflict with actual conditions,
adaptability, and grace of manners, retains its force throughout with an
audience merely in an ideal sense, and relatively to actual conditions at
most asserts itself as an excuse for the poet and a general sympathy for
his position.

(c) As a rule, however, the boundary lines of the intermediate type
fluctuate more than is the case with tragedy or comedy. It is also
exposed to a further danger of breaking away from the true dramatic
type, or ceasing to be genuine poetry. In other words, owing to the fact
that the opposing factors, which have to secure a peaceful conclusion
from out of their own division, are from the start not antithetical to
one another with the emphasis asserted by tragedy; the poet is for
this reason compelled to devote the full strength of his presentation
to the psychological analysis of character, and to make the course
of the situations a mere instrument of such characterization. Or, as
an alternative, he admits a too extensive field for the display of the
material aspect of historical or ethical conditions; and, under the
pressure of such material, he attempts to keep attention alive
only through interest in the series of events evolved. To this class of
composition we may assign a host of our more recent theatrical pieces,
which rather aim at theatrical effect than claim to be poetry. They do
not so much seek to affect us as genuine poetical productions as to
reach our emotions generally as men and women; or they aim on the
one hand simply at recreation, and on the other at the moral education
of public taste; but while doing so they are almost equally concerned to
provide ample opportunity to the actor for the display of his trained art
and virtuosity in the most brilliant manner.

[...]

The Concrete Development of Dramatic Poetry and Its Types

Within the essential distinctions of conception and poetical achievement
which we have just considered the different types of dramatic art assert
themselves, and, for the first time in such association, and in so far as
their development follows either one or the other direction, attain a

really genuine completeness. We have, therefore, in concluding the present work, still to concentrate our inquiry upon the concrete mode under which they receive such a configuration.

(1) Excluding as we shall do for the reasons already given from our subject-matter the origins of such poetry in Oriental literature, the material of first and fundamental importance which engages our attention, as the most valuable phase of genuine tragedy no less than comedy, is the dramatic poetry of the *Greeks*. In other words, in it for the first time we find the human consciousness illuminated with that which in its general terms the tragic and comic situation essentially is; and after these opposed types of dramatic outlook upon human action have been securely and beyond all confusion separated from each other, we mark first in order tragedy, and after that comedy, rise in organic development to the height of their achievement. Of such a successful result the dramatic art of Rome merely returns a considerably attenuated reflection, which does not indeed reach the point secured by the similar effort of Roman literature in epic and lyrical composition. In my examination of the material thus offered my object will be merely to accentuate what is most important, and I shall therefore limit my survey to the tragic point of view of Aeschylus and Sophocles, and to Aristophanes so far as comedy is concerned.

(a) Taking, then, tragedy first, I have already stated that the fundamental type which determines its entire organization and structure is to be sought for in the emphasis attached to the substantive constitution of final ends and their content, as also of the individuals dramatized and their conflict and destiny.

In the tragic drama we are now considering, the general basis or background for tragic action is supplied, as was also the case in the Epos, by that world-condition which I have already indicated as the *heroic*. For only in heroic times, when the universal ethical forces have neither acquired the independent stability of definite political legislation or moral commands and obligations, can they be presented in their primitive jucundity as gods, who are either opposed to each other in their personal activities, or themselves appear as the animated content of a free and human individuality. If, however, what is intrinsically ethical is to appear throughout as the substantive foundation, the universal ground, shall we say, from which the growth of personal action arrests our attention with equal force in its disunion, and is no less brought back again from such divided movement into unity, we shall find that there are two distinct modes under which the ethical content of human action is asserted.

First, we have the simple consciousness, which, in so far as it wills its substantive content wholly as the unbroken identity of its particular aspects, remains in undisturbed, uncriticized, and neutral tranquillity on its own account and as related to others. This undivided and, we may add, purely formal state of mind in its veneration, its faith, and its happiness, however, is incapable of attaching itself to any definite action; it has a sort of dread before the disunion which is implied in such, although it does, while remaining itself incapable of action, esteem at the same time that spiritual courage which asserts itself resolutely and actively in a self-proposed object, as of nobler worth, yet is aware of its inability to undertake such enterprise, and consequently considers that it can do nothing further for such active personalities, whom it respects so highly, than contrast with the energy of their decision and conflict the object of its own wisdom, in other words, the substantive ideality of the ethical Powers.

The *second* mode under which this ethical content is asserted is that of the individual pathos, which urges the active characters with moral self-vindication into opposition to others, and brings them thereby into conflict. The individuals subject to this pathos are neither what, in the modern use of the term, we describe as characters, nor are they mere abstractions. They are rather placed in the vital midway sphere between both, standing there as figures of real stability, which are simply that which they are, without aught of collision in themselves, without any fluctuating recognition of some other pathos, and in so far – in this respect a contrast to our modern irony – elevated, absolutely determinate characters, whose definition, however, discovers its content and basis in a particular ethical power. Forasmuch as, then, the tragic situation first appears in the *antagonism* of individuals who are thus empowered to act, the same can only assert itself in the field of actual human life. It results from the specific character of this alone that a particular quality so affects the substantive content of a given individual, that the latter identifies himself with his entire interest and being in such a content, and penetrates it throughout with the glow of passion. In the blessed gods, however, it is the divine Nature, in its indifference, which is what is essential; in contrast to which we have the contradiction, which in the last instance is not treated seriously, rather is one which, as I have already noticed when discussing the Homeric Epos, becomes eventually a self-resolving irony. These two modes or aspects – of which the one is as important for the whole as the other – namely, the unsevered consciousness of the godlike, and the combating human action, asserted, however, in godlike power and deed, which determines and executes the ethical purpose – supply the two fundamental elements, the mediation of which is displayed by Greek tragedy in its artistic compositions under the form of *chorus* and *heroic figures* respectively.

In modern times, considerable discussion has been raised over the significance of the Greek chorus, and the question has been raised incidentally whether it can or ought to be introduced into modern tragedy. In fact, the need of some such substantial foundation has been experienced; but critics have found it difficult to prescribe the precise manner in which effect should be given to such a change, because they failed to grasp with sufficient penetration the nature of that in which true tragedy consists and the necessity of the chorus as an essential constituent of all that Greek tragedy implies. Critics have, no doubt, recognized the nature of the chorus to the extent of maintaining that in it we find an attitude of tranquil meditation over the whole, whereas the characters of the action remain within the limits of their particular objects and situations, and, in short, receive in the chorus and its observations a standard of valuation of their characters and actions in much the same way as the public discovers in it, and within the drama itself, an objective representative of its own judgment upon all that is thus represented. In this view we have to this extent the fact rightly conceived, that the chorus is, in truth, there as a substantive and more enlightened intelligence, which warns us from irrelevant oppositions, and reflects upon the genuine issue. But, granting this to be so, it is by no means, like the spectator, a wholly disinterested person, at leisure to entertain such thoughts and ethical judgments as it likes which, uninteresting and tedious on its own account, could only be attached for the sake of such reflections. The chorus is the actual substance of the heroic life and action itself: it is, as contrasted with the particular heroes, the common folk regarded as the fruitful earth, out of which individuals, much as flowers and towering trees from their native soil, grow and whereby they are conditioned in this life. Consequently, the chorus is peculiarly fitted to a view of life in which the obligations of State legislation and settled religious dogmas do not, as yet, act as a restrictive force in ethical and social development, but where morality only exists in its primitive form of directly animated human life, and it is merely the equilibrium of unmoved life which remains assured in its stability against the fearful collisions which the antagonistic energies of individual action produces. We are made aware of the fact that an assured asylum of this kind is also a part of our actual existence by the presence of the chorus. It does not, therefore practically co-operate with the action; it executes no right, actively, as against the contending heroes; it merely expresses its judgment as a matter of opinion; it warns, commiserates, or appeals to the divine law, and the ideal forces imminent in the soul, which the imagination grasps in external guise as the sphere of the gods that rule. In this self-expression it is, as we have already seen, lyrical; for it does not act and there are no events for it to narrate in epical form. The content, however, retains at the same time the epic character of substantive universality; and its lyric movement is of such a nature that it can, and in this respect in

37

contrast to the form of the genuine ode, approach at times that of the paean and the dithyramb. We must lay emphatic stress upon this position of the chorus in Greek tragedy. Just as the theatre itself possesses its external ground, its scene and environment, so, too, the chorus, that is the general community, is the spiritual scene; and we may compare it to the architectural temple which surrounds the image of the god, which resembles the heroes in the action. Among ourselves, statues are placed under the open sky without such a background, which also modern tragedy does not require, for the reason that its actions do not depend on this substantive basis, but on the personal volition and personality, no less than the apparently external contingency of events and circumstances.

In this respect it is an entirely false view which regards the chorus as an accidental piece of residuary baggage, a mere remnant from the origins of Greek drama. Of course, it is incontestable that its source is to be traced to the circumstance that, in the festivals of Bacchus, so far as the artistic aspect is concerned, the choral song was of most importance until the introduction and interruption of its course by one reciter, whose relation finally was transformed into and exalted by the real figures of dramatic action. In the blossoming season of tragedy, however, the chorus was not by any means merely retained in honour of this particular phase of the festival and ritual of the god Bacchus; rather it became continuously more elaborate in its beauty and harmonious measures by reason of the fact that its association with the dramatic action is essential and, indeed, so indispensable to it that the decline of tragedy is intimately connected with the degeneration of the choruses, which no longer remain an integral member of the whole, but are degraded to a mere embellishment. In contrast to this, in romantic tragedy, the chorus is neither intrinsically appropriate nor does it appear to have originated from choric songs. On the contrary, the content is here of a type which defeats from the first any attempt to introduce choruses as understood by Greek dramatists. For, even if we go back to the most primitive of those so-called mysteries, morality plays, and farces of a similar character, from which the romantic drama issued, we find that these present no action in that original Greek sense of the term, no outbreak, that is, of opposing forces from the undivided consciousness of life and the godlike. To as little extent is the chorus adapted to the conditions of chivalry and the dominion of kings, in so far as, in such cases, the attitude of the folk is one of mere obedience, or it is itself a party, involved together with the interest of its fortune or misfortune in the course of the action. And in general the chorus entirely fails to secure its true position where the main subject-matter consists of particular passions, ends, and characters, or where any considerable opportunity is admitted to intrigue.

In contrast to the chorus, the *second* fundamental feature of dramatic composition is that of the *individuals* who act in *conflict* with each other. In Greek tragedy it is not at all bad will, crime, worthlessness, or mere misfortune, stupidity, and the like, which act as an incentive to such collisions, but rather, as I have frequently urged, the ethical right to a definite course of action. Abstract evil neither possesses truth in itself, nor does it arouse interest. At the same time, when we attribute ethical traits of characterization to the individuals of the action, these ought not to appear merely as a matter of opinion. It is rather implied in their right or claim that they are actually there as essential on their own account. The hazards of crime, such as are present in modern drama, the useless, or quite as much the so-called noble criminal, with his empty talk about fate, we meet with in the tragedy of ancient literature, rarely, if at all, and for the good reason that the decision and deed depends on the wholly personal aspect of interest and character, upon lust for power, love, honour, or other similar passions, whose justification has its roots exclusively in the particular inclination and individuality. A resolve of this character, whose claim is based upon the content of its object, which it carries into execution in one restricted direction of particularization, violates, under certain circumstances, which are already essentially implied in the actual possibility of conflicts, a further and equally ethical sphere of human volition, which the character thus confronted adheres to, and, by his thus stimulated action, enforces, so that in this way the collision of powers and individuals equally entitled to the ethical claim is completely set up in its movement.

The sphere of this content, although capable of great variety of detail, is not in its essential features very extensive. The principal source of opposition, which Sophocles in particular, in this respect following the lead of Aeschylus, has accepted and worked out in the finest way, is that of the *body politic*, the opposition, that is, between ethical life in its social universality and the family as the natural ground of moral relations. These are the purest forces of tragic representation. It is, in short, the harmony of these spheres and the concordant action within the bounds of their realized content, which constitute the perfected reality of the moral life. In this respect I need only recall the 'Seven before Thebes' of Aeschylus and, as a yet stronger illustration, the 'Antigone' of Sophocles. Antigone reverences the ties of blood-relationship, the gods of the nether world. Creon alone recognizes Zeus, the paramount Power of public life and the commonwealth. We come across a similar conflict in the 'Iphigenia in Aulis', as also in the 'Agamemnon', the 'Choephorae', and 'Eumenides' of Aeschylus, and in the 'Electra' of Sophocles. Agamemnon, as king and leader of his army, sacrifices his daughter in the interest of the Greek folk and the Trojan expedition. He shatters thereby the bond of love as between himself and his daughter and wife, which Clytemnestra retains in the depths of a mother's heart, and in revenge prepares an ignominious death for her husband on his return. Orestes, their son, respects his mother, but is bound to represent the right of his father, the king, and strikes dead the mother who bore him.

A content of this type retains its force through all times, and its presentation, despite all difference of nationality, vitally arrests our human and artistic sympathies.

Of a more formal type is that second kind of essential collision, an illustration of which in the tragic story of Oedipus the Greek tragedians especially favoured. Of this Sophocles has left us the most complete example in his 'Oedipus Rex', and 'Oedipus at Colonus'. The problem here is concerned with the claim of alertness in our intelligence, with the nature of the obligation implied in that which a man carries out with a volition fully aware of its acts as contrasted with that which he has done in fact, but unconscious of and with no intention of doing what he has done under the directing providence of the gods, Oedipus slays his father, marries his mother, begets children in this incestuous alliance, and nevertheless is involved in these most terrible of crimes without active participation either in will or knowledge. The point of view of our profounder modern consciousness of right and wrong would be to recognize that crimes of this description, inasmuch as they were neither referable to a personal knowledge or volition, were not deeds for which the true personality of the perpetrator was responsible. The plastic nature of the Greek on the contrary adheres to the bare fact which an individual has achieved, and refuses to face the division implied by the purely ideal attitude of the soul in the self-conscious life on the one hand and the objective significance of the fact accomplished on the other.

For ourselves, to conclude this survey, other collisions, which either in general are related to the universally accepted association of personal action to the Greek conception of Destiny, or in some measure to more exceptional conditions, are comparatively speaking less important.

In all these tragic conflicts, however, we must above all place on one side the false notion of *guilt* or *innocence*. The heroes of tragedy are quite as much under one category as the other. If we accept the idea as valid that a man is guilty only in the case that a choice lay open to him, and he deliberately decided on the course of action which he carried out, then these plastic figures of ancient drama are guiltless. They act in accordance with a specific character, a specific pathos, for the simple reason that they are this character, this pathos. In such a case there is no lack of decision and no choice. The strength of great characters consists precisely in this that they do not choose, but are entirely and absolutely just that which they will and achieve. They are simply themselves, and never anything else, and their greatness consists in that fact. Weakness in action, in other words, wholly consists in the division of the personal self as such from its content, so that character, volition and final purpose do not appear as absolutely one unified growth; and inasmuch as no assured end lives in the soul as the very substance of the particular personality, as the pathos and might of the individual's entire will, he is still able to turn with indecision from this course to that, and his final decision is that of caprice. A wavering attitude of this description is alien to these plastic creations. The bond between the psychological state of mind and the content of the will is for them indissoluble. That which stirs them to action is this very pathos which implies an ethical justification and which, even in the pathetic aspects of the dialogue, is not enforced in and through the merely personal rhetoric of the heart and the sophistry of passion, but in the equally masculine and cultivated objective presence, in the profound possibilities, the harmony and vitally plastic beauty of which Sophocles was to a superlative degree master. At the same time, however, such a pathos, with its potential resources of collision, brings them to deeds that are both injurious and wrongful. They have no desire to avoid the blame that results therefrom. On the contrary, it is their fame to have done what they have done. One can in fact urge nothing more intolerable against a hero of this type than by saying that he has acted innocently. It is a point of honour with such great characters that they are guilty. They have no desire to excite pity or our sensibilities. For it is not the substantive, but rather the wholly personal deepening of the personality which stirs our individual pain. His securely strong character, however, coalesces entirely with his essential pathos, and this indivisible accord inspires wonder not compassion. The drama of Euripides marks the transition to that.

The final result, then, of the development of tragedy conducts us to this issue and only this, namely, that the twofold vindication of the mutually conflicting aspects is no doubt retained, but the *one-sided* mode is cancelled, and the undisturbed ideal harmony brings back again that condition of the chorus, which attributes without reserve equal honour to all the gods. The true course of dramatic development consists in the annulment of *contradictions* viewed as such, in the reconciliation of the forces of human action, which alternately strive to negate each other in their conflict. Only so far is misfortune and suffering not the final issue, but rather the satisfaction of spirit, as for the first time, in virtue of such a conclusion, the necessity of all that particular individuals experience, is able to appear in complete accord with reason, and our emotional attitude is tranquillized on a true ethical basis; rudely shaken by the calamitous result to the heroes, but reconciled in the substantial facts.

And it is only in so far as we retain such a view securely that we shall be in a position to understand ancient tragedy. We have to guard ourselves therefore from concluding that a *dénouement* of this type is merely a moral issue conformably to which evil is punished and virtue rewarded, as indicated by the proverb that 'when crime turns to vomit, virtue sits down at table'. We have nothing to do here with this wholly personal aspect of a self-reflecting personality and its conception of good and evil, but are concerned with the appearance of the affirmative reconciliation and the equal validity of both powers engaged in conflict, if the collision is complete. To as little extent is the necessity of the issue a blind destiny, or in other words a purely irrational, unintelligible fate, identified with the classical world by many; rather it is the rationality of destiny, albeit it does not as yet appear as self-conscious Providence, the divine final end of which in conjunction with the world and individuals appears on its own account and for others, depending as it does on just this fact that the highest Power paramount over particular gods and mankind cannot suffer this, namely, that the forces, which affirm their self-subsistence in modes that are abstract or incomplete, and thereby overstep the boundary of their warrant, no less than the conflicts which result from them, should retain their self-stability. Fate drives personality back upon its limits, and shatters it, when it has grown overweening. An irrational compulsion, however, an innocence of suffering would rather only excite indignation in the soul of the spectator than ethical tranquillity. From a further point of view, therefore, the reconciliation of *tragedy* is equally distinct from that of the *Epos*. If we look at either Achilles or Odysseus in this respect we observe that both attain their object, and it is right that they do so; but it is not a continuous happiness with which they are favoured; they have on the contrary to taste in its bitterness the feeling of finite condition, and are forced to fight wearily through difficulties, losses and sacrifices. It is in fact a universal demand of truth that in the course of life and all that takes place in the objective world the nugatory character of finite conditions should compel attention. So no doubt the anger of Achilles is reconciled; he obtains from Agamemnon that in respect of which he had suffered the sense of insult; he is revenged upon Hector; the funeral rites of Patroclus are consummated, and the character of Achilles is acknowledged in all its glory. But his wrath and its reconciliation have for all that cost him his dearest friend, the noble Patroclus; and, in order to avenge himself upon Hector for this loss, he finds himself compelled to disengage himself from his anger, to enter once more the battle against the Trojans, and in the very moment when his glory is acknowledged receives the prevision of his early death. In a similar way Odysseus reaches Ithaca at last, the goal of his desire; but he does so alone and in his sleep, having lost all his companions, all the war-booty from Ilium, after long years of endurance and fatigue. In this way both heroes have paid their toll to finite conditions and the claim of nemesis is evidenced in the destruction of Troy and the misfortunes of the Greek heroes. But this nemesis is simply justice as conceived of old, which merely humiliates what is everywhere too exalted, in order to establish once more the abstract balance of fortune by the instrumentality of misfortune, and which merely touches and affects finite existence without further ethical signification. And this is the justice of the Epic in the field of objective fact, the universal reconciliation of simple accommodation. The higher conception of reconciliation in tragedy is on the contrary related to the resolution of specific ethical and substantive facts from their contradiction into their true harmony. The way in which such an accord is established is asserted under very different modes; I propose therefore merely to direct attention to the fundamental features of the actual process herein involved.

First, we have particularly to emphasize the fact, that if it is the one-sidedness of the pathos which constitutes the real basis of collisions this merely amounts to the statement that it is asserted in the action of life, and therewith has become the unique pathos of a particular individual. If this one-sidedness is to be abrogated then it is this individual which, to the extent that his action is exclusively identified with this isolated pathos, must perforce be stripped and sacrificed. For the individual here is merely this single life, and, if this unity is not secured in its stability on its own account, the individual is shattered.

The most complete form of this development is possible when the individuals engaged in conflict relatively to their concrete or objective life appear in each case essentially involved in one whole, so that they stand fundamentally under the power of that against which they battle, and consequently infringe that, which, conformably to their own essential life, they ought to respect. Antigone, for example, lives under the political authority of Creon; she is herself the daughter of a king and the affianced of Haemon, so that her obedience to the royal prerogative is an obligation. But Creon also, who is on his part father and husband, is under obligation to respect the sacred ties of relationship, and only by breach of this can give an order that is in conflict with such a sense. In consequence of this we find immanent in the life of both that which each respectively combats, and they are seized and broken by that very bond which is rooted in the compass of their own social existence. Antigone is put to death before she can enjoy what she looks forward to as bride, and Creon too is punished in the fatal end of his son and wife, who commit suicide, the former on account of Antigone's death, and the latter owing to Haemon's. Among all the fine creations of the ancient and the modern world – and I am

acquainted with pretty nearly everything in such a class, and one ought
to know it, and it is quite possible – the 'Antigone' of Sophocles is from
this point of view in my judgment the most excellent and satisfying
work of art.

The tragic issue does not, however, require in every case, as a means
of removing both over-emphasized aspects and the equal honour which
they respectively claim, the downfall of the contestant parties. The
'Eumenides' ends, as we all know, not with the death of Orestes, or the
destruction of the Eumenides, these avenging spirits of matricide and
filial affection, as opposed to Apollo, who seeks to protect unimpaired
the worth of and reverence for the family chief and king, who
prompted Orestes to slay Clytemnestra, but with Orestes released
from the punishment and honour bestowed on both divinities. At
the same time we cannot fail to see in this adjusted conclusion the
nature of the authority which the Greeks attached to their gods when
they presented them as mere individuals contending with each other.
They appear, in short, to the Athenian of everyday life merely as
definite aspects of ethical experience which the principles of morality
viewed in their complete and harmonious coherence bind together.
The votes of the Areopagus are equal on either side. It is Athene,
the goddess, the life of Athens, that is, imagined in its essential unity,
who adds the white pebble, who frees Orestes, and at the same time
promises altars and a cult to the Eumenides no less than Apollo. As
a contrast to this type of objective reconciliation the settlement may
be, *secondly*, of a more personal character. In other words, the individual
concerned in the action may in the last instance surrender his one-sided
point of view. In this betrayal by personality of its essential pathos,
however, it cannot fail to appear destitute of character; and this
contradicts the masculine integrity of such plastic figures. The
individual, therefore, can only submit to a higher Power and its
counsel or command, to the effect that while on his own account he
adheres to such a pathos, the will is nevertheless broken in its bare
obstinacy by a god's authority. In such a case the knot is not loosened,
but, as in the case of Philoctetes, it is severed by a *deus ex machina*.

But as a *further* and final class, and one more beautiful than the
above rather external mode of resolution, we have the reconciliation
more properly of the soul itself, in which respect there is, in virtue of
the personal significance, a real approach to our modern point of view.
The most perfect example of this in ancient drama is to be found in the
ever admirable 'Oedipus at Colonos' of Sophocles. The protagonist here
has unwittingly slain his father, secured the sceptre of Thebes, and the
bridal bed of his own mother. He is not rendered unhappy by these
unwitting crimes; but the power of divination he has of old possessed
makes him realize, despite himself, the darkness of the experience that

confronts him, and he becomes fearfully, if indistinctly, aware of what
his position is. In this resolution of the riddle in himself he resembles
Adam, losing his happiness when he obtains the knowledge of good
and evil. What he then does, the seer, is to blind himself, then abdicate
the throne and depart from Thebes, very much as Adam and Eve are
driven from Paradise. From henceforward he wanders about a helpless
old man. Finally a god calls the terribly afflicted man to himself the
man, that is, who refusing the request of his sons that he should return
to Thebes, prefers to associate with the Erinyes; the man, in short, who
extinguishes all the disruption in himself and who purifies himself in
his own soul. His blind eyes are made clear and bright, his limbs are
healed, and become a treasure of the city which received him as a free
guest. And this illumination in death is for ourselves no less than for
him the more truly visible reconciliation which is worked out both in
and for himself as individual man, in and through, that is, his essential
character. Critics have endeavoured to discover here the temper of the
Christian life; we are told we have here the picture of a sinner, whom
God receives into His grace; and the fateful misfortunes which expire
in their finite condition are made good with the seal of blessedness in
death. The reconciliation of the Christian religion, however, is an
illumination of the soul, which, bathed in the everlasting waters of
salvation, is raised above mortal life and its deeds. Here it is the heart
itself, for in such a view the spiritual life can effect this, which buries
that life and its deed in the grave of the heart itself, counting the
recriminations of earthly guilt as part and parcel of its own earthly
individuality; and which, in the full assuredness of the eternally
pure and spiritual condition of blessedness, holds itself in itself calm
and steadfast against such impeachment. The illumination of Oedipus,
on the contrary, remains throughout, in consonance with ancient
ideas, the restoration of conscious life from the strife of ethical powers
and violations to the renewed and harmonious unity of this *ethical
content itself*.

There is a further feature in this type of reconciliation, however, and
that is the *personal* or ideal nature of the satisfaction. We may take this
as a point of transition to the otherwise to be contrasted province of
comedy.

(b) That which is comic is, as we have already seen, in general terms
the subjective or personal state, which forces and then dissolves the
action which issues from it by its own effect into and in contradiction,
remaining throughout and in virtue of this process tranquil in its own
self-assurance. Comedy possesses, therefore, for its basis and point of
departure that with which it is possible for tragedy to terminate, that is,
a soul to the fullest extent and eventually reconciled, a joyous state,
which, however much it is instrumental in the marring of its volitional

power, and, indeed, in itself comes to grief, by reason of its asserting voluntarily what is in conflict with its aim, does not therefore lose its general equanimity. A personal self-assurance of this character, however, is, from a further point of view, only possible in so far as the ends proposed, and withal the characters include nothing that is on its own account essentially substantive; or, if they do possess such an intrinsic worth, it is adopted and carried out intentionally under a mode which is totally opposed to the genuine truth contained, in a form, therefore, that is destitute of such truth, so that in this respect, as in the previous case, it is merely that which is itself essentially of no intrinsic importance, but a matter of indifference which is marred, and the individual remains just as he was and unaffected.

Such a view is, too, in its general lines the conception of the old classic comedy, in so far as tradition reflects it in the plays of Aristophanes. We should, however, be careful to notice the distinction whether the individuals in the play are aware that they are comic, or are so merely from the spectator's point of view. It is only the first class that we can reckon as part of the genuine comedy in which Aristophanes was a master. Conformably to such a type, a character is only placed in a ridiculous situation, when we perceive that he himself is not in earnest about the earnestness of his purpose and voluntary effort, so that this earnestness is throughout the means of his own undoing, inasmuch as throughout such a character is unable to enter into any more noble and universally valid interest, which necessarily involves it in a situation of conflict; and, even assuming that he does actually partake of it, merely does so in a way that shows a nature, which, in virtue of its practical existence, has already annihilated that which it appears to strive to bring into operation, so that after all one sees such a coalescence has never been really effected. The comic comes, therefore, rather into play among classes of a lower social order in actual conditions of life, among men who remain much as they are, and neither are able or desire to be anything else; who, while incapable of any genuine pathos, have no doubt whatever as to what they are and do. At the same time the higher nature that is in them is asserted in this that they are not with any seriousness attached to the finite conditions which hem them in, but remain superior to the same and in themselves essentially steadfast and self-reliant against mishap and loss. This absolute freedom of spirit, which brings its own essential comfort from the first in all that a man undertakes, this world of subjective serenity is that to which Aristophanes conducts us. Without a reading of him it is hardly possible to imagine what a wealth of exuberance there is in the human heart.

The interests among which this type of comedy moves are not necessarily taken from spheres opposed to religion, morality, and art.

On the contrary the old Greek comedy remains no doubt within the
limits of this positive and substantive content of human life; but it is
the individual caprice, the vulgar folly and perversity, by reason of
which the characters concerned bring to nought activities which in
their aim have a finer significance. And in this respect an ample and
very pertinent material is supplied Aristophanes partly by Greek gods,
and partly by the life of the Athenian people. In other words, the
configuration of the divine in human impersonation itself possesses, in
its mode of presentation and its particularization, to the extent at least
that it is further enforced in opposition to that which is merely one-
sided and human, the contradiction that is opposed to the nobility
of its significance; it is thus permitted to appear as a purely empty
extension of this personal life which is inadequate wholly to express it.
More particularly, however, Aristophanes revels in the follies of the
common folk, the stupidities of its orators and statesmen, the
blockheadedness of war, and is eager, above all, and with all the
politeness of his satire and the full weight of his ridicule, but also not
without the profoundest meaning, to hand over the new tendencies of
the tragedies of Euripides to the laughter of his fellow-citizens. The
characters he has imported into the substance of his amazing artistic
creations he runs into the mould of fool from the start with a sportive
fancy that seems inexhaustible, so that the very idea of a rational result
is impossible. He treats all alike, whether it be a Strepsiades, who will
join the ranks of philosophers in order to be rid of his debts, or a
Socrates, who offers to instruct the aforesaid Strepsiades and his son,
or Bacchus, whom he makes descend into the lower world, in order
to bring up a genuine tragic poet, and in just the same way Cleon,
the women, and the Greeks, who would like to pump up the goddess
of Peace from the well. The key-note that we find in all these various
creations is the imperturbable self-assurance of such characters one and
all, which becomes all the more emphatic in proportion as they prove
themselves incapable of carrying into effect that which they project.
Our fools here are so entirely unembarrassed in their folly, and also
the more sensible among them possess such a tincture of that which
runs contrary to the very course upon which they are set, that they all,
the more sensible with the rest, remain fixed to this personal attitude
of prodigious imperturbability, no matter what comes next or where
it carries them. It is in fact the blessed laughter of the Olympian gods,
with their untroubled equanimity, now at home in the human breast,
and prepared for all contingencies. And withal we never find
Aristophanes merely a cold or evil-disposed mocker. He was a man
of the finest education, a most exemplary citizen, to whom the weal of
Athens was of really deep importance, and who through thick and thin
shows himself to be a true patriot. What therefore is in the fullest sense

resolved in his comedies is, as already stated, not the divine and what is of ethical import, but the thoroughgoing upside-down-ness which inflates itself into the semblance of these substantive forces, the particular form and distinctive mode of its manifestation, in which the essential thing or matter is already from the first no longer present, so that it can without restriction be simply handed over to the unconcerned play of unqualified personal caprice. But for the very reason that Aristophanes makes explicit the absolute contradiction between the essential nature of the gods, or that of political and social life, and the personal activities of individual persons or citizens, who ought to endow such substantive form with reality, we find in this very triumph of purely personal self-assertion, despite all the profounder insight which the poet displays, one of the greatest symptoms of the degeneracy of Greece. And it is on account of this that these pictures of a wholly unperturbed sense of fundamental well-being are as a matter of fact the last important harvest which we have from the poetry created by the exuberant genius, culture, and wit of the Greek nation.

(2) I shall now direct attention to the dramatic art of the modern world, and here, too, I only propose to emphasize the more general and fundamental features which we find of importance, whether dealing with tragedy or the ordinary drama and comedy.

(a) Tragedy, in the nobility which distinguishes it in its ancient plastic form, is limited to the partial point of view that for its exclusive and essential basis it only enforces as effective the ethically substantive content and its necessary laws; and, on the other hand, leaves the individual and subjective self-penetration of the dramatic characters essentially unevolved; while comedy on its part, to complete what we may regard as the reversed side of such plastic construction, exhibits subjectivity in the unfettered abandonment of its topsy-turvydom and ultimate dissolution.

Modern tragedy accepts in its own province from the first the principle of subjectivity. It makes, therefore, the personal intimacy of character – the character, that is, which is no purely individual and vital embodiment of ethical forces in the classic sense – its peculiar object and content. It, moreover, makes, in a type of concurrence that is adapted to this end, human actions come into collision through the instrumentality of the external accident of circumstances in the way that a contingency of a similar character is also decisive in its effect on the consequence, or appears to be so decisive.

In this connection we would subject to examination the following fundamental points:

First, the nature of the varied *ends* which ought to come into the executive process of the action as the content of the characters therein.

Secondly, the nature of the tragic *characters* themselves, as also of the collisions they are compelled to face.

Thirdly, the nature of the final *issue* and tragic reconciliation, as these differ from those of ancient tragedy.

To start with, we may observe that, however much in romantic tragedy the subjectivity of suffering and passions, in the true meaning of these words, is the focal centre, yet, for all that, it is impossible in human activity that the ground basis of definite ends in the concrete worlds of the family, the State, the Church, and others should be dispensed with, for with activity, man passes wholly into the sphere of true particularity. In so far, however, as in the drama under discussion, it is not the substantive content as such in these spheres of life which constitutes the main interest of individuals, such ends are from a certain point of view particularized in a breadth of extension and variety, as also in exceptional modes of presentment, in which it often happens that what is truly essential is only able to force itself on our attention with attenuated strength. And over and above this fact, these ends receive an entirely altered form. In the province of religion, for example, the content which pre-eminently is asserted is no longer the particular ethical powers exhibited imaginatively under the mode of divine individuals, either in their own person or in the pathos of human heroes. It is the history of Christ, or of saints and the like, which is now set before us. In the political community it is mainly the position of kingship, the power of vassal chiefs, the strife of dynasties, or the particular members of one and the same ruling family which forms the content of the varied picture. Nay, if we take a step further we find as the principal subject-matter questions of civic or private right and other relations of a similar character; and, further, we shall find a similar attention paid to features in the family life which were not yet within the reach of ancient drama. And the reason of this is that, inasmuch as in the spheres of life above-mentioned the principle of the personal life in its independence has asserted its claim, novel phases of existence make their inevitable appearance in each one of them, which the modern man claims to set up as the end and directory of his action.

And, from a further point of view in this drama, it is the right of subjectivity, as above defined, absolutely unqualified, which is retained as the dominating content; and for this reason personal love, honour, and the rest make such an exclusive appeal as ends of human action that, while in one direction other relations cannot fail to appear as the purely external background on which these interests of our modern life are set in motion, in another such relations on their own account actively conflict with the requirements of the more individual state of emotion. Of more profound significance still is wrong and crime, even if a particular character does not deliberately and to start with aim at either, yet does not avoid them to attain his original purpose.

And, furthermore, in contrast to this particularization and individual standpoint, the ends proposed may likewise either in one direction expand to cover the universality and all-inclusive embrace of the content, or they are in another apprehended and carried into execution as themselves intrinsically substantive. In the first respect, I will merely recall to memory that typically philosophical tragedy, the 'Faust' of Goethe, in which, on the one hand, a spirit of disillusion in the pursuit of science, and, on the other, the vital resources of a worldly life and earthly enjoyment – in a word, the attempted mediation in the tragic manner of an individual's wisdom and strife with the Absolute in its essential significance and phenomenal manifestation, offers a breadth of content such as no other dramatic poet has hitherto ventured to include in one and the same composition. The 'Carl Moor' of Schiller is something of the same fashion. He rebels against the entire order of civic society and the collective condition of the world and the humanity of his time, and fortifies himself as such against the same. Wallenstein in the same way conceives a great and far-reaching purpose, the unity and peace of Germany, an object he fails to carry into effect by the means which, in virtue of the fact that they are welded together in an artificial manner, and one that lacks essential coherence, break in pieces and come to nought precisely in the direction where he is most anxious of their success; and he fails in the same way by reason of his opposition to the imperial authority, upon which he himself and his enterprise are inevitably shattered. Such objects of a world-wide policy, such as a Carl Moor or a Wallenstein pursue, are as a rule not accomplished at the hands of a single individual for whom others become obedient instruments; they carry themselves into effect partly with the will of many, partly against and without their knowledge. As an illustration of a conception of objects viewed in their essential significance, I will merely instance certain tragedies of Calderon, in which love, honour, and similar virtues are respectively to the rights and obligations in which they involve the characters of the action, treated as so many unyielding laws of independent force with all the stringency of a code. We find also frequently much the same thing assumed in Schiller's tragic characters, though the point of view is no doubt wholly different, at least to the extent that such individuals conceive and combat for their ends with the assumption they are universal and absolutely valid human rights. So in the early play of 'Kabale und Liebe' Major Ferdinand seeks to defend the rights of Nature against the conveniences of fashionable society, and, above all, claims of the Marquis Posa freedom of thought as an inalienable possession of humanity.

Generally speaking, however, in modern tragedy it is not the substantive content of their object in the interest of which men act, and which is maintained as the stimulus of their passion; rather it is the inner experience of their heart and individual emotion, or the particular qualities of their personality, which insist on satisfaction. For even in the examples already referred to we find that to a real extent in those heroes of Spanish honour and love the content of their ultimate ends is so essentially of a personal character that the rights and obligations deducible from the same are able to fuse in direct concurrence with the individual desires of the heart, and to a large extent, too, in the youthful works of Schiller this continual insistence upon Nature, rights of man, and a converted world somewhat savours of the excess of a wholly personal enthusiasm. And if it came about that Schiller in later years endeavoured to enforce a more mature type of pathos, this was simply due to the fact that it was his main idea to restore once again in modern dramatic art the principle of ancient tragedy.

In order to emphasize still more distinctly the difference which in this respect obtains between ancient and modern tragedy, I will merely refer the reader to Shakespeare's 'Hamlet'. Here we find fundamentally a collision similar to that which is introduced by Aeschylus into his 'Choephorae' and by Sophocles into his 'Electra'. For Hamlet's father, too, and the King, as in these Greek plays, has been murdered, and his mother has wedded the murderer. That which, however, in the conception of the Greek dramatists possesses a certain ethical justification – I mean the death of Agamemnon – in the contrasted case of Shakespeare's play, can only be viewed as an atrocious crime, of which Hamlet's mother is innocent; so that the son is merely concerned in his vengeance to direct his attention to the fratricidal king, and there is nothing in the latter's character that possesses any real claim to his respect. The real collision, therefore, does not turn on the fact that the son, in giving effect to a rightful sense of vengeance, is himself forced to violate morality, but rather on the particular personality, the inner life of Hamlet, whose noble soul is not steeled to this kind of energetic activity, but, while full of contempt for the world and life, what between making up his mind and attempting to carry into effect or preparing to carry into effect its resolves, is bandied from pillar to post, and finally through his own procrastination and the external course of events meets his own doom.

If we now turn, in close connection with the above conclusions, to our *second* point of fundamental importance in modern tragedy – that is to say, the nature of the characters and their collisions – we may summarily take a point of departure from the following general observations.

The heroes of ancient classic tragedy discover circumstances under which they, so long as they irrefragably adhere to the *one* ethical state of pathos which alone corresponds to their own already formed personality, must infallibly come into conflict with an ethical Power which opposes them and possesses an equal ethical claim to recognition. Romantic characters, on the contrary, are from the first placed within a wide expanse of contingent relations and conditions, within which every sort of action is possible; so that the conflict, to which no doubt the external conditions presupposed supply the occasion, essentially abides within the *character* itself, to which the individuals concerned in their *passion* give effect, not, however, in the interests of the ethical vindication of the truly substantive claims, but for the simple reason that they are the kind of men they are. Greek heroes also no doubt act in accordance with their particular individuality; but this individuality, as before noted, if we take for our examples the supreme results of ancient tragedy, is itself necessarily identical with an ethical pathos which is substantive. In modern tragedy the peculiar character in its real significance, and to which it as a matter of accident remains constant, whether it happens to grasp after that which on its own account is on moral grounds justifiable, or is carried into wrong and crime, forms its resolves under the dictate of personal wishes and necessities, or among other things purely external considerations. In such a case, therefore, though we may have a coalescence between the moral aspect of the object and the character, yet, for all that, such a concurrence does not constitute, and cannot constitute – owing to the divided character of ends, passions, and the life wholly personal to the individual – the *essential* basis and objective condition of the depth and beauty of the tragic drama.

From *The Birth of Tragedy**

Friedrich Nietzsche

At this point we need to call upon every aesthetic principle so far
discussed, in order to find our way through the labyrinthine origins of
Greek tragedy. I believe I am saying nothing extravagant when I claim
that the problem of these origins has never even been posed, much
less solved, no matter how often the elusive rags of ancient tradition
have been speculatively sewn together and ripped apart. That tradition
tells us in no uncertain terms that tragedy arose out of the tragic
chorus and was, to begin with, nothing but chorus. We are thus bound
to scan the chorus closely as the archetypal drama, disregarding the
current explanations of it as the idealized spectator, or as representing
the populace over against the noble realm of the set. The latter
interpretation, which sounds so grandly edifying to certain politicians
(as though the democratic Athenians had represented in the popular
chorus the invariable moral law, always right in face of the passionate
misdeeds and extravagances of kings) may have been suggested by a
phrase in Aristotle, but this lofty notion can have had no influence
whatever on the original formation of tragedy, whose purely religious
origins would exclude not only the opposition between the people and
their rulers but any kind of political or social context. Likewise we
would consider it blasphemous, in the light of the classical form of the
chorus as we know it from Aeschylus and Sophocles, to speak of a
'foreshadowing' of constitutional democracy, though others have
not stuck at such blasphemy. No ancient polity ever embodied
constitutional democracy, and one dares to hope that ancient tragedy
did not even foreshadow it.

Much more famous than this political explanation of the chorus is the
notion of A. W. Schlegel, who advises us to regard the chorus as the
quintessence of the audience, as the 'ideal spectator'. If we hold this
view against the historical tradition according to which tragedy was,

* Reprinted from *The Birth of Tragedy and The Genealogy of Morals*, trans. Francis
Golffing (New York: Anchor Doubleday, 1956).

in the beginning, nothing but chorus, it turns out to be a crude, unscholarly, though dazzling hypothesis – dazzling because of the effective formulation, the typically German bias for anything called 'ideal', and our momentary wonder at the notion. For we are indeed amazed when we compare our familiar theatre audience with the tragic chorus and ask ourselves whether the former could conceivably be construed into something analogous to the latter. We tacitly deny the possibility, and then are brought to wonder both at the boldness of Schlegel's assertion and at what must have been the totally different complexion of the Greek audience. We had supposed all along that the spectator, whoever he might be, would always have to remain conscious of the fact that he had before him a work of art, not empiric reality, whereas the tragic chorus of the Greeks is constrained to view the characters enacted on the stage as veritably existing. The chorus of the Oceanides think that they behold the actual Titan Prometheus, and believe themselves every bit as real as the god. Are we seriously to assume that the highest and purest type of spectator is he who, like the Oceanides, regards the god as physically present and real? That it is characteristic of the ideal spectator to rush on stage and deliver the god from his fetters? We had put our faith in an artistic audience, believing that the more intelligent the individual spectator was, the more capable he was of viewing the work of art as art; and now Schlegel's theory suggests to us that the perfect spectator viewed the world of the stage not at all as art but as reality. 'Oh these Greeks!' we moan. 'They upset our entire aesthetic!' But once we have grown accustomed to it, we repeat Schlegel's pronouncement whenever the question of the chorus comes up.

The emphatic tradition I spoke of militates against Schlegel: chorus as such, without stage – the primitive form of tragedy – is incompatible with that chorus of ideal spectators. What sort of artistic genre would it be that derived from the idea of the spectator and crystallized itself in the mode of the 'pure' spectator? A spectator without drama is an absurdity. We suspect that the birth of tragedy can be explained neither by any reverence for the moral intelligence of the multitude nor by the notion of a spectator without drama, and, altogether, we consider the problem much too complex to be touched by such facile interpretations.

An infinitely more valuable insight into the significance of the chorus was furnished by Schiller in the famous preface to his *Bride of Messina*, where the chorus is seen as a living wall which tragedy draws about itself in order to achieve insulation from the actual world, to preserve its ideal ground and its poetic freedom.

Schiller used this view as his main weapon against commonplace naturalism, against the illusionistic demand made upon dramatic poetry. While the day of the stage was conceded to be artificial, the architecture of the set symbolic, the metrical discourse stylized, a larger misconception still prevailed. Schiller was not content to have what constitutes the very essence of poetry merely tolerated as poetic license. He insisted that the introduction of the chorus was the decisive step by which any naturalism in art was openly challenged. This way of looking at art seems to me the one which our present age, thinking itself so superior, has labelled pseudo-idealism. But I very much fear that we, with our idolatry of verisimilitude, have arrived at the opposite pole of all idealism, the realm of the wax-works. This too betrays a kind of art, as do certain popular novels of today. All I ask is that we not be importuned by the pretence that such art has left Goethe's and Schiller's 'pseudo-idealism' behind.

It is certainly true, as Schiller saw, that the Greek chorus of satyrs, the chorus of primitive tragedy, moved on ideal ground, a ground raised high above the common path of mortals. The Greek has built for his chorus the scaffolding of a fictive chthonic realm and placed thereon fictive nature spirits. Tragedy developed on this foundation, and so has been exempt since its beginning from the embarrassing task of copying actuality. All the same, the world of tragedy is by no means a world arbitrarily projected between heaven and earth; rather it is a world having the same reality and credibility as Olympus possessed for the devout Greek. The satyr, as the Dionysiac chorist, dwells in a reality sanctioned by myth and ritual. That tragedy should begin with him, that the Dionysiac wisdom of tragedy should speak through him, is as puzzling a phenomenon as, more generally, the origin of tragedy from the chorus. Perhaps we can gain a starting point for this inquiry by claiming that the satyr, that fictive nature sprite, stands to cultured man in the same relation as Dionysiac music does to civilization. Richard Wagner has said of the latter that it is absorbed by music as lamplight by daylight. In the same manner, I believe, the cultured Greek felt himself absorbed into the satyr chorus, and in the next development of Greek tragedy state and society, in fact all that separated man from man, gave way before an overwhelming sense of unity which led back into the heart of nature. The metaphysical solace (with which, I wish to say at once, all true tragedy sends us away) that, despite every phenomenal change, life is at bottom indestructibly joyful and powerful, was expressed most concretely in the chorus of satyrs, nature beings who dwell behind all civilization and preserve their identity through every change of generations and historical movement.

With this chorus the profound Greek, so uniquely susceptible to the subtlest and deepest suffering, who had penetrated the destructive agencies of both nature and history, solaced himself. Though he had been in danger of craving a Buddhistic denial of the will, he was saved by art, and through art life reclaimed him.

While the transport of the Dionysiac state, with its suspension of all
the ordinary barriers of existence, lasts, it carries with it a Lethean
element in which everything that has been experienced by the
individual is drowned. This chasm of oblivion separates the quotidian
reality from the Dionysiac. But as soon as that quotidian reality enters
consciousness once more it is viewed with loathing, and the consequence
is an ascetic, abulic state of mind. In this sense Dionysiac man might
be said to resemble Hamlet: both have looked deeply into the true
nature of things, they have *understood* and are now loath to act. They
realize that no action of theirs can work any change in the eternal
condition of things, and they regard the imputation as ludicrous or
debasing that they should set right the time which is out of joint.
Understanding kills action, for in order to act we require the veil of
illusion; such is Hamlet's doctrine, not to be confounded with the cheap
wisdom of John-a-Dreams, who through too much reflection, as it were
a surplus of possibilities, never arrives at action. What, both in the case
of Hamlet and of Dionysiac man, overbalances any motive leading to
action, is not reflection but understanding, the apprehension of truth
and its terror. Now no comfort any longer avails, desire reaches beyond
the transcendental world, beyond the gods themselves, and existence,
together with its gulling reflection in the gods and an immortal Beyond,
is denied. The truth once seen, man is aware everywhere of the ghastly
absurdity of existence, comprehends the symbolism of Ophelia's fate
and the wisdom of the wood sprite Silenus: nausea invades him.

Then, in this supreme jeopardy of the will, art, that sorceress expert
in healing, approaches him; only she can turn his fits of nausea into
imaginations with which it is possible to live. These are on the one
hand the spirit of the *sublime*, which subjugates terror by means of art;
on the other hand the *comic* spirit, which releases us, through art, from
the tedium of absurdity. The satyr chorus of the dithyramb was the
salvation of Greek art; the threatening paroxysms I have mentioned
were contained by the intermediary of those Dionysiac attendants.

The satyr and the idyllic shepherd of later times have both been
products of a desire for naturalness and simplicity. But how firmly the
Greek shaped his wood sprite, and how self-consciously and mawkishly
the modern dallies with his tender, fluting shepherd! For the Greek the
satyr expressed nature in a rude, uncultivated state: he did not, for that
reason, confound him with the monkey. Quite the contrary, the satyr
was man's true prototype, an expression of his highest and strongest
aspirations. He was an enthusiastic reveller, filled with transport by
the approach of the god; a compassionate companion re-enacting the
sufferings of the god; a prophet of wisdom born out of nature's womb;
a symbol of the sexual omnipotence of nature, which the Greek was

accustomed to view with reverent wonder. The satyr was sublime and divine – so he must have looked to the traumatically wounded vision of Dionysiac man. Our tricked-out, contrived shepherd would have offended him, but his eyes rested with sublime satisfaction on the open, undistorted limnings of nature. Here archetypal man was cleansed of the illusion of culture, and what revealed itself was authentic man, the bearded satyr jubilantly greeting his god. Before him cultured man dwindled to a false cartoon. Schiller is also correct as regards these beginnings of the tragic art: the chorus is a living wall against the onset of reality because it depicts reality more truthfully and more completely than does civilized man, who ordinarily considers himself the only reality. Poetry does not lie outside the world as a fantastic impossibility begotten of the poet's brain; it seeks to be the exact opposite, an unvarnished expression of truth, and for this reason must cast away the trumpery garments worn by the supposed reality of civilized man. The contrast between this truth of nature and the pretentious lie of civilization is quite similar to that between the eternal core of things and the entire phenomenal world. Even as tragedy, with its metaphysical solace, points to the eternity of true being surviving every phenomenal change, so does the symbolism of the satyr chorus express analogically the primordial relation between the thing in itself and appearance. The idyllic shepherd of modern man is but a replica of the sum of cultural illusions which he mistakes for nature. The Dionysiac Greek, desiring truth and nature at their highest power, sees himself metamorphosed into the satyr.

Such are the dispositions and insights of the revelling throng of Dionysos; and the power of these dispositions and insights transforms them in their own eyes, until they behold themselves restored to the condition of genii, of satyrs. Later the tragic chorus came to be an aesthetic imitation of that natural phenomenon; which then necessitated a distinction between Dionysiac spectators and votaries actually spellbound by the god. What must be kept in mind in all these investigations is that the audience of Attic tragedy discovered *itself* in the chorus of the orchestra. Audience and chorus were never fundamentally set over against each other: all was one grand chorus of dancing, singing satyrs, and of those who let themselves be represented by them. This granted, Schlegel's dictum assumes a profounder meaning. The chorus is the 'ideal spectator' inasmuch as it is the only *seer* – seer of the visionary world of the proscenium. An audience of spectators, such as we know it, was unknown to the Greeks. Given the terraced structure of the Greek theatre, rising in concentric arcs, each spectator could quite literally survey the entire cultural world about him and imagine himself, in the fullness of seeing, as a chorist. Thus we are enabled to view the chorus of primitive prototragedy as the

57

projected image of Dionysiac man. The clearest illustration of this phenomenon is the experience of the actor, who, if he is truly gifted, has before his eyes the vivid image of the role he is to play. The satyr chorus is, above all, a vision of the Dionysiac multitude, just as the world of the stage is a vision of that satyr chorus – a vision so powerful that it blurs the actor's sense of the 'reality' of cultured spectators ranged row on row about him. The structure of the Greek theatre reminds us of a lonely mountain valley: the architecture of the stage resembles a luminous cloud configuration which the Bacchae behold as they swarm down from the mountaintops: a marvellous frame in the centre of which Dionysos manifests himself to them.

Our scholarly ideas of elementary artistic process are likely to be offended by the primitive events which I have adduced here to explain the tragic chorus. And yet nothing can be more evident than the fact that the poet is poet only insofar as he sees himself surrounded by living, acting shapes into whose innermost being he penetrates. It is our peculiar modern weakness to see all primitive aesthetic phenomena in too complicated and abstract a way. Metaphor, for the authentic poet, is not a figure of rhetoric but a representative image standing concretely before him in lieu of a concept. A character, to him, is not an assemblage of individual traits laboriously pieced together, but a personage beheld as insistently living before his eyes, differing from the image of the painter only in its capacity to continue living and acting. What is it that makes Homer so much more vivid and concrete in his descriptions than any other poet? His lively eye, with which he discerns so much more. We all talk about poetry so abstractly because we all tend to be indifferent poets. At bottom the aesthetic phenomenon is quite simple: all one needs in order to be a poet is the ability to have a lively action going on before one continually, to live surrounded by hosts of spirits. To be a dramatist all one needs is the urge to transform oneself and speak out of strange bodies and souls.

Dionysiac excitation is capable of communicating to a whole multitude this artistic power to feel itself surrounded by, and one with, a host of spirits. What happens in the dramatic chorus is the primary *dramatic* phenomenon: projecting oneself outside oneself and then acting as though one had really entered another body, another character. This constitutes the first step in the evolution of drama. This art is no longer that of the rhapsodist, who does not merge with his images but, like the painter, contemplates them as something outside himself; what we have here is the individual effacing himself through entering a strange being. It should be made clear that this phenomenon is not singular but epidemic: a whole crowd becomes rapt in this manner. It is for this reason that the dithyramb differs essentially from any other kind of chorus. The virgins who, carrying laurel branches and singing a processional chant, move solemnly toward the temple of Apollo, retain their identities and their civic names. The dithyrambic chorus on the other hand is a chorus of the transformed, who have forgotten their civic past and social rank, who have become timeless servants of their god and live outside all social spheres. While all the other types of Greek choric verse are simply the highest intensification of the Apollonian musician, in the dithyramb we see a community of unconscious actors all of whom see one another as enchanted.

Enchantment is the precondition of all dramatic art. In this enchantment the Dionysiac reveller sees himself as satyr, and as satyr, in turn, he sees the god. In his transformation he sees a new vision, which is the Apollonian completion of his state. And by the same token this new vision completes the dramatic act.

Thus we have come to interpret Greek tragedy as a Dionysiac chorus which again and again discharges itself in Apollonian images. Those choric portions with which the tragedy is interlaced constitute, as it were, the matrix of the *dialogue*, that is to say, of the entire stage-world of the actual drama. This substratum of tragedy irradiates, in several consecutive discharges, the vision of the drama – a vision on the one hand completely of the nature of Apollonian dream-illusion and therefore epic, but on the other hand, as the objectification of a Dionysiac condition, tending toward the shattering of the individual and his fusion with the original Oneness. Tragedy is an Apollonian embodiment of Dionysiac insights and powers, and for that reason separated by a tremendous gulf from the epic.

On this view the chorus of Greek tragedy, symbol of an entire multitude agitated by Dionysos, can be fully explained. Whereas we who are accustomed to the role of the chorus in modern theatre, especially opera, find it hard to conceive how the chorus of the Greeks should have been older, more central than the dramatic action proper (although we have clear testimony to this effect); and whereas we have never been quite able to reconcile with this position of importance the fact that the chorus was composed of such lowly beings as – originally – goatlike satyrs; and whereas, further, the orchestra in front of the stage has always seemed a riddle to us – we now realize that the stage with its action was originally conceived as pure vision and that the only reality was the chorus, who created that vision out of itself and proclaimed it through the medium of dance, music, and spoken word. Since, in this vision, the chorus beholds its lord and master Dionysos, it remains forever an *attending* chorus; it sees how the god suffers and transforms himself, and it has, for that reason, no need to act. But, notwithstanding its subordination to the god, the chorus remains the highest expression of nature, and, like nature, utters in its enthusiasm oracular words of wisdom. Being compassionate as well as wise, it proclaims a truth that issues from the heart of the world. Thus we see how that fantastic and at first sight embarrassing figure arises, the wise and enthusiastic satyr who is at the same time the 'simpleton' as opposed to the god. The satyr is a replica of nature in its strongest tendencies and at the same time a herald of its wisdom and art. He combines in his person the roles of musician, poet, dancer and visionary.

It is in keeping both with this insight and with general tradition that in the earliest tragedy Dionysos was not actually present but merely imagined. Original tragedy is only chorus and not drama at all. Later an attempt was made to demonstrate the god as real and to bring the visionary figure, together with the transfiguring frame, vividly before the eyes of every spectator. This marks the beginning of drama in the strict sense of the word. It then became the task of the dithyrambic chorus so to excite the mood of the listeners that when the tragic hero appeared they would behold not the awkwardly masked man but a figure born of their own rapt vision. If we imagine Admetus brooding on the memory of his recently departed wife, consuming himself in a spiritual contemplation of her form, and how a figure of similar shape and gait is led toward him in deep disguise; if we then imagine his tremor of excitement, his impetuous comparisons, his instinctive conviction – then we have an analogue for the excitement of the spectator beholding the god, with whose sufferings he has already identified himself, stride on to the stage. Instinctively he would project the shape of the god that was magically present to his mind on to that masked figure of a man, dissolving the latter's reality into a ghostly unreality. This is the Apollonian dream state, in which the daylight world is veiled and a new world – clearer, more comprehensible, more affecting than the first, and at the same time more shadowy – falls upon the eye in ever changing shapes. Thus we may recognize a drastic stylistic opposition: language, colour, pace, dynamics of speech are polarized into the Dionysiac poetry of the chorus, on the one hand, and the Apollonian dream world of the scene on the other. The result is two completely separate spheres of expression. The Apollonian embodiments in which Dionysos assumes objective shape are very different from the continual interplay of shifting forces in the music of the chorus, from those powers deeply felt by the enthusiast, but which he is incapable of condensing into a clear image. The adept no longer obscurely senses the approach of the god: the god now speaks to him from the proscenium with the clarity and firmness of epic, as an epic hero, almost in the language of Homer.

Everything that rises to the surface in the Apollonian portion of Greek tragedy (in the dialogue) looks simple, transparent, beautiful. In this sense the dialogue is a mirror of the Greek mind, whose nature

manifests itself in dance, since in dance the maximum power is only
potentially present, betraying itself in the suppleness and opulence of
movement. The language of the Sophoclean heroes surprises us by its
Apollonian determinacy and lucidity. It seems to us that we can fathom
their innermost being, and we are somewhat surprised that we had
such a short way to go. However, once we abstract from the character
of the hero as it rises to the surface and becomes visible (a character at
bottom no more than a luminous shape projected onto a dark wall, that
is to say, *appearance* through and through) and instead penetrate into the
myth which is projected in these luminous reflections, we suddenly
come up against a phenomenon which is the exact opposite of a
familiar optical one. After an energetic attempt to focus on the sun, we
have, by way of remedy almost, dark spots before our eyes when we
turn away. Conversely, the luminous images of the Sophoclean heroes –
those Apollonian masks – are the necessary productions of a deep look
into the horror of nature; luminous spots, as it were, designed to cure
an eye hurt by the ghastly night. Only in this way can we form an
adequate notion of the seriousness of Greek 'serenity'; whereas we
find that serenity generally misinterpreted nowadays as a condition
of undisturbed complacence.

Sophocles conceived doomed Oedipus, the greatest sufferer of the
Greek stage, as a pattern of nobility, destined to error and misery
despite his wisdom, yet exercising a beneficent influence upon his
environment in virtue of his boundless grief. The profound poet tells
us that a man who is truly noble is incapable of sin; though every law,
every natural order, indeed the entire canon of ethics, perish by his
actions, those very actions will create a circle of higher consequences
able to found a new world on the ruins of the old. This is the poet's
message, insofar as he is at the same time a religious thinker. In his
capacity as poet, he presents us in the beginning with a complicated
legal knot, in the slow unravelling of which the judge brings about his
own destruction. The typically Greek delight in this dialectical solution
is so great that it imparts an element of triumphant serenity to the
work, and thus removes the sting lurking in the ghastly premises of the
plot. In *Oedipus at Colonus* we meet this same serenity, but utterly
transfigured. In contrast to the aged hero, stricken with excess of grief
and passively undergoing his many misfortunes, we have here a
transcendent serenity issuing from above and hinting that by his passive
endurance the hero may yet gain a consummate energy of action. This
activity (so different from his earlier conscious striving, which had
resulted in pure passivity) will extend far beyond the limited experience
of his own life. Thus the legal knot of the Oedipus fable, which had
seemed to mortal eyes incapable of being disentangled, is slowly
loosened. And we experience the most profound human joy as we

witness this divine counterpart of dialectics. If this explanation has done the poet justice, it may yet be asked whether it has exhausted the implications of the myth; and now we see that the poet's entire conception was nothing more nor less than the luminous after-image which kind nature provides our eyes after a look into the abyss. Oedipus, his father's murderer, his mother's lover, solver of the Sphinx's riddle! What is the meaning of this triple fate? An ancient popular belief, especially strong in Persia, holds that a wise *magus* must be incestuously begotten. If we examine Oedipus, the solver of riddles and liberator of his mother, in the light of this Parsee belief, we may conclude that wherever soothsaying and magical powers have broken the spell of present and future, the rigid law of individuation, the magic circle of nature, extreme unnaturalness – in this case incest – is the necessary antecedent; for how should man force nature to yield up her secrets but by successfully resisting her, that is to say, by unnatural acts? This is the recognition I find expressed in the terrible triad of Oedipean fates: the same man who solved the riddle of nature (the ambiguous Sphinx) must also, as murderer of his father and husband of his mother, break the consecrated tables of the natural order. It is as though the myth whispered to us that wisdom, and especially Dionysiac wisdom, is an unnatural crime, and that whoever, in pride of knowledge, hurls nature into the abyss of destruction, must himself experience nature's disintegration. 'The edge of wisdom is turned against the wise man; wisdom is a crime committed on nature': such are the terrible words addressed to us by myth. Yet the Greek poet, like a sunbeam, touches the terrible and austere Memnon's Column of myth, which proceeds to give forth Sophoclean melodies. Now I wish to contrast to the glory of passivity the glory of action, as it irradiates the *Prometheus* of Aeschylus. Young Goethe has revealed to us, in the bold words his Prometheus addresses to Zeus, what the thinker Aeschylus meant to say, but what, as poet, he merely gave us to divine in symbol:

> *Here I sit, kneading men*
> *In my image,*
> *A race like myself,*
> *Made to suffer, weep,*
> *Laugh and delight,*
> *And forget all about you –*
> *As I have forgotten.*

Man, raised to titanic proportions, conquers his own civilization and compels the gods to join forces with him, since by his autonomous wisdom he commands both their existence and the limitations of their sway. What appears most wonderful, however, in the Prometheus poem

– ostensibly a hymn in praise of impiety – is its profound Aeschylean longing for *justice*. The immense suffering of the bold individual, on the one hand, and on the other the extreme jeopardy of the gods, prefiguring a 'twilight of the gods' – the two together pointing to a reconciliation, a merger of their universes of suffering – all this reminds one vividly of the central tenet of Aeschylean speculation in which Moira, as eternal justice, is seen enthroned above men and gods alike. In considering the extraordinary boldness with which Aeschylus places the Olympian world on his scales of justice, we must remember that the profound Greek had an absolutely stable basis of metaphysical thought in his mystery cults and that he was free to discharge all his sceptical velleities on the Olympians. The Greek artist, especially, experienced in respect of these divinities an obscure sense of mutual dependency, a feeling which has been perfectly symbolized in the *Prometheus* of Aeschylus. The titantic artist was strong in his defiant belief that he could create men and, at the least, destroy Olympian gods; this he was able to do by virtue of his superior wisdom, which, to be sure, he must atone for by eternal suffering. The glorious power to *do*, which is possessed by great genius, and for which even eternal suffering is not too high a price to pay – the *artist's* austere pride – is of the very essence of Aeschylean poetry, while Sophocles in his *Oedipus* intones a paean to the *saint*. But even Aeschylus' interpretation of the myth fails to exhaust its extraordinary depth of terror. Once again, we may see the artist's buoyancy and creative joy as a luminous cloud shape reflected upon the dark surface of a lake of sorrow. The legend of Prometheus is indigenous to the entire community of Aryan races and attests to their prevailing talent for profound and tragic vision. In fact, it is not improbable that this myth has the same characteristic importance for the Aryan mind as the myth of the Fall has for the Semitic, and that the two myths are related as brother and sister. The presupposition of the Prometheus myth is primitive man's belief in the supreme value of fire as the true palladium of every rising civilization. But for man to dispose of fire freely, and not receive it as a gift from heaven in the kindling thunderbolt and the warming sunlight, seemed a crime to thoughtful primitive man, a despoiling of divine nature. Thus this original philosophical problem poses at once an insoluble conflict between men and the gods, which lies like a huge boulder at the gateway to every culture. Man's highest good must be bought with a crime and paid for by the flood of grief and suffering which the offended divinities visit upon the human race in its noble ambition. An austere notion, this, which by the dignity it confers on crime presents a strange contrast to the Semitic myth of the Fall – a myth that exhibits curiosity, deception, suggestibility, concupiscence, in short a whole series of principally feminine frailties, as the root of all evil. What distinguishes the Aryan conception is an exalted notion of active sin as the properly Promethean virtue; this notion provides us with the ethical substratum of pessimistic tragedy, which comes to be seen as a justification of human ills, that is to say of human guilt as well as the suffering purchased by that guilt. The tragedy at the heart of things, which the thoughtful Aryan is not disposed to quibble away, the contrariety at the centre of the universe, is seen by him as an interpenetration of several worlds, as for instance a divine and a human, each individually in the right but each, as it encroaches upon the other, having to suffer for its individuality. The individual, in the course of his heroic striving towards universality, de-individuation, comes up against that primordial contradiction and learns both to sin and to suffer. The Aryan nations assign to crime the male, the Semites to sin the female gender; and it is quite consistent with these notions that the original act of *hubris* should be attributed to a man, original sin to a woman. For the rest, perhaps not too much should be made of this distinction, cf. the chorus of wizards in Goethe's *Faust*:

'Tis no mystery to intuit:
Far ahead swift woman scurries,
But no matter how she hurries,
Man in one bold leap will do it.

Once we have comprehended the substance of the Prometheus myth – the imperative necessity of *hubris* for the titanic individual – we must realize the non-Apollonian character of this pessimistic idea. It is Apollo who tranquilizes the individual by drawing boundary lines, and who, by enjoining again and again the practice of self-knowledge, reminds him of the holy, universal norms. But lest the Apollonian tendency freeze all form into Egyptian rigidity, and in attempting to prescribe its orbit to each particular wave inhibit the movement of the lake, the Dionysiac flood tide periodically destroys all the little circles in which the Apollonian will would confine Hellenism. The swiftly rising Dionysiac tide then shoulders all the small individual wave crests, even as Prometheus' brother, the Titan Atlas, shouldered the world. This titanic urge to be the Atlas of all individuals, to bear them on broad shoulders ever farther and higher, is the common bond between the Promethean and the Dionysiac forces. In this respect the Aeschylean Prometheus appears as a Dionysiac mask, while in his deep hunger for justice Aeschylus reveals his paternal descent from Apollo, god of individuation and just boundaries. We may express the Janus face, at once Dionysiac and Apollonian, of the Aeschylean Prometheus in the following formula: 'Whatever exists is both just and unjust, and equality justified in both.' What a world!

3   Historical Materialism and Tragedy

With the advent of Marxism and the emphasis upon human history, including those mechanisms which are responsible for social change, what had been an essentially religious perspective upon tragedy now gradually assumed a much more secular interest. One of the main characteristics of Marxist thinking is its commitment to a totalising explanation of social and cultural phenomena. Lucien Goldmann's emphasis upon the relationship between a 'world vision', and the thought and beliefs of one powerful social class, serves to provide a dynamic structural model of tragic process which extends a number of categories within the classical Marxist tradition. By contrast, the dramatist Bertold Brecht sought to issue a challenge to the Aristotelian conception of tragedy, questioning from a historical-materialist standpoint the need for heroism as such. His concern is with the ways in which Aristotelian definitions of tragedy disempower audiences by demanding an assent to suffering. The validation of suffering which Brecht perceives in tragedy is not so much a mark of the human quality of the sufferer as an indication of the barbarism of a culture. For Brecht the issue is both an ethical and a moral one, but writers such as George Thomson, in his groundbreaking *Aeschylus and Athens*, first published in 1941, sought to contextualise the historical emergence of tragedy within the transitions which were taking place in ancient Greek culture. In a manner which anticipates much modern emphasis upon the relationship between the emergence of tragic form and moments of transition, Thomson sought to align the emerging *form* of tragedy with a growing secularisation of Greek culture. Like Nietzsche, Thomson located the origins of tragedy in the cult of Dionysos, but his interest lies in the congruency of the emergence of the form with that of one social class in ancient Greece.

Walter Benjamin's account of *The Origins of German Tragic Drama* is more difficult to classify. The excerpt included here reads the development of German tragic drama in terms of an engagement with

Nietzsche, though the emphasis upon mourning (*trauers*) is important. Other writers, such as the avant-garde French novelist Alain Robbe-Grillet, or the critic Jonathan Dollimore, have become much more concerned with the proliferation in tragedy of certain myths of human nature, particularly that of humanism. It can be argued that there are strains of a radical humanism in Marxist thought, although certain strands of post-structuralism following in the tradition of Nietzsche and antipathetic to any Marxist totalising account of experience have sought to challenge this. It is Robbe-Grillet's contention that an essential human nature is fundamentally unhistorical, and in this he anticipates the anti-humanism of writers such as Louis Althusser and Michel Foucault for whom humanism was an 'ideology', a product of a particular historical conjuncture. This represents a challenge to the view that it is the function of tragedy to disclose the essence of what it is to be human. Brecht was unhappy with this traditional view, as indeed is the Brazilian theatre director Augusto Boal. In the case of Boal, he takes further the Brechtian critique of Aristotle in his claim that it was the purpose of ancient Greek tragedy to manage politically the emotions of the audience. The Aristotelian concept of *catharsis*, which is generally thought to concern the purging of harmful emotion, will certainly submit to this reading. Boal's account locates tragedy within the purview of a politics, and dissolves the distinction between aesthetics and politics. A study of the formal conditions of tragedy are no longer sufficient; it is now necessary to consider the intricate relationship between aesthetics and politics, and by implication to assess what is radical and what is reactionary in tragedy itself.

The Tragic Vision*

LUCIEN GOLDMANN

Man

> 'That, if we hope, it is against hope.'
>
> Nicolas Pavillon, Bishop of Alet: letter to
> Antoine Arnauld in August 1664

I have in fact already begun the study of tragic man, and I shall be
continuing it in one form or another throughout the book. For it is
impossible to make a clear distinction between the three elements that I
have described as forming the tragic vision – God, the world and man –
since each can exist and be defined only by reference to the two others.
In itself, the world is not contradictory and ambiguous, and not every
mind sees it with these qualities. It only becomes contradictory and
ambiguous when a man lives wholly in order to achieve absolute and
impossible values. Even then, however, a distinction has to be made, for
we must realise that tragic vision occurs only when the two elements
of the paradox are both carried to their final conclusion. Thus, a man
can live for absolute values, and yet do nothing more than vaguely
desire them in his thoughts and dreams. He thus becomes a Romantic
character, and such an attitude is completely opposed to any genuine
tragedy. Or, on the other hand, a man can spend his life in an attempt
to achieve those relative values which are accessible to mankind. His
attitude towards experience may then be that of rationalism or
empiricism if he does not believe in God, or of Thomism if he is a
Catholic. Or, again, if he is a revolutionary he may accept the viewpoint
of dialectical materialism. But whatever he does, he will not be a tragic
character.

Similarly, not every world view sees God as both absent and present
at the same time. It is only the man who is supremely conscious both

* Reprinted from *The Hidden God: A Study of Tragic Vision in the* Pensées *of Pascal and
the Tragedies of Racine,* trans. PHILIP THODY (London: Routledge & Kegan Paul, 1976).

of the demand for absolute values and of the impossibility of ever
satisfying this demand in the real world who sees the paradoxical
nature of the tragic God.

Finally, even if, in the tragedy of refusal, there remains no common
element between God and the world – except, perhaps, the fact that
they are mutually exclusive – they still, thanks to the presence of man
as a mediator, remain part of the same universe. And, in the case of
Pascal, to the supreme mediation of the God who becomes man. For
man, who is a paradoxical being, 'goes infinitely beyond man', and joins
together in his own nature all possible opposites: he is beast and angel,
wretched but great, cursed with radical evil but blessed with the
categorical imperative; he has a dual nature, both divine and worldly,
noumenal and phenomenal, and it is because of this that he sees the
world as contradictory and paradoxical. The God who is absent from the
world when He is looked at from the standpoint of man's wretchedness
becomes present in the world when seen from the standpoint of His
greatness, and of man's demand for justice and truth.

There are two essential characteristics of tragic man which should be
noted if we are to see him as a coherent human reality: the first is that
he makes this absolute and exclusive demand for impossible values; and
the second is that, as a result of this, his demand is for 'all or nothing',
and he is totally indifferent to degrees and approximations, and to any
concept containing the idea of relativity.

It is this rejection of any notion of progression or of degree which
distinguishes the tragic mind from spirituality or mysticism. For if
we leave on one side the question of pantheistic mysticism, which is
obviously incompatible with any type of tragic vision, we shall see that
nothing is more important for the mystic than the idea of the soul
gradually detaching itself from the things of this world and gradually
moving towards God. When the qualitative change finally occurs which
transforms spiritual into mystical experience, and the conceptual
awareness of God is replaced by the ecstacy of His presence, then this
is a result of a journey which the soul has made through different
stages on its path.[1]

The tragic mind can neither conceive nor recognise the existence of
such an experience. However detached a man may be from the world,
he still remains just as *infinitely distant* as ever from any authentic
awareness, until the moment suddenly arrives when, without passing
through any intermediary stage, his inauthentic consciousness enters the
realm of essences. He then leaves the world – or, rather, to use Pascal's
phrase once again, he 'has no love or care for it' – and enters into the
universe of tragedy.

Thus, even though spirituality often precedes mystical experience, and
is in fact one of the paths leading to it, there is only one way of entering

the world of tragedy: by conversion. Tragic man suddenly becomes aware, by a movement which, strictly speaking, is outside time, of the contradiction between the imperfect values of man and the world and the perfection of those to be found in God. It is an event which is difficult to describe, but one which must be understood if we are to study either the tragic characters of Racine – Berenice or Phaedra, for example – or the real life of the nuns and solitaries of Port-Royal.

The most important features of the tragic conversion are that it takes place outside time and independently of any psychological or temporal preparation;[2] and that, whether it be the effect of an intelligible choice or of divine grace, it nevertheless remains entirely foreign to the actual character or the particular will of the individual. We only need to read the letters of Mother Angélique to realise that, for her, conversion is not something which takes place at a particular moment in time. For we constantly see her asking her correspondents to 'pray for her conversion',[3] which thus appears as an event that she has doubtless already experienced, which has nevertheless still to be requested of God. God can always call this conversion into question again, and man is always in danger of losing the grace which made it possible.

The fact remains, however, that 'conversion' is also something that does take place at a particular moment in time, and that it does mark a stage in a particular individual's life. But even from this point of view, it can neither be the result of a decision that any person makes nor the outcome of a series of accidental events and encounters in an individual's life. People we meet or things that happen to us can only be the occasion for divine grace to manifest itself, an occasion which is quite trivial and unimportant when compared to the real significance of the event.

'The first thing that God inspires in the soul on which He deigns to lay His hand in a true and veritable manner,' writes the author at the beginning of the text *On the Conversion of the Sinner,*' is an extraordinary knowledge and awareness by which this soul looks upon both itself and the world in a totally new way.' Lukács also points out that

This moment is both a beginning and an end. It gives man a new memory, and a new concept of what is just and good. . . . Both the occasion and the revelation, the revealer and the revealed, stand face to face, too foreign to each other even to be enemies. For what the occasion reveals is indeed something quite foreign to its own nature, since it is higher and comes from another world. And the soul which has at last found itself looks with a different and a foreign eye upon the life preceding its moment of conversion. This life now seems wholly incomprehensible, quite inauthentic and foreign to the realm of essences; and the soul can do nothing more than dream that it was once other than it is now, for its real existence is the one which it now enjoys. All else is but as the dreams dispersed by the chance ringing of a lone and morning bell.

Now [continues Lukács] the soul stands naked and speaks alone with its naked destiny. Both the soul and its destiny have been stripped of all chance and accidental features, and all the many and different relationships which existed in everyday life have disappeared. . . . Everything vague and uncertain, everything hazy and shaded, has ceased to exist, and there remains only the pure and transparent air which now hides nothing. What we see now are the final question and the final answers.

(*Soul and Form*, pp. 333–8)

In spite of the rather flowery language of the young man of twenty-five who wrote this passage, the central idea is nevertheless clear: worldly existence changes into tragedy and into the universe of the hidden God, who is at one and the same time both absent and present; and, as an inevitable result of this change, tragic man ceases to be able to understand the life that he led before his moment of conversion, and sees that all his earlier values have been overthrown. What was previously great now seems infinitesimally small, and unimportant has now become essential'. Lukács continues: 'Man can no longer tread the paths that he walked before, since he can no longer see which way he should go. With the ease and grace of a bird he now soars up to previously unscaleable heights, and with sure and certain steps crosses unfathomable gulfs' [*Soul and Form*, p. 338, compare fr. 306 of the *Pensées* (E.204) Everyman edn, trans. John Warrington].

It is this instant of conversion which Lukács calls the miracle. Its central characteristic is that it transforms the essential ambiguity of man's life in this world into an unambiguous awareness and an unflinching desire for clarity. An anonymous Jansenist text expresses it in the following way:

There is in our heart so deep an abyss that we cannot sound its depths; we can scarcely make out light from dark or good from evil; vices and virtues are so curiously compounded, and sometimes so apparently similar in feature, that we cannot know which we should avoid and which we should ask of God, nor how we should make our prayers for that which we do require. But the affliction that God, in His infinite mercy, sends down upon us is like a two-edged sword that enters into the very depths of our hearts and minds. There, it cleaves our human thoughts from those which God causes to rise up in our souls, and the spirit of God can then no longer hide itself. We begin to have so clear a knowledge of this spirit that we can no longer be deceived.

It is then that, needing no further demonstration, we behold the
extent of our sins and groan in the sight of God. For then we see that
His rod, though it smite us hard, smites us rightly; and we see how
greatly we need His help and how He is our sole salvation. It is then
that we find it easiest to detach ourselves from the things of this
world, whose nothingness we now see clearly set before us, and
finding no rest here on earth turn to seek it in our Saviour: *Inquietum
est con nostrum donec requiescat in Te.*[4]

This passage, a defence of their faith by the nuns of Port Royal, is an
equally good illustration of two things: the essential nature of Jansenist
conversion, together with the transition which this implies from
complete darkness to absolute clarity; and, with the *Requiescat in Te*, the
difference between this conversion and the attitude of Pascal in the final
years of his life.

For if the fundamental characteristic of tragic man is his demand for
absolute truth, then this involves consequences of which only Pascal,
among the Jansenists of seventeenth-century France, expressed fully in
his work. These consequences concern the problem of certainty. This is,
it is true, primarily a theoretical concept; yet any purely theoretical
certainty runs the risk of being shown to be illusory, and any piece of
abstract reasoning may, when judged by the light of experience, reveal
flaws not noticed by the abstract thinker.

In spite of this, there is no conviction, however powerful, which can
lead to absolute certainty so long as it depends solely upon practical or
emotional considerations and has not found a solid theoretical basis.[5]
Placed between a silent world and a hidden God, tragic man lacks
any completely trustworthy theoretical foundation on which to base
his certainty that God exists. Reason, which is for Pascal what the
understanding is for Kant, the ability to think, cannot say with certainty
either that God does or that He does not exist. This is why, carried to
its final conclusions, Jansenist thought does not lead to the *Requiescat
in Te* but to the phrase in the *Mystery of Jesus*: 'Jesus is suffering the
torment of death until the end of the world. We must not sleep during
all that time.'

But even though it is not a theoretical certainty, God's existence is
nevertheless concrete and real; indeed, it does have a kind of certainty,
that which depends upon will and value and which Kant calls
'practical' certainty. With greater accuracy, Pascal uses a word which
indicates that theory and practice have been synthesised and
transcended: 'certainty of the heart'. Now, practical or theoretico-
practical considerations are not proofs or demonstrations but postulates
and wagers. Both these words indicate the same idea, and Lukács
expresses it in other terms when he says: 'Faith affirms the existence of

this relationship (between empirical reality and essences, between facts and miracles) and makes its permanently unprovable possibility the *a priori* basis for all existence' (*Soul and Form*, p. 335).

[. . .]

World visions and social classes

This second section will inevitably be very different from the first, both in its subject matter and in its greater aspiration to scientific accuracy. I shall therefore begin by explaining why I have not adopted one of the two traditional ways of studying literature and philosophy: that of separating the works from any discussion of their economic, social or political context, or, alternatively, of merely selecting certain arbitrary elements of this context and emphasising them in a spectacular manner.

My starting point is this: facts concerning man always present themselves in a significant pattern, and this pattern can be understood only by explaining how it came into being. Any genuinely scientific study of this pattern must be based upon a knowledge of this development.

In studying Pascal's argument of the water, as in studying Kant's practical postulates and Marx's socialism, I shall adopt this method for both theoretical and practical reasons. Theoretical because it seems to me to be the only one which enables us to see the facts as they really are; and practical because it enables us to justify science by showing how it has a human function. It will also help us to justify man by the image which so exact a knowledge gives us of him.

This is a truly Marxist starting-point, since it implies that practice and theory, sociology and ethics, cannot be separated. Indeed, there cannot, in Marxist thought, be a separation between ethics and sociology, for the simple reason that Marxist value judgements try to be scientific and Marxist science to be practical and revolutionary. It thus abolishes the false distinction between ethics, conceived of as existing outside social structures, and sociology, conceived of as dealing solely with ethically neutral social facts. Thus, when we come to a really scientific study of human life, it is misleading to talk of science, on the one hand, and ethics, on the other. What we must find is an attitude which understands social reality as a whole, in an organic unity which links together both values and actions.

In my view, this attitude can best be described by using the word faith – provided, naturally, that we dissociate it from any exclusively religious connotation. There is, in fact, no other term which so accurately indicates how values are embedded in reality and how many different layers and levels reality reveals when judged by reference to values.

It is certainly dangerous to use the word faith, since Marxist thought has, from the nineteenth century onwards, been strongly opposed to any revealed religious truth and has always, in spite of the fact that it has both integrated and sublated both Augustinianism and eighteenth-century rationalism, maintained a strongly rationalistic bias. Marxism is, in this respect, the inheritor of the development of the Third Estate, of its still recent revolutions and of its doubtless real opposition to Christianity.

This is why the use of the word faith in a Marxist context gives the impression that an attempt is being made to 'Christianise' Marxism or to introduce transcendental values into it. This is, however, a completely false impression. Marxist faith is faith in the future which men make for themselves in and through history. Or, more accurately, in the future that we must make for ourselves by what we do,[6] so that this faith becomes a 'wager' which we make that our actions will, in fact, be successful. The transcendental element present in this faith is not supernatural and does not take us outside or beyond history; it merely takes us beyond the individual. This is sufficient to enable us to claim that Marxist thought leaps over six centuries of Thomist and Cartesian rationalism and renews the Augustinian tradition. It does not, of course, do this by reintroducing the same idea of transcendence, but by affirming two things: that values are founded in an objective reality which can be relatively if not absolutely known (God for Saint Augustine, history for Marx); and that the most objective knowledge which man can obtain of any historical fact presupposes his recognition of the existence of this reality as the supreme value.

There is, however, yet another major difference between the two positions. The God of Saint Augustine exists independently of any human wish or action, whereas the future which we have in history is created by our actions and desires. What characterises Augustinianism is the certainty that God exists, whereas what characterises Marxism is the wager which it places upon the reality that we must create. Pascal's position lies in between the two: he wagers that God exists, and that He is independent of any human will.

The fact that Marxism begins with a wager and that it sees this as a necessary precondition for any knowledge should come as no surprise to anyone familiar with scientific habits of thought. Surely the physicist and chemist set out from the wager that the general physical laws do in fact apply to the particular sector of reality which they happen to be studying? And surely in the seventeenth century – and even more so in the thirteenth – this wager was a new and quite extraordinary thing?

Thus, any objection to the scientific use of the dialectical method must attack not the principle of the wager itself but the actual kind of wager used. There are two main differences between the type of wager adopted in the physical sciences and the type adopted in the sciences which study man. In physics and chemistry the initial wager belongs wholly to the realm of theory, and is linked to practice only in the subordinate domain of technological application. In the sciences concerning man, on the other hand, this wager belongs both to the realm of theory and to that of practice. The second difference is that, in the human sciences, this wager contains an element of finality which is not to be found in the physical sciences, where the initial wager may either give rise to a general law or simply to a number of statistical observations.

In view of the remarkable results obtained by the physical sciences, it is not surprising that the first attempts to conduct a scientific enquiry into social life should have imitated the example which they offered, and have made the same clear distinction between value judgements and empirical observations. However, it is by no means certain that this imitation is entirely valid, and the fact that these methods succeeded in the physical sciences only makes it more probable that they will be equally effective in the sciences of man. The final proof can only be found in the individual studies which are finally produced, but we can nevertheless begin by clearing the ground and dealing with certain prejudices.

All we need to do is to examine how the great tragic thinkers, such as Pascal and Kant, or the great dialectical thinkers, such as Marx and Lukács, go about their work. We note first of all that both Pascal and Kant begin by showing that no empirical observation can show that the initial wager is either right or wrong.[7] For example, they both set out from the problem of the existence of God, and both establish the fact that no scientific proof can be regarded as valid either way. Similarly, Marx and Lukács know that there is no empirical way of proving that progress existed in the past and that it will continue in the present, since the two fundamental values which they recognise – progress and socialism – are linked to specifically human actions and are dependent on them.[8]

'The question of whether human thought can discover objective truth is not a theoretical but a practical one. It is in what he does that man must prove truth, that is to say reality and power, what lies behind his thought. The discussion on whether thought is real or unreal remains a purely scholastic one as long as it is isolated from practice.' 'Social life is essentially practical. All the mysteries which divert theory towards mysticism find their rational solution in human activity and in the understanding of this practical reality.' 'Philosophers so far have merely

interpreted the world. We must change it.'[9] It would be just as absurd
for Pascal or Kant to deny the existence of God on empirical grounds
as it would be for Marx to use the same criterion to assert or deny
the validity of the idea of progress or of humanity's march towards
socialism. In both cases the initial wager depends upon an act of faith,
on 'reasons of the heart' in Pascal, or the validity of reason in Kant and
Marx, a wager which goes beyond and integrates theory and practice.

Thus, no basis can be found in the physical sciences for affirming or
denying the existence of God or of historical progress. All they can
show is that the practising scientist does not need such concepts, unless,
of course, he is talking about the history of physics or chemistry, for in
that case he is dealing with human events.

The fact, however, that the validity of the initial wager in dialectical
or tragic thought can be neither proved nor disproved does not of itself
make this wager a necessary one to make. Could we not study man by
the same methods as those used in the physical sciences?

It is here that, after having established that there is no contradiction
between the idea of the wager and the findings of empirical science,
the champions of tragic and dialectical thought can move on to the
offensive. Pascal and Kant try to show that it is impossible to give an
account of human reality without assuming either that God exists or
that the practical postulates are valid, while Marx and Lukács go even
further. They argue two things: that any theoretical statement about the
structure of reality implies an initial hypothesis, which may or may not
be a wholly conscious one, and which I have called the wager; and that,
in the human sciences, we come up against immediate contradictions
if we make this wager the assumption that reality is governed by
absolutely deterministic laws.

Thus, any discussion about methodology in the human sciences needs
to clear up two points. First of all, accepting the idea that all sciences do
set out from a wager, should we make this explicit, or should we leave
it implicit and try to compose an objective and impartial study free of
all value judgements? Secondly, if it is to be made explicit, which
particular wager is most likely to lead to the most objective and
adequate knowledge of human reality?

The answer to the first question would seem quite obvious, were it
not for the fact that rationalists so frequently base their objections to
any tragic or dialectical thought on the rejection of the notion that
science is based upon a wager. When, in Pascal's imaginary dialogue,
the free thinker reproached the believer with having made 'not this
particular choice, but any choice at all; for the person who says "heads"
and the person who says "tails" are both equally at fault. The correct
thing to do is not to wager at all,' Pascal had his reply ready: 'Yes,' he
said 'but you must place your bet. This is not something which you can

choose either to do or not to do, for you are already embarked.'
Similarly, in the *Theses on Feuerbach* Marx insisted on showing that any
state of awareness must inevitably have some practical intention, and
that 'we are embarked' from the very moment that we make the most
insignificant act of perception: 'Feuerbach, not satisfied with abstract
thought, also appeals to sensible perception, but does not look upon
sensibility as such as forming part of the practical activity of man's
senses.'[10] Now this linking up of intention with awareness always
implies an end; or, as Piaget would say, aims at establishing a balance
– which means, when this end becomes conscious of itself, either
implicitly or explicitly accepting a scale of values.

As far as the second question is concerned, it should be noted that
any wager that absolutely fixed but non-finalistic laws exist in the
domain of the humanities or science is both contradictory and
impossible. This is because in the humanities man is at one and the
same time both the student and the object of study, so that any law
discovered by the student must also be held partly to apply to the
student himself. The denial of meaning and finality in the human
sciences either involves the denial of the meaning and finality of
scientific thought itself or the creation of an unjustifiably privileged
status for the scientist. When we look at this problem from the point
of view of action – and, as we have seen, all ideas are linked to action
and, in the realm of the human sciences, are part of the action itself
– we see that Marx's critique of determinism in the *IIIrd Thesis on
Feuerbach* is equally valid for any purely scientific concept of man
which sees him as bound by certain laws.

> The materialistic doctrine which maintains that men are the products
> of circumstances and education, and that, consequently, different
> men are the product of different circumstances and of a different
> education, forgets that it is men who change these circumstances,
> and that the educator himself needs educating. This is why such a
> doctrine inevitably tends to divide society into two parts, of which
> one is placed above society.

> The coincidence between a change in circumstances and a change in
> human activity can be rationally understood only as an activity which
> effects a qualitative change in reality (*umwälzende Praxis*).

Thus, any general hypothesis about social life must include both the
seeker himself and the kind of investigation he is carrying out. That is
to say, it must imply: (*a*) man's practical activity; (*b*) the meaningful
character of this activity; (*c*) the possibility that he may either succeed
or fail. These three characteristics cannot apply to activity in the
physical sciences, since not only is the seeker himself not part of the

investigation or object he is studying, but this object is created by taking away everything which might be the subject matter of thought or action.

Thus, if we are to arrive at a scientific knowledge of man, we must begin by the wager, or assumption, that history has a meaning. We must, therefore, set out from an act of faith, and the phrase *Credo ut Intelligam* provides a common basis for Augustinian, Pascalian and Marxist epistemology, in spite of the fact that in each of these three cases the 'faith' is of a very different type. In the case of Augustine it is the certainty that God exists; in that of Pascal the wager on His existence; and in that of Marx the wager that history does have an immanent meaning.

As far as the method to be used by dialectical study is concerned, this initial presupposition implies certain consequences. One might, for example, presuppose that history is meaningful only when looked at as a whole, and that each individual series of events, taken by itself, appears meaningless. In that case we should be well advised to give up any hope of carrying out a scientific study of man. It is impossible for man to know history as a whole, both because his interpretation of the past always depends upon future events, and because he himself is inside history and therefore cannot achieve the 'objective' knowledge available to the physical scientist. Thus, if it is assumed that the elements which he is about to study are completely meaningless when abstracted from the whole movement of history, then it is impossible for him to gain any knowledge of them at all.

Thus, when we study man, we must assume both that history itself has a meaning and that individual series of events which constitute history are meaningful as well.

There are several different ways of considering such a relationship between the parts and the whole.[11] My initial assumption, however, is that as we fit the individual series of events into a wider context, we little by little improve our understanding both of the whole and of the parts. Any valid object of study in the human sciences has a complete though relative meaning which is brought out when this object is seen against a wider pattern.

However, this leads up to still greater problems. For even if this initial hypothesis is valid, we still cannot be certain that the events which we have chosen to discuss are in fact meaningful. We might have taken our slice of reality at a completely wrong level, and selected events which cannot be analysed except in terms of a causality applicable to the physical but unsuited to the human sciences. The only way to avoid this danger is to concern ourselves with events that we can see to possess an overall meaning, and it is the quest for this meaning which is the first concern of the scholar.

Thus, in my view, the greatest danger threatening serious scholarship lies in the uncritical acceptance of traditional fields of study, for these may eventually show themselves to be quite meaningless even after the most careful and painstaking examination. For example, Marx points this out in *Capital* when he gives it the subtitle of *A Critique of Political Economy*, and shows that this science falls into error and produces ideological deformations when it studies the production, circulation and distribution of goods instead of dealing with the production, distribution and circulation of exchange values. Similarly, most modern universities continue to study subjects which are really non-existent because they have been badly selected – as, for example, the histories of philosophy, of art, literature and theology, etc.

Take, for example, the history of philosophy, since it is essentially with philosophy that I am concerned. Most great philosophical doctrines are, it is true, significant wholes. But, when they are looked at together – or even in groups – they lose this character. This does not mean, however, that the historian of philosophy should simply limit himself to the admittedly useful task of describing the nature and significance of one philosophical system. Neither should he try to fit it into the unreal and badly conceived pattern known as the 'history of philosophy', and this is why I cannot but agree with the criticisms made by Monsieur Gouhier of the contradictory nature of the concept of 'the history of philosophy'.[12] The historian should always, in my view, see any philosophy within the context of a significant whole made up either of a general current of ideas or of a relatively homogeneous social, economic or ideological group.

Organic analogies are very dangerous – and Marxist thinkers have always underlined this fact – but there is one which may be useful here to illustrate my meaning. A physiologist may study the brain merely as a biological structure, but so long as he remains on this level his research will be incomplete. Any continuation will involve extending the area of his investigations to include the whole of the nervous system of which this brain forms part. It is no use his just comparing this brain to a number of others, each of which is studied in isolation from the total organism of which it forms part. If he does this, he will be concerned not with the brains as biological structures but simply as structures of a similar type. This is merely an example, since no serious biologist has ever thought of doing anything so absurd, but it does illustrate a number of weaknesses in the modern approach to the humanities. There are, in fact, a number of traditional historians of philosophy who do just this, and as long as they are concerned with just one philosophical system they are, admittedly, still dealing with a valid subject in a valid manner. But when such an historian goes straight from Kant to Hegel, for example, and makes no attempt to fit each philosopher into his artistic and literary environment – and, above all, into the social and economic circumstances in which he lived – then he is making the same mistake as the biologist who tries to study a series of brains without fitting any one of them to the body of which it formed part. He will fail to explain anything at all and will simply provide a series of more or less accurately described but nevertheless isolated and lifeless examples. This is why there are a number of very good histories of philosophy which tell us about the structure of each particular philosophical system taken individually, but very few – perhaps none at all – which show any organic link between the different systems. This is because, if this link does exist, it joins together not the philosophical systems as such, but the civilisations of which these systems were parts, and which must themselves be studied as social, economic and cultural wholes if this link is to be discovered.

However, the history of philosophy must always set out from what individual philosophers actually wrote. It is not every writer whose works can be looked on as constituting a significant whole. Only a very small number of highly privileged writers have this distinction, and it is precisely because their work has such a coherence that it possesses artistic, literary or philosophical worth. The concept of 'world vision' is an extremely useful one in any attempt to discover this meaning, and I shall here be using it to study the work of Pascal and Racine. However, in addition to actually describing their work, it is also very useful to discover in what circumstances this work came to be written. It is rarely sufficient to concentrate solely on the personal life of the writer in question, and the scholar must often deal first of all with the general climate of thought and feeling, of which the philosophical system or literary work provides the most coherent expression. This climate – which can be called group consciousness, or, in certain definite cases which I shall be describing later, class consciousness – can also provide a historical explanation as to why a particular work came to be written in its present form.

This climate does itself constitute a significant whole, but one which is among the least autonomous and the most difficult to describe. The historian must deal with it, but he must also go further: he must examine and elucidate this climate against the background of the wider economic, social, political and ideological life of which it forms part.

These are my reasons for maintaining that any scientific study of a literary work of a philosophical system must involve linking it with the social, economic and political life of the group whose world view or vision it expresses. Although a more precise definition of what constitutes such a group could be left to be determined in each particular case, it is nevertheless possible to make the following observation: any valid literary work of philosophical system takes in the whole of human life. It thus follows that the only groups whose world view is likely to find expression in such works or systems are those whose ideas or activities tend towards the creation of a complete vision of man's social life; and that, in the modern world – from the seventeenth century onwards – artistic, literary and philosophical works have been associated with social classes and closely linked with the consciousness which each class has of itself.[13]

It will now be clear that, in my view, any valid and scientific study of Pascal's *Pensées* or Racine's tragedies will be based not only upon a careful analysis of their structure but also upon an attempt to fit them into the intellectual and emotional climate which is closest to them. That is to say, they should first of all be studied as part of the whole movement of Jansenism, seen both as a spiritual and as an intellectual phenomenon, and then in relation to the economic and social life of the group or class which found its expression in the Jansenist movement. This book is thus a study of Racine and Pascal with special respect to the expression which Jansenism gave to the social, economic and political situation of the *noblesse de robe* in seventeenth-century France.

This study will consist of three stages, but these will not necessarily be presented in chronological order. In the first the text will be seen as the expression of a world vision; in the second this world vision will be more closely analysed as constituting a whole made up of the intellectual and social life of the group; and in the third the thoughts and feelings of the members of the group will be seen as an expression of their economic and social life. It must be fully recognised, however, that this is a schematic view of a much more complex phenomenon, and that there are many other causes which contributed to the significant whole constituted by Pascal's *Pensées* and Racine's tragedies. The historian must never forget these, and he must remain equally aware of the fact that the social, economic and political activity of the class he is studying can be understood only by reference to the social, economic and political activity of the whole of the society of which this class forms part.

There are, however, two contradictory qualities to this programme: dialectically, it is indispensable; from a practical point of view, however, it can never be carried out at the present moment, even if only a provisional degree of accuracy were required. In fact, as we go up the scale – from the work to the vision, from the vision to the class and from the class to society as a whole – the same difficulty keeps recurring: the facts to be taken into account become increasingly numerous, so much so that it is almost impossible for one man to deal adequately with them.

This difficulty is particularly important when the dialectical method is being used, since this method begins by rejecting any *a priori* principles.

If we are to bring out the essential qualities of a meaningful structure, we must examine all the individual empirical facts[14] which go to constitute it. And it is only when these facts are known and assimilated that we can begin to see what kind of conceptual pattern they form. Of course, the scholar does not set out from an absolute zero, since not only the work itself, but also the climate of opinion which it reflects and the society in which it came to birth have already been analysed by earlier students. The main difficulty lies in the fact that their analyses have set out from a number of different points of view. And since very few of them reflect dialectical considerations, their usefulness is rather limited.

What I mean is this: the dialectical historian is trying to find the whole structural meaning represented by each of the individual wholes which I have mentioned – the text, the world vision, the social class. (Whether he finds it or not has nothing to do with the success or failure of his initial wager.) And it is a fact that, up to the present, most scholars have not given serious attention to this question, either with regard to the texts or to the intellectual and economic life of the society. This is particularly true of the traditional methods still used for studying the history of the seventeenth century, and which are in sharp contrast to those used by historians such as Mathiez, Pirenne, Lucien Febvre, Daniel Guérin for the period of the French Revolution. Thus, in studying Jansenism it has not been enough for me simply to read a certain number of historical works and to think about their content. I have had to go back to primary sources and think out the whole question of the relationship between literature and society in a new perspective.

This was fortunately possible in so far as the texts were concerned, but was much more difficult when I was dealing with the intellectual and emotional climate of the various Jansenist groups under discussion.

It is important to note that my initial hypothesis that Jansenist sensibility existed as a significant structure did enable me to discover a set of facts and documents, now published elsewhere, which has changed our traditional picture of the 'Friends of Port-Royal'.[15] This discovery is not a decisive proof that my method is a valid one, but does nevertheless create a strong presumption in its favour. But even as far as this second level is concerned, there is still much to be done in the direction of a serious exploration of the life and thought of the Jansenist group.

Less progress, however, could be expected in the study of the link between the social and economic circumstances of the *noblesse de robe* and its ideas and feelings. Too much work still has to be done on this question, which is nevertheless essential to a real understanding of Pascal and Racine.

However, rather than simply neglect this problem or simply accept at their face value the results of the remarkable studies that already exist, but which have been written from entirely different points of view, I have devoted a chapter to it. It immediately follows this one, and is to be looked upon simply as a hypothesis based upon a number of facts noted in the work of other historians and in the *mémoires* of the seventeenth century. I will, however, make one or two remarks about the probable validity of this hypothesis, while insisting on the fact that it can be finally confirmed or rejected only by a detailed and thorough examination of primary sources.

It is based first of all on the fact that it provides an explanation for a whole collection of apparently unrelated facts. One should, it is true, always mistrust the apparent elegance which over-simplification offers in intellectual matters, but when a hypothesis offers a new explanation for a phenomenon it should perhaps first of all be appreciated for its possible fertility. Thus, if we take into consideration my contention that a change in the balance of power between the different social classes in seventeenth-century France did have repercussions in the field of theology and philosophy we shall very probably be able to see connections which earlier scholars have missed.

Moreover, if it brings together within the framework of a single significant structure a large number of facts taken from widely different sources, all foreign to the realms of the original hypothesis, then this hypothesis becomes worth noting and exploring.

I should like to conclude by answering a criticism made of one of my earlier books. I have been attacked for trying to fit Kant into a highly schematic and over-generalised conception of the history of Western bourgeois thought. My reply is that schematisation is an inevitable stage through which any serious dialectical study must pass, since the dialectical historian is compelled to fit any significant set of facts into a totality which he is obliged to sketch out in a schematic manner. If he had been fully acquainted with this totality, then he would have concentrated on describing it, but the problem would then only have been postponed and would have recurred at a higher level. But there is nothing contradictory or reprehensible about this, for this schematisation is by no means arbitrary. The dialectical historian sets out from the significant structure of the facts which he intends to study, and aims to fit this structure into another and more comprehensive one that will provide an historical framework for it. This, alone, limits the possible schematisations open to him, especially when one considers that he must constantly defer to the facts themselves, which have almost inevitably been brought to light by studies written from a completely different standpoint from his own. Any serious historical study must, in my view, have two starting-points: the facts themselves, and a conceptual schematisation intended to make them comprehensible. And it is in the very nature of dialectical thought that, as more facts are revealed, they will modify the original schematisation. This is an inevitable characteristic of any serious dialectical research, which must always be moving from the whole to the parts and from the parts back to the whole again. These are the principles governing the present work, and which provide a framework that, in the very nature of things, will always remain provisional, since the discovery of each new fact will inevitably modify the initial hypothesis.

Notes

1. And this without taking into consideration the separation so often described by the psychologists of mysticism between the 'fine point' and the other faculties of the soul; a separation which is completely foreign to the tragic soul, for whom only what is essential has real existence and yet which also sees everything existing as equally essential.

2. This is the most complex aspect of the tragic mind, and the one which has given rise to the most misunderstanding. For us, and for any historian, psychologist or sociologist, tragic conversion is the final stage in a whole temporal and psychic evolution without which it would be quite incomprehensible. But its content is the absolute negation of such a process or evolution. Everything temporal or psychological forms part of this world, and has therefore no existence for the tragic mind, which has moved out of time and into eternity and life in the eternal instant.

   A psychologist with whom I once discussed the characters of Bérénice and Phaedra made a remark which I shall quote precisely because it illustrates the most dangerous form of misunderstanding, and one that one must avoid at all costs. 'Racine,' he said, 'left out any description of the way in which the two "conversions" were prepared in the psychology of the individual because this was not necessary to the structure of the play; what the critic must do, however, is to supply the description of how these two conversions came about, and thus restore the individualistic psychology neglected by Racine.' In my view, this would involve altering the psychology of these two characters, or, rather, attributing to them a psychological development that completely destroyed their tragic nature.

3. See the letters of 3 June, 14 August, 17 August and 9 November, 1637; 15 November 1639; April 1644 (to Antoine Arnauld); 16 March and 14 May, 1649; 24 September 1652 in *Lettres écrits à un provincial*.

4. In the *Défense de la foi des religieuses de Port-Royal et de leurs directeurs sur tous les faits alleguez par M. Chamaillard dans les deux libelles*, etc. . . . , 1667, p. 59.

5. It is the problem of the *Fidens quarens intellectum* from the *Prosologion* of Saint Anselm to the *Theses on Feuerbach*.

6. There is a considerable difference between the way in which the two ideas are formulated. 'Men make' implies that an attempt is being made to see human history from outside. 'We make' indicates the practical perspective implied by faith and action.

7. Cf. KANT, *Critique of Practical Reason*, Vol. V, pp. 120 and 146 of the German Academy edition. Cf. p. 224 and p. 227 of LEWIS WHITE BECK's translation, University of Chicago Press 1949.

8. Whenever mention is made in this book of Georg Lukács as a Marxist thinker and theoretician, I am referring to the book which he published in 1923 on *History and Class Consciousness*, and that he now disowns and declares to be 'wrong and out of date'.

9. Second, eighth and ninth of the *Theses on Feuerbach*.

10. Fifth thesis. It may perhaps be objected that if Marx is right this is valid not only for the humanities but also for chemistry and physics as well. Of course! And this is why I said earlier that any science sets out from an initial wager. However, the wager which lies at the basis of the physical sciences – the wager on the causal or statistical rationality of the sector of the universe which we are studying and which we can in no way influence, and on the technical utilisation of the laws governing it – is today universally accepted, and, moreover, has been confirmed by so many technical triumphs that only philosophers, who are at the periphery of such activity, ever think of calling it into question.

The comparison may appear rather a far-fetched one, but it might nevertheless be suggested that the person who would perhaps correspond to Pascal's unbeliever – that is to say, someone who doubted the rational and comprehensible character of the physical universe – no longer exists. It is therefore no longer necessary to write apologies to convince him.

11. The most important hypothesis would be that of a totality that was meaningful as a whole, and made up both of a certain number of relative wholes – among which would be historical research itself – and of a certain number of non-significant elements that do not form part of any relative significant whole. This is not only a possible but also a probable hypothesis. However, the choice between it and the one put forward in this chapter could be made only on the basis of a fairly large number of actual research projects completed.

12. I refrain from quoting Monsieur Gouhier in the text because of a difference in our terminologies which might lead to misunderstanding. In the sense in which I speak of 'world vision', he keeps to the German terms 'Weltanschauung'. For him the expression 'world vision' is a conceptual tool which fulfils a different, though entirely legitimate, function. If I understand him rightly, he uses it to place a philosopher's or writer's work not in the context of the consciousness of a social class but in that of the individual's consciousness and biography. No doubt such a concept is indispensable. I have repeatedly said that when one is studying a set of particular facts, specifically in the form of a collection of texts, one has to place the facts in the widest possible number of significant wholes. A philosophical work should be interpreted and its origin explained as the expression both of the consciousness of a social class and the consciousness of the individual. There are, however, two points on which I differ from M. Gouhier. The first is a question of practice rather than principle, and may in the last resort be decided by the nature of the topic, the stage which the enquiry has reached and, above all, by the personality and aptitudes of the investigator. The question is whether it is easier to proceed from the individual and the individual's consciousness to the consciousness of the class, or vice versa. In principle, and subject to exceptions, the latter procedure is the one I think generally valid. Monsieur Gouhier, though he does not explicitly say so,

seems to prefer the former. The second point seems to me to go deeper.
M. Gouhier gives the word 'essence' a rationalistic and a-temporal meaning.
This leads him to construct abstract essences with concrete particular facts.
Accordingly, he distinguishes between, on the one hand, 'The history of
philosophies', which can be either the description of several essences or the
study of an essence, and, on the other, the history of individual world visions,
which he rightly sees as a conceptual instrument for studying individual
facts. This leads him to write, in *L'Histoire et sa philosophie* (*Introduction aux
Méditations Cartesiennes de Malebranche*, pp. 149–50), that: 'Continuity and
essence belong to the same pattern of thinking, for in the philosophy of
philosophy according to Dilthey, as in the phenomenology of Max Scheler,
or in Marxist humanism, the Weltanshauungen represent types of essences:
the concept of "world vision", on the other hand, has been defined in such
a way as to provide a useful tool for studying a history without essences.'

'Thus the different problems raised by the history of philosophy,' continues
Monsieur Gouhier, 'may perhaps be regarded as constituting really only one
problem: is it legitimate to link together two types of research which differ
so completely from each other and talk about "The history of philosophy"?
The two disciplines covered by the title seem to me to be sufficiently different
to exist separately side by side.'

For dialectical thought, however, there is no opposition between essences
and individual facts, since, by its very nature, an essence is an individualising
concept. Essence is the insertion of abstract individual facts into a coherent
whole, by a process of conceptualisation which makes them concrete; and,
indeed, for the biologist and the psychologist, the individual is himself a
relative whole having both structure and meaning. In order to go from
the text to the individual author, Monsieur Gouhier feels the need for an
instrument which is similar to the Weltanschauung: the individual world
vision, which enables him to fit the individual element – the text – into the
whole made up of one person's life and mode of thought. Like Monsieur
Gouhier, I hold that the two forms of history – individual and social – must
exist side by side and that they do in fact throw light on each other, but it
does not seem to me that one can talk about a difference of nature between
the two. If we give the word 'essence' a rationalistic and a-temporal meaning,
then they are both 'histories without essence'; if, on the other hand, we give
it a dialectical meaning they are both histories which try to incorporate
essences, and which do so in so far as they succeed in transforming partial
and abstract facts into concrete ones. Obviously I agree with Monsieur
Gouhier in holding that, in the last analysis, there is no valid history either
of 'philosophy' or of 'philosophies', and that we must combine the study of a
particular set of ideas as an expression of one person's life and thought with
an examination of the history of the society in which those ideas occurred,
seeing them both as the product of one individual and of the degree of
consciousness attained by a particular class. Any attempt at writing history
presupposes the existence of significant structures, and these can be made up
either of individuals, classes, particular philosophical systems or works of
literature. Philosophy, however, taken as a whole and in isolation, does
not constitute such a structure.

13. Cf. LUCIEN GOLDMANN, *Sciences humaines et Philosophie* (Paris: Presses
Universitaires de France, 1952).

14. The research may, of course, subsequently lead to a modification of the
actual subject matter and its reconstitution in a different form, from which

certain original elements have been eliminated but to which others have been added. There is always a dialectical relationship – what Piaget called a 'return bounce' – between the activity of study and research and the object that the scholar began by examining.

15. Cf. *Correspondance de Martin de Barcos*, edited by Lucien Goldmann (Presses Universitaires de France, 1955).

From *A Short Organum for the Theatre*[*]

BERTOLD BRECHT

Prologue

The following sets out to define an aesthetic drawn from a particular
kind of theatrical performance which has been worked out in practice
over the past few decades. In the theoretical statements, excursions,
technical indications occasionally published in the form of notes to the
writer's plays, aesthetics have only been touched on casually and with
comparative lack of interest. There you saw a particular species of
theatre extending or contracting its social functions, perfecting or sifting
its artistic methods and establishing or maintaining its aesthetics – if the
question arose – by rejecting or converting to its own use the dominant
conventions of morality or taste according to its tactical needs. This
theatre justified its inclination to social commitment by pointing to the
social commitment in universally accepted works of art, which only fail
to strike the eye because it was the accepted commitment. As for the
products of our own time, it held that their lack of any worthwhile
content was a sign of decadence: it accused these entertainment
emporiums of having degenerated into branches of the bourgeois
narcotics business. The stage's inaccurate representations of our social
life, including those classed as so-called Naturalism, led it to call for
scientifically exact representations; the tasteless rehashing of empty
visual or spiritual palliatives, for the noble logic of the multiplication
table. The cult of beauty, conducted with hostility towards learning and
contempt for the useful, was dismissed by it as itself contemptible,
especially as nothing beautiful resulted. The battle was for a theatre
fit for the scientific age, and where its planners found it too hard to
borrow or steal from the armoury of aesthetic concepts enough weapons
to defend themselves against the aesthetics of the Press they simply
threatened 'to transform the means of enjoyment into an instrument of

[*] Reprinted from *Brecht on Theatre: The Development of an Aesthetic*, ed. and trans.
JOHN WILLETT (New York: Hill & Wang, 1966).

instruction, and to convert certain amusement establishments into organs of mass communication ('Notes to the opera *Mahagonny*'): i.e. to emigrate from the realm of the merely enjoyable. Aesthetics, that heirloom of a by now depraved and parasitic class, was in such a lamentable state that a theatre would certainly have gained both in reputation and in elbowroom if it had rechristened itself thaëter. And yet what we achieved in the way of theatre for a scientific age was not science but theatre, and the accumulated innovations worked out during the Nazi period and the war – when practical demonstration was impossible – compel some attempt to set this species of theatre in its aesthetic background, or anyhow to sketch for it the outlines of a conceivable aesthetic. To explain the theory of theatrical alienation except within an aesthetic framework would be impossibly awkward.

Today one could go so far as to compile an aesthetics of the exact sciences. Galileo spoke of the elegance of certain formulae and the point of an experiment; Einstein suggests that the sense of beauty has a part to play in the making of scientific discoveries; while the atomic physicist R. Oppenheimer praises the scientific attitude, which 'has its own kind of beauty and seems to suit mankind's position on earth'.

Let us therefore cause general dismay by revoking our decision to emigrate from the realm of the merely enjoyable, and even more general dismay by announcing our decision to take up lodging there. Let us treat the theatre as a place of entertainment, as is proper in an aesthetic discussion, and try to discover which type of entertainment suits us best.

1

'Theatre' consists in this: in making live representations of reported or invented happenings between human beings and doing so with a view to entertainment. At any rate that is what we shall mean when we speak of theatre, whether old or new.

2

To extend this definition we might add happenings between humans and gods, but as we are only seeking to establish the minimum we can leave such matters aside. Even if we did accept such an extension we should still have to say that the 'theatre' set-up's broadest function was to give pleasure. It is the noblest function that we have found for 'theatre'.

3

From the first it has been the theatre's business to entertain people, as it also has of all the other arts. It is this business which always gives it its particular dignity; it needs no other passport than fun, but this it has got to have. We should not by any means be giving it a higher status if we were to turn it e.g. into a purveyor of morality: it would on the contrary run the risk of being debased, and this would occur at once if it failed to make its moral lesson enjoyable, and enjoyable to the senses at that: a principle, admittedly, by which morality can only gain. Not even instruction can be demanded of it: at any rate, no more utilitarian lesson than how to move pleasurably, whether in the physical or in the spiritual sphere. The theatre must in fact remain something entirely superfluous, though this indeed means that it is the superfluous for which we live. Nothing needs less justification than pleasure.

4

Thus what the ancients, following Aristotle, demanded of tragedy is nothing higher or lower than that it should entertain people. Theatre may be said to be derived from ritual, but that is only to say that it becomes theatre once the two have separated; what it brought over from the mysteries was not its former ritual function, but purely and simply the pleasure which accompanied this. And the catharsis of which Aristotle writes – cleansing by fear and pity, or from fear and pity – is a purification which is performed not only in a pleasurable way, but precisely for the purpose of pleasure. To ask or to accept more of the theatre is to set one's own mark too low.

5

Even when people speak of higher and lower degrees of pleasure, art stares impassively back at them; for it wishes to fly high and low and to be left in peace, so long as it can give pleasure to people.

6

Yet there are weaker (simple) and stronger (complex) pleasures which the theatre can create. The last-named, which are what we are dealing with in great drama, attain their climaxes rather as cohabitation does through love: they are more intricate, richer in communication, more contradictory and more productive of results.

7

And different periods' pleasures varied naturally according to the system under which people lived in society at the time. The Greek demos [literally: the demos of the Greek circus] ruled by tyrants had to be entertained differently from the feudal court of Louis XIV. The theatre was required to deliver different representations of men's life together: not just representations of a different life, but also representations of a different sort.

8

According to the sort of entertainment which was possible and
necessary under the given conditions of men's life together the
characters had to be given varying proportions, the situations to be
constructed according to varying points of view. Stories have to be
narrated in various ways, so that these particular Greeks may be able to
amuse themselves with the inevitability of divine laws where ignorance
never mitigates the punishment; these French with the graceful self-
discipline demanded of the great ones of this earth by a courtly code
of duty; the Englishmen of the Elizabethan age with the self-awareness
of the new individual personality which was then uncontrollably
bursting out.

9

And we must always remember that the pleasure given by
representations of such different sorts hardly ever depended on the
representation's likeness to the thing portrayed. Incorrectness, or
considerable improbability even, was hardly or not at all disturbing, so
long as the incorrectness had a certain consistency and the improbability
remained of a constant kind. All that mattered was the illusion of
compelling momentum in the story told, and this was created by all
sorts of poetic and theatrical means. Even today we are happy to
overlook such inaccuracies if we can get something out of the spiritual
purifications of Sophocles or the sacrificial acts of Racine or the
unbridled frenzies of Shakespeare, by trying to grasp the immense or
splendid feelings of the principal characters in these stories.

10

For of all the many sorts of representation of happenings between
humans which the theatre has made since ancient times, and which
have given entertainment despite their incorrectness and improbability,
there are even today an astonishing number that also give entertainment
to us.

11

In establishing the extent to which we can be satisfied by
representations from so many different periods – something that can
hardly have been possible to the children of those vigorous periods
themselves – are we not at the same time creating the suspicion that we
have failed to discover the special pleasures, the proper entertainment
of our own time?

12

And our enjoyment of the theatre must have become weaker than that
of the ancients, even if our way of living together is still sufficiently like

theirs for it to be felt at all. We grasp the old works by a comparatively new method – empathy – on which they rely little. Thus the greater part of our enjoyment is drawn from other sources than those which our predecessors were able to exploit so fully. We are left safely dependent on beauty of language, on elegance of narration, on passages which stimulate our own private imaginations: in short, on the incidentals of the old works. These are precisely the poetical and theatrical means which hide the imprecisions of the story. Our theatres no longer have either the capacity or the wish to tell these stories, even the relatively recent ones of the great Shakespeare, at all clearly: i.e. to make the connection of events credible. And according to Aristotle – and we agree there – narrative is the soul of drama. We are more and more disturbed to see how crudely and carelessly men's life together is represented, and that not only in old works but also in contemporary ones constructed according to the old recipes. Our whole way of appreciation is starting to get out of date.

13
It is the inaccurate way in which happenings between human beings are represented that restricts our pleasure in the theatre. The reason: we and our forebears have a different relationship to what is being shown.

14
For when we look about us for an entertainment whose impact is immediate, for a comprehensive and penetrating pleasure such as our theatre could give us by representations of men's life together, we have to think of ourselves as children of a scientific age. Our life as human beings in society – i.e. our life – is determined by the sciences to a quite new extent.

15
A few hundred years ago a handful of people, working in different countries but in correspondence with one another, performed certain experiments by which they hoped to wring from Nature her secrets. Members of a class of craftsmen in the already powerful cities, they transmitted their discoveries to people who made practical use of them, without expecting more from the new sciences that personal profit for themselves.

Crafts which had progressed by methods virtually unchanged during a thousand years now developed hugely; in many places, which became linked by competition, they gathered from all directions great masses of men, and these, adopting new forms of organization, started producing on a giant scale. Soon mankind was showing powers whose extent it would till that time scarcely have dared to dream of.

16

It was as if mankind for the first time now began a conscious and
co-ordinated effort to make the planet that was its home fit to live on.
Many of the earth's components, such as coal, water, oil, now became
treasures. Steam was made to shift vehicles; a few small sparks and the
twitching of frogs' legs revealed a natural force which produced light,
carried sounds across continents, etc. In all directions man looked about
himself with a new vision, to see how he could adapt to his
convenience familiar but as yet unexploited objects. His surroundings
changed increasingly from decade to decade, then from year to year,
then almost from day to day. I who am writing this write it on a
machine which at the time of my birth was unknown. I travel in the
new vehicles with a rapidity that my grandfather could not imagine; in
those days nothing moved so fast. And I rise in the air: a thing that my
father was unable to do. With my father I already spoke across the
width of a continent, but it was together with my son that I first saw
the moving pictures of the explosion at Hiroshima.

17

The new sciences may have made possible this vast alteration and
all-important alterability of our surroundings, yet it cannot be said
that their spirit determines everything that we do. The reason why
the new way of thinking and feeling has not yet penetrated the great
mass of men is that the sciences, for all their success in exploiting and
dominating nature, have been stopped by the class which they brought
to power – the bourgeoisie – from operating in another field where
darkness still reigns, namely that of the relations which people have to
one another during the exploiting and dominating process. This
business on which all alike depended was performed without the new
intellectual methods that made it possible ever illuminating the mutual
relationships of the people who carried it out. The new approach to
nature was not applied to society.

18

In the event people's mutual relations have become harder to
disentangle than ever before. The gigantic joint undertaking on which
they are engaged seems more and more to split them into two groups;
increases in production lead to increases in misery; only a minority gain
from the exploitation of nature, and they only do so because they
exploit men. What might be progress for all then becomes advancement
for a few, and an ever-increasing part of the productive process gets
applied to creating means of destruction for mighty wars. During these
wars the mothers of every nation, with their children pressed to them,
scan the skies in horror for the deadly inventions of science.

19

The same attitude as men once showed in face of unpredictable natural catastrophes they now adopt towards their own undertakings. The bourgeois class, which owes to science an advancement that it was able, by ensuring that it alone enjoyed the fruits, to convert into domination, knows very well that its rule would come to an end if the scientific eye were turned on its own undertakings. And so that new science which was founded about a hundred years ago and deals with the character of human society was born in the struggle between rulers and ruled. Since then a certain scientific spirit has developed at the bottom, among the new class of workers whose natural element is large-scale production; from down there the great catastrophes are spotted as undertakings by the rulers.

20

But science and art meet on this ground, that both are there to make men's life easier, the one setting out to maintain, the other to entertain us. In the age to come art will create entertainment from that new productivity which can so greatly improve our maintenance, and in itself, if only it is left unshackled, may prove to be the greatest pleasure of them all.

21

If we want now to surrender ourselves to this great passion for producing, what ought our representations of men's life together to look like? What is that productive attitude in face of nature and of society which we children of a scientific age would like to take up pleasurably in our theatre?

22

The attitude is a critical one. Faced with a river, it consists in regulating the river; faced with a fruit tree, in spraying the fruit tree; faced with movement, in constructing vehicles and aeroplanes; faced with society, in turning society upside down. Our representations of human social life are designed for river-dwellers, fruit farmers, builders of vehicles and upturners of society, whom we invite into our theatres and beg not to forget their cheerful occupations while we hand the world over to their minds and hearts, for them to change as they think fit.

23

The theatre can only adopt such a free attitude if it lets itself be carried along by the strongest currents in its society and associates itself with those who are necessarily most impatient to make great alterations there. The bare wish, if nothing else, to evolve an art fit for the times must drive our theatre of the scientific age straight out into the suburbs, where it can stand as it were wide open, at the disposal of those who live hard and produce much, so that they can be fruitfully entertained there with their great problems. They may find it hard to pay for our art, and immediately to grasp the new method of entertainment, and we shall have to learn in many respects what they need and how they need it; but we can be sure of their interest. For these men who seem so far apart from natural science are only apart from it because they are being forcibly kept apart; and before they can get their hands on it they have first to develop and put into effect a new science of society; so that these are the true children of the scientific age, who alone can get the theatre moving if it is to move at all. A theatre which makes productivity its main source of entertainment has also to take it for its theme, and with greater keenness than ever now that man is every-where hampered by men from self-production: i.e. from maintaining himself, entertaining and being entertained. The theatre has to become geared into reality if it is to be in a position to turn out effective representations of reality, and to be allowed to do so.

24

But this makes it simpler for the theatre to edge as close as possible to the apparatus of education and mass communication. For although we cannot bother it with the raw material of knowledge in all its variety, which would stop it from being enjoyable, it is still free to find enjoyment in teaching and inquiring. It constructs its workable representations of society, which are then in a position to influence society, wholly and entirely as a game: for those who are constructing society it sets out society's experiences, past and present alike, in such a manner that the audience can 'appreciate' the feelings, insights and impulses which are distilled by the wisest, most active and most passionate among us from the events of the day or the century. They must be entertained with the wisdom that comes from the solution of problems, with the anger that is a practical expression of sympathy with the underdog, with the respect due to those who respect humanity, or rather whatever is kind to humanity, in short, with whatever delights those who are producing something.

25

And this also means that the theatre can let its spectators enjoy the particular ethic of their age, which springs from productivity. A theatre which converts the critical approach – i.e. our great productive method – into pleasure finds nothing in the ethical field which it must do and a great deal that it can. Even the wholly anti-social can be a source of enjoyment to society so long as it is presented forcefully and on the grand scale. It then often proves to have considerable powers of understanding and other unusually valuable capacities, applied admittedly to a destructive end. Even the bursting flood of a vast catastrophe can be appreciated in all its majesty by society, if society knows how to master it; then we make it our own.

26

For such an operation as this we can hardly accept the theatre as we see it before us. Let us go into one of these houses and observe the effect which it has on the spectators. Looking about us, we see somewhat motionless figures in a peculiar condition: they seem strenuously to be tensing all their muscles, except where these are flabby and exhausted. They scarcely communicate with each other; their relations are those of a lot of sleepers, though of such as dream restlessly because, as is popularly said of those who have nightmares, they are lying on their backs. True, their eyes are open, but they stare rather than see, just as they listen rather than hear. They look at the stage as if in a trance: an expression which comes from the Middle Ages, the days of witches and priests. Seeing and hearing are activities, and can be pleasant ones, but these people seem relieved of activity and like men to whom something is being done. This detached state, where they seem to be given over to vague but profound sensations, grows deeper the better the work of the actors, and so we, as we do not approve of this situation, should like them to be as bad as possible.

27

As for the world portrayed there, the world from which slices are cut in order to produce these moods and movements of the emotions, its appearance is such, produced from such slight and wretched stuff as a few pieces of cardboard, a little miming, a bit of text, that one has to admire the theatre folk who, with so feeble a reflection of the real world, can move the feelings of their audience so much more strongly than does the world itself.

28

In any case we should excuse these theatre folk, for the pleasures which they sell for money and fame could not be induced by an exacter representation of the world, nor could their inexact renderings be presented in a less magical way. Their capacity to represent people can be seen at work in various instances; it is especially the rogues and the minor figures who reveal their knowledge of humanity and differ one from the other, but the central figures have to be kept general, so that it is easier for the onlooker to identify himself with them, and at all costs each trait of character must be drawn from the narrow field within which everyone can say at once: that is how it is.

For the spectator wants to be put in possession of quite definite sensations, just as a child does when it climbs on to one of the horses on a roundabout: the sensation of pride that it can ride, and has a horse; the pleasure of being carried, and whirled past other children; the adventurous daydreams in which it pursues others or is pursued, etc. In leading the child to experience all this the degree to which its wooden seat resembles a horse counts little, nor does it matter that the ride is confined to a small circle. The one important point for the spectators in these houses is that they should be able to swap a contradictory world for a consistent one, one that they scarcely know for one of which they can dream.

29

That is the sort of theatre which we face in our operations, and so far it has been fully able to transmute our optimistic friends, whom we have called the children of the scientific era, into a cowed, credulous, hypnotized mass.

30

True, for about half a century they have been able to see rather more faithful representations of human social life, as well as individual figures who were in revolt against certain social evils or even against the structure of society as a whole. They felt interested enough to put up with a temporary and exceptional restriction of language, plot and spiritual scope; for the fresh wind of the scientific spirit nearly withered the charms to which they had grown used. The sacrifice was not especially worth while. The greater subtlety of the representations subtracted from one pleasure without satisfying another. The field of human relationships came within our view, but not within our grasp. Our feelings, having been aroused in the old (magic) way, were bound themselves to remain unaltered.

31

For always and everywhere theatres were the amusement centres of a class which restricted the scientific spirit to the natural field, not daring to let it loose on the field of human relationships. The tiny proletarian section of the public, reinforced to a negligible and uncertain extent by renegade intellectuals, likewise still needed the old kind of entertainment, as a relief from its predetermined way of life.

32

So let us march ahead! Away with all obstacles! Since we seem to have landed in a battle, let us fight! Have we not seen how disbelief can move mountains? Is it not enough that we should have found that

something is being kept from us? Before one thing and another there
hangs a curtain: let us draw it up!

33

The theatre as we know it shows the structure of society (represented
on the stage) as incapable of being influenced by society (in the
auditorium). Oedipus, who offended against certain principles
underlying the society of his time, is executed: the gods see to that; they
are beyond criticism. Shakespeare's great solitary figures, bearing on
their breast the star of their fate, carry through with irresistible force
their futile and deadly outbursts; they prepare their own downfall; life,
not death, becomes obscene as they collapse; the catastrophe is beyond
criticism. Human sacrifices all round! Barbaric delights! We know that
the barbarians have their art. Let us create another.

34

How much longer are our souls, leaving our 'mere' bodies under cover
of the darkness, to plunge into those dreamlike figures up on the stage,
there to take part in the crescendos and climaxes which 'normal' life
denies us? What kind of release is it at the end of all these plays (which
is a happy end only for the conventions of the period–suitable
measures, the restoration of order–), when we experience the dreamlike
executioner's axe which cuts short such crescendos as so many excesses?
We slink into *Oedipus*, for taboos still exist and ignorance is no excuse
before the law. Into *Othello*; for jealously still causes us trouble and
everything depends on possession. Into *Wallenstein*; for we need to be
free for the competitive struggle and to observe the rules, or it would
peter out. This deadweight of old habits is also needed for plays like
Ghosts and *The Weavers*, although there the social structure, in the shape
of a 'setting', presents itself as more open to question. The feelings,
insights and impulses of the chief characters are forced on us, and so
we learn nothing more about society than we can get from the 'setting'.

35

We need a type of theatre which not only releases the feelings, insights
and impulses possible within the particular historical field of human
relations in which the action takes place, but employs and encourages
those thoughts and feelings which help transform the field itself.

36

The field has to be defined in historically relative terms. In other words
we must drop our habit of taking the different social structures of past
periods, then stripping them of everything that makes them different; so
that they all look more or less like our own, which then acquires from
this process a certain air of having been there all along, in other words

of permanence pure and simple. Instead we must leave them their distinguishing marks and keep their impermanence always before our eyes, so that our own period can be seen to be impermanent too. (It is of course futile to make use of fancy colours and folklore for this, such as our theatres apply precisely in order to emphasize the similarities in human behaviour at different times. We shall indicate the theatrical methods below.)

37

If we ensure that our characters on the stage are moved by social impulses and that these differ according to the period, then we make it harder for our spectator to identify himself with them. He cannot simply feel: that's how I would act, but at most can say: if I had lived under those circumstances. And if we play works dealing with our own time as though they were historical, then perhaps the circumstances under which he himself acts will strike him as equally odd; and this is where the critical attitude begins.

38

The 'historical conditions' must of course not be imagined (nor will they be so constructed) as mysterious Powers (in the background); on the contrary, they are created and maintained by men (and will in due course be altered by them): it is the actions taking place before us that allow us to see what they are.

39

If a character responds in a manner historically in keeping with his period, and would respond otherwise in other periods, does that mean that he is not simply 'Everyman'? It is true that a man will respond differently according to his circumstances and his class; if he were living at another time, or in his youth, or on the darker side of life, he would infallibly give a different response, though one still determined by the same factors and like anyone else's response in that situation at that time. So should we not ask if there are any further differences of response? Where is the man himself, the living, unmistakeable man, who is not quite identical with those identified with him? It is clear that his stage image must bring him to light, and this will come about if this particular contradiction is recreated in the image. The image that gives historical definition will retain something of the rough sketching which indicates traces of other movements and features all around the fully-worked-out figure. Or imagine a man standing in a valley and making a speech in which he occasionally changes his views or simply utters sentences which contradict one another, so that the accompanying echo forces them into confrontation.

40

Such images certainly demand a way of acting which will leave the spectator's intellect free and highly mobile. He has again and again to make what one might call hypothetical adjustments to our structure, by mentally switching off the motive forces of our society or by substituting others for them: a process which leads real conduct to acquire an element of 'unnaturalness', thus allowing the real motive forces to be shorn of their naturalness and become capable of manipulation.

41

It is the same as when an irrigation expert looks at a river together with its former bed and various hypothetical courses which it might have followed if there had been a different tilt to the plateau or a different volume of water. And while he in his mind is looking at a new river, the socialist in his is hearing new kinds of talk from the labourers who work by it. And similarly in the theatre our spectator should find that the incidents set among such labourers are also accompanied by echoes and by traces of sketching.

42

The kind of acting which was tried out at the Schiffbauerdamm Theater in Berlin between the First and Second World Wars, with the object of producing such images, is based on the 'alienation effect' (A-effect). A representation that alienates is one which allows us to recognize its subject, but at the same time makes it seem unfamiliar. The classical and medieval theatre alienated its characters by making them wear human or animal masks; the Asiatic theatre even today uses musical and pantomimic A-effects. Such devices were certainly a barrier to empathy, and yet this technique owed more, not less, to hypnotic suggestion than do those by which empathy is achieved. The social aims of these old devices were entirely different from our own.

43

The old A-effects quite remove the object represented from the spectator's grasp, turning it into something that cannot be altered; the new are not odd in themselves, though the unscientific eye stamps anything strange as odd. The new alienations are only designed to free socially-conditioned phenomena from that stamp of familiarity which protects them against our grasp today.

44

For it seems impossible to alter what has long not been altered. We are always coming on things that are too obvious for us to bother to understand them. What men experience among themselves they think of as 'the' human experience. A child, living in a world of old men, learns how things work there. He knows the run of things before he can walk. If anyone is bold enough to want something further, he only wants to have it as an exception. Even if he realizes that the arrangements made for him by 'Providence' are only what has been provided by society he is bound to see society, that vast collection of beings like himself, as a whole that is greater than the sum of its parts and therefore not in any way to be influenced. Moreover, he would be used to things that could not be influenced; and who mistrusts what he is used to? To transform himself from general passive acceptance to a corresponding state of suspicious inquiry he would need to develop that detached eye with which the great Galileo observed a swinging chandelier. He was amazed by this pendulum motion, as if he had not expected it and could not understand its occurring, and this enabled him to come on the rules by which it was governed. Here is the outlook, disconcerting but fruitful, which the theatre must provoke with its representations of human social life. It must amaze its public, and this can be achieved by a technique of alienating the familiar.

45

This technique allows the theatre to make use in its representations of the new social scientific method known as dialectical materialism. In order to unearth society's laws of motion this method treats social situations as processes, and traces out all their inconsistencies. It regards nothing as existing except in so far as it changes, in other words is in disharmony with itself. This also goes for those human feelings, opinions and attitudes through which at any time the form of men's life together finds its expression.

46

Our own period, which is transforming nature in so many and different ways, takes pleasure in understanding things so that we can interfere. There is a great deal to man, we say; so a great deal can be made out of him. He does not have to stay the way he is now, nor does he have to be seen only as he is now, but also as he might become. We must not start with him; we must start on him. This means, however, that I must not simply set myself in his place, but must set myself facing him, to represent us all. That is why the theatre must alienate what is shows.

47

In order to produce A-effects the actor has to discard whatever means he has learnt of getting the audience to identify itself with the characters which he plays. Aiming not to put his audience into a trance, he must not go into a trance himself. His muscles must remain loose, for a turn of the head, e.g. with tautened neck muscles, will 'magically' lead the spectators' eyes and even their heads to turn with it, and this can only detract from any speculation or reaction which the gesture may bring about. His way of speaking has to be free from parsonical sing-song and from all those cadences which lull the spectator so that the sense gets lost. Even if he plays a man possessed he must not seem to be possessed himself, for how is the spectator to discover what possessed him if he does?

48

At no moment must he go so far as to be wholly transformed into the character played. The verdict: 'he didn't act Lear, he was Lear' would be an annihilating blow to him. He has just to show the character, or rather he has to do more than just get into it; this does not mean that if he is playing passionate parts he must himself remain cold. It is only that his feelings must not at bottom be those of the character, so that the audience's may not at bottom be those of the character either. The audience must have complete freedom here.

49

This principle – that the actor appears on the stage in a double role, as Laughton and as Galileo; that the showman Laughton does not disappear in the Galileo whom he is showing; from which this way of acting gets its name of 'epic' – comes to mean simply that the tangible, matter-of-fact process is no longer hidden behind a veil; that Laughton is actually there, standing on the stage and showing us what he imagines Galileo to have been. Of course the audience would not forget Laughton if he attempted the full change of personality, in that they would admire him for it; but they would in that case miss his own opinions and sensations, which would have been completely swallowed up by the character. He would have taken its opinions and sensations and made them his own, so that a single homogeneous pattern would emerge, which he would then make ours. In order to prevent this abuse the actor must also put some artistry into the act of showing. An illustration may help: we find a gesture which expresses one-half of his attitude – that of showing – if we make him smoke a cigar and then imagine him laying it down now and again in order to show us some further characteristic attitude of the figure in the play. If we then subtract any element of hurry from the image and do not read slackness into its refusal to be taut we shall have an actor who is fully capable of leaving us to our thoughts, or to his own.

50

There needs to be yet a further change in the actor's communication of these images, and it too makes the process more 'matter-on-fact'. Just as the actor no longer has to persuade the audience that it is the author's character and not himself that is standing on the stage, so also he need not pretend that the events taking place on the stage have never been rehearsed, and are now happening for the first and only time. Schiller's distinction is no longer valid: that the rhapsodist has to treat his material as wholly in the past: the mime his, as wholly here and now.[1] It should be apparent all through his performance that 'even at the start and in the middle he knows how it ends' and he must 'thus maintain a calm independence throughout'. He narrates the story of his character by vivid portrayal, always knowing more than it does and treating its 'now' and 'here' not as a pretence made possible by the rules of the game but as something to be distinguished from yesterday and some other place, so as to make visible the knotting-together of the events.

51

This matters particularly in the portrayal of large-scale events or ones where the outside world is abruptly changed, as in wars and revolutions. The spectator can then have the whole situation and the whole course of events set before him. He can for instance hear a woman speaking and imagine her speaking differently, let us say in a few weeks' time, or other women speaking differently at that moment but in another place. This would be possible if the actress were to play as though the woman had lived through the entire period and were now, out of her memory and her knowledge of what happened next, recalling those utterances of hers which were important at the time; for what is important here is what became important. To alienate an individual in this way, as being 'this particular individual' and 'this particular individual at this particular moment', is only possible if there are no illusions that the player is identical with the character and the performance with the actual event.

52

We shall find that this has meant scrapping yet another illusion: that everyone behaves like the character concerned. 'I am doing this' has become 'I did this', and now 'he did this' has got to become 'he did this, when he might have done something else'. It is too great a simplification if we make the actions fit the character and the character fit the actions: the inconsistencies which are to be found in the actions and characters of real people cannot be shown like this. The laws of motion of a society are not to be demonstrated by 'perfect examples', for 'imperfection' (inconsistency) is an essential part of motion and of the thing moved. It is only necessary – but absolutely necessary – that there should be something approaching experimental conditions. i.e. that a counter-experiment should now and then be conceivable. Altogether this is a way of treating society as if all its actions were performed as experiments.

53

Even if empathy, or self-identification with the character, can be usefully indulged in at rehearsals (something to be avoided in a performance) it has to be treated just as one of a number of methods of observation. It helps when rehearsing, for even though the contemporary theatre has applied it in an indiscriminate way it has none the less led to subtle delineation of personality. But it is the crudest form of empathy when the actor simply asks: what should I be like if this or that were to happen to me? what would it look like if I were to say this and do that? – instead of asking: have I ever heard somebody saying this and doing that? in order to piece together all sorts of elements with which to construct a new character such as would allow the story to have taken place – and a good deal else. The coherence of the character is in fact shown by the way in which its individual qualities contradict one another.

54

Observation is a major part of acting. The actor observes his fellow-men with all his nerves and muscles in an act of imitation which is at the same time a process of the mind. For pure imitation would only bring out what had been observed; and this is not enough, because the original says what it has to say with too subdued a voice. To achieve a character rather than a caricature, the actor looks at people as though they were playing him their actions, in other words as though they were advising him to give their actions careful consideration.

55

Without opinions and objectives one can represent nothing at all. Without knowledge one can show nothing; how could one know what would be worth knowing? Unless the actor is satisfied to be a parrot or a monkey he must master our period's knowledge of human social life by himself joining in the war of the classes. Some people may feel this to be degrading, because they rank art, once the money side has been settled, as one of the highest things; but mankind's highest decisions are in fact fought out on earth, not in the heavens; in the 'external' world, not inside people's heads. Nobody can stand above the warring classes, for nobody can stand above the human race. Society cannot snare a common communication system so long as it is split into warring classes. Thus for art to be 'unpolitical' means only to ally itself with the 'ruling' group.

56

So the choice of viewpoint is also a major element of the actor's art, and it has to be decided outside the theatre. Like the transformation of nature, that of society is a liberating act; and it is the joys of liberation which the theatre of a scientific age has got to convey.

57

Let us go on to examine how, for instance, this viewpoint affects the actor's interpretation of his part. It then becomes important that he should not 'catch on' too quickly. Even if he straightway establishes the most natural cadences for his part, the least awkward way of speaking it, he still cannot regard its actual pronouncement as being ideally natural, but must think twice and take his own general opinions into account, then consider various other conceivable pronouncements; in short, take up the attitude of a man who just wonders. This is not only to prevent him from 'fixing' a particular character prematurely, so that it has to be stuffed out with after-thoughts because he has not waited to register all the other pronouncements, and especially those of the other characters; but also and principally in order to build into the character that element of 'Not – But' on which so much depends if society, in the shape of the audience, is to be able to look at what takes place in such a way as to be able to affect it. Each actor, moreover, instead of concentrating on what suits him and calling it 'human nature', must go above all for what does not suit him, is not his speciality. And along with his part he must commit to memory his first reactions, reserves, criticisms, shocks, so that they are not destroyed by being 'swallowed up' in the final version but are preserved and perceptible; for character and all must not grow on the audience so much as strike it.

58

And the learning process must be co-ordinated so that the actor learns as the other actors are learning and develops his character as they are developing theirs. For the smallest social unit is not the single person but two people. In life too we develop one another.

59

Here we can learn something from our own theatres' deplorable habit of letting the dominant actor, the star, 'come to the front' by getting all the other actors to work for him: he makes his character terrible or wise by forcing his partners to make theirs terrified or attentive. Even if only to secure this advantage for all, and thus to help the story, the actors should sometimes swap roles with their partners during rehearsal, so that the characters can get what they need from one another. But it is also good for the actors when they see their characters copied or portrayed in another form. If the part is played by somebody of the opposite sex the sex of the character will be more clearly brought out; if it is played by a comedian, whether comically or tragically, it will gain fresh aspects. By helping to develop the parts that correspond to his own, or at any rate standing in for their players, the actor strengthens the all-decisive social standpoint from which he has to present his character. The master is only the sort of master his servant lets him be, etc.

60

A mass of operations to develop the character are carried out when it is introduced among the other characters of the play, and the actor will have to memorize what he himself has anticipated in this connection from his reading of the text. But now he finds out much more about himself from the treatment which he gets at the hands of the characters in the play.

61

The realm of attitudes adopted by the characters towards one another is what we call the realm of gest. Physical attitude, tone of voice and facial expression are all determined by a social gest: the characters are cursing, flattering, instructing one another, and so on. The attitudes which people adopt towards one another include even those attitudes which would appear to be quite private, such as the utterances of physical pain in an illness, or of religious faith. These expressions of a gest are usually highly complicated and contradictory, so that they cannot be rendered by any single word and the actor must take care that in giving his image the necessary emphasis he does not lose anything, but emphasizes the entire complex.

62

The actor masters his character by paying critical attention to its manifold utterances, as also to those of his counterparts and of all the other characters involved.

Note

1. Letter to Goethe, 26.12.1797.

Trauerspiel and Tragedy*

Walter Benjamin

With his insight into the connection of tragedy to legend, and the independence of the tragic from the ethos, Nietzsche's work lays the foundation for theses such as this. It is not necessary to refer to the prejudice of the next generation of scholars in order to explain the delay, not to say the laboriousness, with which these insights exerted their influence. It was rather that the Schopenhauerian and Wagnerian metaphysics necessarily vitiated the best aspects of Nietzsche's work. They are already influential in the definition of myth. 'The myth leads the world of manifestation to its limits where it denies itself and seeks to flee back again into the womb of the true and only reality ... Thus we use the experiences of the truly aesthetic listener to bring to mind the tragic artist himself as he creates his figures like a fecund divinity of individuation (so his work can hardly be understood as an "imitation of nature") and as his vast Dionysian impulse then devours his entire world of manifestations, in order to let us sense beyond it, and through its destruction, the highest artistic primal joy, in the bosom of the primordially One.'[1] For Nietzsche, as is sufficiently clear from this passage, the tragic myth is a purely aesthetic creation, and the interplay of Apollonian and Dionysian energy remains equally confined to the aesthetic sphere, as appearance and the dissolution of appearance. Nietzsche's renunciation of any understanding of the tragic myth in historical-philosophical terms is a high price to pay for his emancipation from the stereotype of a morality in which the tragic occurrence was usually clothed. The classic formulation of this renunciation is as follows: 'For to our humiliation *and* exaltation, one thing above all must be clear to us. The entire comedy of art is neither performed for our betterment or education nor are we the true authors of this art world. On the contrary, we may assume that we are merely images and artistic projections for the true author, and that we have our highest dignity in

* Reprinted from *The Origin of German Tragic Drama*, trans. John Osborne (London: Verso, 1985).

our significance as works of art – for it is only as an *aesthetic
phenomenon* that the existence and the world are eternally *justified* –
while of course our consciousness of our own significance hardly differs
from that which the soldiers painted on canvas have of the battle
represented on it.'[2] The abyss of aestheticism opens up, and this brilliant
intuition was finally to see all its concepts disappear into it, so that
gods and heroes, defiance and suffering, the pillars of the tragic edifice,
fall away into nothing. Where art so firmly occupies the centre of
existence as to make man one of its manifestations instead of
recognizing him above all as its basis, to see man's existence as the
eternal subject of its own creations instead of recognizing him as its
own creator, then all sane reflection is at an end. And whether, with the
removal of man from the centre of art, it is Nirvana, the slumbering
will to life, which takes his place, as in Schopenhauer, or whether it is
the 'dissonance become man'[3] which, as in Nietzsche, has created both
the manifestations of the human world and man himself, it makes no
difference; it is the same pragmatism. For what does it matter whether
it is the will to life or the will to destroy life which is supposed to
inspire every work of art, since the latter, as a product of the absolute
will, de-values itself along with the world? The nihilism lodged in the
depths of the artistic philosophy of Bayreuth nullified – it could do no
other – the concept of the hard, historical actuality of Greek tragedy.
'Image sparks, lyrical poems, which in their highest development are
called tragedies and dramatic dithyrambs'[4] – tragedy is dissolved into
visions of the chorus and the spectators. Nietzsche argues that one must
'always keep in mind that the public at an Attic tragedy found itself in
the chorus of the orchestra, and there was at bottom no opposition
between public and chorus; everything is merely a great sublime chorus
of dancing and singing satyrs or of those who permit themselves to be
represented by such satyrs ... The satyr chorus is, first of all, a vision of
the Dionysian mass of spectators, just as the world of the stage, in turn,
is a vision of this satyr chorus.'[5] It is not permissible to lay such
extreme emphasis on the Apollonian illusion, a pre-condition of the
aesthetic dissolution of tragedy. As far as the philologist is concerned
'there is no basis in the cult for the tragic chorus';[6] while the ecstatic,
whether in the form of the mass or the individual, is – so long as he is
not transfixed – only to be conceived in the state of most violent action.
It is not possible to make the chorus, which intervenes in the tragedy in
a considered and reflective way, at the same time into the subject which
experiences the visions; especially not a chorus which would be both
itself the vision of a mass of people and the bearer of further visions.
Above all, there is no kind of unity between the choruses and the
public. This needs to be said, insofar as the gulf between them, the
orchestra, does not demonstrate it by its very presence.

Nietzsche turned his back on the tragic theories of the epigones without refuting them. For he saw no reason to take issue with their central doctrine of tragic guilt and tragic atonement, because he was only too willing to leave the field of moral debates to them. His neglect of such criticism barred the way to those concepts from the philosophy of history or the philosophy of religion in which the definition of tragedy is ultimately expressed. Wherever the discussion begins there is one, apparently unchallengeable, prejudice which it cannot tolerate. This is the assumption that the actions and attitudes encountered in fictional characters may be used in the discussion of moral problems in a similar way to an anatomical model. Although, in general, one hardly dare treat it so unquestioningly as a faithful imitation of nature, the work of art is unhesitatingly accepted as the exemplary copy of moral phenomena without any consideration of how susceptible such phenomena are to representation. The object in question here is not the significance of moral content for the criticism of a work of art; the question is a different one, indeed a double one. Do the actions and attitudes depicted in a work of art have moral significance as images of reality? And: can the content of a work of art, in the last analysis, be adequately understood in terms of moral insights? Their assent to – or rather their failure to consider – these two questions is what, more than anything else, determines the character of the customary interpretation and theory of the tragic. And yet a negative answer is precisely what is required to show the necessity of understanding the moral content of tragic poetry, not as its last word, but as one aspect of its integral truth: that is to say in terms of the history of philosophy. Certainly, the denial of the first proposition can, in different contexts, be more readily justified than that of the second, which is primarily the concern of a philosophy of art. But this much is true even of the former: fictional characters exist only in literature. They are woven as tightly into the totality of the literary work as are the subjects of Gobelins into their canvas, so that they cannot be removed from it as individuals. In this respect the human figure in literature, indeed in art as such, differs from the human figure in reality, where physical isolation, which in so many ways is only apparent isolation, has its true meaning as a perceptible expression of moral seclusion with God. 'Thou shalt not make unto thee any graven image' – this is not only a warning against idolatry. With incomparable emphasis the prohibition of the representation of the human body obviates any suggestion that the sphere in which the moral essence of man is perceptible can be reproduced. Everything moral is bound to life in its extreme sense, that is to say where it fulfils itself in death, the abode of danger as such. And from the point of view of any kind of artistic practice this life, which concerns us morally, that is in our unique individuality, appears as something negative, or at least should appear so. For art cannot, for its part, allow itself, in its works, to be appointed a councillor of the conscience and it cannot permit what is represented, rather than the actual representation, to be the object of attention. The truth content of this totality, which is never encountered in the abstracted lesson, least of all the moral lesson, but only in the critical elaboration of the work itself,[7] includes moral warnings only in the most indirect form.[8] Where they obtrude as the main purpose of the investigation, which is the case in the criticism of tragedy as practised by the German idealists – how typical is Solger's essay on Sophocles![9] – then this means that the very much more worthwhile struggle to ascertain the place of a work or a form in terms of the history of philosophy has been abandoned in favour of a cheap reflection which is figurative, and therefore less relevant than any moral doctrine, however philistine. As far as tragedy is concerned, this struggle will find reliable guidance in the consideration of its relationship to legend.

Wilamowitz gives the following definition: 'an Attic tragedy is a self-contained piece of heroic legend, poetically adapted in the sublime style for presentation by a chorus of Attic citizens and two or three actors, and intended for performance as part of the public worship at the shrine of Dionysus'.[10] Elsewhere he writes: 'thus any consideration ultimately leads back to the relationship of tragedy to legend. Tragedy has its essential roots in legend, from here it derives its special strengths and weaknesses, and herein lies the difference between Attic tragedy and every other kind of dramatic poetry'.[11] This is where the philosophical definition of tragedy has to begin, and it will do so with the perception that tragedy cannot be understood simply as legend in dramatic form. For legend is, by its very nature, free of tendentiousness. Here the streams of tradition, which surge down violently, often from opposite directions, have finally come to rest beneath the epic surface which conceals a divided, many-armed river-bed. Tragic poetry is opposed to epic poetry as a tendentious re-shaping of the tradition. The Oedipus-theme shows just how intensively and how significantly it was able to re-shape it.[12] Nevertheless, older theoreticians such as Wackernagel, are right when they declare that invention is incompatible with tragedy. For the re-shaping of the legend is not motivated by the search for tragic situations, but it is undertaken with a tendentious purpose which would lose all its significance if the tendency were not expressed in terms of the legend, the primordial history of the nation. The signature of tragedy does not therefore consist in a 'conflict of levels'[14] between the hero and the environment as such, which is what Scheler declares to be characteristic in his study *Zum Phänomen des Tragischen*, but the unique Greek form of such conflicts. Where is this to be sought? What tendency is hidden in the tragic? For what does the hero die? Tragic poetry is based on the idea of sacrifice. But in respect of its victim, the hero, the tragic sacrifice differs from any other kind, being at once a first and a final sacrifice. A final sacrifice in the sense of the atoning sacrifice to gods who are upholding an ancient right; a first sacrifice in the sense of the representative action, in which new aspects of the life of the nation become manifest. These are different from the old, fatal obligations in that they do not refer back to a command from above, but to the life of the hero himself; and they destroy him because they do not measure up to the demands of the individual will, but benefit only the life of the, as yet unborn, national community. The tragic death has a dual significance: it invalidates the ancient rights of the Olympians, and it offers up the hero to the unknown god as the first fruits of a new harvest of humanity. But this dual power can also reside in tragic suffering, as Aeschylus depicts it in the *Oresteia*, and Sophocles in *Oedipus*. If the expiatory character of the sacrifice stands out less prominently in this form, all the clearer is its transformation, in which the subjection of the hero to death is replaced by a paroxysm which just as surely does justice to the old conception of gods and sacrifice, as it is patently clad in the form of the new conception. Death thereby becomes salvation: the crisis of death. One of the oldest examples is the replacement of the execution of the victim at the altar with his escape from the knife of the sacrificial priest; the destined victim thus runs around the altar, finally seizing it, so that the altar becomes a place of refuge, the angry god a merciful god, the victim a prisoner and servant of god. This is the whole schema of the *Oresteia*. In its narrow concentration on the subject of death, its absolute dependence on the community, and above all in the absence of any guarantee of finality from the solution and salvation with which it concludes, this agonal prophecy is free of all epic-didactic elements. But what justification have we for speaking of an 'agonal' representation? For the hypothetical derivation of the tragic event from the sacrificial race around the *thymele* is scarcely enough to provide such a justification. This shows, in the first instance, that the Attic stage plays took the form of contests. Not only did the dramatists compete with each other, but also the protagonists, even the *choragi*. But the inner justification lies in the dumb anguish which every tragic performance both communicates to the spectators and displays in its characters. Here it comes about in the speechless contest of the *agon*. In his analysis of 'meta-ethical man', Franz Rosenzweig has demonstrated that the inarticulacy of the tragic hero, which distinguishes the main figure in Greek tragedy from all his successors, is one of the foundation stones of the theory of tragedy.

'For this is the mark of the self, the seal of its greatness and the token of its weakness alike: it is silent. The tragic hero has only one language that is completely proper to him: silence. It has been so from the very beginning. The tragic devised itself the artistic form of the drama precisely so as to be able to present silence . . . In his silence the hero burns the bridges connecting him to god and the world, elevates himself above the realm of personality, which in speech, defines itself against others and individualizes itself, and so enters the icy loneliness of the self. The self knows of nothing other than itself; its loneliness is absolute. How else can it activate this loneliness, this rigid and defiant self-sufficiency, except in silence. And so it is in the tragedies of Aeschylus, as even contemporaries noticed.'[15] Yet tragic silence, as presented in this important description, must not be thought of as being dominated by defiance alone. Rather, this defiance is every bit as much a consequence of the experience of speechlessness as a factor which intensifies the condition. The content of the hero's achievements belongs to the community, as does speech. Since the community of the nation denies these achievements, they remain unarticulated in the hero. And he must therefore all the more forcefully enclose within the confines of his physical self every action and every item of knowledge the greater and the more potentially effective it is. It is the achievement of his *physis* alone, not of language, if he is able to hold fast to his cause, and he must therefore do so in death. Lukács has the same thing in mind when, in his account of tragic decision, he observes: 'The essence of these great moments in life is the pure experience of selfhood.'[16] A passage in Nietzsche shows more clearly that the meaning of tragic silence had not escaped him. Although he had no suspicion of its significance as a manifestation of the agonal in the tragic sphere, he nevertheless puts his finger on it in his contrast of image and speech. Tragic 'heroes speak, as it were, more superficially than they act; the myth does not at all obtain adequate objectification in the spoken word. The structure of the scenes and the visual images reveal a deeper wisdom than the poet himself can put into words and concepts.'[17] This can, of course, hardly be a question of failure, as Nietzsche goes on to suggest. The greater the discrepancy between the tragic word and the situation – which can no longer be called tragic when there is no discrepancy – the more surely has the hero escaped the ancient statutes to which, when they finally overtake him, he throws only the dumb shadow of his being, the self, as a sacrifice, while his soul finds refuge in the word of a distant community. The tragic presentation of legend thereby acquired inexhaustible topicality. In the presence of the suffering hero the community learns reverence and gratitude for the word with which his death endowed it – a word which shone out in another place as a new gift whenever the poet extracted some new meaning from the legend. Tragic silence, far more than tragic pathos, became the storehouse of an experience of the sublimity of linguistic expression, which is generally so much more intensely alive in ancient than in later literature. The decisive confrontation with the demonic world-order which takes place in Greek literature also gives tragic poetry its signature in terms of the history of philosophy. The tragic is to the demonic what the paradox is to ambiguity. In all the paradoxes of tragedy – in the sacrifice, which, in complying with ancient statutes, creates new ones, in death, which is an act of atonement but which sweeps away only the self, in the tragic ending, which grants the victory to man, but also to god – ambiguity, the stigma of the daimons, is in decline. There are indications of this everywhere, however slight. For instance in the silence of the hero, which neither looks for nor finds any justification, and therefore throws suspicion back on to his persecutors. For its meaning is inverted: what appears before the public is not the guilt of the accused but the evidence of speechless suffering, and the tragedy which appeared to be devoted to the judgment of the hero is transformed into a hearing about the Olympians in which the latter appears as a witness and, against the will of the gods, displays the honour of the demi-god.[18] The profound Aeschylean impulse to justice[19] inspires the anti-Olympian prophecy of all tragic poetry. 'It was not in law but in tragedy that the head of the genius first emerged above the cloud of guilt, for in tragedy the hold of demonic fate is broken. Not, however, in the replacement of the inscrutable pagan concatenation of guilt and atonement by the purity of man, absolved and reconciled with the pure god. It is rather that in tragedy pagan man realizes that he is better than his gods, but this realization strikes him dumb, and it remains unarticulated. Without declaring itself, it secretly endeavours to gather strength . . . There is here no question whatever of a restitution of the "moral order of the universe", but it is the attempt of moral man, still dumb, still inarticulate – as such he bears the name of hero – to raise himself up amid the agitation of that painful world. The paradox of the birth of the genius in moral speechlessness, moral infantility, constitutes the sublime element in tragedy.'[20]

It would be otiose to point out that the sublimity of the content is not explained by the rank and lineage of the characters, were it not for the fact that the royal status of so many heroes has been the source of certain curious speculations and obvious confusions. Both have arisen from a consideration of this royal status as such, in the modern sense. Yet it could not be more obvious that it is an incidental factor, arising from the material of the tradition on which tragic poetry is based. For in primeval times it is the ruler who occupies the central position here, so that royal descent is an indication of the dramatic character's origin in the heroic age. This is the sole significance attaching to this descent, but it is, of course, a decisive significance. For the forthrightness of the heroic self – which is not a character-trait, but the historical-philosophical signature of the hero – corresponds to his position of authority. By contrast to this simple state of affairs, Schopenhauer's interpretation of kingship in tragedy seems to be one of those levellings into the universally human which obscure the essential difference between ancient and modern drama. 'For the heroes of their tragedies the Greeks generally took royal persons and the moderns for the most part have done the same. This is certainly not because rank gives more dignity to the person who acts or suffers; and as it is merely a question of setting human passions in play, the relative worth of the objects by which this is done is a matter of indifference, and farms achieve as much as is achieved by kingdoms . . . Persons of great power and prestige are nevertheless best adapted for tragedy, because the misfortune in which we should recognize the fate of human life must have sufficient magnitude, in order to appear terrible to the spectator, be he who he may . . . But the circumstances that plunge a bourgeois family into want and despair are in the eyes of the great or wealthy often very insignificant, and can be removed by human aid, sometimes indeed by a trifle; therefore such spectators cannot be tragically shaken by them. On the other hand, the misfortunes of the great and powerful are unconditionally terrible, and are inaccessible even to help from outside; for kings must either help themselves through their own power, or be ruined. In addition to this is the fact that the fall is greatest from a height. Bourgeois characters lack the height from which to fall.'[21] What is here explained as the tragic character's dignity of rank – and explained in a thoroughly baroque way on the basis of the unhappy events of the 'tragedy' – has nothing whatever to do with the status of the timeless heroic figures; the princely estate does, however, have for the modern *Trauerspiel* the exemplary and far more precise significance which has been considered in the appropriate context. What distinguishes the *Trauerspiel* from Greek tragedy in respect of this deceptive affinity has not yet been perceived even by the most recent research. There is an extreme, involuntary irony about Borinski's commentary on Schiller's tragic experiments in *Die Braut von Messina*, which, because of the romantic attitude, could not but revert sharply to the *Trauerspiel*; following Schopenhauer, Borinski observes, with reference to the high rank of the characters, which is persistently emphasized by the chorus: 'How right were renaissance poetics – not in a spirit of "pedantry", but in a vital human way – to adhere rigidly to the "kings and heroes" of ancient tragedy.'[22]

Schopenhauer conceived of tragedy as *Trauerspiel*; of the great German metaphysicians after Fichte there is scarcely another so lacking in sympathy for Greek drama. In modern drama he saw a higher stage of development, and in this comparison, however inadequate it may be, he did at least locate the problem. 'What gives to everything tragic, whatever the form in which it appears, the characteristic tendency to the sublime, is the dawning of the knowledge that the world and life can afford us no true satisfaction, and are therefore not worth our attachment to them. In this the tragic spirit consists; accordingly, it leads to resignation. I admit that rarely in the tragedy of the ancients is this spirit of resignation seen and directly expressed . . . Stoic equanimity is fundamentally distinguished from Christian resignation by the fact that it teaches only calm endurance and unruffled expectation of unalterably necessary evils, but Christianity teaches renunciation, the giving up of willing. In just the same way the tragic heroes of the ancients show resolute and stoical subjection under the unavoidable blows of fate; the Christian tragedy, on the other hand, shows the giving up of the whole will to live, cheerful abandonment of the world in the consciousness of its worthlessness and vanity. But I am fully of the opinion that the tragedy of the moderns is at a higher level than that of the ancients.'[23] This diffuse appreciation, inhibited by anti-historical metaphysics, needs only to be contrasted with a few sentences by Rosenzweig for us to realize what progress has been made in the philosophical history of the drama with the discoveries of this thinker. 'This is one of the profoundest differences between the new tragedy and the old . . . its figures are all different from each other, different in the way every personality is different from another . . . In ancient tragedy this was not so; here only the actions were different; the hero, as tragic hero, always remained the same, always the same self, defiantly buried in itself. The demand that he be essentially conscious, that is to say conscious when he is alone with himself, is repugnant to the necessarily limited consciousness of the modern hero. Consciousness always demands clarity; limited consciousness is imperfect . . . The goal of modern tragedy is therefore quite unknown to ancient tragedy: it is the tragedy of the absolute man in his relationship to the absolute object . . . The barely recognized goal . . . is as follows: to replace the unlimited multiplicity of characters with one absolute character, a modern hero, who is every bit as much a single and unchanging hero as the ancient hero. This point of convergence, at which the lines of all tragic characters would meet, this absolute man . . . is none other than the saint. The tragedy of the saint is the secret longing of the tragedian . . . It makes no difference . . . whether this is an attainable goal for the tragic poet or not; even if it is beyond the reach of tragedy as a work of art, it is, nonetheless, for the modern consciousness, the exact counterpart to the hero of ancient tragedy.'[24] The 'modern tragedy', whose deduction from ancient tragedy is the object of these sentences, bears – it hardly needs saying – the far from insignificant name: *Trauerspiel*. With this the reflections which conclude the above passage transcend the theoretical nature of the problem. The *Trauerspiel* is confirmed as a form of the tragedy of the saint by means of the martyr-drama. And if one only learns to recognize its characteristics in many different styles of drama from Calderón to Strindberg it must become clear that this form, a form of the mystery play, still has a future.

Here it is a question of its past. This leads us far back to a turning-point in the history of the Greek spirit itself: the death of Socrates. The martyr-drama was born from the death of Socrates as a parody of tragedy. And here, as so often, the parody of a form proclaims its end. Wilamowitz testifies to the fact that it meant the end of tragedy for Plato: 'Plato burnt his tetralogy; not because he was renouncing the ambition to be a poet in the sense of Aeschylus, but because he recognized that the tragedian could no longer be the teacher and master of the nation. He did of course attempt – so great was the power of tragedy – to create a new art form of tragic character, and he created a new cycle of legend to replace the obsolete heroic legends, the legend of Socrates.'[25] This legend of Socrates is a comprehensive secularization of the heroic legend by the submission of its demonic paradoxes to reason. Superficially, of course, the death of the philosopher resembles tragic death. It is an act of atonement according to the letter of an ancient law, a sacrificial death in the spirit of a new justice which contributes to the establishment of a new community. But this very similarity reveals most clearly the real significance of the agonal character of the genuinely tragic: that silent struggle, that mute flight of the hero, which in the [Platonic] *Dialogues*, has given way to such a brilliant display of speech and consciousness. The agonal has disappeared from the drama of Socrates – even in his philosophical struggles it is only a question of going through the motions – and in one stroke the death of the hero has been transformed into that of a martyr. Like the Christian hero of the faith – which explains both the sympathy of many a father of the Church and the hatred of Nietzsche, who unerringly detected this – Socrates dies voluntarily, and voluntarily, with inexpressible superiority and without any defiance, he becomes mute as he becomes silent. 'But that he was sentenced to death, not exile, Socrates himself seems to have brought about with perfect awareness and without any natural awe of death . . . *The dying Socrates* became the new ideal, never seen before, of noble Greek youths.'[26] Plato could not have indicated more

115

expressively the remoteness of this ideal from that of the tragic hero than he did by making immortality the subject of his master's final conversation. If, according to the *Apology*, the death of Socrates could still have appeared to be tragic – in much the same way as death in the *Antigone*, where it is already illuminated by an all too rational concept of duty – the Pythagorean tone of the *Phaedo*, on the other hand shows this death to be free of all tragic association. Socrates looks death in the face as a mortal – the best and most virtuous of mortals, one may insist – but he recognizes it as something alien, beyond which, in immortality, he expects to return to himself. Not so the tragic hero; he shrinks before death as before a power that is familiar, personal, and inherent in him. His life, indeed, unfolds from death, which is not its end but its form. For tragic existence acquires its task only because it is intrinsically subject to the limits of both linguistic and physical life which are set within it from its very beginning. This has been expressed in many different ways. Perhaps nowhere better than in a casual reference to tragic death as 'merely ... the outward sign that the soul has died'.[27] The tragic hero may, indeed, be described as soulless. Out of his profound inner emptiness echo the distant, new divine commands, and from this echo future generations learn their language. Just as in the ordinary creature the activity of life is all-embracing, so, in the tragic hero, is the process of dying, and tragic irony always arises whenever the hero – with profound but unsuspected justification – begins to speak of the circumstances of his death as if they were the circumstances of life. 'The determination of the tragic character to die is also ... only apparently heroic, only in a context of human psychology; the dying heroes of tragedy – thus, approximately, wrote a young tragedian – have already long been dead before they actually die.'[28] In his spiritual-cum-physical existence the hero is the framework of the tragic process. If the 'power of the framework', as it has appropriately been called, is really one of the essential features which distinguish the ancient attitude from the modern, in which the infinite and varied range of feelings or situations seems to be self-evident, then this power cannot be separated from that of tragedy itself. 'It is not the intensity but the duration of high feeling which makes the high man.' This monotonous duration of heroic feeling is vouchsafed solely in the pre-ordained framework of the hero's life. The oracle in tragedy is more than just a magical incantation of fate; it is a projection of the certainty that there is no tragic life which does not take place within its framework. The necessity which appears to be built into the framework, is neither a causal nor a magical necessity. It is the unarticulated necessity of defiance, in which the self brings forth its utterances. At the slightest breath of the word it would melt away like snow before the south wind. But the only word which could bring this about is an unknown one. Heroic defiance contains this word enclosed within it; that is what distinguishes it from the *hubris* of a man whose hidden significance is no longer acknowledged by the fully developed consciousness of the community.

Only antiquity could know tragic *hubris*, which pays for the right to be silent with the hero's life. The hero, who scorns to justify himself before the gods, reaches agreement with them in a, so to speak, contractual process of atonement which, in its dual significance, is designed not only to bring about the restoration but above all the undermining of an ancient body of law in the linguistic constitution of the renewed community. Athletic contests, law, and tragedy constitute the great agonal trinity of Greek life – in his *Griechische Kulturgeschichte* Jacob Burckhardt refers to the *agon* as a scheme[29] – and they are bound together under the sign of this contract. 'Legislation and legal procedure were founded in Hellas in the struggle against self-help and the law of the jungle. Where the tendency to take law into one's own hands declined, or the state succeeded in restraining it, the trial did not at once assume the character of a search for a judicial decision, but that of an attempt at conciliation . . . In the framework of such a procedure the principal aim was not to establish the absolute right, but to prevail upon the injured party to renounce vengeance; and so sacral forms for proof and verdict could not but acquire a particularly high significance, because of the impact they had even on the losers.'[30] In antiquity the trial – especially the criminal trial – is a dialogue, because it is based on the twin roles of prosecutor and accused, without official procedure. It has its chorus: partly in the sworn witnesses (in ancient Cretan law, for instance, the parties proved their case with the help of compurgators, that is to say character-witnesses, who originally stood surety for the right of their party with weapons in the trial by ordeal), partly in the array of comrades of the accused begging the court for mercy, and finally in the adjudicating assembly of the populace. The important and characteristic feature of Athenian law is the Dionysian outburst, the fact that the intoxicated, ecstatic word was able to transcend the regular perimeter of the *agon*, that a higher justice was vouchsafed by the persuasive power of living speech than from the trial of the opposed factions, by combat with weapons or prescribed verbal forms. The practice of the trial by ordeal is disrupted by the freedom of the *logos*. This is the ultimate affinity between trial and tragedy in Athens. The hero's word, on those isolated occasions when it breaks through the rigid armour of the self, becomes a cry of protest. Tragedy is assimilated in this image of the trial; here too a process of conciliation takes place. So it is that in Sophocles and Euripides the heroes learn 'not to speak . . . only to debate'; and this explains why 'the love-scene is quite alien to ancient drama'.[31] But if in the mind of the dramatist the

myth constitutes the negotiation, his work is at one and the same time
a depiction and a revision of the proceedings. And with the inclusion
of the amphitheatre the dimensions of this whole trial have increased.
The community is present at this re-opening of the proceedings as the
controlling, indeed as the adjudicating authority. For its part it seeks to
reach a decision about the settlement, in the interpretation of which the
dramatist renews the memory of the achievements of the hero. But the
conclusion of the tragedy is always qualified by a *non liquet*. The
solution is always, it is true, a redemption; but only a temporary,
problematic, and limited one. The satyric drama which precedes or
follows the tragedy is an expression of the fact that the élan of comedy
is the only proper preparation for, or reaction to, the *non liquet* of the
represented trial. And even this is not free from the awe which
surrounds the inscrutable conclusion: 'The hero, who awakens fear and
pity in others, himself remains an unmoved, rigid self. And again in the
spectator these emotions are at once turned inwards, and make him,
too, a totally self-enclosed self. Each keeps to himself; each remains self.
No community emerges. And yet there is an element common to them
all. The selves do not come together, and yet the same note resounds
in them all, the feeling of their own self.'[32] A disastrous and enduring
effect of the forensic dramaturgy of tragedy has been the doctrine of the
unities. This most concrete explanation of the unities is overlooked even
in the profound interpretation which argues: 'Unity of place is the self-
evident, immediately obvious symbol of this remaining-at-a-standstill
amid the perpetual change of surrounding life; hence the technically
necessary way to its expression. The tragic is but a single moment: that
is what is meant by the unity of time.'[33] There is, of course, no doubt
about this – the temporally limited emergence of the hero from the
underworld lends the greatest emphasis to this interruption of the
passage of time. Jean Paul's rhetorical question about tragedy is nothing
less than a disavowal of the most astonishing divination: 'who will
present gloomy worlds of shades at public festivals before a crowd?'[34]
None of his contemporaries imagined anything of the kind. But here, as
always, the most fruitful layer of metaphysical interpretation is to be
found on the level of the pragmatic. Here unity of place is the court of
judgment; unity of time, the duration of the court session, which has
always been limited – either by the revolution of the sun or otherwise;
and unity of action, that of the proceedings. These are the circumstances
which make the conversations of Socrates the irrevocable epilogue of
tragedy. In his own lifetime the hero not only discovers the word, but
he acquires a band of disciples, his youthful spokesmen. His silence, not
his speech, will now be informed with the utmost irony. Socratic irony,
which is the opposite of tragic irony. What is tragic is the indiscretion
by which, unconsciously, the truth of heroic life is touched upon: the

self, whose reticence is so profound that it does not stir even when
it calls out its own name in its dreams. The ironic silence of the
philosopher, the coy, histrionic silence, is conscious. In place of the
sacrificial death of the hero Socrates sets the example of the pedagogue.
But, in Plato's work, the war which the rationalism of Socrates declared
on tragic art is decided against tragedy with a superiority which
ultimately affected the challenger more than the object challenged. For
this does not happen in the rational spirit of Socrates, so much as in the
spirit of the dialogue itself. At the end of the *Symposium*, when Socrates,
Agathon, and Aristophanes are seated alone, facing one another – why
should it not be the sober light of his dialogues which Plato allows to
fall over the discussion of the nature of the true poet, who embodies
both tragedy and comedy, as dawn breaks over the three? The dialogue
contains pure dramatic language, unfragmented by its dialectic of tragic
and comic. This purely dramatic quality restores the mystery which had
gradually become secularized in the forms of Greek drama: its language,
the language of the new drama, is, in particular, the language of the
Trauerspiel.

Given the equation of the tragedy and the *Trauerspiel* it ought to have
seemed very odd that the *Poetics* of Aristotle make no mention of
mourning [*Trauer*] as the resonance of the tragic. But far from it, it has
often been believed that modern aesthetics has, in the concept of the
tragic, itself discovered a feeling, the emotional reaction to tragedy and
Trauerspiel. Tragedy is a preliminary stage of prophecy. It is a content,
which exists only in language: what is tragic is the word and the silence
of the past, in which the prophetic voice is being tried out, or suffering
and death, when they are redeemed by this voice; but a fate in the
pragmatic substance of its entanglements is never tragic. The *Trauerspiel*
is conceivable as pantomime; the tragedy is not. For the struggle against
the demonic character of the law is dependent on the word of the
genius. The evaporation of the tragic under the scrutiny of psychology
goes hand in hand with the equation of tragedy and *Trauerspiel*. The
very name of the latter already indicates that its content awakens
mourning in the spectator. But it does not by any means follow that
this content could be any better expressed in the categories of empirical
psychology than could the content of tragedy – it might far rather mean
that these plays could serve better to describe mourning than could the
condition of grief. For these are not so much plays which cause
mourning, as plays through which mournfulness finds satisfaction: plays
for the mournful. A certain ostentation is characteristic of these people.
Their images are displayed in order to be seen, arranged in the way
they want them to be seen. Thus the Italian renaissance theatre, which
is in many ways an influential factor in the German baroque, emerged

from pure ostentation, from the *trionfi*,[35] the processions with explanatory recitation, which flourished in Florence under Lorenzo de Medici. And in the European *Trauerspiel* as a whole the stage is also not strictly fixable, not an actual place, but it too is dialectically split. Bound to the court, it yet remains a travelling theatre; metaphorically its boards represent the earth as the setting created for the enactment of history; it follows its court from town to town. In Greek eyes, however, the stage is a cosmic *topos*. 'The form of the Greek theatre recalls a lonely valley in the mountains: the architecture of the scene appears like a luminous cloud formation that the Bacchants swarming over the mountains behold from a height – like the splendid frame in which the image of Dionysus is revealed to them.'[36] Whether this beautiful description is correct or not, whether or not the courtroom analogy, the statement 'the scene becomes a tribunal', must hold good for every excited community, the Greek trilogy is, in any case, not a repeatable act of ostentation, but a once-and-for-all resumption of the tragic trial before a higher court. As is suggested by the open theatre and the fact that the performance is never repeated identically, what takes place is a decisive cosmic achievement. The community is assembled to witness and to judge this achievement. The spectator of tragedy is summoned, and is justified, by the tragedy itself; the *Trauerspiel*, in contrast, has to be understood from the point of view of the onlooker. He learns how, on the stage, a space which belongs to an inner world of feeling and bears no relationship to the cosmos, situations are compellingly presented to him. The linguistic indications of the connection between mourning and ostentation, as it finds expression in the theatre of the baroque, are terse. For instance: 'T[rauer] bühne' 'fig. the earth as a setting for mournful events . . .'; 'das T[rauer] gepränge; das T[rauer] gerüst, a frame draped in cloth and furnished with decorations, emblems, etc., on which the body of a prominent person is displayed in his coffin (catafalque, *castrum doloris, Trauerbühne*)'.[37] The word *Trauer* is always to hand for these compounds, and it extracts the marrow of its significance, so to speak, from its companion word.[38] The following words of Hallmann are thoroughly characteristic of the extreme sense in which the term is used in the baroque, a sense which is not at all governed by aesthetic considerations: 'Solch Trauerspiel kommt aus deinen Eitelkeiten! | Solch Todten-Tantz wird in der Welt gehegt!'[39]

Notes

1. Cf. WILHELM DILTHEY, *Weltanschauung und Analyse des Menschen seit Renaissance und Reformation. Abhandlungen zur Geschichte der Philosophie und Religion* (Gesammelte Schriften, II) (Leipzig, Berlin, 1923), p. 445.

2. MARTIN OPITZ, *Prosodia Germanica, Oder Buch von der Deudschen Pocterey*. Nunmehr zum siebenden mal correct gedruckt, Frankfurt a.M., n.d. [ca 1650], pp. 30–1.

3. *Die Aller Edelste Belustigung Kunst- und Tugendliebender Gemühter* [Aprilgespräch]/beschrieben und fürgestellt von Dem Rüstigen [Johann Rist] (Frankfurt, 1666), pp. 241–2.

4. A[ugust] A[dolf] von H[augwitz], *Prodomus Poeticus, Oder: Poetischer Vortrab* (Dresden, 1684), p. 78 [of the pagination of *Schuldige Unschuld Oder Maria Stuarda* (fn.)].

5. ANDREAS GRYPHIUS, *Trauerspiele*, hrsg. von Hermann Palm (Tübingen, 1882) (Bibliothek des litterarischen Vereins in Stuttgart, 162), p. 635 (*Amilius Paulus Papinianus*, fn.).

6. BERNHARD ERDMANNSDORFFER, *Deutsche Geschichte vom Westfälischen Frieden bis zum Regierungsantritt Friedrich's des Grossen*. 1648–1740, I (Berlin, 1892) (Allgemeine Geschichte in Einzeldarstellungen, 3, 7), p. 102.

7. MARTIN OPITZ, *L. Annaei Senecae Trojanerinnen* (Wittenberg, 1625), p. 1 (of the unpaginated preface).

8. JOHANN KLAI; quoted from: KARL WEISS, *Die Wiener Haupt / und Staatsactionen. Ein Beitrag zur Geschichte des deutschen Theaters* (Vienna, 1854), p. 14.

9. Cf. CARL SCHMITT, *Politische Theologie. Vier Kapitel zur Lehre von der Souverenatität* (Munich, Leipzig, 1922), pp. 11–12.

10. Cf. AUGUST KOBERSTEIN, *Geschichte der deutschen Nationalliteratur vom Anfang des siebzehnten bis zum zweiten Viertel des achtzehnten Jahrhunderts*. 5., umgearb. Aufl. von Karl Bartsch (Leipzig, 1872) (Grundriss der Geschichte der deutschen Nationalliteratur, 2), p. 15.

11. SCHMITT, *Politische Theologie*, p. 14.

12. Ibid.

13. WILHELM HAUSENSTEIN, *Vom Geist des Barock*, 3–5 Aufl. (Munich, 1921), p. 42.

14. [Christian Hofmann von Hofmannswaldau], *Helden-Briefe* (Leipzig, Breslau, 1680), pp. 8–9 (of the unpaginated preface).

15. SIGMUND BIRKEN, *Deutsche Redebind- und Dichtkunst* (Nuremberg, 1679), p. 242.

16. GRYPHIUS, *Trauerspiele*, p. 61 (*Leo Armenius* II, 433 ff.).

17. JOHANN CHRISTIAN HALLMANN, *Trauer- Freuden- und Schäffer-Spiele* (Breslau, n.d. [1684]), p. 17 (of the pagination of *Die beleidigte Liebe oder die grossmütige Mariamne* [I, 477/478]). – cf. ibid., p. 12 (I, 355).

18. [Diego Saavedra Fajardo], *Abris Eines Christlich-Politischen Printzens / In CI Sinn-Bildern / Zuvor auss dem spanischen ins Lateinisch: Nun in Teutsch versetzet* (Coloniae, 1674), p. 897. [Don Diego Saavedra Faxardo, *The Royal Politician represented in one hundred emblems*, done into English by Sir JA. ASTRY, London, 1700, II, 210.]

19. KARL KRUMBACHER, 'Die griechische Literatur des Mittelalters', *Die Kultur der Gegenwart. Ihre Entwicklung und ihre Ziele*, hrsg. von Paul Hinneberg, Teil I, Abt. 8, Die griechische und lateinische Literatur und Sprache. Von U. v. Wilamowitz-Moellendorff [et al.] (Leipzig, Berlin, 1912³), p. 367.

20. [Anon], *Die Glorreiche Marter Joannes von Nepomuck*.

21. Ibid.

22. JOSEPH [Felix] KURZ, *Prinzessin Pumphia* (Vienna, 1883) (Wiener Neudrucke, 2), p. 1 (reproduction of the old title-page).

23. *Lorentz Gratians Staats-kluger Catholischer Ferdinand / aus dem Spanischen übersetzet von Daniel Caspern von Lohenstein* (Breslau, 1676), p. 123.

24. Cf. WILLI FLEMMING, *Andreas Gryphius und die Bühne* (Halle a.d.S., 1921), p. 386.

25. Gryphius, *Trauerspiele*, p. 212 (*Catharina von Georgien*, III, 438).
26. Cf. Marcus Landau, 'Die Dramen von Herodes und Mariamne', *Zeitschrift für vergleichende Literaturgeschichte*, NF VIII (1895), pp. 175–212 and pp. 279–317, and NF IX (1896), pp. 185–223.
27. Cf. Hausenstein, *Vom Geist des Barock*, p. 94.
28. Herbert Cysarz, *Deutsche Barockdichtung. Renaissance, Barock, Rokoko* (Leipzig, 1924), p. 31.
29. Daniel Casper von Lohenstein, *Sophonisbe* (Frankfurt, Leipzig, 1724), p. 73 (IV, 504 ff.).
30. Gryphius, *Trauerspiele*, p. 213 (*Catharina von Georgien*, III, 457 ff.). – cf. Hallmann, *Trauer-, Freuden- und Schäferspiele, Mariamne*, p. 86 (V, 351).
31. [Josef Anton Stranitzky], *Wiener Haupt- und Staatsaktionen*. Eingeleitet und hrsg. von Rudolf Payer von Thurn, I (Vienna, 1908) (Schriften des Literarischen Vereins in Wien, 10), p. 301 (*Die Gestürzte Tyrannay in der Person dess Messinischen Wüttrichs* Pelifonte, II, 8).
32. [Georg Philipp Harsdörffer], *Poetischen Trichters zweyter Theil* (Nuremberg, 1648), p. 84.
33. Julius Wilhelm Zincgref, *Emblematum Ethico-Politicorum Centuria*, 2nd edn (Frankfurt, 1624), Embl. 71.
34. [Claudius Salmasius], *Königliche Verthätigung für Carl den I. geschrieben an den durch-läuchtigsten König von Grossbritannien Carl den Andern*, 1650.
35. Cf. Paul Stachel, *Seneca und das deutsche Renaissance drama. Studienen zur Literatur- und Stilgeschichte des 16. und 17. Jahrhunderts* (Berlin, 1907), p. 29.
36. Cf. Gotthold Ephraim Lessing, *Sämtliche Schriften*. Neue rechtmässige Ausg., hrsg von Karl Lachmann, VII (Berlin, 1839), pp. 7 ff. (*Hamburgische Dramaturgie*, 1. und 2. Stück).
37. Hallmann, *Trauer-, Freuden- und Schäferspiele, Mariamne*, p. 27 (II, 263/264).
38. Ibid., p. 112 (fn.).
39. Birken, *Deutsche Redebind- und Dichtkunst*, p. 323.

Aristotle's Coercive System of Tragedy*

Augusto Boal

What does tragedy imitate?

Tragedy imitates human acts. Human acts, not merely human activities. For Aristotle, man's soul was composed of a rational part and of another, irrational part. The irrational soul could produce certain activities such as eating, walking or performing any physical movement without greater significance than the physical act itself. Tragedy, on the other hand, imitated solely man's actions, determined by his rational soul.

Man's rational soul can be divided into:

(a) faculties
(b) passions
(c) habits.

A *faculty* is everything man is able to do, even though he may not do it. Man, even if he does not love, is able to love; even if he does not hate, he is able to hate; even if a coward, he is capable of showing courage. Faculty is pure potentiality and is immanent to the rational soul.

But, even though the soul has all the faculties, only some of them attain realization. These are the passions. A *passion* is not merely a 'possibility', but a concrete fact. Love is a passion once it is expressed as such. As long as it is simply a possibility it will remain a faculty. A passion is an 'enacted' faculty, a faculty that becomes a concrete act.

Not all passions serve as subject matter for tragedy. If a man, in a given moment, happens to exert a passion, that is not an action worthy

---

* Reprinted from *Theater of the Oppressed*, trans. Charles A. and Maria-Odilia Leal McBride (London: Pluto Press, 1979).

of tragedy. It is necessary that that passion be constant in the man; that is, that by its repeated exertion it has become a *habit*. Thus we conclude that tragedy imitates man's actions, but only those produced by the habits of his rational soul. Animal activity is excluded, as well as the faculties and passions that have not become habitual.

To what end is a passion, a habit, exerted? What is the purpose of man? Each part of man has a purpose: the hand grabs, the mouth eats, the leg walks, the brain thinks, etc.; but as a whole being, what purpose does man have? Aristotle answers; the good is the aim of all man's actions. It is not an abstract idea of good, but rather the concrete good, diversified in all the different sciences and the different arts which deal with particular ends. Each human action, therefore, has an end limited to that action, but all actions as a whole have as their purpose the supreme good of man. What is the supreme good of man? Happiness!

Thus far we are able to say that tragedy imitates man's actions, those of his rational soul, directed to the attainment of his supreme end, happiness. But in order to understand which actions they are, we have to know first what happiness is.

What is happiness?

The types of happiness, says Aristotle, are three: one that derives from material pleasures, another from glory, and a third from virtue.

For the average person, happiness consists in possessing material goods and enjoying them. Riches, honours, sexual and gastronomic pleasures, etc. – that is happiness. For the Greek philosopher, human happiness on this level differs very little from the happiness that animals can also enjoy. This happiness, he says, does not deserve to be studied in tragedy.

On a second level, happiness is glory. Here man acts according to his own virtue, but his happiness consists in the recognition of his actions by others. Happiness is not in the virtuous behaviour itself, but in the fact that that behaviour is recognized by others. Man, in order to be happy, needs the approval of others.

Finally, the superior level of happiness is that of the man who acts virtuously and asks no more. His happiness consists in acting in a virtuous manner, whether others recognize him or not. This is the highest degree of happiness: the virtuous exercise of the rational soul.

Now we know that tragedy imitates the actions of the rational soul – passions transformed into habits – of the man in search of happiness, which is to say, virtuous behaviour. Very well. But now we need to know what is meant by 'virtue'.

124

And what is virtue?

Virtue is the behaviour most distant from the possible extremes of behaviour in any given situation. Virtue cannot be found in the extremes: both the man who voluntarily refuses to eat and the glutton harm their health. This is not virtuous behaviour; to eat with moderation is. The absence of physical exercise, as well as the too violent exercise, ruins the body; moderate physical exercise constitutes virtuous behaviour. The same is true of the moral virtues. Creon thinks only of the good of the State, while Antigone thinks only of the good of the Family and wishes to bury her dead, traitorous brother. The two behave in a non-virtuous manner, for their conduct is extreme. Virtue would be found somewhere in the middle ground. The man who gives himself to all pleasures is a libertine, but the one who flees from all pleasures is an insensitive person. The one who confronts all dangers is foolhardy, but he who runs from all dangers is a coward.

Virtue is not exactly the average, for a soldier's courage is much closer to temerity than to cowardice. Nor does virtue exist in us 'naturally'; it is necessary to learn it. The things of nature lack man's ability to acquire habits. The rock cannot fall upward nor can fire burn downward. But we can cultivate habits which will allow us to behave virtuously.

Nature, still according to Aristotle, gives us faculties, and we have the power to change them into actions (passions) and habits. The one who practices wisdom becomes wise, he who practices justice becomes just, and the architect acquires his virtue as an architect by constructing buildings. Habits, not faculties! Habits, not merely ephemeral passions!

Aristotle goes farther and states that the formation of habits should begin in childhood and that a youth cannot practise politics because he needs first to learn all the virtuous habits taught by his elders, the legislators who instruct the citizens in virtuous habits.

Thus we know now that vice is extreme behaviour and virtue is behaviour characterized neither by excess nor deficiency. But if any given behaviour is to be seen as either vicious or virtuous, it must fulfil four indispensable conditions: wilfulness, freedom, knowledge, and constancy. These terms call for explanation. But let us bear in mind what we already know: that for Aristotle tragedy imitates the actions of man's rational soul (habitual passions) as he searches for happiness, which consists in virtuous behaviour. Little by little our definition is becoming more complex.

Necessary characteristics of virtue

A man can behave in a totally virtuous manner and, in spite of that, not be considered virtuous; or he may behave in a vicious manner and not be considered vicious. In order to be considered virtuous or vicious, human action must meet four conditions.

First Condition: Wilfulness

Wilfulness excludes the accidental. That is, man acts because he decides to act voluntarily, by his will and not by accident.

One day a mason put a stone on a wall in such a way that a strong wind blew it down. A pedestrian happened to be passing by, and the rock fell on him. The man died. His wife sued the mason, but the latter defended himself by saying that he had not committed any crime since he had not had the intention of killing the pedestrian. That is, his behaviour was not vicious – he merely had an accident. But the judge did not accept this defence and found him guilty based on the fact that there was no wilfulness in causing the death, but there was in placing the stone in a position such that it could fall and cause a death. In this respect there was wilfulness.

If man acts because he wishes to, there we find virtue or vice. If his action is not determined by his will, one can speak neither of vice nor virtue. The one who does good without being aware of it is not for that a good person. Nor is he bad who causes harm involuntarily.

Second Condition: Freedom

Here, exterior coercion is excluded. If a man commits an evil act because someone forces him with a gun to his head, one cannot in this case speak of vice. Virtue is free behaviour, without any sort of exterior pressure.

In this case, too, a story is told – this time of a woman who, on being abandoned by her lover, decided to kill him, and so she did. Taken to court, she declared in her defence that she had not acted freely: her irrational passion forced her to commit the crime. According to her, there was no guilt here, no crime.

As before, the judge disagreed, ruling that passion is an integral part of a person, part of one's soul. Though there is no freedom when coercion comes from without, acts based upon inner impulse must be regarded as freely undertaken. The woman was condemned.

Third Condition: Knowledge

It is the opposite of ignorance. The person who acts has before him an option whose terms he knows. In court a drunken criminal asserted that he had committed no crime because he was not conscious of what he was doing when he killed another man, and was therefore ignorant of his own actions. Also in this case, the drunk was condemned. Before he started drinking he had full knowledge that the alcohol was going to lead him to a state of unconsciousness; therefore he was guilty of letting himself fall into a state in which he lost consciousness of what he was doing.

In relation to this third condition of virtuous behaviour, the conduct of characters such as Othello and Oedipus may seem questionable. With regard to both, we find discussions of the existence or nonexistence of knowledge (on which their virtue or vice would hinge). To my way of thinking the argument can be resolved as follows. Othello does not know the truth; this is correct. Iago lies to him about the infidelity of Desdemona, his wife, and Othello, blind with jealousy, kills her. But the tragedy of Othello goes far beyond a simple murder: his tragic flaw (and soon we will discuss the concept of *hamartia*, tragic flaw) is not that of having killed Desdemona. Nor is this habitual behaviour. But what indeed is a habit is his constant pride and his unreflective temerity. In several moments of the play Othello tells how he flung himself against his enemies, how he acted without reflecting upon the consequences of his actions. This, or his excessive pride, is the cause of his misfortune. And of these qualities, Othello is fully conscious, has full knowledge.

Also in the case of Oedipus, one must ask, what is his true flaw (hamartia)? His tragedy does not consist in having killed his father or married his mother. Those are not habitual acts either, and habit is one of the basic characteristics of virtuous or vicious behaviour. But if we read the play with care, we will see that Oedipus, in all the important moments of his life, reveals his extraordinary pride, his arrogance, the vanity which leads him to believe that he is superior to the gods themselves. It is not the Moirai (the Fates) that lead him to his tragic end; he himself, by his own decision, moves toward his misfortune. It is intolerance that causes him to kill an old man, who happens to be his father, because the latter did not treat him with the proper respect at a crossroads. And when he deciphers the enigma of the Sphinx, once more it is because of pride that he accepts the throne of Thebes and the hand of the Queen, a woman old enough to be his mother. And she really was! A person to whom the oracles (a kind of 'voodoo witch doctor' or 'seer' of the time) had said that he was going to marry his own mother and kill his own father would have to be a little careful and abstain from killing men old enough to be his father or marrying women old enough to be his mother. Why did he not exercise such care? Because of pride, haughtiness, intolerance, because he believed himself to be a worthy adversary of the gods. These are his flaws, his vices. To know or not the identity of Jocasta and Laius is secondary. Oedipus himself, when he recognizes his error, acknowledges these facts.

We conclude, therefore, that the third condition present in virtuous behaviour consists in the agent's knowing the true terms of the option. He who acts in ignorance practices neither virtue nor vice.

Fourth Condition: Constancy

Since virtues and vices are habits, not merely passions, it is necessary that virtuous or vicious behaviour also be constant. All the heroes of the Greek tragedies act consistently in the same manner. When the tragic flaw of the character consists precisely in his incoherence, that character must be introduced as coherently incoherent. Once more, neither accident nor chance characterize vice and virtue.

Thus those whom tragedy imitates are the virtuous men who, upon acting, show wilfulness, freedom, knowledge, and constancy. These are the four conditions necessary for the exercise of virtue, which is man's way to happiness. But is virtue one, or are there different degrees of virtue?

The degrees of virtue

Each art, each science, has its corresponding virtue, because each has its own end, its own good. The virtue of the horseman is to ride a horse well; the virtue of the ironsmith is to manufacture good iron tools. The virtue of the artist is to create a perfect work of art. That of the physician is to restore the health of the sick. That of the legislator is to make perfect laws that will bring happiness to the citizens.

While it is true that each art and each science has its own virtue, it is also true as we have already seen, that all the arts and all the sciences are interdependent and that some are superior to others, to the extent by which they are more complex than others and study or include larger sectors of human activity. Of all the arts and sciences, the sovereign art and science is Politics, because nothing is alien to it. Politics has for its field of study the totality of the relationships of the totality of men. Therefore the greatest good – the attainment of which would entail the greatest virtue – is the political good.

Tragedy imitates those actions of man which have the good as their goal; but it does not imitate actions which have minor ends, of secondary importance. Tragedy imitates actions that are directed toward the highest goal, the political good. And what is the political good?

There is no doubt: the highest good is the political one, and the political good is justice!

What is justice?

In the *Nicomachaean Ethics*, Aristotle proposes to us (and we accept) the principle that the just is that which is equal, and the unjust that which is unequal. In any division, the people that are equal should receive equal parts and those who (by any criterion) are unequal should receive unequal parts. Up to here we are in agreement. But we must define the criteria of inequality, because no one will want to be unequal in an inferior sense while all will want to be unequal in a superior one.

Aristotle himself was opposed to the *talion law* (an eye for an eye, a tooth for a tooth) because, he said, if the people were not equal, their eyes and teeth would not be equal either. Thus one would have to ask: whose eye for whose eye? If it was a master's eye for a slave's eye, it did not seem right to Aristotle, because for him those eyes were not equal in value. If it was a man's tooth for a woman's tooth, neither did Aristotle find here an equivalent value.

Then our philosopher utilizes an apparently honest argument to determine criteria of equality to which no one can object. He asks, should we begin with ideal, abstract principles and descend to reality or, on the contrary, should we look at concrete reality and from there ascend toward the principles? Far from any romanticism, he answers: obviously we should start with concrete reality. We must examine empirically the real, existing inequalities and upon them base our criteria of inequality.

This leads us to accept as 'just' the *already existing* inequalities. For Aristotle, therefore, justice is already contained in reality itself as it is. He does not consider the possibility of *transforming the already existing inequalities*, but simply accepts them. And for this reason he decides that since free men and slaves do exist in reality (abstract principles do not matter), that will be the first criterion of inequality. To be a man is *more* and to be a woman is *less* – this is shown by concrete reality, according to Aristotle. Thus free men would rank highest; then would come free women, followed by male slaves, with the poor female slaves at the bottom.

That was Athenian democracy, which was based on the supreme value of 'freedom'. But not all societies were based on that same value; the oligarchies, for example, were based on the supreme value of wealth. There the men who owned more were considered superior to those who had less. Always starting with reality as it is. . . .

Thus we come to the conclusion that justice is not equality: justice is proportionality. And the criteria of proportionality are given by the political system actually in force in a particular city. Justice will always be proportionality, but the criteria which determine the latter will vary depending upon whether the system is a democracy, an oligarchy, a dictatorship, a republic, or other.

And how are the criteria of inequality established so that all become aware of them? Through laws. And who makes the laws? If the inferior human beings (women slaves, the poor) made them, they would, according to Aristotle, make inferior laws just as their authors are inferior. In order to have superior laws, it is necessary that they be made by superior beings: free men, wealthy men. . . .

The body of laws of a city, of a country, is put together and systematized in a constitution. The constitution, therefore, is the expression of the political good, the maximum expression of justice.

Finally, with the help of the *Nicomachaean Ethics*, we can arrive at a clear conclusion regarding what tragedy is for Aristotle. Its widest and most complete definition would be the following:

> Tragedy imitates the actions of man's rational soul, his passions turned into habits, in his search for happiness, which consists in virtuous behaviour, remote from the extremes, whose supreme good is justice and whose maximum expression is the Constitution.

In the final analysis, happiness consists in obeying the laws. This is Aristotle's message, clearly spelled out.

For those who make the laws, all is well. But what about those who do not make them? Understandably, they rebel, not wishing to accept the criteria of inequality provided by present reality, since they are criteria subject to modification, as is reality itself. In those cases, says the philosopher, sometimes war is necessary.

In what sense can theatre function as an instrument for purification and intimidation?

We have seen that the population of a city is not *uniformly* content. If there is inequality, no one wants it to be to his disadvantage. It is necessary to make sure that all remain, if not uniformly satisfied, at least uniformly passive with respect to those criteria of inequality. How to achieve this? Through the many forms of repression: politics, bureaucracy, habits, customs – and Greek tragedy.

This statement may seem somewhat daring, but it is nothing more than the truth. Of course, the system presented by Aristotle in his

Poetics, the functional system of tragedy (and all the forms of theatre which to this day follow its general mechanism) is not *only* a system of repression. Other, more 'aesthetic', factors clearly enter into it. And there are many other apsects that ought likewise to be taken into account. But it is important to consider especially this fundamental aspect: its repressive function.

And why is the repressive function the fundamental aspect of the Greek tragedy and of the Aristotelian system of tragedy? Simply because, according to Aristotle, the principle aim of tragedy is to provoke catharsis.

The ultimate aim of tragedy

The fragmentary nature of the *Poetics* has obscured the solid connection existing among its parts, as well as the hierarchy of the parts within the context of the whole. Only this fact explains why marginal observations, of little or no importance, have been taken to be central concepts of Aristotelian thought. For example, when dealing with Shakespeare or the medieval theatre, it is very common to decide that such and such a play is not Aristotelian because it does not obey the 'law of the three unities'. Hegel's objection to this view is contained in his *The Philosophy of Fine Art*:

> The inalterability of one exclusive *locale* of the action proposed belongs to the type of those rigid rules which the French in particular have deduced from classic tragedy and the critique of Aristotle thereupon. As a matter of fact, Artistotle merely says that the duration of the tragic action should not exceed at the most the length of a day. He does not mention the unity of place at all. . . .[1]

The disproportionate importance that is given to this 'law' is incomprehensible, since it has no more validity than would the statement that only the works that contain a prologue, five episodes and choral chants, and an exode are Aristotelian. The essence of Aristotelian thought cannot reside in structural aspects such as these. To emphasize these minor aspects is, in effect, to compare the Greek philosopher to the modern and abundant professors of dramaturgy, especially the Americans, who are no more than cooks of theatrical menus. They study the typical reactions of certain chosen audiences and from there extract conclusions and rules regarding how the perfect work should be written (equating perfection to box office success).

Aristotle, on the contrary, wrote a completely organic poetics, which is the reflection, in the field of tragedy and poetry, of all his philosophical contribution; it is the practical and concrete application of that philosophy specifically to poetry and tragedy.

For this reason, every time we find imprecise or fragmentary statements, we should immediately consult other texts written by the author. S. H. Butcher does precisely this, with crystal clear results, in his book *Aristotle's Theory of Poetry and Fine Art*.[2] He tries to understand the *Poetics* from the perspective of the *Metaphysics, Politics, Rhetoric,* and above all, the three *Ethics*. To him we owe mainly the clarification of the concept of catharsis.

Nature tends toward certain ends; when it fails to achieve those objectives, art and science intervene. Man, as part of nature, also has certain ends in view: health, gregarious life in the State, happiness, virtue, justice, etc. When he fails in the achievement of those objectives, the art of tragedy intervenes. This correction of man's actions is what Aristotle calls *catharsis*.

Tragedy, in all its qualitative and quantitative aspects, exists as a function of the effect it seeks, catharsis. All the unities of tragedy are structured around this concept. It is the centre, the essence, the purpose of the tragic system. Unfortunately, it is also the most controversial concept. Catharsis is correction: what does it correct? Catharsis is purification: what does it purify?

Butcher helps us with a parade of opinions of such illustrious people as Racine, Milton, and Jacob Bernays.

Racine

In tragedy, he wrote:

> the passions are shown only to reveal all the disorder of which they are the cause; and vice is always painted with colours that make us know and hate the deformity . . . this is what the first tragic poets had in mind, more than anything else. Their theatre was a school where the virtues were taught fully as well as in the philosopher's schools. For this reason Aristotle wanted to provide rules for the dramatic poem . . . It is to be desired that our works should be as solid and as full of useful instructions as the ones of those poets.[3]

As we see, Racine emphasizes the doctrinal, moral aspect of tragedy; and this is fine, but there is one correction to be made: Aristotle did not advise the tragic poet to portray vicious characters. The tragic hero should suffer a radical change in the course of his life – from happiness to adversity – but this should happen not as a consequence of vice, but rather as a result of some error or weakness (see Chapter 13 of the *Poetics*). Soon we shall examine the nature of this *hamartia*.

It is necessary to understand also that the presentation of the error of weakness was not designed to make the spectator, in his immediate perception of it, feel repugnance or hatred. On the contrary, Aristotle suggested that the mistake or weakness be treated with some understanding. Almost always the state of 'fortune' in which the hero is found at the beginning of the tragedy is due precisely to this fault and not to his virtues. Oedipus is King of Thebes because of a weakness in his character, that is, his pride. And indeed the efficacy of a dramatic process would be greatly diminished if the fault were presented from the beginning as despicable, the error as abominable. It is necessary, on the contrary, to show them as acceptable in order to destroy them later through the theatrical, poetic processes. Bad playwrights in every epoch fail to understand the enormous efficacy of the transformations that take place before the spectators' eyes. Theatre is change and not simple presentation of what exists: it is becoming and not being.

[. . .]

How Aristotle's coercive system of tragedy functions

The spectacle begins. The tragic hero appears. The public establishes a kind of empathy with him.

The action starts. Surprisingly, the hero shows a flaw in his behaviour, a hamartia; and even more surprising, one learns that it is by virtue of this same hamartia that the hero has come to his present state of happiness.

Through empathy, the same hamartia that the spectator may possess is stimulated, developed, activated.

Suddenly, something happens that changes everything. (Oedipus, for example, is informed by Teiresias that the murderer he seeks is Oedipus himself.) The character, who because of a hamartia had climbed so high, runs the risk of falling from those heights. This is what the *Poetics* classifies as *peripeteia*, a radical change in the character's destiny. The spectator, who up to then had his own hamartia stimulated, starts to feel a growing fear. The character is now on the way to misfortune. Creon is informed of the death of his son and his wife; Hippolytus cannot convince his father of his innocence, and the latter impels his son, unintentionally, to death.

Peripeteia is important because it lengthens the road from happiness to misfortune. The taller the palm tree, the greater the fall, says a popular Brazilian song. That way creates more impact.

The peripeteia suffered by the character is reproduced in the spectator as well. But it could happen that the spectator would follow the character empathically until the moment of the peripeteia and then detach himself at that point. In order to avoid that, the tragic character must also pass through what Aristotle calls *anagnorisis* – that is, through the recognition of his flaw as such and, by means of reasoning, the explanation of it. The hero accepts his error, hoping that, empathically, the spectator will also accept as bad his own hamartia. But the spectator has the great advantage of having erred only vicariously: he does not really pay for it.

Finally, so that the spectator will keep in mind the terrible consequences of committing the error not just vicariously but in actuality, Aristotle demands that tragedy have a terrible end, which he calls *catastrophe*. The happy end is not permitted, though the character's physical destruction is not absolutely required. Some die; others see their loved ones die. In any case, the catastrophe is always such that not to die is worse than death.

Those three interdependent elements (peripeteia, anagnorisis, catastrophe) have the ultimate goal of provoking catharsis in the spectator (as much or more than in the character); that is, their purpose is to produce a purgation of the hamartia, passing through three clearly defined stages:

First Stage: Stimulation of the hamartia; the character follows an ascending path toward happiness, accompanied empathically by the spectator. Then comes a moment of reversal: the character, with the spectator, starts to move from happiness toward misfortune; fall of the hero.

Second Stage: The character recognizes his error – *anagnorisis*. Through the empathic relationship *dianoia-reason*, the spectator recognizes his own error, his own hamartia, his own anticonstitutional flaw.

Third Stage: Catastrophe; the character suffers the consequences of his error, in a violent form, with his own death or with the death of loved ones.

Catharsis: The spectator, terrified by the spectacle of the catastrophe, is purified of his hamartia.

The words '*Amicus Plato, sed magis amicus veritas*' ('I am Plato's friend, but I am more of a friend of truth!') are attributed to Aristotle. In this we agree entirely with Aristotle: we are his friends, but we are much better friends of truth. He tells us that poetry, tragedy, theatre have nothing to do with politics. But reality tells us something else. His own *Poetics* tells us it is not so. We have to be better friends of reality: all of man's activities – including, of course, all the arts, especially theatre – are political. And theatre is the most perfect artistic form of coercion.

Different types of conflict: hamartia and social ethos

As we have seen, Aristotle's coercive system of tragedy requires:

a) the creation of a conflict between the character's ethos and the ethos of the society in which he lives; something is not right!

b) the establishment of a relationship called empathy, which consists in allowing the spectator to be guided by the character through his experiences; the spectator – feeling as if he himself is action – enjoys the pleasures and suffers the misfortunes of the character, to the extreme of thinking his thoughts.

c) that the spectator experience three changes of a rigorous nature: *peripeteia, anagnorisis,* and *catharsis;* he *suffers a blow* with regard to his fate (the action of the play), *recognizes the error* vicariously committed and *is purified of the antisocial characteristic* which he sees in himself.

This is the essence of the coercive system of tragedy. In the Greek theatre the system functions [in the manner discussed above]; but in its essence, the system survived and has continued to be utilized down to our own time, with various modifications introduced by new societies. Let us analyse some of these modifications.

First Type: Hamartia Versus the Perfect Social Ethos (classical type)

This is the most classical case studied by Aristotle. Consider again the example of Oedipus. The perfect social ethos is presented through the Chorus or through Teiresias in his long speech. The collision is head-on. Even after Teiresias has declared that the criminal is Oedipus himself, the latter does not accept it and continues the investigation on his own. Oedipus – the perfect man, the obedient son, the loving husband, the model father, the statesman without equal, intelligent, handsome, and sensitive – has nevertheless a tragic flaw: his pride! Through it he climbs to the peak of his glory, and through it he is destroyed. The balance is re-established with the catastrophe, with the terrifying vision of the protagonist's hanged mother-wife and his eyes torn out.

Second Type: Hamartia Versus Hamartia Versus the Perfect Social Ethos

The tragedy presents two characters who meet, two tragic heroes, each one with his flaw, who destroy each other before an ethically perfect society. This is the typical case of Antigone and Creon, both very fine persons in every way with the exception of their respective flaws. In these cases, the spectator must necessarily *empathize with both characters,* not only one, since the tragic process must purify him of two hamartias. A spectator who empathizes only with Antigone can be led to think that Creon possesses the truth, and vice versa. The spectator must purify himself of the 'excess', whatever direction it takes – whether excess of love of the State to the detriment of the Family, or excess of love of the Family to the detriment of the good of the State.

Often, when the anagnorisis of the character is perhaps not enough to convince the spectator, the tragic author utilizes the direct reasoning of the Chorus, possessor of common sense, moderation, and other qualities.

In this case also the catastrophe is necessary in order to produce, through fear, the catharsis, the purification of evil.

Third Type: Negative Hamartia Versus the Perfect Social Ethos

This type is completely different from the two presented before. Here the ethos of the character is presented in a negative form; that is, he has all the faults and only a single virtue, and not as was taught by Aristotle, all the virtues and only one fault, flaw, or mistake of judgment. Precisely because he possesses that small and solitary virtue the character is saved, the catastrophe is avoided, and instead a happy end occurs.

It is important to note that Aristotle clearly objected to the happy end, but we should note, too, that the coercive character of his whole system is the true essence of his political *Poetics;* therefore, in changing a characteristic as important as the composition of the ethos of the character, the structural mechanism of the end of the work is inevitably changed also, in order to maintain the purgative effect.

This type of catharsis, produced by 'negative hamartia versus the perfect social ethos', was often used in the Middle Ages. Perhaps the best known medieval drama is *Everyman.*

It tells the story of the character named Everyman, who when it comes time to die, tries to save himself, has a dialogue with Death, and analyses all his past actions. Before Everyman and Death passes a whole series of characters who accuse Everyman and reveal the sins committed by him: the material goods, the pleasures, etc. Everyman finally recognizes all the sins he has committed, admits the complete absence of any virtue in his actions, but at the same time trusts in divine mercy. This faith is his only virtue. This faith and his repentance save him, for the greater glory of God. . . .

The anagnorisis (recognition of his sins) is practically accompanied by the birth of a new character, and the latter is saved. In tragedy, the acts of the character are irremediable; but in this type of drama, the acts of the character can be forgiven provided he decides to change his life completely and become a 'new' character.

The idea of a new life (and this one is the forgiven life, since the sinning character ceases to be a sinner) can be seen clearly in *Condemned for Faithlessness* (*El condenado por desconfiado*) by Tirso de Molina. The hero, Enrique, has all the worst faults to be found in a person: he is a drunkard, murderer, thief, scoundrel – no defect, crime, or vice is alien to him. Wickedness that the Devil himself might envy. He has the most perverted ethos that dramatic art has ever invented. At his side is Pablo, the pure one, incapable of committing the slightest, most forgivable little sin, an immaculate spirit, insipid, empty, the image of perfection!

But something very strange happens to this pair which will cause their fate to be exactly the opposite of what one would expect. Enrique, the bad one, knows himself to be evil and a sinner, and never doubts that divine justice will condemn him to burn in the flames of the deepest and darkest corner of hell. And he accepts the divine wisdom and its justice. On the other hand, Pablo sins by wanting to keep himself pure. At every instant he wonders if God will truly realize that his life has been one of sacrifice and want. He ardently wishes to die and move immediately to heaven, so that he can possibly begin there a more pleasant life.

The two of them die, and to the surprise of some, the divine verdict is as follows: Enrique, in spite of all the crimes, robberies, drunkenness, treasons, etc., goes to heaven, because his firm belief in his punishment glorified God; Pablo, on the other hand, did not truly believe in God, since he doubted his salvation; therefore, he goes to hell with all his virtues.

That, in rough outline, is the play. Observed from the point of view of Enrique, it is clearly a case of a thoroughly evil ethos, possessing a single virtue. The exemplary effect is obtained through the happy end and not through the catastrophe. Observed from the point of view of Pablo, it is a conventional, classical, Aristotelian scheme. Everything in Pablo was virtue, with the exception of his tragic flaw – doubting God. For him there is indeed a catastrophe!

Fourth Type: Negative Hamartia Versus Negative Social Ethos

The word 'negative' is employed here in the sense of referring to a model that is the exact opposite of the original positive model – without reference to any moral quality. As, for instance, in a photographic negative, where all that is white shows up black and vice versa.

This type of ethical conflict is the essence of 'romantic drama', and *Camille* (*La Dame aux camélias*) is its best example. The hamartia of the protagonist, as in the preceding case, displays an impressive collection of negative qualities, sins, errors, etc. On the other hand, the social ethos (that is, the moral tendencies, ethics) of the society – contrary to the preceding example (third type) – is here entirely in agreement with the character. All her vices are perfectly acceptable, and she would suffer nothing for having them.

In *Camille* we see a corrupted society, which accepts prostitution, and Marguerite Gauthier is the best prostitute – individual vice is defended and accepted by the vicious society. Her profession is perfectly acceptable, her house frequented by society's most respected men (considering that it is a society whose principal value is money, her house is frequented by financiers) . . . Marguerite's life is full of happiness! But, poor girl, all her faults are accepted, though not her only virtue. Marguerite falls in love. Indeed, she truly loves someone. Ah, no, not that. Society cannot permit it; it is a tragic flaw and must be punished.

Here, from the ethical point of view, a sort of triangle is established. Up to now we have analysed conflicts in which the 'social ethics' was the same for the characters as for the spectators; now a dichotomy is presented: the author wishes to show a social ethics accepted by the society portrayed on stage, but he himself, the author, does not share that ethics, and proposes another. The universe of the work is one, and our universe, or at least our momentary position during the spectacle, is another. Alexander Dumas (Dumas fils) says in effect: here you see what this society is like, and it is bad, but we are not like that, or we are not like that in our innermost being. Thus, Marguerite has all the virtues that society believes to be virtues; a prostitute must practise her profession of prostitute with dignity and efficiency. But Marguerite has a flaw which prevents her from practising her profession well – she falls in love. How can a woman in love with *one* man serve with equal fidelity *all* men (all those who can pay)? Impossible. Therefore, falling in love, for a prostitute, is not a virtue but a vice.

But we, the spectators, who do not belong to the universe of the work, can say the exact opposite: a society which allows and encourages prostitution is a society which must be changed. Thus the triangle is established: to love, for us is a virtue, but in the universe of the work, it is a vice. And Marguerite Gauthier is destroyed precisely because of that vice (virtue).

Also in this kind of romantic drama, the catastrophe is inevitable. And the romantic author hopes that the spectator will be purified not of the tragic flaw of the hero, but rather of the whole ethos of society.

The same modification of the Aristotelian scheme is found in another romantic drama, *An Enemy of the People*, by Ibsen. Here again, the character, Dr Stockman, embodies an ethos identical to that of the society in which he lives, a society based on profit, on money; but he also possesses a flaw: he is an honest man! This the society cannot tolerate. The powerful impact this work usually has stems from the fact that Ibsen shows (whether intentionally or not) that societies based on profit find it impossible to foster an 'elevated' morality.

Capitalism is fundamentally immoral because the search for profit, which is its essence, is incompatible with its official morality, which preaches superior human values, justice, etc.

Dr Stockman is destroyed (that is, he loses his position in society, as does his daughter, who becomes an outcast in a competitive society) precisely because of his basic virtue, which is here considered vice, error, or tragic flaw.

Fifth Type: Anachronistic Individual Ethos Versus Contemporary Social Ethos

This is the typical case of Don Quixote: his social ethos is perfectly synchronized with the ethos of a society that no longer exists. This past society, now nonexistent, enters into a confrontation with the contemporary society and the resultant conflicts are inevitable. The anachronistic ethos of Don Quixote, knight errant and lordly Spanish hidalgo, cannot live peacefully in a time when the bourgeoisie is developing – the bourgeoisie which changes all values and for whom all things become money, as money comes to equal all things.

A variation of the 'anachronistic ethos' is that of the 'diachronic ethos': the character lives in a moral world made up of values which society honours in word but not in deed. In *José, from Birth to Grave*, the character, José da Silva, embodies all the values that the bourgeoisie claims as its own, and his misfortune comes precisely because he believes in those values and rules his life by them: a 'self-made man', he works more than he has to, is devoted to his employers, avoids causing labour troubles, etc. In short, a character who follows *The Laws of Success* of Napoleon Hill, or *How to Win Friends and Influence People* of Dale Carnegie. That is tragedy! And what a tragedy!

Notes

1. G. W. F. HEGEL, *The Philosophy of Fine Art*, trans. F. P. B. OSMASTON, 4 vols (London: G. Bell & Sons, Ltd., 1920), 4:257.
2. S. H. BUTCHER, *Aristotle's Theory of Poetry and Fine Art*, 4th edn (New York: Dover Publications, Inc., 1951).

3. 'Les passions n'y sont présentées aux yeux que pour montrer tout le désordre dont elles sont cause; et le vice y est peint partout avec des couleurs qui en font connaître et haïr la difformité ... et c'est ce que les premiers poètes tragiques avaient en vue sur toute chose. Leur théâtre était une école où la vertu n'était pas moins bien enseignée que dans les écoles des philosophes. Aussi Aristote a bien voulu donner des règles due pòeme dramatique ... Il serait à souhaiter que nos ouvrages fussent aussi solides et aussi pleins d'utiles instructions que ceux de ces poètes.' Cited in Butcher, *Aristotle's Theory*, pp. 243–4 note.

4 Tradition and Innovation

In an important short essay written in 1949, the American playwright, Arthur Miller, posed the question of whether in the light of modern psychiatry, tragedy was any longer possible. His own *The Death of A Salesman* may be read as an answer to this question, especially when we consider that Miller perceived the assertion that tragedy depended upon the noble status of the protagonist to be nothing more than 'a clinging to the outward forms of tragedy' (*The Theatre Essays of Arthur Miller*, p. 5). It is Miller's contention, shared to some extent, at least implicitly, by George Steiner, that the advent of psychiatry and sociology have been responsible for the essentially untragic belief that 'all our miseries, our indignities, are born and bred within our minds', and that this acts as a severe break on 'action', and particularly on 'heroic action'. In another essay which Miller wrote a month later, 'The Nature of Tragedy', he draws a distinction between pathos and tragedy, arguing that the precise difference between the two resides in the suggestion that 'tragedy brings us not only sadness, sympathy, identification and even fear; it also, unlike pathos, brings us knowledge or enlightenment'. For Miller the knowledge which it brings is ultimately an ethical knowledge: 'knowledge pertaining to the right way of living in the world' (ibid., p. 9). However, in this second essay Miller offers a more positive interpretation of tragedy than we might find either in Brecht or in Steiner. He perceives tragedy as being 'inseparable from a certain modest hope regarding the human animal. And it is the glimpse of this brighter possibility that raises sadness out of the pathetic toward the tragic' (ibid., p. 10).

In 1961 George Steiner published his influential *The Death of Tragedy*. His contention was that with the advent of, for example, Christianity and Marxism, the tragic sense of the world became eroded. In his view, tragedy emerges from the collective life of a culture, from what he identifies, in a telling phrase, as 'the ripening of collective emotion' (p. 324). Where modern writers such as T. S. Eliot, Sartre, or Eugene O'Neill have returned to classical models, they have not

141

so much breathed new life into old mythologies as enhanced 'the old, stolen bottles with new wine' (p. 325).

It was precisely this gloomy prognostication that prompted Raymond William's rejoinder in 1966. Williams sought to justify the continued validity of tragedy as a viable experience, and in order to argue his case, he adduced a critical history of tragedy which has proved both persuasive and influential. Williams's historicising of tragedy follows on from the writings of Brecht and in some ways shares certain methodological concerns with the work of Walter Benjamin. It is Williams's contention that as society changes so does the form of tragedy: the form itself is not fixed. This emphasis upon the contingent nature of tragedy poses a serious challenge to the essentialist formalism of a writer such as Steiner, and proposes a different kind of history of the genre.

From *The Death of Tragedy**

GEORGE STEINER

We are entering on large, difficult ground. There are landmarks worth noting from the outset.

All men are aware of tragedy in life. But tragedy as a form of drama is not universal. Oriental art knows violence, grief, and the stroke of natural or contrived disaster; the Japanese theatre is full of ferocity and ceremonial death. But that representation of personal suffering and heroism which we call tragic drama is distinctive of the western tradition. It has become so much a part of our sense of the possibilities of human conduct, the *Oresteia, Hamlet,* and *Phèdre* are so ingrained in our habits of spirit, that we forget what a strange and complex idea it is to re-enact private anguish on a public stage. This idea and the vision of man which it implies are Greek. And nearly till the moment of their decline, the tragic forms are Hellenic.

Tragedy is alien to the Judaic sense of the world. The book of Job is always cited as an instance of tragic vision. But that black fable stands on the outer edge of Judaism, and even here an orthodox hand has asserted the claims of justice against those of tragedy:

> So the Lord blessed the latter end of Job more than the beginning: for he had fourteen thousand sheep, and six thousand camels, and a thousand yoke of oxen, and a thousand she-asses.

God has made good the havoc wrought upon His servant; he has compensated Job for his agonies. But where there is compensation, there is justice, not tragedy. This demand for justice is the pride and burden of the Judaic tradition. Jehovah is just, even in His fury. Often the balance of retribution or reward seems fearfully awry, or the proceedings of God appear unendurably slow. But over the sum of time, there can be no doubt that the ways of God to man are just. Not only are they just, they are rational. The Judaic spirit is vehement in its

---

* Reprinted from *The Death of Tragedy* (New York: Alfred A. Knopf, 1968).

143

conviction that the order of the universe and of man's estate is accessible to reason. The ways of the Lord are neither wanton nor absurd. We may fully apprehend them if we give to our inquiries the clear-sightedness of obedience. Marxism is characteristically Jewish in its insistence on justice and reason, and Marx repudiated the entire concept of tragedy. 'Necessity', he declared, 'is blind only in so far as it is not understood.'

Tragic drama arises out of precisely the contrary assertion: necessity is blind and man's encounter with it shall rob him of his eyes, whether it be in Thebes or in Gaza. The assertion is Greek, and the tragic sense of life built upon it is the foremost contribution of the Greek genius to our legacy. It is impossible to tell precisely where or how the notion of formal tragedy first came to possess the imagination. But the *Iliad* is the primer of tragic art. In it are set forth the motifs and images around which the sense of the tragic has crystallized during nearly three thousand years of western poetry: the shortness of heroic life, the exposure of man to the murderousness and caprice of the inhuman, the fall of the City. Note the crucial distinction: the fall of Jericho or Jerusalem is merely just, whereas the fall of Troy is the first great metaphor of tragedy. Where a city is destroyed because it has defied God, its destruction is a passing instant in the rational design of God's purpose. Its walls shall rise again, on earth or in the kingdom of heaven, when the souls of men are restored to grace. The burning of Troy is final because it is brought about by the fierce sport of human hatreds and the wanton, mysterious choice of destiny.

There are attempts in the *Iliad* to throw the light of reason into the shadow-world which surrounds man. Fate is given a name, and the elements are shown in the frivolous and reassuring mask of the gods. But mythology is only a fable to help us endure. The Homeric warrior knows that he can neither comprehend nor master the workings of destiny. Patroclus is slain, and the wretch Thersites sails safely for home. Call for justice or explanation, and the sea will thunder back with its mute clamour. Men's accounts with the gods do not balance.

The irony deepens. Instead of altering or diminishing their tragic condition, the increase in scientific resource and material power leaves men even more vulnerable. This idea is not yet explicit in Homer, but it is eloquent in another major tragic poet, in Thucydides. Again, we must observe the decisive contrast. The wars recorded in the Old Testament are bloody and grievous, but not tragic. They are just or unjust. The armies of Israel shall carry the day if they have observed God's will and ordinance. They shall be routed if they have broken the divine covenant or if their kings have fallen into idolatry. The Peloponnesian Wars, on the contrary, are tragic. Behind them lie obscure fatalities and misjudgements. Enmeshed in false rhetoric and driven by political

compulsions of which they can give no clear account, men go out to
destroy one another in a kind of f[...]d. We are still
waging Peloponnesian war[...]rial world and our
positive science have grow[...] y achievements
turn against us, making politics [...] rs more bestial.

The Judaic vision sees in disaster a specific moral fault or failure of
understanding. The Greek tragic poets assert that the forces which
shape or destroy our lives lie outside the governance of reason or
justice. Worse than that: there are around us daemonic energies which
prey upon the soul and turn it to madness or which poison our will so
that we inflict irreparable outrage upon ourselves and those we love.
Or to put it in the terms of the tragic design drawn by Thucydides: our
fleets shall always sail toward Sicily although everyone is more or less
aware that they go to their ruin. Eteocles knows that he will perish at
the seventh gate but goes forward nevertheless:

We are already past the care of gods.
For them our death is the admirable offering.
Why then delay, fawning upon our doom?

Antigone is perfectly aware of what will happen to her, and in the
wells of his stubborn heart Oedipus knows also. But they stride to their
fierce disasters in the grip of truths more intense than knowledge. To
the Jew there is a marvellous continuity between knowledge and action;
to the Greek an ironic abyss. The legend of Oedipus, in which the
Greek sense of tragic unreason is so grimly rendered, served that great
Jewish poet Freud as an emblem of rational insight and redemption
through healing.

Not that Greek tragedy is wholly without redemption. In the
Eumenides and in *Oedipus at Colonus*, the tragic action closes on a
note of grace. Much has been made of this fact. But we should, I think,
interpret it with extreme caution. Both cases are exceptional; there is
in them an element of ritual pageant commemorating special aspects
of the sanctity of Athens. Moreover, the part of music in Greek tragedy
is irrevocably lost to us, and I suspect that the use of music may have
given to the endings of these two plays a solemn distinctness, setting
the final moments at some distance from the terrors which went before.

I emphasize this because I believe that any realistic notion of tragic
drama must start from the fact of catastrophe. Tragedies end badly.
The tragic personage is broken by forces which can neither be fully
understood nor overcome by rational prudence. This again is crucial.
Where the causes of disaster are temporal, where the conflict can be
resolved through technical or social means, we may have serious drama,
but not tragedy. More pliant divorce laws could not alter the fate of

Agamemnon; social psychiatry is no answer to *Oedipus*. But saner economic relations or better plumbing *can* resolve some of the grave crises in the dramas of Ibsen. The distinction should be borne sharply in mind. Tragedy is irreparable. It cannot lead to just and material compensation for past suffering. Job gets back double the number of she-asses; so he should, for God has enacted upon him a parable of justice. Oedipus does not get back his eyes or his sceptre over Thebes.

Tragic drama tells us that the spheres of reason, order, and justice are terribly limited and that no progress in our science or technical resources will enlarge their relevance. Outside and within man is *l'autre*, the 'otherness' of the world. Call it what you will: a hidden or malevolent God, blind fate, the solicitations of hell, or the brute fury of our animal blood. It waits for us in ambush at the crossroads. It mocks us and destroys us. In certain rare instances, it leads us after destruction to some incomprehensible repose.

None of this, I know, is a definition of tragedy. But any neat abstract definition would mean nothing. When we say 'tragic drama' we know what we are talking about; not exactly, but well enough to recognize the real thing. In one instance, however, a tragic poet does come very near to giving an explicit summary of the tragic vision of life. Euripides' *Bacchae* stands in some special proximity to the ancient, no longer discernible springs of tragic feeling. At the end of the play, Dionysus condemns Cadmus, his royal house, and the entire city of Thebes to a savage doom. Cadmus protests: the sentence is far too harsh. It is utterly out of proportion with the guilt of those who fail to recognize or have insulted the god. Dionysus evades the question. He repeats petulantly that he has been greatly affronted; then he asserts that the doom of Thebes was predestined. There is no use asking for rational explanation or mercy. Things are as they are, unrelenting and absurd. We are punished far in excess of our guilt.

It is a terrible, stark insight into human life. Yet in the very excess of his suffering lies man's claim to dignity. Powerless and broken, a blind beggar hounded out of the city, he assumes a new grandeur. Man is ennobled by the vengeful spite or injustice of the gods. It does not make him innocent, but it hallows him as if he had passed through flame. Hence there is in the final moments of great tragedy, whether Greek or Shakespearean or neo-classic, a fusion of grief and joy, of lament over the fall of man and of rejoicing in the resurrection of his spirit. No other poetic form achieves this mysterious effect; it makes of *Oedipus, King Lear*, and *Phèdre* the noblest yet wrought by the mind.

From antiquity until the age of Shakespeare and Racine, such accomplishment seemed within the reach of talent. Since then the tragic voice in drama is blurred or still.

From *Modern Tragedy**

RAYMOND WILLIAMS

Tragedy and contemporary ideas

In the suffering and confusion of our own century, there has been great
pressure to take a body of work from the past and to use it as a way
of rejecting the present. That there has been tragedy (or chivalry, or
community) but that lacking this belief, that rule, we are now incapable
of it, is a common response of this kind. And of course it is necessary,
if this position is to be maintained, to reject ordinary contemporary
meanings of tragedy, and to insist that they are a misunderstanding.

Yet tragic experience, because of its central importance, commonly
attracts the fundamental beliefs and tensions of a period, and tragic
theory is interesting mainly in this sense, that through it the shape and
set of a particular culture is often deeply realised. If, however, we think
of it as a theory about a single and permanent kind of fact, we can end
only with the metaphysical conclusions that are built into any such
assumption. Chief among these is the assumption of a permanent,
universal and essentially unchanging human nature (an assumption
taken over from one kind of Christianity to 'ritual' anthropology and
the general theory of psycho-analysis). Given such an assumption, we
have to explain tragedy in terms of this unchanging human nature or
certain of its faculties. But if we reject this assumption (following a
different kind of Christianity, a different psychological theory, or the
evidence of comparative anthropology) the problem is necessarily
transformed. Tragedy is then not a single and permanent kind of fact,
but a series of experiences and conventions and institutions. It is not
a case of interpreting this series by reference to a permanent and
unchanging human nature. Rather, the varieties of tragic experience
are to be interpreted by reference to the changing conventions and
institutions. The universalist character of most tragic theory is then
at the opposite pole from our necessary interest.

* Reprinted from *Modern Tragedy* (London: Chatto & Windus, 1966).

The most striking fact about modern tragic theory is that it is rooted in very much the same structure of ideas as modern tragedy itself, yet one of its paradoxical effects is its denial that modern tragedy is possible, after almost a century of important and continuous and insistent tragic art. It is very difficult to explain why this should be so. Part of the explanation seems to be the incapacity to make connections which is characteristic of this whole structure. But it is also significant that the major original contributions to the theory were made in the nineteenth century, before the creative period of modern tragedy, and have since been systematised by men deeply conditioned, by their academic training, to a valuation of the past against the present, and to a separation between critical theory and creative practice.

It is in any case necessary to break the theory if we are to value the art: in the simple sense, to see it as a major period of tragic writing, directly comparable in importance with the great periods of the past; and, more crucially, to see its controlling structure of feeling, the variations within this and their connections with actual dramatic structures, and to be able to respond to them critically, in the full sense. In my second part I shall discuss modern tragedy directly, but following the historical analysis already outlined it is worth trying to engage, critically, the major points of the theory. These are, as I see them: order and accident; the destruction of the hero; the irreparable action and its connections with death; and the emphasis of evil.

Order and Accident

The argument that there is no significant tragic meaning in 'everyday tragedies' seems to rest on two related beliefs: that the event itself is not tragedy, but only becomes so through shaped response (with the implication that tragedy is a matter of art, where such responses are embodied, rather than of life where they are not); and that significant response depends on the capacity to connect the event with some more general body of facts, so that it is not mere accident but is capable of bearing a general meaning.

My doubts here are radical. I do not see how it is finally possible to distinguish between an event and response to an event, in any absolute way. It is of course possible to say that *we* have not responded to an event, but this does not mean that response is absent. We can properly see the difference between a response which has been put into a communicable form and one which has not, and this will be relevant. But, in the case of ordinary death and suffering, when we see mourning and lament, when we see men and women breaking under their actual loss, it is at least not self-evident to say that we are not in the presence of tragedy. Other responses are of course possible: indifference, justification (as so often in war), even relief or rejoicing. But where the suffering is felt, where it is taken into the person of another, we are clearly within the possible dimensions of tragedy. We can of course ourselves react to the mourning and lament of others with our own forms of indifference and justification, even relief and rejoicing. But if we do, we should be clear what we are doing. That the suffering has communicated to those most closely involved but not to us may be a statement about the suffering, about those involved, or (which we often forget) about ourselves.

Obviously the possibility of communication to ourselves, we who are not immediately involved, depends on the capacity to connect the event with some more general body of facts. This criterion, which is now quite conventional, is indeed very welcome, for it poses the issue in its most urgent form. It is evidently possible for some people to hear of a mining disaster, a burned-out family, a broken career or a smash on the road without feeling these events as tragic in the full sense. But the starkness of such a position (which I believe to be sincerely held) is of course at once qualified by the description of such events as *accidents* which, however painful or regrettable, do not connect with any general meanings. This view is made even stronger when the unavailable meanings, for a particular event, are described as universal or permanent.

The central question that needs to be asked is what kind of general (or universal or permanent) meaning it is which interprets events of the kind referred to as accidents. Here at least (if not at a much earlier stage) we can see that the ordinary academic tradition of tragedy is in fact an ideology. What is in question is not the process of connecting an event to a general meaning, but the character and quality of the general meaning itself.

I once heard it said that if 'you or I' went out and got run over by a bus, that would not be tragedy. I was not sure how to take this: as engagingly modest; as indifferent and offensive; or as a quite alien ideology. I remembered Yeats –

some blunderer has driven his car on to the wrong side of the road – that is all

– or again

if war is necessary, or necessary in our time and place, it is best to forget its suffering as we do the discomfort of fever.

This has come a long way from Hegel's description of 'mere sympathy', which he distinguished from 'true sympathy' because it lacked 'genuine content': 'an accordant feeling with the ethical claim at the same time associated with the sufferer'. It is also some way from Bradley's restatement of this: 'no mere suffering or misfortune, no suffering that does not spring in great part from human agency, and in some degree from the agency of the sufferer, is tragic, however pitiful or dreadful it may be'. Here the 'ethical claim', a positive and representative content, has been changed to the more general concept of 'agency'. But what is really significant is the subsequent separation of both ethical content and human agency from a whole class of ordinary suffering.

Yeats, with his 'if war is necessary, or necessary in our time and place', may have been simply eccentric, but the exclusion from tragedy of certain kinds of suffering, as 'mere suffering', is characteristic and significant. There is the exclusion, already evident in the language of Hegel, of ordinary suffering, and this is surely the unconscious attachment of significant suffering to (social) nobility. But there is also the related and deeper exclusion of all that suffering which is part of our social and political world, and its actual human relations. The real key, to the modern separation of tragedy from 'mere suffering', is the separation of ethical control and, more critically, human agency, from our understanding of social and political life.

What we encounter again and again in the modern distinction between tragedy and accident, and in the related distinction between tragedy and suffering, is a particular view of the world which gains much of its strength from being unconscious and habitual. The social character of this view can be seen in its ordinary examples, as well as in its deprecating language of 'you or I'. It is not as if the event chosen for argument was a death by lightning, at the far edge of the possible spectrum. The events which are not seen as tragic are deep in the pattern of our own culture: war, famine, work, traffic, politics. To see no ethical content or human agency in such events, or to say that we cannot connect them with general meanings, and especially with permanent and universal meanings, is to admit a strange and particular bankruptcy, which no rhetoric of tragedy can finally hide.

We can only distinguish between tragedy and accident if we have some conception of a law or an order to which certain events are accidental and in which certain other events are significant. Yet wherever the law or order is partial (in the sense that only certain events are relevant to it) there is an actual alienation of some part of human experience. Even in the most traditional general orders, there has been this factual alienation. The definition of tragedy as dependent on the history of a man of rank was just such an alienation: some deaths mattered more than others, and rank was the actual dividing line – the death of a slave or a retainer was no more than incidental and was certainly not tragic. Ironically, our own middle-class culture began by

appearing to reject this v ⟨…⟩ of a citizen could be as real as
the tragedy of a prince. ⟨…⟩ not so much rejection of
the real structure of feeling ⟨…⟩ gic category to a
newly rising class. Yet its even⟨…⟩ nd. As in other
bourgeois revolutions, extending the ⟨…⟩ or suffrage, the
arguments for the limited extension becam⟨…⟩ arguments for a
general extension. The extension from the princ⟨…⟩ he citizen became
in practice an extension to all human beings. Yet the character of the
extension largely determined its content, until the point was reached
where tragic experience was theoretically conceded to all men, but the
nature of this experience was drastically limited.

The important element in the earlier emphasis on rank in tragedy was
always the *general* status of the man of rank. His fate was the fate of the
house or kingdom which he at once ruled and embodied. In the person
of Agamemnon or of Lear the fate of a house or a kingdom was
literally acted out. It was of course inevitable that this definition should
fail to outlast its real social circumstances, in its original form. It was
in particular inevitable that bourgeois society should reject it: the
individual was neither the state nor an element of the state, but an
entity in himself. There was then both gain and loss: the suffering of a
man of no rank could be more seriously and more directly regarded,
but equally, in the stress on the fate of an individual, the general and
public character of tragedy was lost. Eventually, as we shall see, new
definitions of general and public interest were embodied in new kinds
of tragedy. But, meanwhile, the idea of a tragic order had to co-exist
with the loss of any such actual order. What happened, at the level of
theory, was then the abstraction of order, and its mystification.

One practical consequence intervened. Rank in tragedy became the
name-dropping, the play with titles and sonorities, of costume drama.
What had formerly been a significant relationship, of the king
embodying his people and embodying also the common meanings of
life and the world, became an empty ceremonial: a play of bourgeois
man calling himself King or Duke (as in our own twentieth-century
version of honours and nobility, in which a retiring Prime Minister is
called an Earl and a civil servant of a particular grade a Knight).
Sometimes indeed the ceremonial was even more alienated, and the
names were Agamemnon or Caesar: a social order withered to a
classical education.

But the main effects were more serious. What had been a whole lived
order, connecting man and state and world, became, finally, a purely
abstract order. Tragic significance was made to depend on an event's
relation to a supposed nature of things, yet without the specific
connections which had once provided a particular relation and action
of this kind. Hegel's insistence on ethical substance, and his connection

of this with a process of historical embodiment of the Idea, was a major attempt to meet the new situation. Marx pushed the connection further, into a more specific history. But, increasingly, the idea of the permanent 'nature of things' became separated from any action that could be felt as contemporary, to the point where even Nietzsche's brutal rationalisation of suffering could be welcomed as specific. The whole meaning of 'accident' changed. Fate or Providence had been beyond man's understanding, so that what he saw as accident was in fact design, or was a specifically limited kind of event outside this design. The design in any case was embodied in institutions, through which man could hope to come to terms with it. But when there is an idea of design, without specific institutions at once metaphysical and social, the alienation is such that the category of accident is stressed and enlarged until it comes to include almost all actual suffering, and especially the effects of the existing and non-metaphysical social order. This is then either newly generalised as a *blind* fate, accident taking over from design as a plan of the universe, and becoming objective rather than subjective; or significant suffering, and therefore tragedy, is pushed back in time to periods when fully connecting meanings were available, and contemporary tragedy is seen as impossible because there are now no such meanings. The living tragedies of our own world can then not be negotiated at all. They cannot be seen in the light of those former meanings, or they are, however regrettable, accidents. New kinds of relation and new kinds of law, to connect with and interpret our actual suffering, are the terms of contemporary tragedy. But to see new relations and new laws is also to change the nature of experience, and the whole complex of attitudes and relationships dependent on it. To *find* significance is to be capable of tragedy, but of course it was easier to find insignificance. Then behind the facade of the emphasis on order, the substance of tragedy withered.

The effect of this development is not only on theory; it is also on critical method. If we are to think of the relations between tragedy and order, we have to think of relations and connections substantial enough to be embodied in an action. The abstraction of order, on the other hand, emerges as a critical procedure, corresponding to the idea that the tragic action is a kind of putting experience to the order, for ratification or containment. That is to say, it makes the order exist before the action: the abstract beliefs of fifth-century Athens are expounded as a 'background' to its tragic drama; the abstract beliefs of the 'Elizabethan world' are expounded as a 'background' to Marlowe and Shakespeare and Webster. Often, in fact, these expositions are circular; the general beliefs are derived from the works and then reapplied to them, in an abstract and static way (the case of Greek religion is especially to this point).

But the relations between order and tragedy are always more dynamic than such accounts and procedures suggest. Order, in tragedy, is the *result* of the action, even where it entirely corresponds, in an abstract way, with a pre-existing conventional belief. It is not so much that the order is illustrated as that it is recreated. In any living belief, this is always the relation between experience and conviction. Specifically, in tragedy, the creation of order is directly related to the fact of disorder, through which the action moves. Whatever the character of the order that is finally affirmed, it has been literally created in this particular action. The relation between the order and the disorder is direct.

There is an evident variation in the nature of tragic disorder. It can be the pride of man set against the nature of things, or it can be a more general disorder which in aspiration man seeks to overcome. There seems to be no continuing tragic cause, at the simple level of content. In different cultures, disorder and order both vary, for they are parts of varying general interpretations of life. We should see this variation, not so much as an obstacle to discovering a single tragic cause or tragic emotion, as an indication of the major cultural importance of tragedy as a form of art.

The tragic meaning is always both culturally and historically conditioned, but the artistic process in which a particular disorder is both experienced and resolved is more widely available and important. The essence of tragedy has been looked for in the pre-existing beliefs and in the consequent order, but it is precisely these elements that are most narrowly limited, culturally. Any attempt to abstract these orders, as definitions of tragedy, either misleads or condemns us to a merely sterile attitude towards the tragic experience of our own culture. The ideas of order matter, critically, only when they are in solution in particular works; as precipitates they are of only documentary interest.

The correlate of this, in our own time, is that our ideas of order are, while the mainstream of the culture holds, still in solution, and often unnoticed. I shall try to show, in my studies of modern tragedies, how firm and general our own ideas of order and disorder are, even though they are oriented to a pervasive individualism, and hardly seem in the same world as the definitions of tragic order and disorder which we have taken from the past and generalised as permanent tragic ideas. But tragic meanings, which differ in different cultures and are general only within particular cultures, operate in important tragedy more as actors than as background. The real action embodies the particular meaning, and all that is common, in the works we call tragedies, is the dramatisation of a particular and grievous disorder and its resolution.

When we look, then, for the historical conditions of tragedy, we shall not look for particular kinds of belief: in fate, in divine government, or in a sense of the irreparable. The action of isolating extreme suffering and then of re-integrating it within a continuing sense of life can occur in very different cultures, with very different fundamental beliefs. It is often argued that these beliefs need to be both common and stable, if tragedy is to occur. Some such argument lies behind the assertion that tragedy was dependent, in the past, on ages of faith, and is impossible now, because we have no faith. That the beliefs which are brought into action or question need to be reasonably common I would not deny. We have, as we shall see, our own beliefs of this kind, and we are surely capable of avoiding the simple trap of calling some beliefs 'faiths' and others not.

The question of stability is much more important. I would not deny the possibility of tragedy when there are stable beliefs, but it is in this direction that an historical examination seems to take us. What is commonly asserted, about the relation between tragedy and stability of belief, seems to be almost the opposite of the truth. Of course if beliefs are simply abstracted, and taken out of their context as lived behaviour and working institutions, it is possible to create the impression of stability, the reiteration of received interpretations, even when the real situation is quite evidently one of instability or indeed disintegration. The most remarkable case of this kind is the description of an Elizabethan and Jacobean sense of order – the persistence of late mediaeval beliefs – in almost total disregard of the extraordinary tensions of a culture moving towards violent internal conflict and substantial transformation. The ages of comparatively stable belief, and of comparatively close correspondence between beliefs and actual experience, do not seem to produce tragedy of any intensity, though of course they enact the ordinary separations and tensions and the socially sanctioned ways of resolving these. The intensification of this common procedure, and the possibility of its permanent interest, seem to depend more on an extreme tension between belief and experience than on an extreme correspondence. Important tragedy seems to occur, neither in periods of real stability, nor in periods of open and decisive conflict. Its most common historical setting is the period preceding the substantial breakdown and transformation of an important culture. Its condition is the real tension between old and new: between received beliefs, embodied in institutions and responses, and newly and vividly experienced contradictions and possibilities. If the received beliefs have widely or wholly collapsed, this tension is obviously absent; to that extent their real presence is necessary. But beliefs can be both active and deeply questioned, not so much by other beliefs as by insistent immediate experience. In such situations, the common process of dramatising and resolving disorder and suffering is intensified to the level which can be most readily recognised as tragedy.

The Destruction of the Hero

The most common interpretation of tragedy is that it is an action in which the hero is destroyed. This fact is seen as irreparable. At a simple level this is so obviously true that the formula usually gets little further examination. But it is of course still an interpretation, and a partial one. If attention is concentrated on the hero alone, such an interpretation naturally follows. We have been very aware of the kind of reading which we can describe as *Hamlet* without the Prince, but we have been almost totally unaware of the opposite and equally erroneous reading of the Prince of Denmark without the State of Denmark. It is this unity that we must now restore.

Not many works that we call tragedies in fact end with the destruction of the hero. Outside the undeveloped mediaeval form, most of the examples that we could offer come, significantly, from modern tragedy. Certainly in almost all tragedies the hero is destroyed, but that is not normally the end of the action. Some new distribution of forces, physical or spiritual, normally succeeds the death. In Greek tragedy this is ordinarily a religious affirmation, but in the words or presence of the chorus, which is then the ground of its social continuity. In Elizabethan tragedy it is ordinarily a change of power in the state, with the arrival of a new, uncommitted or restored Prince. There are many factual variations of this reintegrative action, but their general function is common. Of course these endings are now normally read as merely valedictory or as a kind of tidying-up. To our consciousness, the important action has ended, and the affirmation, settlement, restoration or new arrival are comparatively minor. We read the last chapters of Victorian novels, which bring the characters together and settle their future directions, with a comparable indifference or even impatience. This kind of reparation is not particularly interesting to us, because not really credible. Indeed it looks much too like a solution, which twentieth-century critics agree is a vulgar and intrusive element in any art. (It is not the business of the artist, or even the thinker, to provide answers and solutions, but simply to describe experiences and to raise questions.) Yet of course it is no more and no less a solution than its commonplace twentieth-century alternative. To conclude that there is no solution is also an answer.

When we now say that the tragic experience is of the irreparable, because the action is followed right through until the hero is dead, we are taking a part for the whole, a hero for an action. We think of tragedy as what happens to the hero, but the ordinary tragic action is what happens through the hero. When we confine our attention to the hero, we are unconsciously confining ourselves to one kind of experience which in our own culture we tend to take as the whole. We are unconsciously confining ourselves to the individual. Yet over a very wide range we see this transcended in tragedy. Life does come back, life ends the play, again and again. And the fact that life does come back, that its meanings are reaffirmed and restored, after so much suffering and after so important a death, has been, quite commonly, the tragic action.

What is involved, of course, is not a simple forgetting, or a picking-up for the new day. The life that is continued is informed by the death; has indeed, in a sense, been created by it. But in a culture theoretically limited to individual experience, there is no more to say, when a man has died, but that others also will die. Tragedy can then be generalised not as the response to death but as the bare irreparable fact.

'The Irreparable Action'

Human death is often the form of the deepest meanings of a culture. When we see death, it is natural that we should draw together – in grief, in memory, in the social duties of burial – our sense of the values of living, as individuals and as a society. But then, in some cultures or in their breakdown, life is regularly read back from the fact of death, which can seem not only the focus but also the source of our values. Death, then, is absolute, and all our living simply relative. Death is necessary, and all other human ends are contingent. Within this emphasis, suffering and disorder of any kind are interpreted by reference to what is seen as the controlling reality. Such an interpretation is now commonly described as a tragic sense of life.

What is not usually noticed, in this familiar and now formal procession, is precisely the element of convention. To read back life from the fact of death is a cultural and sometimes a personal choice. But that it is a choice, and a variable choice, is very easily forgotten. The powerful association of a particular rhetoric and a persistent human fact can give the appearance of permanence to a local and temporary and even sectional response. To tie any meaning to death is to give it a powerful emotional charge which can at times obliterate all other experience in its range. Death is universal, and the meaning tied to it quickly claims universality, as it were in its shadow. Other readings of life, other interpretations of suffering and disorder, can be assimilated to it with great apparent conviction. The burden of proof shifts continually from the controversial meaning to the inescapable experience, and we are easily exposed, by fear and loss, to the most conventional and arbitrary conclusions.

The connection between tragedy and death is of course quite evident, but in reality the connection is variable, as the response to death is variable. What has happened in our own century is that a particular post-liberal and post-Christian interpretation of death has been imposed as an absolute meaning, and as identical with all tragedy. What is generalised is the loneliness of man, facing a blind fate, and this is the fundamental isolation of the tragic hero. The currency of this experience is of course sufficiently wide to make it relevant to much modern tragedy. But the structure of the meaning still needs analysis. To say that man dies alone is not to state a fact but to offer an interpretation. For indeed men die in so many ways: in the arms and presence of family and neighbours; in the blindness of pain, or the blankness of sedation; in the violent disintegration of machines and in the calm of sleep. To insist on a single meaning is already rhetorical, but to insist on the meaning of loneliness is to interpret life as much as death. However men die, the experience is not only the physical dissolution and ending; it is also a change in the lives and relationships of others, for we know death as much in the experience of others as in our own expectations and endings. And just as death enters, continually, our common life, so any statement about death is in a common language and depends on common experience. The paradox of 'we die alone' or 'man dies alone' is then important and remarkable: the maximum substance that can be given to the plural 'we', or to the group-name 'man', is the singular loneliness. The common fact, in a common language, is offered as a proof of the loss of connection.

But then, as we become aware of this structure of feeling, we can look through it at the experience which it has offered to interpret. It is using the names of death and tragedy, but it has very little really to do with the tragedies of the past, or with death as a universal experience. Rather, it has correctly identified, and then blurred, the crisis around which one main kind of contemporary tragic experience moves. It blurs it because it offers as absolutes the very experiences which are now most unresolved and most moving. Our most common received interpretations of life put the highest value and significance on the individual and his development, but it is indeed inescapable that the individual dies. What is most valuable and what is most irreparable are then set in an inevitable relation and tension. But to generalise this particular contradiction as an absolute fact of human existence is to fix and finally suppress the relation and tension, so that tragedy becomes not an action but a deadlock. And then to claim this deadlock as the whole meaning of tragedy is to project into history a local structure that is both culturally and historically determined.

It is characteristic of such structures that they cannot even recognise as possible any experience beyond their own structural limits; that such varying and possible statements as 'I die but I shall live', 'I die but we shall live', or 'I die but we do not die' become meaningless, and can even be contemptuously dismissed as evasions. The whole fact of community is reduced to the singular recognition, and it is angrily denied that there can be any other. Yet what seems to me most significant about the current isolation of death, is not what it has to say about tragedy or about dying, but what it is saying, through this, about loneliness and the loss of human connection, and about the consequent blindness of human destiny. It is, that is to say, a theoretical formulation of liberal tragedy, rather than any kind of universal principle.

The tragic action is about death, but it need not end in death, unless this is enforced by a particular structure of feeling. Death, once again, is a necessary actor but not the necessary action. We encounter this alteration of pattern again and again in contemporary tragic argument. The most spectacular example, perhaps, is the resurgence of the concept of evil.

The Emphasis of Evil

Evil, of course, is a traditional name, but, like other names, it has been appropriated by a particular ideology which then offers itself as the whole tragic tradition. In recent years especially, we have been continually rebuked by what is called the fact of transcendent evil, and the immense social crisis of our century is specifically interpreted in this light or darkness. The true nature of man, it is argued, is now dramatically revealed, against all the former illusions of civilisation and progress. The concentration camp, especially, is used as an image of an absolute condition, in which man is reduced, by men, to a thing. The record of the camps is indeed black enough, and many other examples could be added. But to use the camp as an image of an absolute condition is, in its turn, a blasphemy. For while men created the camps, other men died, at conscious risk, to destroy them. While some men imprisoned, other men liberated. There is no evil which men have created, of this or any other kind, which other men have not struggled to end. To take one part of this action, and call it absolute or transcendent, is in its turn a suppression of other facts of human life on so vast a scale that its indifference can only be explained by its role in an ideology.

The appropriation of evil to the theory of tragedy is then especially significant. What tragedy shows us, it is argued, is the fact of evil as inescapable and irreparable. Mere optimists and humanists deny the fact of transcendent evil, and so are incapable of tragic experience. Tragedy is then a salutary reminder, indeed a theory, against the illusions of humanism.

But this can only be maintained if the tragic action can be reduced and simplified, in ways very similar to the simplifications of tragic order and the tragic individual and the irreparable death. Evil, as it is now widely used, is a deeply complacent idea. For it ends, and is meant to end, any actual experience. It ends, among other things, the normal action of tragedy. It is not that any of us can deny, or wish to deny, the description, as evil, of particular actions. But when we abstract and generalise it, we remove ourselves from any continuing action, and deliberately break both response and connection.

The current emphasis of evil is not, we must remind ourselves, the Christian emphasis. Within that structure, evil was certainly generalised, but so also was good, and the struggle of good and evil in our souls and in the world could be seen as a real action. Evil was the common disorder which was yet overcome in Christ. As such, for all the magnitude of its name, it has commonly operated within the terms of the tragic action.

Culturally, evil is a name for many kinds of disorder which corrode or destroy actual life. As such, it is common in tragedy, though in many particular and variable forms: vengeance or ambition or pride or coldness or lust or jealousy or disobedience or rebellion. In every case it is only fully comprehensible within the valuations of a particular culture or tradition. It may indeed be possible, in any particular ideology, to generalise it until it appears as an absolute and even singular force. As a common name, also, it appears to take on a general character. But we cannot then say that tragedy is the recognition of transcendent evil. Tragedy commonly dramatises evil, in many particular forms. We move away from actual tragedies, and not towards them, when we abstract and generalise the very specific forces that are so variously dramatised. We move away, even more decisively, from a common tragic action, when we interpret tragedy as only the dramatisation and recognition of evil. A particular evil, in a tragic action, can be at once experienced and lived through. In the process of living through it, and in a real action seeing its moving relations with other capacities and other men, we come not so much to the recognition of evil as transcendent but to its recognition as actual and indeed negotiable.

This is of course far from its simple abolition, which is the opposite and yet complementary error to its recognition as transcendent, just as the proposition that man is naturally good is the complementary error to the proposition that man is naturally evil. Within a religious culture, man is seen as naturally limited, but within a liberal culture man is seen as naturally absolute, and good and evil are then alternative absolute names. They are not, however, the only alternatives. It is equally possible to say that man is not 'naturally' anything: that we both create and transcend our limits, and that we are good or evil in particular ways and in particular situations, defined by pressures we at once receive and can alter and can create again. This continuing and varying activity is the real source of the names, which can only in fantasy be abstracted to explain the activity itself.

Tragedy, as such, teaches nothing about evil, because it teaches many things about many kinds of action. Yet it can at least be said, against the modern emphasis on transcendent evil, that most of the great tragedies of the world end not with evil absolute, but with evil both experienced and lived through. A particular tragic hero may put out his eyes when he sees the evil that he has committed, but we see him do this, in a continuing action. Yet that blindness, which was part of the action, is now abstracted and generalised, as an absolute blindness: a rejection of particulars, a refusal to look into sources and causes and versions of consequence. The affirmation of absolute evil, which is now so current, is, under pressure, a self-blinding; the self-blinding of a culture which, lacking the nerve to inquire into its own nature, would have not only actors but also spectators put out their eyes. What is offered as tragic significance is here, as elsewhere, a significant denial of the possibility of *any* meaning.

If I am right in seeing this fundamental pattern in the orthodox modern idea of tragedy, both negative and positive conclusions follow. Negatively, we must say that what is now offered as a total meaning of tragedy is in fact a particular meaning, to be understood and valued historically. Some would go further and dispense with tragedy as an idea at all. There is a certain attraction in accepting the consequences of historical criticism, and cutting out all general considerations because they have been shown to be variable. A sophisticated and mainly technical criticism will then supervene: the meanings do not matter, but we can look at how they are expressed, in particular arrangements of words. It is in fact doubtful if in any case this can be done. If the words matter, the meanings will matter, and to ignore them formally is usually to accept some of them informally.

I believe that the meanings matter as such; in tragedy especially, because the experience is so central and we can hardly avoid thinking about it. If we find a particular idea of tragedy, in our own time, we find also a way of interpreting a very wide area of our experience; relevant certainly to literary criticism but relevant also to very much else. And then the negative analysis is only part of our need. We must try also, positively, to understand and describe not only the tragic theory but also the tragic experience of our own time.

Tragedy and revolution

The most complex effect of any really powerful ideology is that it directs us, even when we think we have rejected it, to the same kind of fact. Thus, when we try to identify the disorder which is at the root of our tragic experiences, we tend to find elements analogous to former tragic systems, as the ideology has interpreted them. We look, almost unconsciously, for a crisis of personal belief: matching a lost belief in immortality with a new conviction of mortality, or a lost belief in fate with a new conviction of indifference. We look for tragic experience in our attitudes to God or to death or to individual will, and of course we often find tragic experience cast in these familiar forms. Having separated earlier tragic systems from their actual societies, we can achieve a similar separation in our own time, and can take it for granted that modern tragedy can be discussed without reference to the deep social crisis, of war and revolution, through which we have all been living. That kind of interest is commonly relegated to politics, or, to use the cant word, sociology. Tragedy, we say, belongs to deeper and closer experience, to man not to society. Even the general disorders, which can hardly escape the most limited attention, and which equally can hardly be said to involve only societies and not men, can be reduced to symptoms of the only kind of disorder we are prepared to recognise: the fault in the soul. War, revolution, poverty, hunger; men reduced to objects and killed from lists; persecution and torture; the many kinds of contemporary martyrdom: however close and insistent the facts, we are not to be moved, in a context of tragedy. Tragedy, we know, is about something else.

Yet the break comes, in some minds. In experience, suddenly, the new connections are made, and the familiar world shifts, as the new relations are seen. We are not looking for a new universal meaning of tragedy. We are looking for the structure of tragedy in our own culture. Once we begin to doubt, in experience and then in analysis, the ordinary twentieth-century idea, other directions seem open.

Tragedy and Social Disorder

Since the time of the French Revolution, the idea of tragedy can be seen as in different ways a response to a culture in conscious change and movement. The action of tragedy and the action of history have been consciously connected, and in the connection have been seen in new ways. The reaction against this, from the mid-nineteenth century, has been equally evident: the movement of spirit has been separated from the movement of civilisation. Yet even this negative reaction seems, in its context, a response to the same kind of crisis. The academic tradition, on the whole, has followed the negative reaction, but it is difficult to hear its ordinary propositions and feel that they are only about a set of academic facts. They sound, insistently, like propositions about contemporary life, even when they are most negative and most consciously asocial. The other nineteenth-century tradition, in which tragedy and history were consciously connected, seems then deeply relevant. In experience and in theory we have to look again at this relation.

We must ask whether tragedy, in our own time, is a response to social disorder. If it is so, we shall not expect the response to be always direct. The disorder will appear in very many forms, and to articulate these will be very complex and difficult. A more immediate difficulty is the ordinary separation of social thinking and tragic thinking. The most influential kinds of explicitly social thinking have often rejected tragedy as in itself defeatist. Against what they have known as the idea of tragedy, they have stressed man's powers to change his condition and to end a major part of the suffering which the tragic ideology seems to ratify. The idea of tragedy, that is to say, has been explicitly opposed by the idea of revolution: there has been as much confidence on the one side as on the other. And then to describe tragedy as a response to social disorder, and to value it as such, is to break, apparently, from both major traditions.

The immediate disturbance is radical, for the fault in the soul was a recognition of a kind; it was close to the experience, even when it added its ordinary formulas. From the other position, from the recognition of social disorder, there is a habit of easy abstraction which the scale of the disorder almost inevitably supports. As we recognise history, we are referred to history, and find it difficult to acknowledge men like ourselves. Before, we could not recognise tragedy as social crisis; now, commonly, we cannot recognise social crisis as tragedy. The facts of disorder are caught up in a new ideology, which cancels suffering as it finds the name of a period or a phase. From day to day we can make everything past, because we believe in the future. Our actual present, in which the disorder is radical, is as effectively hidden as when it was merely politics, for it is now only politics. It seems that we have jumped from one blindness to another, and with the same visionary confidence. The new connections harden, and no longer connect.

What seems to matter, against every difficulty, is that the received ideas no longer describe our experience. The most common idea of revolution excludes too much of our social experience. But it is more than this. The idea of tragedy, in its ordinary form, excludes especially that tragic experience which is social, and the idea of revolution, again in its ordinary form, excludes especially that social experience which is tragic. And if this is so, the contradiction is significant. It is not a merely formal opposition, of two ways of reading experience, between which we can choose. In our own time, especially, it is the connections between revolution and tragedy – connections lived and known but not acknowledged as ideas – which seem most clear and significant.

The most evident connection is in the actual events of history, as we all quite simply observe them. A time of revolution is so evidently a time of violence, dislocation and extended suffering that it is natural to feel it as tragedy, in the everyday sense. Yet, as the event becomes history, it is often quite differently regarded. Very many nations look back to the revolutions of their own history as to the era of creation of the life which is now most precious. The successful revolution, we might say, becomes not tragedy but epic: it is the origin of a people, and of its valued way of life. When the suffering is remembered, it is at once either honoured or justified. That particular revolution, we say, was a necessary condition of life.

Contemporary revolution is of course very different. Only a post-revolutionary generation is capable of that epic composition. In contemporary revolution, the detail of suffering is insistent, whether as violence or as the reshaping of lives by a new power in the state. But further, in a contemporary revolution, we inevitably take sides, though with different degrees of engagement. And a time of revolution is ordinarily a time of lies and of suppressions of truths. The suffering of the whole action, even when its full weight is acknowledged, is commonly projected as the responsibility of this party or that, until its very description becomes a revolutionary or counter-revolutionary act. There is a kind of indifference which comes early whenever the action is at a distance. But there is also an exposure to the scale of suffering, and to the lies and campaigns that are made from it, which in the end is also indifference. Revolution is a dimension of action from which, for initially honourable reasons, we feel we have to keep clear.

Thus the social fact becomes a structure of feeling. Revolution as such is in a common sense tragedy, a time of chaos and suffering. It is almost inevitable that we should try to go beyond it. I do not rely on what is almost certain to happen: that this tragedy, in its turn, will become epic. However true this may be, it cannot closely move us; only heirs can inherit. Allegiance to even a probable law of history, which has not, however, in the particular case, been lived through, becomes quite quickly an alienation. We are not truly responding to this action but, by projection, to its probable composition.

The living alternative is quite different in character. It is neither the rejection of revolution, by its simple characterisation as chaos and suffering, nor yet the calculation of revolution, by laws and probabilities not yet experienced. It is, rather, a recognition; the recognition of revolution as a whole action of living men. Both the wholeness of the action, and in this sense its humanity, are then inescapable. It is this recognition against which we ordinarily struggle.

Revolution and Disorder

As we have reduced tragedy to the death of the hero, so we have reduced revolution to its crisis of violence and disorder. In simple observation, these are often the most evident effects, but in the whole action they are both preceded and succeeded, and much of their meaning depends on this fact of continuity. Thus it is strange that from our whole modern history revolution should be selected as the example of violence and disorder: revolution, that is, as the critical conflict and resolution of forces. To limit violence and disorder to the decisive conflict is to make nonsense of that conflict itself. The violence and disorder are in the whole action, of which what we commonly call revolution is the crisis.

The essential point is that violence and disorder are institutions as well as acts. When a revolutionary change has been lived through, we can usually see this quite clearly. The old institutions, now dead, take on their real quality as systematic violence and disorder; in that quality, the source of the revolutionary action is seen. But while such institutions are still effective, they can seem, to an extraordinary extent, both settled and innocent. Indeed they constitute, commonly, an order, against which the very protest, of the injured and oppressed, seems the source of disturbance and violence. Here, most urgently, in our own time, we need to return the idea of revolution, in its ordinary sense of the crisis of a society, to its necessary context as part of a whole action, within which alone it can be understood.

Order and disorder are relative terms, although each is experienced as an absolute. We are aware of this relativism, through history and comparative studies: intellectually aware, though that is often not much use to us, under the pressure of fear or interest or in the simple immediacy of our local and actual world. In the ideas of both tragedy and revolution, this dimension and yet also these difficulties are at once encountered. I have already argued that the relation between tragedy and order is dynamic. The tragic action is rooted in a disorder, which indeed, at a particular stage, can seem to have its own stability. But the whole body of real forces is engaged by the action, often in such a way that the underlying disorder becomes apparent and terrible in overtly tragic ways. From the whole experience of this disorder, and through its specific action, order is recreated. The process of this action is at times remarkably similar to the real action of revolution.

Yet revolution, at least in its feudal form as rebellion, is often, in many valued tragedies, the disorder itself. The restoration of 'lawful' authority is there literally the restoration of order. But the essential consideration lies deeper than this, below the false consciousness of feudal attitudes to rebellion. It is not difficult to see that the feudal definitions of lawful authority and rebellion are, at the political level, at worst timeserving, at best partisan. The majesty of kings is usually the political façade of successful usurpers and their descendants. What challenges it, as an action, is of the same human kind as what established it. Yet the investment of political power with religious or magical sanctions is also, in its most important examples, a vehicle for the expression of a fundamental conception of order, and indeed of the nature of life and of man. Characteristically, this is a conception of a static order, and of a permanent human condition and nature. Around such conceptions, real values are formed, and the threat to them overrides the temporary and arbitrary association of them with a particular figure or system. When connections of this kind are a living reality, the tragic action, whatever its local form, can have the widest human reference.

In its actual course, the tragic action often undercuts the ordinary association between fundamental human values and the acknowledged social system: the claims of actual love contradict the duties of family; the awakened individual consciousness contradicts the assigned social role. In the transition from a feudal to a liberal world, such contradictions are common and are lived out as tragedy. Yet the identification between a permanent order and a social system is still not really challenged. The contradictions and disorders are normally seen in terms of the identification, which has been blurred by human error but which the tragic action essentially restores. The figures of the true and false kings, of the lawful authority and his erring deputy, are dramatic modes of just this structure of feeling. There is a close relation between such dramatic modes and the type of argument common to political reformers and even political revolutionaries, in England in the seventeenth century, in which it was claimed that nothing new was being proposed or fought for, but only the restoration of the true and ancient constitution. This consciousness contained the most radical and even revolutionary actions. In tragedy, the stage was at last reached when there was scepticism about the possibility of any social order, and then resolution was seen as altogether outside the terms of civil society. A religious or quasi-religious withdrawal restored order by supernatural or magical intervention, and the tragic action came full circle.

Liberalism

Liberal tragedy inherited this separation between ultimate human values
and the social system, but in a mode which it finally transformed.
Slowly, in the development of liberal consciousness, the point of
reference became not a general order but the individual, who as such
embodied all ultimate values, including (in the ordinary emphasis of
Protestantism) divine values. I shall trace the course of liberal tragedy
to the point where new contradictions, in this absolute conception of the
individual, led to deadlock and then to final breakdown (a breakdown
of which I expect to see many further examples).

But the great current of liberalism had other effects, and is especially
responsible for the sharp opposition between the idea of tragedy and the
idea of revolution which we find so clearly in our own time. Liberalism
steadily eroded the conceptions of a permanent human nature and of a
static social order with connections to a divine order. From these
erosions, and from the alternative conception of the possibility of
human and social transformation, the early idea of revolution, in the
modern sense, took its origins. Rebellion became revolution, and the
most important human values became associated not with the received
order but with development, progress and change. The contrast between
the ordinary ideas of tragedy and of revolution seemed then quite stark.
Revolution asserted the possibility of man altering his condition;
tragedy showed its impossibility, and the consequent spiritual effects.
On that opposition, we are still trying to rest.

Yet the essential history has already changed. The liberal idea of
revolution and the feudal idea of tragedy are no longer the only
alternatives, and to go on offering to choose between them is to be
merely stranded in time. To understand this we must see what
happened to the liberal idea of revolution.

It is at first sight surprising that so open and positive a movement
as liberalism should ever have produced tragedy at all. Yet each of the
literary movements which took their origins from liberalism came to a
point where the most decisive choices were necessary, and where, while
some chose, others merely divided. The nature of these choices is in the
end essentially a matter of attitudes toward revolution. It is in this
process that we are still engaged.

Naturalism

The literature of naturalism is the most obvious example. It seems now
the true child of the liberal enlightenment, in which the traditional ideas

of a fate, an absolute order, a design beyond human powers, were replaced by a confidence in reason and in the possibility of a continually expanding capacity for explanation and control. In politics this produced a new social consciousness of human destiny; in philosophy, analysis of the ideologies of religion and of social custom, together with new schemes of rational explanation; in literature, a new emphasis on the exact observation and description of the contemporary social world. But the literature of naturalism, finally, is a bastard of the enlightenment. Characteristically, it detached the techniques of observation and description from the purposes which these were intended to serve. What became naturalism, and what distinguished it from the more important movement of realism, was a mechanical description of men as the creatures of their environment, which literature recorded as if man and thing were of the same nature. The tragedy of naturalism is the tragedy of passive suffering, and the suffering is passive because man can only endure and can never really change his world. The endurance is given no moral or religious valuation; it is wholly mechanical, because both man and his world, in what is now understood as rational explanation, are the products of an impersonal and material process which though it changes through time has no ends. The impulse to describe and so change a human condition has narrowed to the simple impulse to describe a condition in which there can be no intervention by God or man, the human act of will being tiny and insignificant within the vast material process, universal or social, which at once determines and is indifferent to human destiny.

This naturalism, at once the most common theory and the most ordinary practice of our literature, began in liberalism but ends, ironically, as a grotesque version of the system originally challenged by liberalism, just as atheism ends as a grotesque version of faith. A living design became a mechanical fate, and the latter is even further from man than the former; more decisively alienated from any image of himself. But then this development had real causes. It is, essentially, a deliberate arrest of the process of enlightenment, at the point of critical involvement. As such it corresponds to the deliberate arrest and subsequent decadence of liberalism, at the point where its universal principles required the transformation of its social programme, and where men could either go on or must go back. Everywhere in the nineteenth century we see men running for cover from the consequences of their own beliefs. In our own century, they do not even have to run; the temporary covers have become solid settlements. The universal principles of human liberation have become an embarrassment to men who, benefiting themselves from change of this kind, see before them an infinitely extending demand, of other classes and other peoples, which threatens to submerge and destroy their own newly-won identity. A few

men hold to their principles, and make their commitment to a general
social revolution. But the majority compromise, evade, or seek to delay,
and the most destructive form of this breakdown – for simple reaction
is easily recognised – is the characteristic substitution of evolution for
revolution as a social model.[1]

The whole point of the new theories of social evolution, most evident
in the theory of administered reform, was the separation of historical
development from the actions of the majority of men, or even, in its
extreme forms, from all men. Society, in this view, was an impersonal
process, a machine with certain built-in properties. The machine might
be described or regulated, but was not, ultimately, within human
control. Social change, at its maximum, was the substitution of one
group of fitters for another. Social description, at its best, was neutral
and mechanical. The process, so to say, would build up, would evolve,
and we must watch it, go with it, not get in its modernising way. Any
attempt to assert a general human priority, over the process as a whole,
is then of course seen as childish: the mere fantasy of revolution.

The extent to which almost all our politics has been re-shaped to this
mechanical materialism hardly needs emphasis. But what has to be said
is that this movement of mind, claiming its origins in reason, was
theoretically and factually a mystification of real social activity, and as
such discredited reason itself. It thus worked, finally, to the same effect
as the other major movement which sought to express the values of
liberalism but which seemed for so long to have so different a direction:
the whole current of subjectivism and Romanticism.

Romanticism

Utilitarianism, the most common English form of mechanical
materialism, had sought liberal values in the reform of civil society.
Romanticism, on the other hand, sought liberal values in the
development of the individual. In its early stages, Romanticism was
profoundly liberating, but, partly because of the inadequacy of any
corresponding social theory, and partly because of the consequent
decline from individualism to subjectivism, it ended by denying its own
deepest impulses, and even reversing them. Almost all our revolutionary
language in fact comes from the Romantics, and this has been a real
hindrance as well as an incidental embarrassment. Romanticism is the
most important expression in modern literature of the first impulse of
revolution: a new and absolute image of man. Characteristically, it
relates this transcendence to an ideal world and an ideal human society;
it is in Romantic literature that man is first seen as making himself.

But of course when this is particularised, to social criticism and construction, it encounters fundamental obstacles. It is easier to visualise the ideal in an exotic or fabled community (or an historical community transformed by these elements). The existing social world is seen as so hostile to what is most deeply human that even what begins as social criticism tends to pass into nihilism. For more than a century, the fate of this Romantic tradition was uncertain. Some part of its force inspired the developing idea of total social revolution. A related part, while moving in this direction, got no further, finally, than the images of revolution: the flag, the barricade, the death of martyr or prisoner. But perhaps the major part went in a quite different direction, towards the final separation of revolution from society.

The decisive element, here, was the Romantic attitude to reason. In form, Romanticism can seem a negative reaction to the Enlightenment: its stress on the irrational and the strange seems an absolute contradiction of the stress on reason. But there is, here, a curious dialectic. Romanticism was not proposing what the Enlightenment had opposed; the one version of man was as new as the other. Yet, because this was not seen, the essential unity of these movements, as programmes for human liberation, was disastrously narrowed and confused. What the Romantics criticised as reason was not the reasoning activity, but the abstraction and final alienation of this activity, into what was called a rational but was in fact a mechanical system. Such criticism, and notably the English Romantic critique of utilitarianism, was not only humane; it was also on the side of man as a creative and active being. The eventual collapse to irrationalism can be understood only in terms of the earlier collapse to rationalism. The alienation of reason, from all the other activities of man, changed reason from an activity to a mechanism, and society from a human process to a machine. The protest against this was inevitable, but to stay with society as a human process involved commitments to social action which were indeed difficult to make. Under the pressure of difficulty and the disillusion of failure, the Romantic vision of man became in its turn alienated. The alienation of the rational, into a system of mechanical materialism, was matched by an alienation of the irrational, which has become complete only in our own century.

Thus, while one major part of the liberal idea of revolution had run into the mechanics of social evolution and administered reform, another major part had run into the parody of revolution, in nihilism and its many derivatives. To the former society was a machine, which would go its own predestined way in its own time. To the latter, society was the enemy of human liberation: man could free himself only by rejecting or escaping from society, and by seeing his own deepest activities, in love, in art, in nature, as essentially asocial and even anti-social.

Ironically, just as mechanical materialism had produced a new kind of fate, the 'evolutionary' society from which man's activity and aspiration were shut out, so nihilism, also, produced a version of fate: the separation of humanity from society, but also the internalisation of what had once been an external design. In its later variants, especially, nihilism emphasised and generalised the irrational as more powerful than social man. From its assumption of hostility between personal liberation and the social fact, it rationalised an irrationality, more dark and destructive than any known gods. In its last stages, the dream of human liberation was the nightmare of an ineradicable destructive instinct and the death wish.

The End of Liberalism

The liberal idea of revolution was finally hemmed in on both sides: by its reduction to a mechanical and impersonal process, and by the channelling of personal revolt into an ideology which made social construction seem hopeless, because man as such was deeply irrational and destructive. In Western societies, the contrast of these positions is now normally offered as total, so that we see ourselves as having to choose between them. In politics we are offered not revolution, or even substantial change, but what is widely called modernisation: that is, a separation of change from value. We are asked to go along with what is supposed to be an inevitable evolutionary process, or to bend, whatever its direction, to the 'wind of change' (which is an exact expression of just this alienation in that it blows from elsewhere and is rationalised as a natural force). Or, alternatively, we reject politics, and see the reality of human liberation as internal, private and apolitical, even under the shadow of politically willed war or politically willed poverty or politically willed ugliness and cruelty.

Yet in fact, since 1917, we have been living in a world of successful social revolutions. In this sense it is true to say that our attitude to the revolutionary societies of our own time is central and probably decisive in all our thinking. What our own ideology, in its many variants, has theoretically excluded, has happened or seems to have happened elsewhere. And then there are not really many choices left. We can actively oppose or seek to contain revolution elsewhere, as in national practice we have been continually doing. Militancy and indifference serve this tactic almost equally well. Or we can support revolution elsewhere, in a familiar kind of romanticism, for which the images lie ready in the mind. Or, finally – I am stating my own position – we can work to understand and participate in revolution as a social reality: that is to say, not only as an action now in progress among real men, but also, and therefore, as an activity immediately involving ourselves.

It is here that the relation between revolution and tragedy is inescapable and urgent. It may still be possible, for some thinkers, to interpret actual revolution in the received ideology of rationalism. We can all see the constructive activity of the successful revolutionary societies, and we can take this as evidence of the simple act of human liberation by the energy of reason. I know nothing I welcome more than this actual construction, but I know also that the revolutionary societies have been tragic societies, at a depth and on a scale that go beyond any ordinary pity and fear. At the point of this recognition, however, where the received ideology of revolution, its simple quality as liberation, seems most to fail, there is waiting the received ideology of tragedy, in either of its common forms: the old tragic lesson, that man cannot change his condition, but can only drown his world in blood in the vain attempt; or the contemporary reflex, that the taking of rational control over our social destiny is defeated or at best deeply stained by our inevitable irrationality, and by the violence and cruelty that are so quickly released when habitual forms break down. I do not find, in the end, that either of these interpretations covers enough of the facts, but also I do not see how anyone can still hold to that idea of revolution which simply denied tragedy, as an experience and as an idea.

Socialism and Revolution

Socialism, I believe, is the true and active inheritor of the impulse to human liberation which has previously taken so many different forms. But in practice, I also believe, it is an idea still forming, and much that passes under its name is only a residue of old positions. I do not mean only such a movement as Fabianism, with its cast of utilitarianism and its mechanical conceptions of change. I mean also a main current in Marxism, which though Marx may at times have opposed it is also profoundly mechanical, in its determinism, in its social materialism, and in its characteristic abstraction of social classes from human beings. I can see that it is possible, with such habits of mind, to interpret revolution as only constructive and liberating. Real suffering is then at once non-human: is a class swept away by history, is an error in the working of the machine, or is the blood that is not and never can be rose water. The more general and abstract, the more truly mechanical, the process of human liberation is ordinarily conceived to be, the less any actual suffering really counts, until even death is a paper currency.

But then I do not believe, as so many disillusioned or broken by actual revolution have come to believe, that the suffering can be laid to the charge of the revolution alone, and that we must avoid revolution if we are to avoid suffering. On the contrary, I see revolution as the inevitable working through of a deep and tragic disorder, to which we can respond in varying ways but which will in any case, in one way or another, work its way through our world, as a consequence of any of our actions. I see revolution, that is to say, in a tragic perspective, and it is this I now seek to define.

Marx's early idea of revolution seems to me to be tragic in this sense:

> A class must be formed which has *radical chains*, a class in civil society which is not a class of civil society, a class which is the dissolution of all classes, a sphere of society which has a universal character because its sufferings are universal, and which does not claim a *particular redress* because the wrong which is done to it is not a *particular wrong* but *wrong in general*. There must be formed a sphere of society which claims no *traditional* status but only a *human* status . . . a sphere finally which cannot emancipate itself without emancipating itself from all the other spheres of society, without therefore emancipating all these other spheres; which is, in short, a *total loss* of humanity and which can only redeem itself by a *total redemption of humanity*.
>
> (*Zur Kritik der Hegelschen Rechts-Philosophie: Einleitung*)

So absolute a conception distinguishes revolution from rebellion, or, to put it another way, makes political revolution into a general human revolution:

> In all former revolutions the form of activity was always left unaltered, and it was only a question of redistributing this activity among different people, of introducing a new division of labour. The communist revolution, however, is directed against the former *mode* of activity, does away with *labour*, and abolishes all class rule along with the classes themselves. . . .
>
> (*Die Deutsche Ideologie*)

> The *social life* from which the worker is shut out . . . is *life* itself, physical and cultural life, human morality, human activity, human enjoyment, real human existence. . . . As the irremediable exclusion from this life is much more complete, more unbearable, dreadful, and contradictory, than the exclusion from political life, so is the ending of this exclusion, and even a limited reaction, a *revolt* against it, more fundamental, as *man* is more fundamental than the *citizen, human life* more than *political life*.
>
> (*Vorwärts* (1844))

This way of seeing revolution seems to me to stand. Whatever we have learned, since Marx wrote, about actual historical development, and thence about the agencies and tactics of revolution, does not affect the idea itself. We need not identify revolution with violence or with a sudden capture of power. Even where such events occur, the essential transformation is indeed a long revolution. But the absolute test, by which revolution can be distinguished, is the change in the *form* of activity of a society, in its deepest structure of relationships and feelings. The incorporation of new groups of men into the pre-existing form and structure is something quite different, even when it is accompanied by an evident improvement of material conditions and by the ordinary changes of period and local colour. In fact the test of a pre-revolutionary society, or of a society in which the revolution is still incomplete, is in just this matter of incorporation. A society in which revolution is necessary is a society in which the incorporation of all its people, *as whole human beings*, is in practice impossible without a change in its fundamental form of relationships. The many kinds of partial 'incorporation' – as voters, as employees, or as persons entitled to education, legal protection, social services and so on – are real human gains, but do not in themselves amount to that full membership of society which is the end of classes. The reality of full membership is the capacity to direct a particular society, by active mutual responsibility and co-operation, on a basis of full social equality. And while this is the purpose of revolution, it remains necessary in all societies in which there are, for example, subordinate racial groups, landless landworkers, hired hands, the unemployed, and suppressed or discriminate minorities of any kind. Revolution remains necessary, in these circumstances, not only because some men desire it, but because there can be no acceptable human order while the full humanity of any class of men is in practice denied.

The Tragedy of Revolution

This idea of 'the total redemption of humanity' has the ultimate cast of resolution and order, but in the real world its perspective is inescapably tragic. It is born in pity and terror: in the perception of a radical disorder in which the humanity of some men is denied and by that fact the idea of humanity itself is denied. It is born in the actual suffering of real men thus exposed, and in all the consequences of this suffering: degeneration, brutalisation, fear, hatred, envy. It is born in an experience of evil made the more intolerable by the conviction that it is not inevitable, but is the result of particular actions and choices.

And if it is thus tragic in its origins – in the existence of a disorder that cannot but move and involve – it is equally tragic in its action, in that it is not against gods or inanimate things that its impulse struggles, nor against mere institutions and social forms, but against other men. This, throughout, has been the area of silence, in the development of the idea. What is properly called utopianism, or revolutionary romanticism, is the suppression or dilution of this quite inevitable fact.

There are many reasons why men will oppose such a revolution. There are the obvious reasons of interest or privilege, for which we have seen men willing to die. There is the deep fear that recognition of the humanity of others is a denial of our own humanity, as our whole lives have known it. There is the flight in the mind from disturbance of a familiar world, however inadequate. There is the terror, often justified, of what will happen when men who have been treated as less than men gain the power to act. For there will of course be revenge and senseless destruction, after the bitterness and deformity of oppression. And then, more subtly, there are all the learned positions, from an experience of disorder that is as old as human history and yet also is continually re-enacted: the conviction that any absolute purpose is delusion and folly, to be corrected by training, by some social ease where we are, or by an outright opposition to this madness which would destroy the world.

From all these positions, revolution is practically opposed, in every form from brutal suppression and massive indoctrination to genuine attempts to construct alternative futures. And all our experience tells us that this immensely complicated action between real men will continue as far ahead as we can foresee, and that the suffering in this continuing struggle will go on being terrible. It is very difficult for the mind to accept this, and we all erect our defences against so tragic a recognition. But I believe that it is inevitable, and that we must speak of it if it is not to overwhelm us.

In some Western societies we are engaged in the attempt to make this total revolution without violence, by a process of argument and consensus. It is impossible to say if we shall succeed. The arrest of humanity, in many groups and individuals, is still severe and seems often intractable. At the same time, while the process has any chance of success, nobody in his senses would wish to alter its nature. The real difficulty, however, is that we have become introverted on this process, in a familiar kind of North Atlantic thinking, and the illusions this breeds are already of a tragic kind.

Thus we seek to project the result of particular historical circumstances as universal, and to identify all other forms of revolution as hostile. The only consistent common position is that of the enemies of revolution everywhere, yet even they, at times, speak a liberal rhetoric. It is a very deep irony that, in ideology, the major conflict in the world is between different versions of the absolute rights of man. Again and again, men in Western societies act as counter-revolutionaries, but in the name of an absolute liberation. There are real complexities here, for revolutionary regimes have also acted, repeatedly and brutally, against every kind of human freedom and dignity. But there are also deep and habitual forms of false consciousness. Only a very few of us, in any Western society, have in fact renounced violence, in the way that our theory claims. If we believe that social change should be peaceful, it is difficult to know what we are doing in military alliances, with immense armament and weapons of indiscriminate destruction. The customary pretence that this organised violence is defensive, and that it is wholly dedicated to human freedom, is literally a tragic illusion. It is easy to move about in our own comparatively peaceful society, repeating such phrases as 'a revolution by due course of law', and simply failing to notice that in our name, and endorsed by repeated majorities, other peoples have been violently opposed in the very act of their own liberation. The bloody tale of the past is always conveniently discounted, but I am writing on a day when British military power is being used against 'dissident tribesmen' in South Arabia, and I know this pattern and its covering too well, from repeated examples through my lifetime, to be able to acquiesce in the ordinary illusion. Many of my countrymen have opposed these politics, and in many particular cases have ended them. But it is impossible to believe that as a society we have yet dedicated ourselves to human liberation, or even to that simple recognition of the absolute humanity of all other men which is the impulse of any genuine revolution. To say that in our own affairs we have made this recognition would also be too much, in a society powered by great economic inequality and by organised manipulation. But even if we had made this recognition, among ourselves, it would still be a travesty of any real revolutionary belief. It is only when the recognition is general that it can be authentic, for in practice every reservation, in a widely communicating world, tends to degenerate into actual opposition.

Our interpretation of revolution as a slow and peaceful growth of consensus is at best a local experience and hope, at worst a sustained false consciousness. In a world determined by the struggle against poverty and against the many forms of colonial and neo-colonial domination, revolution continually and inescapably enters our society, in the form of our own role in those critical areas. And here it is not only that we have made persistent errors, and that we comfort ourselves with the illusion of steady progress when the gap between wealth and poverty is actually increasing in the world, and when the consciousness of exploitation is rapidly rising. It is also that the revolutionary process has become, in our generation, the ordinary starting point of war. It is very remarkable, in recent years, how the struggles for national liberation and for social change, in many different parts of the world, have involved the major powers in real and repeated dangers of general war. What are still, obtusely, called 'local upheavals', or even 'brushfires', put all our lives in question, again and again. Korea, Suez, the Congo, Cuba, Vietnam, are names of our own crisis. It is impossible to look at this real and still active history without a general sense of tragedy: not only because the disorder is so widespread and intolerable that in action and reaction it must work its way through our lives, wherever we may be; but also because, on any probable estimate, we understand the process so little that we continually contribute to the disorder. It is not simply that we become involved in this general crisis, but that we are already, by what we do and fail to do, participating in it.

There is, here, a strange contradiction. The two great wars we have known in Europe, and the widespread if still limited awareness of the nature of nuclear war, have induced a kind of inert pacifism which is too often self-regarding and dangerous. We say, understandably, that we must avoid war at all costs, but what we commonly mean is that we will avoid war at any cost but our own. Relatively appeased in our own situation, we interpret disturbance elsewhere as a threat to peace, and seek either to suppress it (the 'police action' to preserve what we call law and order; the fire brigade to put out the 'brushfire'), or to smother it with money or political manoeuvres. So deep is this contradiction that we regard such activities, even actual suppression, as morally virtuous; we even call it peacemaking. But what we are asking is what, in a limited consciousness, we have ourselves succeeded in doing: to acquiesce in a disorder and call it order; to say peace where there is no peace. We expect men brutally exploited and intolerably poor to rest and be patient in their misery, because if they act to end their condition it will involve the rest of us, and threaten our convenience or our lives.

In these ways, we have identified war and revolution as the tragic dangers, when the real tragic danger, underlying war and revolution, is a disorder which we continually re-enact. So false a peacemaking, so false an appeal to order, is common in the action of tragedy, in which, nevertheless, all the real forces of the whole situation eventually work themselves out. Even if we were willing to change, in our attitudes to others and even more in our real social relations with them, we might still not, so late in the day, avoid actual tragedy. But the only relevant response, to the tragedy of this kind that we have already experienced, is that quite different peacemaking which is the attempt to resolve rather than to cover the determining tragic disorder. Any such resolution would mean changing ourselves, in fundamental ways, and our unwillingness to do this, the certainty of disturbance, the probability of secondary and unforeseen disorder, put the question, inevitably, into a tragic form.

The only consciousness that seems adequate in our world is then an exposure to the actual disorder. The only action that seems adequate is, really, a participation in the disorder, as a way of ending it. But at this

point another tragic perspective opens. I find that I still agree with
Carlyle, when he wrote in *Chartism*:

> Men who discern in the misery of the toiling complaining millions
> not misery, but only a raw material which can be wrought upon and
> traded in, for one's own poor hide-bound theories and egoisms; to
> whom millions of living fellow-creatures, with beating hearts in their
> bosoms, beating, suffering, hoping, are 'masses', mere 'explosive
> masses for blowing-down Bastilles with', for voting at hustings for *us*:
> such men are of the questionable species.

I have already argued the questionable nature of our many kinds of
failure to commit ourselves to revolution. I would now repeat, with
Carlyle, and with much real experience since he wrote, the questionable
nature of a common kind of commitment. It is undoubtedly true that a
commitment to revolution can produce a kind of hardening which even
ends by negating the revolutionary purpose. Some people make the false
commitment – the use of the misery of others – from the beginning. The
most evident example is in Fascism, which is false revolution in just this
sense. But, under real historical pressures, this hardening and negation
occur again and again in authentic revolutionary activity, especially in
isolation, under fire, and in scarcity so extreme as to threaten survival.
The enemies of the revolutionary purpose then seize on the evidence of
hardening and negation: either to oppose revolution as such, or to
restore the convenient belief that man cannot change his condition, and
that aspiration brings terror as a logical companion.

But this tragic aspect of revolution, which we are bound to
acknowledge, cannot be understood in such ways. We have still to
attend to the whole action, and to see actual liberation as part of the
same process as the terror which appals us. I do not mean that the
liberation cancels the terror; I mean only that they are connected, and
that this connection is tragic. The final truth in this matter seems to be
that revolution – the long revolution against human alienation –
produces, in real historical circumstances, its own new kinds of
alienation, which it must struggle to understand and which it must
overcome, if it is to remain revolutionary.

I see this revolutionary alienation in several forms. There is the simple
and yet bloody paradox that in the act of revolution its open enemies
are easily seen as 'not men'. The tyrant, as he is killed, seems not a man
but an object, and his brutality draws an answering brutality, which can
become falsely associated with liberation itself. But it is not only a matter
of the open enemies. Under severe pressure, the revolutionary purpose
can become itself abstracted and can be set as an idea above real men.
The decisive connection between present and future, which can only be

a connection in experience and in continuing specific relations, is at once suppressed and replaced. There is then the conversion of actual misery and actual hope into a merely tactical 'revolutionary situation'. There is the related imposition of an idea of the revolution on the real men and women in whose name it is being made. The old unilinear model, by which revolution is abstractly known, is imposed on experience, including revolutionary experience. Often only this abstracted idea can sustain men, at the limits of their strength, but the need to impose it, in just such a crisis, converts friends into enemies, and actual life into the ruthlessly moulded material of an idea. The revolutionary purpose, born in what is most human and therefore most various, is negated by the single and often heroic image of revolutionary man, arrested at a stage in the very process of liberation and, persistent, becoming its most inward enemy.

In such ways, the most active agents of revolution can become its factual enemies, even while to others, and even to themselves, they seem its most perfect embodiment. But while we see this merely as accident, as the random appearance of particular evil men, we can understand nothing, for we are evading the nature of the whole action, and projecting its general meaning on to individuals whom we idealise or execrate. Elevating ourselves to spectators and judges, we suppress our own real role in any such action, or conclude, in a kind of indifference, that what has happened was inevitable and that there is even a law of inevitability. We see indeed a certain inevitability, of a tragic kind, as we see the struggle to end alienation producing its own new kinds of alienation. But, while we attend to the whole action, we see also, working through it, a new struggle against the new alienation: the comprehension of disorder producing a new image of order; the revolution against the fixed consciousness of revolution, and the authentic activity reborn and newly lived. What we then know is no simple action: the heroic liberation. But we know more also than simple reaction, for if we accept alienation, in ourselves or in others, as a permanent condition, we must know that other men, by the very act of living, will reject this, making us their involuntary enemies, and the radical disorder is then most bitterly confirmed.

The tragic action, in its deepest sense, is not the confirmation of disorder, but its experience, its comprehension and its resolution. In our own time, this action is general, and its common name is revolution. We have to see the evil and the suffering, in the factual disorder that makes revolution necessary, and in the disordered struggle against the disorder. We have to recognise this suffering in a close and immediate experience, and not cover it with names. But we follow the whole action: not only the evil, but the men who have fought against evil; not only the crisis, but the energy released by it, the spirit learned in it. We make the connections, because that is the action of tragedy, and what we learn in suffering is again revolution, because we acknowledge others as men and any such acknowledgement is the beginning of struggle, as the continuing reality of our lives. Then to see revolution in this tragic perspective is the only way to maintain it.

Continuity

I began from the gap between tragic theory and tragic experience, and went on to inquire into the history of the idea of tragedy, and to criticise what I see as a dominant contemporary ideology. I then argued the relationship between tragedy and history, and in particular the contemporary relationship between tragedy and revolution. In the rest of the book my emphasis will be different. What I have written about tragedy and revolution is in a sense a preface to my third part. What I have written more generally, on tragic ideas and experiences, needs another kind of discussion, of modern tragic literature, and this is the substance of my second part. The test of what I have argued will come again there, in a quite different form.

Note

1. Evolution in this Fabian sense is different again from both Darwinism and the competitive struggle for life. Yet it shares with the latter a metaphorical quality, still essentially unrelated to the scientific theory. For behind the idea of social evolution was an unconscious attachment to the development of a *single* form. Social development was unconsciously based on the experience of one type of Western society, and its imperialist contacts with more 'primitive' societies. The real social and cultural variation of human history was thus reduced to a single model: unilinear and predictable. Even Marxists took over this limited model, and its rigidity has been widely experienced in some twentieth-century communist practice. A more adequate understanding of both natural and cultural evolution would have made so mechanical and unilinear a model untenable, for it would have emphasised both variation and creativity and thus a more genuinely open and (in the full sense) revolutionary future.

5 Psychoanalysis and Tragedy

Freud's well-known account of the Oedipus complex is the starting-point for any psychoanalytical reading of tragedy. Despite the concerns of dramatists such as Arthur Miller about the debilitating effect of the preoccupation with psychiatry as far as tragedy is concerned, questions concerning the tragic subject, the interior motivations of the protagonist, begin with Freud. In Freudian psychoanalysis the 'unconscious' replaces that Dionysiac energy which, as we saw, was for Nietzsche the mainspring of tragic action. In one sense, the Freudian concern with subjectivity has served to complicate the concern with 'character' in tragedy. Moreover, Freud is preoccupied, especially in an essay he wrote entitled 'Some Character Types', with the question of guilt and its functioning as an obstacle to success. The division within the protagonist between the desire for success, and the guilt that attends upon it, is derived, according to Freud, from a universal conscience which he calls 'an inherited power in the mind', and which he argues 'was originally acquired from the Oedipus complex'. Guilt, therefore, and the operations of conscience, are reactions to 'the two great criminal intentions of killing the father and having sexual relations with the mother'. What the Freudian unconscious represses, is a triangulated Oedipal drama, which is manifest in everyday life through a variety of symptoms which the psychoanalyst 'reads'.

It is in Lacan's re-reading of Freud, and especially in his suggestion that 'the unconscious is structured like a language', that Freudian psychoanalysis is brought into step with the concerns of post-structuralism. What in Nietzsche was a division and a conflict of energies, becomes in Marxist accounts a structured conflict between social classes. In Lacan the division at the centre of subjectivity is articulated differently, and in such a way as to expose the various stages through which the infant travels to full subjecthood. We see in Lacan a residue of the Hegelian dialectic, combined with the awareness that language itself can never figure forth the object of its concerns as pure presence. Lacan's concern, then, is with how subjects become aware of their own subjectivity, how they produce for themselves an *imaginary* unity, and how, once having acquired a coherent sense of themselves, they enter into the *symbolic* order where they are subjected to pressure to conform to the demands of the social order itself. Beginning from an analysis of the Aristotelian notion of catharsis as 'purgation', Lacan proceeds to investigate the subjectivity of Antigone, and focusing on the signifiers which go to make up the text, he aims to analyse what he calls 'the fantasm that guides feminine desire'. He insists that 'tragedy is an action' and that it is not concerned with any 'true event'; rather, he argues, 'The hero and that which is around him are situated with relation to the goal of desire.' The economy of desire in Lacan is complicated, and it is tied up with the question of signification. In a lucid discussion of this topic, Catherine Belsey has defined the Lacanian category of desire as 'a metonym (a displaced version) of the want-to-be' that necessarily characterizes a human life divided between the unmasterable symbolic and the unreachable, inextricable real. And desire itself is split between the quest for satisfaction in the real, 'a refusal of the signifier', and the desire of (for) the Other, the origin of meaning, which entails a 'lack of being'. She goes on, 'This must be so because if the subject longs to find the real again, it also yearns to find the self which is perpetually created and destroyed by the signifier' (*Desire: Love Stories in Western Culture* (Oxford, 1994), p. 60).

In the writing of André Green, these difficult Lacanian insights are brought to bear directly on tragic drama in the theatre. In Green's account, what tragic drama stages is the 'scene' of the Other, the unconscious, offering a generic space for 'the unveiling, the revelation, of some original kinship relation, which never works more effectively than through a sudden reversal of fortune, a peripeteia' (Green, p. 8). Green uses the dramatic theory of Artaud to counterbalance the pronouncements of Aristotle, and argues for theatrical activity as a form of listening to the unconscious. He is aware, of course, that after Freud – and we might add also, after Lacan – it is possible to listen to the unconscious differently. Green also counters the claim that psychoanalytical criticism 'pathologizes' the object of its enquiry, preferring to suggest that it actually permits the recognition 'in all the products of mankind the traces of the conflicts of the unconscious' (p. 200). For him, crucial to the mechanisms of tragedy is the notion that 'The satisfaction of desire cannot be separated from submission to the sanction of the prohibition that weighs upon it' (p. 200). In a complicated passage, Green sees the work of the artist as being commensurate with those processes of symbolic activity which are at work in dream or fantasy. For him the text of a tragedy is not a means of exposing the unconscious to the spectator's view, but rather it 'sets up a communication between a sentient corporeal space and the textual space of the work'. 'Between the two' he continues, 'stand prohibition and its censor; the symbolic activity is the disguise and the exclusion of the unacceptable, and the substitution of the excluded term by another less unacceptable one, more capable of slipping into the area that is closed to it' (p. 201). In a methodical way Green charts the progress of psychoanalysis and its application to tragedy as a theatrical form.

The Splendour of Antigone*

JACQUES LACAN

I told you that I would talk about *Antigone* today.

I am not the one who has decreed that *Antigone* is to be a turning point in the field that interests us, namely, ethics. People have been aware of that for a long time. And even those who haven't realized this are not unaware of the fact that there are scholarly debates on the topic. Is there anyone who doesn't evoke *Antigone* whenever there is a question of a law that causes conflict in us even though it is acknowledged by the community to be a just law?

And what is one to think of the scholars' contribution to the discussion of *Antigone*? What is one to think of it when one has, like me, gone over the ground for one's own interest and for the interest of those one is speaking to?

Well now, while I have tried to omit nothing that seemed important in all that has been said on the question, so as not to deprive either you or me of the help that I might derive from this lengthy historical survey, I have nevertheless often had the impression that I was lost in quite extraordinary byways. One learns that the opinions formulated by the pens of our great thinkers over the centuries are strange indeed.

The meaning of catharsis

Antigone is a tragedy, and tragedy is in the forefront of our experiences as analysts – something that is confirmed by the references Freud found in *Oedipus Rex* as well as in other tragedies. He was attracted by his need of the material he found in their mythical content. And if he himself didn't expressly discuss *Antigone* as tragedy, that doesn't mean to say it cannot be done at this crossroads to which I have brought you.

* Reprinted from *The Ethics of Psychoanalysis 1959–1960*, ed. JACQUES-ALAIN MILLER, Book VII, trans. with notes DENNIS PORTER (London: Routledge, 1992).

It seems to me to be what it was for Hegel, although in a different way, namely, the Sophoclean tragedy that is of special significance.

In an even more fundamental way than through the connection to the Oedipus complex, tragedy is at the root of our experience, as the key word 'catharsis' implies.

For you the word is no doubt more or less closely associated with the term 'abreaction', which presupposes that the problem outlined by Freud in his first work with Breuer, namely, that of discharge, has already been broached – discharge in an act, indeed motor discharge, of something that is not so simple to define, and that we still have to say remains a problem for us, the discharge of an emotion that remains unresolved. For that is what is involved here: an emotion or a traumatic experience may, as far as the subject is concerned, leave something unresolved, and this may continue as long as a resolution is not found. The notion of unfulfilment suffices to fill the role of comprehensibility which is required here.

Read over Freud and Breuer's opening pages and, in the light of what I have attempted to focus on for your benefit in our experience, you will see how difficult it now is to be content with the word 'fulfilment' that is employed in this context, and to state simply, as Freud does, that the action may be discharged in the words that articulate it.

That catharsis which in this text is linked to the problem of abreaction, and which is already specifically invoked in the background, has its origins in the thought of classical antiquity. It is centred on Aristotle's formula at the beginning of Chapter VI of his *Poetics*: Aristotle there explains at length, in a classification of the genres, what must be present for a work to be defined as a tragedy.

The passage is a long one and we will return to it later. One finds there a description of the distinguishing characteristics of tragedy, of its composition, and of what, for example, distinguishes it from epic discourse. I simply put on the blackboard the end point or final words of this passage, what in logical causality is known as its τέλος. It is formulated by Aristotle as δί ἐλέου καὶ φόβου περαίνουσα τὴν τῶν τοιούτων παθημάτων κάθαρσιν. That is to say, a means of accomplishing the purgation of the emotions by a pity and fear similar to this.

These words which seem so simple have over the centuries produced a flood – indeed a whole world – of commentaries, whose history I can't even begin to trace here.

The references I will make to this history are highly selective and to the point. We usually translate the word 'catharsis' by something like 'purgation'. And thus, all of us here, especially if we are doctors, are, from the school desks of our so-called secondary schools on, more or less familiar with the term 'purgation', which has a certain Moliéresque meaning. And this is the case because the Moliéresque element here merely echoes an ancient medical concept, namely, in Molière's own words, the one which involves the elimination of 'peccant humours'.

Moreover, that is not very far from what the term still, in fact, evokes. But it also has a different resonance. And to make you sense it right away, I can simply point out what in the course of our work here I recently expounded for you with reference to the name of the Cathars.

What are the Cathars? They are the pure. $Ka\theta\alpha\rho\delta s$ is a pure person. And the word in its original sense doesn't mean illumination or discharge, but purification.

Doubtless in classical antiquity, too, the term 'catharsis' was already used in a medical context, in Hippocrates, for example, with a specifically medical meaning; it is linked to forms of elimination, to discharge, to a return to normality. But, on the other hand, in other contexts it is linked to purification and especially to ritual purification. Hence the ambiguity which we, as you might suspect, are far from the first to discover.

So as to refer to a specific individual, I will mention the name of Denis Lambin, who reinterprets Aristotle in order to emphasize the ritual function of tragedy and the ceremonial sense of purification. It's not a matter of affirming that he is more or less right than someone else, but of simply identifying the sphere in which the question is raised.

We shouldn't, in fact, forget that the term catharsis is strangely isolated in the context of the *Poetics*. It's not that it isn't developed and commented on there, but we will learn very little about it until some new papyrus is discovered. I assume you know that what we have of the *Poetics* is only a part, roughly half, in fact. And in the half that we have there is only the passage referred to which discusses catharsis. We know that there was more because at the beginning of Book VIII, in the numbering of Didot's classic edition of the *Politics*, Aristotle speaks of 'that catharsis which I discussed elsewhere in the *Poetics*'. In Book VIII his subject is catharsis in connection with music, and as things turned out, it is there that we learn much more about catharsis.

In this text catharsis has to do with the calming effect associated with a certain kind of music, from which Aristotle doesn't expect a given ethical effect, nor even a practical effect, but one that is related to excitement. The music concerned is the most disturbing kind, the kind that turned their stomachs over, that made them forget themselves, in the same way that hot jazz (*le hot*) or rock 'n' roll does for us; it was the kind of music that in classical antiquity gave rise to the question of whether or not it should be prohibited.

Well now, says Aristotle, once they have experienced the state of exaltation, the Dionysian frenzy stimulated by such music, they become calm. That's what catharsis means as it is evoked in Book VIII of the *Politics*.

Yet not everyone enters into such states of excitement, even if everyone is in the position of being at least slightly susceptible. There are the παθητικοί as opposed to the ἐνθουσιαστικοί. The former are in the position of being prey to other passions, namely, fear and pity. Well, it turns out that a form of catharsis or calming effect will be granted them by a certain music also, by the music, one may assume, that has a role in tragedy. And this comes about through pleasure, Aristotle tells us, leaving us once again to reflect on what might be meant by pleasure and at what level and why it is invoked on this occasion. What is this pleasure to which one returns after a crisis that occurs in another dimension, a crisis that sometimes threatens pleasure, for we all know to what extremes a certain kind of ecstatic music may lead? It is at this point that the topology we have defined – the topology of pleasure as the law of that which functions previous to that apparatus where desire's formidable centre sucks us in – perhaps allows us to understand Aristotle's intuition better than has been the case heretofore.

In any case, before I go on to define the beyond of the apparatus referred to as the central point of that gravitational pull, I want to emphasize that element in modern literature which has given rise to the use of the term catharsis in its medical sense.

The medical notion of Aristotelian catharsis is, in effect, more or less current in a sphere that goes far beyond the realm of our colleagues, the writers, critics, and literary theoreticians. But if one seeks to determine the culminating moment of this conception of catharsis, one reaches a point of origin beyond which the concept is much broader and where it is far from obvious that the word catharsis has only the medical connotation.

The triumph of the latter conception of its meaning has a source to which it is worth making an erudite reference here. The paper in question is by Jakob Bernays and it appeared in a review in Breslau. I couldn't tell you why Breslau is involved, since I wasn't able to consult enough biographical material on this Jakob Bernays. If I am to believe Jones's book on Freud, the latter, as you will probably have realized, belongs to the same family from which Freud took his wife, namely, a distinguished Jewish bourgeois family, that had long since acquired a form of nobility in the sphere of German culture. Jones refers to Michael Bernays as a professor in Munich, who was condemned by his family as a political apostate, as someone who changed his political allegiance for the sake of his career. As for Jakob Bernays, if I am to believe the person who looked into this for me, he is simply mentioned as someone who had a distinguished career as a Latinist and a Hellenist. Nothing further is said except that he didn't achieve his academic success at the same cost as Michael.

What I have here is an 1880 version of two papers by Jakob Bernays, reprinted in Berlin, on the subject of Aristotle's theory of drama. They are excellent. It is rare to find such a satisfying work by an academic in general, and even more so by a German academic. It is as clear as crystal. And it is no accident if the virtual universal adoption of the medical notion of catharsis occurs at that time.

It is a pity that Jones, who was himself so knowledgeable, didn't believe it appropriate to place a greater emphasis on the personality and the work of Jakob Bernays; little attention has been paid to him. It is nevertheless difficult to imagine that Freud, who was by no means indifferent to the reputation of the Bernays' family, wasn't aware of him. It would have been a way of referring Freud's original use of the word catharsis to its best source.

Having said that, I will now return to what most concerns us in this commentary on *Antigone*, namely, the essence of tragedy.

Hegel's weakness

Tragedy – we are told in a definition that we can hardly avoid paying attention to, since it appeared scarcely a century after the time of the birth of tragedy – has as its aim catharsis, the purgation of the τιαθήματα, of the emotions of fear and pity.

How is one to understand that formula? We will approach the problem from the perspective imposed on us by what we have articulated on the subject of the proper place of desire in the economy of the Freudian Thing. Will this allow us to take the additional step required by this historical revelation?

If the Aristotelian formulation appears at first sight to be so closed, it is due to the loss of a part of Aristotle's work as well as to a certain conditioning within the very possibilities of thought. Yet is it so closed to us after all as a consequence of the progress made in our discussions of ethics here over the past two years? What in particular has been said about desire enables us to bring a new element to the understanding of the meaning of tragedy, above all by means of the exemplary approach suggested by the function of catharsis – there are no doubt more direct approaches.

In effect, *Antigone* reveals to us the line of sight that defines desire.

This line of sight focuses on an image that possesses a mystery which up till now has never been articulated, since it forces you to close your

eyes at the very moment you look at it. Yet that image is at the centre
of tragedy, since it is the fascinating image of Antigone herself. We
know very well that over and beyond the dialogue, over and beyond
the question of family and country, over and beyond the moralizing
arguments, it is Antigone herself who fascinates us, Antigone in her
unbearable splendour. She has a quality that both attracts us and
startles us, in the sense of intimidates us; this terrible, self-willed victim
disturbs us.

It is in connection with this power of attraction that we should look
for the true sense, the true mystery, the true significance of tragedy –
in connection with the excitement involved, in connection with the
emotions and, in particular, with the singular emotions that are fear and
pity, since it is through their intervention, δι' ἐλέου καὶ φόβου, through
the intervention of pity and fear, that we are purged, purified of
everything of that order. And that order, we can now immediately
recognize, is properly speaking the order of the imaginary. And we are
purged of it through the intervention of one image among others.

And it is here that a question arises. How do we explain the
dissipatory power of this central image relative to all the others that
suddenly seem to descend upon it and disappear? The articulation of the
tragic action is illuminating on the subject. It has to do with Antigone's
beauty. And this is not something I invented; I will show you the
passage in the song of the Chorus where that beauty is evoked, and I
will prove that it is the pivotal passage. It has to do with Antigone's
beauty and with the place it occupies as intermediary between two
fields that are symbolically differentiated. It is doubtless from this place
that her splendour derives, a splendour that all those who have spoken
worthily of beauty have never omitted from its definition.

Moreover, as you know, this is the place that I am attempting to
define. I have already come close to it in previous lectures, and I
attempted to grasp it the first time by means of the second death
imagined by Sade's heroes – death insofar as it is regarded as the point
at which the very cycles of the transformations of nature are
annihilated. This is the point where the false metaphors of being (*l'étant*)
can be distinguished from the position of Being (*l'être*) itself, and we
find its place articulated as such, as a limit, throughout the text of
Antigone, in the mouths of all the characters and of Tiresias. But how
can one also not fail to see this position in the action itself? Given that
the middle of the play is constituted of a time of lamentation,
commentary, discussions, and appeals relative to an Antigone
condemned to a cruel punishment. Which punishment? That of being
buried alive in a tomb.

The central third of the text is composed of a detailed series of vowel
gradations, which informs us about the meaning of the situation or fate

of a life that is about to turn into certain death, a death lived by anticipation, a death that crosses over into the sphere of life, a life that moves into the realm of death.

It is surprising that dialecticians or indeed aestheticians as eminent as Hegel and Goethe haven't felt obliged to take account of this whole field in their evaluation of the effect of the play.

The dimension involved here is not unique to *Antigone*. I could suggest that you look in a number of places and you will find something analogous without having to search too hard. The zone defined in that way has a strange function in tragedy.

It is when passing through that zone that the beam of desire is both reflected and refracted till it ends up giving us that most strange and most profound of effects, which is the effect of beauty on desire.

It seems to split desire strangely as it continues on its way, for one cannot say that it is completely extinguished by the apprehension of beauty. It continues on its way, but now more than elsewhere, it has a sense of being taken in, and this is manifested by the splendour and magnificence of the zone that draws it on. On the other hand, since its excitement is not refracted but reflected, rejected, it knows it to be most real. But there is no longer any object.

Hence these two sides of the issue. The extinction or the tempering of desire through the effect of beauty that some thinkers, including Saint Thomas, whom I quoted last time, insist on. On the other hand, the disruption of any object, on which Kant insists in *The Critique of Judgment*.

I was talking to you just now of excitement. And I will take a moment to have you reflect on the inappropriate use that is made of this word in the usual translation into French of *Triebregung*, namely, 'émoi pulsionne', 'instinctual excitement'.[1] Why was this word so badly chosen? 'Emoi' (excitement) has nothing to do with emotion nor with being moved. 'Emoi' is a French word that is linked to a very old verb, namely, 'émoyer' or 'esmayer', which, to be precise, means 'faire perdre à quelqu'un ses moyens', as I almost said, although it is a play on words in French, 'to make someone lose' not 'his head', but something closer to the middle of the body, 'his means'. In any case a question of power is involved. 'Esmayer' is related to the old gothic word 'magnan' or 'mögen' in modern German. As everybody knows, a state of excitement is something that is involved in the sphere of your power relations; it is notably something that makes you lose them.

We are now in a position to be able to discuss the text of *Antigone* with a view to finding something other than a lesson in morality.

A thoroughly irresponsible individual wrote a short time ago that I am powerless to resist the seductions of the Hegelian dialectic. The reproach was formulated at a time when I was beginning to articulate for you the dialectic of desire in terms that I have continued to employ since. And I don't know if the reproach was deserved at the time, but no one could claim that the individual involved is especially sensitive to these things. It is in any case true that Hegel nowhere appears to me to be weaker than he is in the sphere of poetics, and this is especially true of what he has to say about *Antigone.*

According to Hegel, there is a conflict of discourses, it being assumed that the discourses of the spoken dialogues embody the fundamental concerns of the play, and that they, moreover, move toward some form of reconciliation. I just wonder what the reconciliation of the end of *Antigone* might be. Further, it is not without some astonishment that one learns that, in addition, this reconciliation is said to be subjective.

Let us not forget that in Sophocles's last play, *Oedipus at Colonus,* Oedipus's final malediction is addressed to his sons; it is the malediction that gives rise to the catastrophic series of dramas to which *Antigone* belongs. *Oedipus at Colonus* ends with Oedipus's last curse, 'Never to have been born were best . . .' How can one talk of reconciliation in connection with a tone like that?

I am not tempted to regard my own indignation as particularly worthy; others have had a similar reaction before me. Goethe notably seems to have been somewhat suspicious of such a view, and so was Erwin Rohde. When I went and looked up his *Psyche* recently, a work that I made use of to bring together classical antiquity's different conceptions of the immortality of the soul, and that is an admirable work, which I strongly recommend, I was pleased to come across an expression of the author's astonishment at the traditional interpretation of *Oedipus at Colonus.*

Let us now attempt to wash our brains clean of all we have heard about *Antigone* and look in detail at what goes on there.

The function of the Chorus

What does one find in *Antigone?* First of all, one finds Antigone.

Have you noticed that she is only ever referred to throughout the play with the Greek word ἡ παῖς, which means 'the child'? I say that as a way of coming to the point and of enabling you to focus your eye on the style of the thing. And, of course, there is the action of the play.

The question of the action in tragedy is very important. I don't know why someone whom I'm not very fond of, probably because he is always being shoved under my nose, someone called La Bruyère, said that we have arrived too late in a world that is too old in which everything has already been said. It's not something I've noticed. As far as the action of tragedy is concerned, there's still a lot to be said. It's far from being resolved.

To return to Erwin Rohde, whom I complimented just now, I was astonished to find that in another chapter he explains a curious conflict between the tragic author and his subject, a conflict that is caused by the following: the laws of the genre oblige the author to choose as a frame a noble action in preference to a mythic action. I suppose that is so that everyone already knows what it's all about, what's going on. The action has to be emphasized in relation to the ethos, the personalities, the characters, the problems, and so forth, of the time. If that's true, then Mr Anouilh was right to give us his little fascist Antigone. The conflict that results from the dialogue between the poet and his subject is, according to Erwin Rohde, capable of generating conflicts between action and thought, and in this connection, echoing a great many things that have already been said before, he refers with some relevance to the figure of Hamlet.

It's entertaining, but it must be difficult for you to accept, if what I explained last year about *Hamlet* meant anything to you. *Hamlet* is by no means a drama of the importance of thought in the face of action. Why on the threshold of the modern period would *Hamlet* bear witness to the special weakness of future man as far as action is concerned? I am not so gloomy, and nothing apart from a cliché of decadent thought requires that we should be, although it is a cliché Freud himself falls into when he compares the different attitudes of Hamlet and Oedipus toward desire.

I don't believe that the drama of Hamlet is to be found in such a divergence between action and thought nor in the problem of the extinction of his desire. I tried to show that Hamlet's strange apathy belongs to the sphere of action itself, that it is in the myth chosen by Shakespeare that we should look for its motives; we will find its origin in a relationship to the mother's desire and to the father's knowledge of his own death. And to take a step further, I will mention here the moment at which our analysis of *Hamlet* is confirmed by the analysis I am leading up to on the subject of the second death.

Don't forget one of the effects in which the topology I refer to may be recognized. If Hamlet stops when he is on the point of killing Claudius, it is because he is worried about that precise point I am trying to define here: simply to kill him is not enough, he wants him to suffer hell's eternal torture. Under the pretext that we have already busied ourselves a great deal with this hell, should we see it as beneath our dignity to make a little use of it in the analysis of a text? Even if he doesn't believe in hell any more than we do, even if he's not at all sure about it, since he does after all question the notion – 'To sleep, perchance to dream . . .'

– it is nevertheless true that Hamlet stops in the middle of his act because he wants Claudius to go to hell.

The reason why we are always missing the opportunity of pointing to the limits and the crossing-points of the paths we follow is because we are unwilling to come to grips with the texts, preferring to remain within the realm of what is considered acceptable or, in other words, the realm of prejudices. If I were not to have taught you anything more than an implacable method for the analysis of signifiers, then it would not have been in vain – at least I hope so. I even hope that that is all you will retain. If it is true that what I teach represents a body of thought, I will not leave behind me any of those handles which will enable you to append a suffix in the form of an '-ism'. In other words, none of the terms that I have made use of here one after the other – none of which, I am glad to see from your confusion, has yet managed to impress itself on you as the essential term, whether it be the symbolic, the signifier or desire – none of the terms will in the end enable anyone of you to turn into an intellectual cricket on my account.

Next then in a tragedy, there is a Chorus. And what is a Chorus? You will be told that it's you yourselves. Or perhaps that it isn't you. But that's not the point. Means are involved here, emotional means. In my view, the Chorus is people who are moved.

Therefore, look closely before telling yourself that emotions are engaged in this purification. They are engaged, along with others, when at the end they have to be pacified by some artifice or other. But that doesn't mean to say that they are directly engaged. On the one hand, they no doubt are, and you are there in the form of a material to be made use of; on the other hand, that material is also completely indifferent. When you go to the theatre in the evening, you are preoccupied by the affairs of the day, by the pen that you lost, by the cheque that you will have to sign the next day. You shouldn't give yourselves too much credit. Your emotions are taken charge of by the healthy order displayed on the stage. The Chorus takes care of them. The emotional commentary is done for you, The greatest chance for the survival of classical tragedy depends on that. The emotional commentary is done for you. It is just sufficiently silly; it is also not without firmness; it is more or less human.

Therefore, you don't have to worry; even if you don't feel anything, the Chorus will feel in your stead. Why after all can one not imagine that the effect on you may be achieved, at least a small dose of it, even if you didn't tremble that much? To be honest, I'm not sure if the spectator ever trembles that much. I am, however, sure that he is fascinated by the image of Antigone.

In this he is a spectator, but the question we need to ask is, What is he a spectator of? What is the image represented by Antigone? That is the question.

Let us not confuse this relationship to a special image with the spectacle as a whole. The term spectacle, which is usually used to discuss the effect of tragedy, strikes me as highly problematic if we don't delimit the field to which it refers.

On the level of what occurs in reality, an auditor rather than a spectator is involved. And I can hardly be more pleased with myself since Aristotle agrees with me; for him the whole development of the arts of theatre takes place at the level of what is heard, the spectacle itself being no more than something arranged on the margin. Technique is not without significance, but it is not essential; it plays the same role as elocution in rhetoric. The spectacle here is a secondary medium. It is a point of view that puts in its place the modern concerns with *mise en scène* or stagecraft. The importance of *mise en scène* should not be underrated, and I always appreciate it both in the theatre and in the cinema. But we shouldn't forget that it is only important – and I hope you will forgive the expression – if our third eye doesn't get a hard-on; it is, so to speak, jerked off a little with the *mise en scène*.

In this connection I have no intention of giving myself up to the morose pleasure I was denouncing earlier by affirming a supposed decline in the spectator. I don't believe in that at all. From a certain point of view, the audience must always have been at the same level. *Sub specie aeternitatis* everything is equal, everything is always there, although it isn't always in the same place.

But I would just mention in passing that you really have to be a student in my seminar – by which I mean someone especially alert – to find something in the spectacle of Fellini's *La Dolce Vita*.

I am amazed at the murmur of pleasure that that name seems to have aroused among a significant number of you here today. I am ready to believe that this effect is only due to the moment of illusion produced by the fact that the things I say are calculated to emphasize a certain mirage, which is, in effect, the only one aimed at in the series of cinematographic images referred to. But it isn't reached anywhere except at one single moment. That is to say at the moment when early in the morning among the pines on the edge of the beach, the jet-setters suddenly begin to move again after having remained motionless and almost disappearing from the vibration of the light; they begin to move toward some goal that pleased a great many of you, since you associated it with my famous Thing, which in this instance is some disgusting object that has been caught by a net in the sea. Thank goodness, that hadn't yet been seen at the moment I am referring to. Only the jet-setters start to walk, and they remain almost always as invisible, just like statues moving among trees painted by Uccello. It is a rare and unique moment. Those of you who haven't been should go and observe what I've been teaching you here. It happens right at the end, so that you can take your seats at the right moment, if there are any seats left.

Now we are ready for *Antigone*.

Our Antigone is on the point of entering the action of the play, and we will follow her.

Note

1. There is an additional problem in English, since the equivalent for the German 'Triebe' and the French 'pulsion', i.e., 'drive', has no adjectival form.

The Psychoanalytic Reading of Tragedy*

ANDRÉ GREEN

What right has the psychoanalyst to meddle in the business of tragedy? Freud proceeded with extreme caution in his search among the common stock of culture for examples of the expression of the unconscious. Today, when psychoanalysis is less concerned to seek validations outside its own field of practice, is it still proper to seek material for interpretation in works of art? Many people, including some psychoanalysts, believe that the period must now end in which psychoanalytic investigation turned to cultural productions, myths or works of art, to provide evidence for a possible mapping of the unconscious outside the domain of neurosis. Psychoanalysis has provided enough proof of its scientific character, and ought to confine its efforts to the strict framework, defined by its own rigorous parameters, of psychoanalytic treatment. The view is well founded; the field of psychoanalysis will always remain the locus in which the exchanges between analyst and analysand unfold. When the analyst ventures outside the analytic situation, in which he is in direct contact with the unconscious, as it were, he must proceed with caution. The work of art is handed over to the analyst; it can say nothing more than is incorporated in it and cannot, like the analysand, offer an insight into the work of the unconscious *in statu nascendi*. It cannot reveal the state of its functioning through the operation that consists in analysing by free association – that is to say, by providing material that reveals its nature in the very act by which it makes itself known. It does not possess any of the resources that make analysis bearable: that of going back on what one has said, rejecting the intolerable connection at the moment when it presents itself, putting off the moment of an emerging awareness, even denying, by one of the many ways available to the analysand, the correctness of an interpretation or the obviousness of some truth brought by repetition to the front of the stage and needing

* Reprinted from *The Tragic Effect: The Oedipus Complex in Tragedy* trans. ALAN SHERIDAN (Cambridge: Cambridge University Press, 1979).

to be deciphered. The work remains obstinately mute, closed in upon itself, without defences against the treatment that the analyst may be tempted to subject it to.

It would be illusory to believe that one can use a work to provide proof of psychoanalytic theories. Psychoanalysts know that this enterprise is vain, since no degree of consciousness can overcome unconscious resistance. In certain cases, it happens that a fragment of psychical reality manages to overcome repression and seems to emerge with exceptional ease. One then has regretfully to admit, powerless to do anything about it, that the effect is usually followed by a reactivation of the psychical conflict of which this fragment is an integral part. Persuasion, whatever those unacquainted with psychoanalytic experience may think, has never been one of the analyst's instruments; however much he is tempted to use it to get himself out of some impasse in a difficult case, its use will always prove disappointing. The same can be said when the analyst presents the results of his analytic work on some cultural object. If he does not stay close enough to the lines of force that govern the architecture of his object, the truth that even a partly correct analysis contains runs a strong risk of not being recognized, for all its rightness, because the factors opposed to crossing the barriers of the censor find solid support in objections which, though superficial, are reinforced by rationalization. It is therefore particularly necessary to be vigilant in the account of any such investigation. In psychoanalytic treatment, the repetition compulsion again and again offers to disclose the meaning of a conflictual organization, which one can then approach in a fragmentary way. In the analysis of a work of art, everything is said in a single utterance by whoever assumes the task of interpretation, and no inkling is given of the long process of elaboration that has made it possible to arrive at the conclusions now advanced in connected form.

These few remarks are not intended to reassure those who fear the intrusion of psychoanalysis into a domain in which it could have a restricting effect. No interpretation can avoid constraining the work, in the sense that it necessarily forces it into the frame provided by a certain conceptual approach. The work may then be seen from a different perspective, with a new meaning that enlarges it by inserting it in a wider frame of reference. To speak is above all to choose this restricted economy within the enclosure of discourse, in order to give oneself ways towards a development that is impossible if one says nothing.

These warnings are primarily intended to remind myself of the conditions that govern this venture of literary interpretation, that should guide my initial grasp of the work and the subsequent development of my analysis. In any case, the psychoanalyst has less need to defend himself against the charge of violating the work by imposing his version on it, in that a whole recent current of criticism makes it clear that no

197

one is entirely free of this charge when he comes into contact with a work, that every work is itself a kind of reading, calling for a new reading that is the reader's only access to it. Any reading is by definition interpretative; an attribution of meanings is always going on even in the person who thinks himself the most humble of exegetes. Where is a tyrannical relation between reader and text most likely to become established: in the reader who admits his reading is a conjectural enquiry forcing the decipherer to find his way even as he attempts to draw the implicit map of the work, or in the reader who rules out any movement from his own position and merely repeats old schemata that he supposes to be eternal, though historical analysis would show that they are merely the fossilization of acquired knowledge? Who abuses cultural products most: he who seeks in them for a new vision that he supposes them to be still capable of producing, despite the accumulation of readings already in existence, or he who dispenses with radical questioning and brings to the works a mere paraphrastic commentary saturated with the presuppositions of common knowledge? It is just because psychoanalysis provides this radical questioning, this conjectural interrogation, this appeal to what is not given from the outset as cause of an effect, that it has a role in the renewal of criticism.

But even as part of this movement, its role will be a difficult one. Psychoanalysis will always be suspect. It will be criticized, for example, for setting up a relation between the author and the work, as if it were doing so in the spirit of the old biographical criticism, which saw the work as an extension of the experiences of the author's life. Yet psychoanalysis sees it in a relation of discontinuity with them. Biographical criticism saw the work as an echo or a reverberation of some event whose influence was measured in a relation of immediate understanding, according to an implicit scale of common feelings. The link established between author and work by psychoanalysis does not postulate a direct influence between the events of a life and the content of the work, but situates these historical elements in a conflict. These elements are set in the perspective of another problematic, which has been essentially misunderstood because it belongs to repressed childhood, the modes of combination of present and past no longer being accessible to the individual who experiences them, even though they may have a considerable conscious charge. So the work becomes the other network, by which rehandled modes of combination echo what has been reawakened of the unknown past by the present. This repeated past provides the material for a new relation, which keeps a significatory link with its roots that will help to illuminate it retrospectively. A hypothesis about the meaning of this relation for the author helps us to grasp the coherence of the work, which gains in comprehensibility without losing any of its mystery. The reawakening of some significatory constellation underlies this mobilization, which has transformatory power by virtue of its identity with the things from which it is separated by repression. This content is doubly articulated: by the original complexual organization and by the repetition manifested in the present 'event'. None of this puts the author at the mercy of his conflicts – at least, no more than anyone else, since each of us is the system of relations of the various agencies at work in the conflict.

Would it be possible, anyway, to show that there is no relation between a man and his creation? (This is not a thread I mean to follow here, but I must draw attention to the suspiciously passionate way in which any link between author and work is usually 'refuted'.) From what power could creation be nourished if not from those at work in the creator? The psychoanalytic point of view cannot accept that we have disposed of the problem of the genesis of works of art when we have invoked some absolute mystery of creation where the desire to create is not rooted in its unconscious ramifications. Nor can we be content with the idea that the work has the existential signification of a 'supersession' – a view, admittedly, expressed less often by the creator than by commentators on his production. The creator himself always remains aware of its character as a temporary halt on a journey whose aim is above all to ensure the stock of means that will enable him to continue the search.

In the last resort, what people fear most of all about the psychoanalyst is the threat that he will apply some pathological label to the creator or his creations. The keywords in the psychoanalytic vocabulary – though they have value only when placed in the structural ensemble from which they derive their coherence – continue to intimidate; no one feels secure from the unpleasant feeling he would have if, unexpectedly, this vocabulary were applied to him. In our time, this fear has taken on a curiously paradoxical form. We all talk about the pervert and proclaim our potential brotherhood with him; but the mere mention of the word 'normality' is ruthlessly pounced on and denounced. Yet the psychoanalytic texts never postulate a norm – analysts have been attacked enough by physicians and psychiatrists for doing just that – except as a relative term that must be posited somewhere if we are to understand differences of degree or gradations between one structure and another. Resistance to psychoanalytic terminology makes itself felt as soon as it emerges from an unthreatening world of generalization, a world in which its resort to metaphorical terms allows us to harbour the secret hope that we are dealing with the language of some new mythology. It is easy to forget that psychoanalysis has been persecuted precisely for abolishing the frontiers between health and illness and showing the presence in the so-called normal man of all the potentialities whose pathological forms reflect back a magnified, caricatural image. It was Roland Barthes who wrote this condemnation of traditional criticism: 'It wishes to preserve in the work an absolute value, untouched by any of those unworthy "other elements" represented by history and the lower depths of the *psyche*: what it wants is not a constituted work, but a *pure* work, in which any compromise with the world, any misalliance with desire, is avoided'.[1] These remarks can be applied to a good deal of the new criticism, or to those upholders of a theory of writing who defend a sort of literary absolutism.

When a psychoanalyst enters the universe of tragedy, it is not to 'pathologize' this world; it is because he recognizes in all the products of mankind the traces of the conflicts of the unconscious. And although it is true that he must not, as Freud rightly remarked, expect to find there a perfect correspondence with what his experience has led him to observe, he is right in thinking that works of art may help him to grasp the articulation of actual but hidden relations, in the cases that he studies, through the increased distortions that accompany the return of the repressed. Freud never thought that he had anything to teach gifted creators of authentic genius, and he never hid his envy of the exceptional gifts that allowed them, if not direct access, at least considerably easier access to the relations that govern the unconscious.

The exploitation of these gifts is directed towards obtaining the 'bonus of pleasure' that is made possible through the displacements of sublimation; this would tend to establish a relation of disjunction between the product of artistic creation and the symptom. For the first has the effect of negating the action of repression; but the second, because it is the expression of the return of the repressed, erupts into the consciousness only after paying the entrance fee of displeasure at the prohibition of satisfaction. Satisfaction, then, is indissolubly linked to the need for punishment associated with the guilt engendered by desire, whose symptom thus becomes its herald. The satisfaction of desire cannot be separated from submission to the sanction of the prohibition that weighs upon it.

This difference between symptom and creation now makes it possible to indicate their resemblance, if not their similarity. In both symptom and creation, the processes of symbolic activity are at work, as they are also in the dream or the fantasy. So artistic creation, 'pathological' creation and dream creation are linked by symbolic activity, their difference being situated in the accommodation that each offers to the tension between the satisfaction bound up with the realization of desire and the satisfaction bound up with the observance of its prohibition. Neurosis, Freud would say, is the individual, asocial solution of the problems posed to the human condition. At the social level, morality and religion propose other solutions. Between the two, at the meeting-point of the individual and society, between the personal resonance of the work's content and its social function, art occupies a transitional position, which qualifies the domain of illusion, which permits an inhibited and displaced *jouissance*[2] obtained by means of objects that both are and are not what they represent.

Breaking the action of repression does not mean exposing the unconscious in all its starkness, but revealing the effective relation between the inevitable disguising and the indirect unveiling that the work allows to take place. The unconscious sets up a communication between a sentient, corporeal space and the textual space of the work. Between the two stand prohibition and its censor; the symbolic activity is the disguise and the exclusion of the unacceptable, and the substitution of the excluded term by another less unacceptable one, more capable of slipping incognito into the area that is closed to it. Indeed, if every text is a text only because it does not yield itself up in its entirety at a first reading, how can we account for this essential dissimulation other than by some prohibition that hangs over it? We can infer the presence of this prohibition by what it allows to filter through of a conflict of which it is the outcome, marked by the lure it offers, calling on us to traverse it from end to end. We shall often feel a renewed disappointment, faced by its refusal to take us anywhere except to the point of origin from which it took its own departure.

The trans-narcissistic object

The products of artistic creation are evidence of work. Every examination of them travels, however briefly, the route of their birth. These products set up in the field of illusion a new category of objects related to psychical reality. Their relation with the objects of fantasy enables us to understand their function more clearly. The objects of fantasy, which, on their admission to consciousness, had to undergo distortion and adjustments to make them compatible with conscious logic, remain, as I said above, occult; the reticence of their message testifies to the precariousness of this cover. But the veil that hides them also corresponds to another requirement. They are an integral part of an equilibrium in which the realizations of desire that are carried out through them are inseparable from a condition of appropriation by the subject, which is necessary to feed his narcissistic idealization. The unity of the fantasy is inseparable from the narcissistic unity that it helps to form. The types of objects to which artistic creations correspond are on the other hand characteristically objects of ejection, expulsion: objects put into circulation through disappropriation by their creator, who expects their appropriation by others to authenticate their paternity. The upsurge of desire that gave them birth is repeated at each new reception. This enables us to map out in such productions the narcissistic double of their creator, which is neither his own image, nor his own personality, but a projected construction, a configuration formed in place of the narcissistic idealization of the recipient of the work.

Thus the structures of fantasy face in two directions. First, towards the object, they sustain desire and help to form whatever serves in fulfilling it: dream, symptom or sexual activity – the means placed at the disposal of the discharge and the channels open to it. Second, they serve the search for an idealizing subjective unit involving the renunciation of the satisfaction of a complete discharge (aesthetic *jouissance* being subjected to the inhibition of the aim of the drive), but in which the narcissistic construction of the other is accepted. So the objects of artistic creation may properly be called *trans-narcissistic*: that is to say, they bring the narcissisms of producer and consumer into communication in the work. The communication of the two fields of this double orientation will give us a clue to whatever may arouse, as an after-effect, the desire fantasy, through the mediation of this narcissistic idealization.

The psychoanalytic approach to the work of art need not involve a study of the personality of the artist, but there is no need to exclude the possibility. It is enough to be aware of this narcissistic construction that is the artist's double, and to seek to map out the points of impact at which the desire fantasy is set in motion, even if this fantasy inevitably fails to satisfy its recipient. But, through the disjunctions so revealed, we may posit hypotheses concerning the mode of articulation that holds its parts together.

No doubt there is a risk – and adventurous hermeneuts have often been criticized for just this – that one may shape the work into a lock (or discover a lock in it) to fit one's own particular key. The objection need not be taken seriously. A work only allows itself to take the form of a lock if it can be so taken – if its material permits it to do so and if its form suggests it. The important thing is not that one should be able to insert a key, but that one should know what would be revealed by the door that one hopes to open. What one interprets of a corpus of work depends on the way in which one segments it – the originality of the segmentation is inseparable from the originality of what one discovers. And this discovery is not possible without the mode of segmentation proper to it and the body of references that supports it. Such an interpretation does not say everything about the work, but confines itself to the particular aspect of the work that concerns it, without bothering about the rest, without necessarily even touching on it; and the rest cannot be reached except by adopting another mode of segmentation.

Can one, then, say anything one likes about the work? No, for the discovery is set against the coherence of the system that corresponds to the interpretation, and the coherence of the work that may accept or reject this interpretation. It is not a question of reaching an infinity of juxtaposed and contradictory insights, nor of leaving the field open to the most extravagant and arbitrary interpretations, but of attaining a mode of reading that does not deny other modes of interpretation, but which takes as its aim the revelation of the unconscious effects of the spectacle.

It must be repeated, at the risk of being boring, that psychoanalytic interpretation is not exhaustive, but specific. No other approach can replace its particular discourse, just as this discourse cannot be substituted for any other. No doubt, one will come up against other competing interpretations – especially at the level of significations. This collision cannot be avoided. One must set the different readings side by side, and decide which provides most information, which is most revealing.

Our aim, therefore, is to rediscover, in a work whose specific nature is the labour of representation unfolding according to its own procedures, an analogue of what Freud described in his first intuitions about the functioning of the psychical apparatus. This process is the play of a pluri-functional system, which never progresses continuously and in a single direction; it goes back over inscriptions that have already been traced and slides away from obstacles; it reproduces its message with a distortion that forces us back to it; receives some new impulsion that overcomes a resistance; or breaks into fragments. It recomposes these dissociated fragments into a new message incorporating other elements from another fragmented totality, preserving at the essential level that nucleus of intelligibility without which no new crossing of the boundary can be made. It preserves itself from annihilation and consequent oblivion by a protective distortion which prevents it being recognized. The work of representation, which unceasingly maintains an effect of tension in the spectator, is the reconstitution of the process of formation of the fantasy, just as the analysis of the dream, through the resistance to the work of association and to the regroupings that this work operates, replicates the construction of the dream process.

This brings us, then, to our object: the psychoanalytic reading of a tragedy, a reading situated in the potential space between text and representation. Here a question inevitably arises: how are we to understand the *jouissance* felt by the spectator of a tragedy, when the spectacle arouses pity and terror? This question brings us back to Aristotle's problem, for which Freud tried to provide a new answer.

The work of art, says Freud, offers an 'incentive bonus' to whoever experiences it. 'We give the name of an *incentive bonus*, or a *fore-pleasure*, to a yield of pleasure such as this, which is offered to us so as to make possible the release of still greater pleasure arising from deeper psychical sources'.[3] There is a discharge, then, but it is a partial discharge, desexualized by aim-inhibition and displacement of sexual pleasure. But we still have to account for the effect of tragedy.

How may we extend or replace the hypothesis of catharsis as a purging of the passions? Tragedy certainly gives pleasure, but pleasure tinged with pain: a mixture of terror and pity. But there is no tragedy without a tragic hero, that is, without an idealized projection of an ego that finds here the satisfaction of its megalomaniac designs. The hero is the locus of an encounter between the power of the bard, who brings the fantasy to life, and the desire of the spectator, who sees his fantasy embodied and represented. The spectator is the ordinary person to whom nothing of importance happens. The hero is the man who lives through exceptional adventures in which he performs his exploits, and who, in the last resort, must pay the gods dearly for the power he acquires in this way. Becoming a demi-god, he enters into competition with the gods, and so must be crushed by them, thus assuring the triumph of the father.

The spectator's pleasure will be compounded of his movement of identification with the hero (pity, compassion) and his masochistic movement (terror). Every hero, and therefore every spectator, is in the position of the son in the Oedipal situation: the son must become (move towards being) like the father. He must be brave and strong, but he must not do everything the father does. He must show proper respect for the father's prerogative (his *having*), namely those of paternal power, sexual possession of the mother, and physical power, the right of life and death over his children. In this respect, the father, even when dead, indeed especially when dead, sees this power still further increased in the beyond: totem and taboo.

Tragedy, then, is the representation of the fantasy myth of the Oedipus complex, which Freud identified as the constitutive complex of the subject. Thus the frontiers between the 'normal' individual, the neurotic and the hero became blurred in the subjective structure that is the subject's relation to his progenitors. The encounter between myth and tragedy is obviously not fortuitous. First, because every history, whether it is individual or collective, is based on a myth. In the case of the individual, this myth is known as fantasy. Second, because Freud himself includes myth in the psychoanalytic field: 'It seems quite possible to apply the psychoanalytic views derived from dreams to products of ethnic imagination such as myths and fairy-tales'.[4] (In his study of the structure of myths, Lévi-Strauss refers to the myth, without further explanation, as an 'absolute object'.) Freud rejects the traditional interpretation òf myths as mere attempts to explain natural phenomena, or as cult practices that have become unintelligible. It is highly likely that he would have much to say about the structuralist interpretation. For the essential function of these collective productions was, in Freud's view, the assuaging of unsatisfied or unsatisfiable desires. This is my interpretation too; it finds support in the foundations of the Oedipus complex, which forbids parricide and incest and so condemns the subject to seek other solutions if he is to satisfy these desires. Tragedy is, at a collective level, one of these substitute solutions. The psychoanalytic reading of tragedy, therefore, will have as its aim the mapping of the traces of the Oedipal structure concealed in its formal organization, through an analysis of the symbolic activity, which is masked from the spectator's perception and acts on him unknown to himself.

Freud and his successors

This chapter belongs to the tradition, established by Freud, of psychoanalytic criticism. Indeed, Freud is my major point of reference, a reference extended by the new developments that have given fresh life to Freudian thought. It is well known that since Freud's death, psychoanalytic thinking which in his work formed an organically linked whole has been split into various, sometimes contradictory, polarities. Thus the theoretical contributions of Melanie Klein and Jacques Lacan[5] provide two antinomian faces of psychoanalysis.

In the present grouping of the psychoanalytic world, one must, if one is not to condemn oneself to sectarianism, choose the group that includes the others, if I may borrow Euler's image. So it is sometimes surprising to observe that the ensemble that includes other ensembles bears a strange resemblance to the body of doctrine formed by Freudian theory, which has the advantages of completeness and balance. If one claims to be returning to Freud, one is under an obligation to respect the totality of his thought.[6]

In studying tragedy, one should not pay undue attention to the combinatory of signifiers (representatives of the drive), at the expense of the role of the affect. It is here that the reading between text and representation avoids the drawbacks of a disembodied formalization (the combinatory) or of a subjective construct (the emotional power of the spectacle).[7] The analysis of the text will stress its formalization: the reference to the representation-spectacle will emphasize its quasi-visceral role as discharge. There is a long-standing opposition between those who write about tragedy and those who act it or see it acted. The psychoanalyst must be attentive to the *text in representation* or the *representation of a text*.

Writing and representation

We often hear it said that the work cannot be reduced to its significations. The constitution of the signified by the action of the signifier is undoubtedly its essential nature. That which seems to elude psychoanalytic investigation forces us here to recognize its limits. But it is often a study of the latent signified, the relation of the manifest to the latent, that is most likely to throw light on the form of the signifier at any given point. In the long succession of signifiers in linked sequence which constitutes the work, the unconscious signified rises between two signifiers from the gulf or absence in which it resides and determines the difference between the 'natural' form of discourse and its literary form – not in order to express what has to be said, but in order to indicate, by veiling it, what needs to be hidden.

My constant concern will be to show the double articulation of the theatrical fantasy: that of the scene, which takes place on the stage, and is given an ostensible significance for the spectator; and that of the other scene that takes place – although everything is said aloud and intelligibly and takes place in full view – unknown to the spectator, by means of this chain-like mode and its unconscious logic.

But where does the operation of writing enter into this? This, it might be objected, is where the specificity of the work is to be found.

What about Aeschylus, Shakespeare and Racine as writers? This brings us to some of the crucial questions of contemporary criticism. In literature, should we allow privilege to the signifier or the signified? Why, for whom does one write? Put like that, the question cannot be answered. Signifier and signified are *relata* that necessarily refer back to one another, since the segmentation of the one cannot but affect the other by the same division. What is at issue, then, is not so much which has precedence over the other as the nature of the relation between them.

The resistance to the signified that is becoming so strongly marked in the present state of criticism is a sign of rejection and mistrust. Because it has for too long been linked with 'psychology', the signified has, so to speak, run out of breath. It is obvious that the work is not merely the signified that it overlays: it is the work of formalization without which there can be no work of art, but merely an expression of intention. If the work were merely what it signifies, what difference would there be between writing as literature and the writing of a treatise on psychology, a political manifesto or an advertising brochure? But this reference back to the specificity of the literary conceals a suspicion about the signified – especially, as I have said, if this signified is that of psychoanalysis.

It has recently been objected that psychoanalysis has turned away from 'the becoming literary of the literal' (Derrida, 340). The originality of the literary signifier appears to have been misunderstood by psychoanalytic criticism which, for the most part, remains an 'analysis of literary, or rather, non-literary signifieds'. Although it is true that literature sets out to be an exploration through the practice of the possibilities of language, it stumbles sooner or later upon the unspoken aspect of the work, on what we now call its 'unreadability', as the navel-cord from which it draws all its strength. Nothing appears to be external to this writing, whose links with representation have been undone. But what if writing *is* representation, as in the theatre? Do we not find here a defeat for that ambition, always present in non-theatrical literary forms, the ambition to be free of all direct reference to representation? It is facile to say that a literary statement can only refer to the whole body of other statements. This evident fact is meaningful only because every text demonstrates in this way the distance between itself and its object, in the process of once more traversing that distance. The object at which it is directed can never be embodied in any text; yet what emerges from this confrontation is not an endless dizzy round of texts, but the absence that inhabits them all. This is the absence of the work summing up all other texts, and cancelling them out by occupying the space of the written text, which has no difference, which is unique, which recovers the unity of the past and renders all further effort vain. This body of the letter is distilled from the text only to return to it in the representation of the nature and elements of writing. (And if there is a whole literature exploiting the artifices of representation, punctuation, layout and the addition of non-written signs, is it not precisely in order to displace one kind of unsaid and replace it by another? If one wishes to serve the text, one must first ask oneself in what service the text is supposed to be acting. To whom does the text speak? Who speaks through the text?) This is proof, if proof were needed, that the process of literature is not to become the stigmata of the relation between writing and representation, but to establish the relation between two systems of representation, writing's system of representation being unable to take any other way than that of the representation of the non-represented in representation.

There is much to be said about this operation of the non-represented: this book is an attempt to say something about it. But it should be clear that it is in the *absence of representation* that this operation is carried out and not in a deliverance from representation. The way in which certain literary 'integrists' make use of Freud's writings does not always reveal a clear understanding of them. If one wishes to refer to a 'trace', rather than to a signifier/signified opposition, how can the trace obstruct every relation with representation – even in the diastem, the spacing and the difference that call it into being? The confusion between the unrepresentable and the non-represented seems to be the source of errors of interpretation. Not that the two are unrelated. The non-represented refers us back to the sense of lack that obtrudes in the 'too full' of any representation; in its plenitude, this representation tries to block the outlet, because it is itself the result of the pressure of this lack, which can still be traced in it. The fact that this lack is at the origin of the unrepresentability of the process of writing refers back all the more inevitably to the non-representable, because it is blocked, of the non-represented. The trace maintains itself between the threat of being worn away – so causing the collapse of the whole signifying system – and its own persistence, which is revelatory of its nature, if only through reference back to all the other traces of the thing that it reveals or rather distorts as it unveils. This revelation is not continuous with its own nature, but is caught up in another web, in another texture. 'In its implications the distortion of a text resembles a murder: the difficulty is not perpetrating the deed, but getting rid of its traces' (*S.E.*, xxiii, 43). The great virtue of the concept of 'trace' is that it provides an opposition to the notion of language as a presence in itself: for it points to an absence in language. It is this absence inhabiting language that is revealing; without being confused with a materialization of the lack, absence conveys the lack in its effect and makes it possible to sustain a discourse on this absence and not to cement the identity of absence and non-existence.[8]

Yet, despite the many attempts to eliminate it from discourse, one still finds representation elsewhere, for instance in ideology, short-circuiting the individual signified. The desire to prevent creative subjectivity from being a fetish and to merge writing into the impersonality of the revolutionary movement is praiseworthy enough in its modesty. It shows us above all that 'readability' is easier when, overleaping several mediations, it is dissolved in the social body. If psychoanalysis, in centring its attention on the signified, has overleapt the mediations of the literary, we have now to say that literary 'integrism', forced by its own process to challenge a literally repressed signified, conceives no mediation between literature and ideology. Despite its overt professions, this 'integrism' reduces the value of the passion of writing, of reading and of the power of repetition to engender both the process and the challenge to it. It falls into the same willed search for 'lucidity' that it condemns elsewhere. It thus cancels itself out, in the sense that it is its own debtor. What I deprecate in this approach is not, therefore, that it neglects the signified, but that it adopts too readily the thesis of an elusive signified. The unsaid is the absence of the signified, not its ungraspability. The effect of this absence is the condition of the investment produced by what the counter-investment keeps separate. In this respect, literary exchange is, like all exchange, an exchange of desire, with a view to a deferred, postponed *jouissance*.

The originality of the literary signified can only reside, therefore, at our level of exploration, in the literalness of the unsaid of the signified. This unsaid, whose effects are displaced on the occasion of the conjoint reading–writing of the literary product (since all writing is a reading and vice versa), will be established by a study of the relation between the manifest signified and the difference between the literary signifier and the ordinary signifier. This difference has the function of introducing the effect of deception by which the web of the latent signified is attracted, caught and held in its network. But this attempt never manages to make the two planes coincide and, at each reading–writing, the project fails and the difference is unveiled in the substitution in which something else is revealed. It is the constantly renewed and never successful attempt which replicates the difference between the ordinary signifier and the literary signifier (a difference that is supposed to imprison what refuses to be named in the manifest) through the genre, construction and organization of the work. Repetition hollows out the bed in which this disparity must be filled and, by rendering it more perceptible, apprehends it. Theatrical representation multiplies this difference between the ordinary signifier and the literary signifier by stressing all the non-literary signifiers, the physical means at the disposal of the actor: prosody, phrasing, use of the body, which are here not only seen but exploited – one can see how it is, in fact, almost as much a duplication of difference as an increase of it. It is this time-lag in the oppositions between the signifiers of language (ordinary and literary) and the non-linguistic signifiers that serve, as it were, as a transmission belt for another duplication, that of the opposition between the spoken words of the play and its staging in scenes, acts, and so on.

Notes

1. ROLAND BARTHES, *Critique et Vérité* (Paris: Seuil, 1966), p. 37.
2. [There is no adequate translation in English for the French '*jouissance*'. 'Enjoyment' conveys the sense, contained in '*jouissance*', of 'enjoyment' of rights, of property, etc. Unfortunately, the word has lost much of its Shakespearean power in modern English. In French, '*jouissance*' also has the sexual connotation of 'ejaculation'. ('*Jouir*' is the slang equivalent of 'to come'.) Green is using the term here in the Lacanian sense, in contra-distinction with

'pleasure'. For Lacan, pleasure obeys the law of homoeostasis that Freud evokes in 'Beyond the Pleasure Principle', whereby, through discharge, the psyche seeks the lowest possible level of tension. *Jouissance* transgresses this law and, in that respect, it is beyond the pleasure principle.]

3. *Standard Edition of the Complete Psychological Works* 23 vols (London: Hogarth Press, 1953–66), vol. 9, p. 153.

4. Ibid., vol. 13, p. 185.

5. In a work like this, my debt to Jacques Lacan is probably more important than any other, after that to Freud himself. This is not the place to explain why my approach, when applied to works of art, tends to push into the background my points of disagreement with Lacan's theory. However, these points will be indirectly present whenever I refer, in my analysis, to other theorizations, whether psychoanalytic or not.

6. The reformulation of Freud's thought is made necessary by knowledge that we have gained since his time. This knowledge cannot simply be added to Freud's work, but requires a re-elaboration of theory. If we are to safeguard the truth of the Freudian heritage we must take care that the Freudian language as a whole does not break down into a number of new dialects.

7. The role of the affect is particularly stressed by Freud in his analysis of Michelangelo's 'Moses'. This analysis is carried out according to the strictest rules of the combinatory, through the examination of the function of detail, but is aroused, solicited, by a powerful affect that keeps Freud rooted to the ground before the 'Moses'. The direction of gazes is then reversed: Freud feels that he is under the gaze of Moses, 'as though I myself belonged to the mob upon whom his eye is turned'. Similarly, Freud insists on the fact that the understanding required by the analyst cannot be an intellectual one: 'What he aims at is to awaken in us the same emotional attitude, the same mental constellation as that which in him produced the impetus to create' (Standard Edition, vol. 13, pp. 12–13). One could hardly state more clearly the indissolubility of the affect and the representative of the drive.

8. An elucidation of these points is to be found in my article, '*L'objet* (a) de J. Lacan', *Cahiers pour l'analyse*, no. 3.

6 Feminism and Tragedy

There is no shortage of theoretical writings demonstrating how tragedy victimises its feminine representations, but these only constitute a feminist discourse if such a discourse demands the rejection of tragedy as a meaningful representation of significant human activity. The proposition (see Bamber, for example) that tragedy is anti-feminist requires a syllogistic counter-proposition: if tragedy is anti-feminist, then feminism must perforce be anti-tragic. Feminist critics of Renaissance tragedy (for example, Woodbridge, Callaghan, Neely, Bamber, Figes, Sprengnether) who have drawn attention to the ways in which the genre of tragedy victimises its female characters have not generally been concerned with the fact that the genre also, with equal frequency and intensity, victimises its males, even or especially those in the plays who themselves victimise females. If tragedy's masculine representations are murdering ministers, they are not thereby redeemed or rewarded in that function.

Feminist critics of classical Greek and Roman tragedy (for example, Sarah B. Pomeroy, Nicole Loraux, Elisabeth Bronfen, Mary Lefkowitz) point the study of tragedy in a different direction. In Greek tragedy, they note, difference sometimes implies a distinction that is not necessarily hierarchical, and in some cases when it is, the hierarchy represented places the feminine at the top. For Pomeroy, the mirror held up to nature by Greek tragedy is a magnifying mirror; it reflects not ordinary social reality but the extraordinary epic mythology that provided the plots of these plays. Where Greek tragedy makes significant alterations from its mythic sources in regard to the roles of women in its stories, as in Aeschylus's *Agamemnon*, it does so by elevating their importance in the action of their plays and enlivening their characterisation. It often designates a female tragic protagonist. The extent to which such representation reflects anything like the social reality of patriarchal Athens varies according to scholarship that traces the foundations of Athenian culture to a disputed matriarchal root in the Bronze Age and the degree to which that buried foundation is remembered in the tragic drama that emerged some 700 years afterwards. If Greek tragedy offers a representation of the *ideal*, the foregrounding of the feminine is evidently an important component in that ideal. On the other hand, if tragedy represents a patriarchal *ideology*, Pomeroy argues, it is vitally important to bear in mind the distinction between ideology and statements of fact, both as presented in the action of tragedy and as preserved in records of real social life. Tragedy, we must remember, represents not what *is* but what *might be*, and when it revives old social myths, it does so to provoke a new interrogation of traditional notions such as the feminine submission to masculine will, acceptance of social isolation, and a willingness to die, if necessary, by suicide.

In Greek tragedy, Loraux argues, not only is suicide often required of women, but the very means of self-annihilation is dictated by customary representation: not the specifically masculine mode of penetration by sword or knife-blade, but strangulation, the most degraded and shameful way out of intolerable circumstances, and one, moreover, which left the body intact and unstained while silencing it by closing off the voice. 'Hanging is a woman's way of death,' a specific social inflection whose violation (as in the sword deaths of Deianira, Eurydice and Euripides's Iocasta) forms part of the shaped and coded discourse of tragic drama. But deviations from custom are found in representations of male suicides (Ajax, Haemon) as well as female; when tragedy represents transgressive behaviour, it imaginatively interrogates any and all social distinctions, including those of gender. 'In tragedy,' says Loraux, 'male and female behaviour can disregard the division of humanity into men and women,' thereby showing 'how each character – whether by conformity or by deviation – lives out a destiny as an individual man or woman.' There are dimensions of both reality and imagination to these lives, while the city would like to make them fundamentally a matter of social reality.

These feminist critics offer a radical revaluation of tragedy insofar as their readings refocus attention on the foregrounded representation of the feminine. What emerges from their respective readings is a view of the feminine *subject* not as nemesis or antagonistic to the masculine, but rather as the representation of a heroic human potential in her own right. Furthermore, they remind us that we tend to read tragedy for messages about its original audiences that we believe, based on what we have come to understand as the informing ideology of the drama's producing culture, 'must' have been the prevailing system of belief, especially in regard to representations of social and political hierarchy. But as these scholars have discovered, what modern readers and audiences believe about ancient cultures is, like any system of belief, subject to the changes that a revivified inquiry is likely to bring about. Social status, as Pomeroy argues, is never an immutable 'fact'; it shifts not only with the passage of time and from place to place, but also, and perhaps more importantly, with the difference a different perspective, a point of view that does not necessarily seek to reaffirm what has long been accepted, can make in the reception and understanding of what tragedy represents.

Images of Women in the Literature of Classical Athens*

SARAH B. POMEROY

Women in Tragedy versus Real Women

If respectable Athenian women were secluded and silent, how are we
to account for the forceful heroines of tragedy and comedy? And why
does the theme of strife between woman and man pervade Classical
drama? Before proceeding to complex explanations which are directly
concerned with women, it is necessary to repeat the truism that the
dramatists examined multiple aspects of man's relationship to the
universe and to society; accordingly, their examination of another basic
relationship – that between man and woman – is not extraordinary. It is
rather the apparent discrepancy between women in the actual society
and the heroines on the stage that demands investigation. Several
hypotheses have been formulated in an attempt to explain the conflict
between fact and fiction.

Many plots of tragedy are derived from myths of the Bronze Age
preserved by epic poets. As we have observed, the royal women of epic
were powerful, not merely within their own homes but in an external
political sense. To the Athenian audience familiar with the works of
Homer, not even an iconoclast like Euripides could have presented
a silent and repressed Helen or Clytemnestra. Likewise, the Theban
epic cycle showed the mutual fratricide of the sons of Oedipus. The
surviving members of the family were known to be Antigone and
Ismene. Sophocles could not have presented these sisters as boys.
In short, some myths that provided the plots of Classical tragedies
described the deeds of strong women, and the Classical dramatist could
not totally change these facts.

Those who believe in the historical existence of Bronze Age
matriarchy also propose an answer to our questions: the male–female
polarity discernible in Bronze Age myths can be explained by referring

* Reprinted from *Goddesses, Whores, Wives and Slaves: Women in Classical Antiquity*
(New York: Schocken Books, 1975).

to an actual conflict between a native pre-Hellenic matriarchal society and the patriarchy introduced by conquering invaders.

The Bronze Age origin of these myths does not explain why Athenian tragic poets, living at least seven hundred years later in a patriarchal society, not only found these stories congenial but accentuated the power of their heroines. For example, in the *Odyssey* Aegisthus is the chief villain in the murder of Agamemnon, but in the tragedies of Aeschylus a shift was made to highlight Clytemnestra as the prime mover in the conspiracy. Electra, the daughter of Clytemnestra, is a colourless figure in mythology, and in the *Odyssey* Orestes alone avenges his father; but two dramatists elevated Electra and created whole plays around her and her dilemma. Similarly, Sophocles is thought to have been responsible for the story of the conflict between Creon and Antigone. Homer, it is true, showed how Calypso and Circe could unman even the hero Odysseus, who more easily survived other ordeals, but these two were immortal females. The mortal women in epic, however vital, are not equivalent in impact to tragic heroines, nor is their power such as to produce the male–female conflicts that tragedy poses in a pervasive and demanding way.

A number of scholars find a direct relationship between real women living in Classical Athens and the heroines of tragedy.[1] They reason that the tragic poets found their models not in the Bronze Age but among the real women known to them. From this theory they deduce that real women were neither secluded nor repressed in Classical times. They use as evidence, for example, the fact that tragic heroines spent much time conversing out-of-doors without worrying about being seen. This argument lacks cogency, since the scenes of tragedy are primarily out-of-doors and female characters could scarcely be portrayed if they had to be kept indoors. The proponents of this argument question how dramatists could have become so familiar with feminine psychology if they never had a chance to be with women. They ignore the fact that playwrights were familiar with their female relatives, as well as with the numerous resident aliens and poor citizen women who did move freely about the city. At least one group of women – the wives of citizens with adequate means – probably was secluded.

It is not legitimate for scholars to make judgments about the lives of real women solely on the basis of information gleaned from tragedy. When an idea expressed in tragedy is supported by other genres of ancient sources, then only is it clearly applicable to real life. Ismene's statement that the proper role of women is not to fight with men[2] can be said to reflect real life, since it agrees with information derived from Classical oratory and from comedy. But when Clytemnestra murders her husband, or Medea her sons, or when Antigone takes credit for an act of civil disobedience, we cannot say that these actions have much to do with the lives of real women in Classical Athens, although isolated precedents in Herodotus could be cited for passionate, aggressive women (including a barbarian queen who contrived the murder of her husband with his successor; another who opposed men in battle; and a third who cut off the breasts, nose, ears, lips, and tongue of her rival's mother).[3] However, as images of women in Classical literature written by men, heroines such as Clytemnestra, Medea, and Antigone are valid subjects for contemplation.

Retrospective psychoanalysis has been used to analyse the experience of young boys in Classical Athens, and thus to explain the mature dramatist's depiction of strong heroines According to the sociologist Philip Slater, the Athenian boy spent his early formative years primarily in the company of his mother and female slaves.[4] The father passed the day away from home, leaving the son with no one to defend him from the mother. The relationship between mother and son was marked by ambiguity and contradiction. The secluded woman nursed a repressed hostility against her elderly, inconsiderate, and mobile husband. In the absence of her husband, the mother substituted the son, alternately pouring forth her venom and doting on him. She demanded that he be successful and lived vicariously through him. The emotionally powerful mother impressed herself upon the imagination of the young boy, becoming the seed, as it were, which developed into the dominant female characters of the mature playwright's mind. The Classical dramatist tended to choose those myths of the Bronze Age that were most fascinating to him, since they explored certain conflicts that existed within his own personality. The 'repressed mother' explanation works in inverse ratio to the power of the heroines produced by the son: the more repressed his mother was and the more ambivalent her behaviour, the more dreadful were the heroines portrayed by the dramatist-son.

Slater's theory is an interesting attempt to answer a difficult question. Some readers may abhor the interpretation of Classical antiquity by means of psychoanalytic approaches. But since the myths of the past illuminate the present, it appears valid to examine them with the critical tools of the present. Still, there are problems with Slater's analysis, just as there were with the more traditional ones. First, although adult Athenians lived sex-segregated lives, it is far from certain that fathers were distant from children. Inferences from the modern 'commuting father' have too much influenced Slater's view of antiquity. In fact, comedy shows a closeness between fathers and children: children could accompany fathers when they were invited out, and a father claimed to have nursed a baby and bought toys for him.[5] Second, the reader would have to accept Slater's premise that women constrained in a patriarchal society would harbour rage, whether or not they themselves were aware of it. The epitaphs of women assumed that their lives were satisfactory, although this evidence may be somewhat discounted since the inscriptions were selected by the surviving members of the family, most probably male. But even today many believe that women can find happiness in the role of homemaker, particularly when traditional expectations are being fulfilled. Thus Athenian women may well have lacked the internal conflict of, say, Roman women, who were plagued with the frustrations arising from relative freedom which confronted them with the realm of men, but tantalizingly kept its trophies just beyond their grasp. Is it more reasonable to suggest from a modern viewpoint that the boredom of tasks like constant weaving must have driven Athenian women to insanity, or, in contrast, to call attention to the satisfaction women may have felt at jobs well done?

I am not convinced that we can learn much about the Athenian mother from Slater, but his work is useful for the analysis of the male playwright's creative imagination. For explanations of the powerful women in tragedy, we must look to the poets, and to other men who judged the plays and selected what they thought best. The mythology about women is created by men and, in a culture dominated by men, it may have little to do with flesh-and-blood women. This is not to deny that the creative imagination of the playwright was surely shaped by some women he knew. But it was also moulded by the entire milieu of fifth-century Athens, where separation of the sexes as adults bred fear of the unfamiliar; and finally by the heritage of his literary past, including not only epic but Archaic poetry, with its misogynistic element.

Misogyny was born of fear of women. It spawned the ideology of male superiority. But this was ideology, not statement of fact; as such, it could not be confirmed, but was open to constant doubt. Male status was not immutable. Myths of matriarchies and Amazon societies showed female dominance. Three of the eleven extant comedies of Aristophanes show women in successful opposition to men. A secluded wife like Phaedra may yearn for adultery; a wife like Creusa may have borne an illegitimate son before her current marriage; a good wife like Deianira can murder her husband. These were the nightmares of the victors: that some day the vanquished would arise and treat their ex-masters as they themselves had been treated.

Most important, in the period between Homer and the tragedians, the city-state, with established codes of behaviour, had evolved, and the place of women as well as of other disenfranchised groups in the newly organized society was an uncomfortable one. Many tragedies show women in rebellion against the established norms of society. As the *Oresteia* of Aeschylus makes clear, a city-state such as Athens flourished only through the breaking of familial or blood bonds and the subordination of the patriarchal family within the patriarchal state. But women were in conflict with this political principle, for their interests

217

were private and family-related. Thus, drama often shows them acting
out of the women's quarters, and concerned with children, husbands,
fathers, brothers, and religions deemed more primitive and family-
oriented than the Olympian, which was the support of the state. This is
the point at which the image of the heroine on the stage coincides with
the reality of Athenian women.

Masculine and feminine roles in tragedy

The proper behaviour of women and men is explored in many
tragedies. This is not to say that it is the primary theme of any tragedy.
Aeschylus' *Agamemnon* is about the workings of justice, but the
discussion of this tragedy in these pages will set aside the principal
idea and focus on the secondary theme of sex roles and antagonisms.

Womanly behaviour was characterized then, as now, by
submissiveness and modesty. Ismene in *Antigone*, Chrysothemis in
the plays dealing with the family of Agamemnon, Tecmessa in *Ajax*,
Deianira in *Trachinian Women*, and the female choruses in tragedy act
the role of 'normal' women. Because of the limitations of 'normal'
female behaviour, heroines who act outside the stereotype are
sometimes said to be 'masculine'. Again, it is not a compliment to a
woman to be classified as masculine. Aristotle judged it inappropriate
for a female character to be portrayed as manly or clever.[6]

Heroines, like heroes, are not normal people. While in a repressively
patriarchal culture, most women – like Ismene – submit docilely, some
heroines – like Clytemnestra, Antigone, and Hecuba – adopt the
characteristics of the dominant sex to achieve their goals. The
psychoanalyst A. Adler termed the phenomenon 'masculine protest'.[7]
In *Agamemnon*, the first play of the *Oresteia* trilogy, Aeschylus shows
Clytemnestra with political power, planning complex strategies
involving the relaying of signal beacons from Troy, outwitting her
husband in persuading him to tread upon a purple carpet, and finally
planning and perpetrating his murder. Unrepentant, she flaunts her
sexual freedom by announcing that the death of Cassandra has brought
an added relish of pleasure to her, and that her situation will be secure
as long as her lover Aegisthus lights the fire on her hearth (1435–6,
1446–7). The double entendre is especially shocking because a woman
traditionally lit the fire on her father's or husband's hearth.

Thus the chorus of old men of Argos considers that her ways are
masculine and reminds her that she is a woman, addressing her as 'my
lady' (351). When it quizzes her as though she were a silly child she
answers with a brilliant, complex speech displaying her knowledge of

geography (268–316; cf. 483–7). To a chorus slow to digest the fact that
she has murdered Agamemnon, Clytemnestra impatiently retorts, 'You
are examining me as if I were a foolish woman' (1401). The chorus
continues to meditate upon the fact that their king has been killed by a
woman (1453–4). Had Aegisthus himself performed the murder, as he
was reputed to have done in the *Odyssey*, the chorus would better have
accepted it. The old men find the reversal of sex roles in Clytemnestra
and Aegisthus monstrous (1633–5; 1643–5).

In the *Eumenides*, which was the final play of the *Oresteia*, Aeschylus
restores masculine and feminine to their proper spheres. Orestes, who
chose to murder his mother in vengeance for her murder of his father, is
defended by Apollo and Athena. The power of the uncanny, monstrous
female spirits of vengeance (formerly called 'Erinyes' or 'Furies') is
tempered and subordinated to the rule of the patriarchal Olympians,
Henceforth, as Eumenides, or fair-minded spirits, they will have a
proper place in the affections of civilized people.

The portrayal of the masculine woman as heroine was fully developed
in Sophocles' *Antigone*. The play opens with the daughters of Oedipus
lamenting the laws established by the tyrant Creon. Their brother
Polyneices lies dead, but Creon has forbidden that the corpse be buried,
as punishment for the dead man's treachery against his native land.
While Antigone urges that they perform the burial rites, her sister
Ismene seizes upon the excuse that they are not men. 'We were born
women, showing that we were not meant to fight with men' (61–2). She
uses the frequently significant verb *phyō*, implying that it is by nature
(*physis*) rather than by man-made convention that women do not
attempt to rival men.

Creon, a domineering ruler, reveals particular hostility in his relations
with the opposite sex. His prejudices are patriarchal. He cannot
understand his son Haemon's love for Antigone, but refers to a wife as
a 'field to plough' (569). The sentiments of Apollo in Aeschylus'
Eumenides (657–61) must be recalled here: since the male seed is all-
important, any female will suffice. Apollo's idea is restated by Orestes
in Euripides' *Orestes*.[8] Simone de Beauvoir, in *The Second Sex*, traced the
phallus/plough–woman/furrow as a common symbol of patriarchal
authority and subjugation of woman.[9] Moreover, as modern feminists
have pointed out, the repressive male cannot conceive of an equal
division of power between the sexes, but fears that women, if permitted,
would be repressive in turn. So Creon, the domineering male, is
constantly anxious about being bested by a woman and warns his
son against such a humiliation (484, 525, 740, 746, 756).

On the other hand, Ismene – perhaps because she stayed at Thebes
while Antigone shared the exile of her father – has been indoctrinated

into the beliefs of patriarchal society: men are born to rule, and women to obey. Antigone bitterly rejects her sister's notion of the natural behaviour of women. Polyneices is buried secretly, and Creon, the guard, and the chorus all suppose that only a man could have been responsible (248, 319, 375). Thereupon forced to confess to Creon that she has in fact buried her brother, Antigone refers to herself with a pronoun in the masculine gender (464). Creon, in turn, perceives her masculinity and refers to Antigone by a masculine pronoun and participle (479, 496). He resolves to punish her, declaring, 'I am not a man, she is the man if she shall have this success without penalty' (484–5). (Similarly, Herodotus notes that Queen Artemisia, who participated in Xerxes' expedition against Greece, was considered masculine, and that the Athenians were so indignant that a woman should be in arms against them that for her capture alone they offered a financial reward.[10])

Feeling, then, that in daring to flout his commands Antigone has acted as a man – for a true woman would be incapable of opposition – Creon, when he declares sentence upon the sisters, asserts that 'they must now be women'. However, he continues to refer to them in the masculine gender (579–80). The repeated use of a masculine adjective to modify a feminine noun is noteworthy, because in Classical Greek, adjectives regularly agree with the gender of the modified noun (the masculine gender may be used in reference to a woman when a general statement is made).[11]

We may note the male orientation of the Greek language, in which general human truths, though conceived as referring specifically to women, can be cast in the masculine gender. Perhaps this grammatical explanation will suffice when the change in gender is sporadic. However, the masculine gender used to refer to a female in specific rather than general statements – a rare occurrence in Greek – occurs with significant frequency in *Antigone*. It is, I believe, a device used by the playwright in characterizing the heroine who has become a masculine sort of woman. In her penultimate speech, Antigone explains her willingness to die for the sake of a brother, though not for a husband or child.

> For had I been a mother, or if my husband had died, I would never have taken on this task against the city's will. In view of what law do I say this? If my husband were dead I might find another, and another child from him if I lost a son. But with my mother and father hidden in the grave, no other brother could ever bloom for me.
>
> (905–12)

Herodotus also relates a story about a woman who, when offered the life of a husband, a son, or a brother, chooses a brother for the same reason as Antigone.[12]

A number of Sophoclean scholars have judged the speech spurious, or pronounced the sentiments unworthy of the heroine.[13] They consider the choice of a brother over a child bizarre. And yet, in the context of Classical Athens, Antigone's choice is reasonable. Mothers could not have been as attached to children as the ideal mother is nowadays. The natural mortality of young children would seem to discourage the formation of strong mother–child bonds. In addition, patriarchal authority asserted that the child belonged to the father, not the mother. He decided whether a child should be reared, and he kept the child upon dissolution of a marriage, while the woman returned to the guardianship of her father or, if he were dead, her brother. Thus the brother–sister bond was very precious.

The preference for the brother is also characteristic of the masculine woman, who may reject the traditional role of wife and mother as a result of being inhibited by external forces from displaying cherishing or nurturing qualities.[14] The masculine woman often allies herself with the male members of her family. In this context we may note Antigone's firm and repeated denunciations of her sister (538–9, 543, 546–7, 549). She also judges her mother harshly, blaming her for the 'reckless guilt of the marriage bed', while the chorus, seeing only her father's disposition in her, calls her 'cruel child of a cruel father' (862, 471–2). Her disregard of her sister is so complete that she actually refers to herself as the sole survivor of the house of Oedipus (941).[15]

In the end, Antigone reverts to a traditional female role. She laments that she dies a virgin, unwed and childless (917–18), and commits suicide after being entombed alive by Creon. In Classical mythology, suicide is a feminine and somewhat cowardly mode of death. Ajax, like Deianira, Jocasta, and Creon's wife Eurydice, had killed himself because he could not live with unbearable knowledge. Haemon, like Phaedra, Alcestis, Laodamia, Dido, Evadne, and Hero, kills himself for love, justifying Creon's earlier concern over his 'womanish' tendencies. Of all tragic heroines, Antigone was the most capable of learning through suffering and achieving a tragic vision comparable to that of Oedipus. Her death erased that possibility.

The fate of Haemon illustrates the destructive quality of love. The chorus gives voice to this idea:

Love, invincible love, who keeps vigil on the soft cheek of a young girl, you roam over the sea and among homes in wild places, no one can escape you, neither man nor god, and the one who has you is possessed by madness. You bend the minds of the just to wrong, so here you have stirred up this quarrel of son and father. The love-kindling light in the eyes of the fair bride conquers.

(781–96)[16]

Antigone is a complex and puzzling play. According to Athenian law, Creon was Antigone's guardian, since he was her nearest male relative.[17] As such, he was responsible for her crime in the eyes of the state, and his punishing her was both a private and public act. He was also the nearest male relative of his dead nephews, and he, not Antigone, was responsible for their burial. Creon put what he deemed to be the interests of the state before his personal obligations.

The differences between Creon and Antigone are traditional distinctions between the sexes. According to Freud. 'Women spread around them their conservative influence . . . Women represent the interests of the family and sexual life; the work of civilization has become more and more men's business.'[18] The civilizing inventions of men are listed by the chorus of *Antigone*: sailing, navigation, ploughing, hunting, fishing, domesticating animals, verbal communication, building houses, and the creation of laws and government (332–64). These were mainly masculine activities.

The Greeks assumed that men were bearers of culture. For example, according to myth, Cadmus brought the alphabet to Greece; Triptolemus – albeit prompted by the goddess Demeter – brought the use of the plough; while Daedalus was credited with the scissors the saw, and other inventions. The specific achievements of women – which were probably in the realm of clothing manufacture, food preparation, gardening, and basketmaking, and the introduction of olive culture by Athena – do not appear in Sophocles' list, nor in a similar list in Aeschylus' *Prometheus Bound*.[19]

Creon's lack of insight into the necessity of the duality of male and female led to the death of Antigone and to his own annihilation as well. Creon's wife died cursing him. Moreover, in a society where sons were expected to display filial obedience, Haemon chose Antigone over his father and his choice was not held against him. His death was not a punishment for disobedience. *Antigone* and many other tragedies show the effect of overvaluation of the so-called masculine qualities (control, subjugation, culture, excessive cerebration) at the expense of the so-called feminine aspects of life (instinct, love, family ties) which destroys men like Creon. The ideal, we can only assume – since Sophocles formulates no solution – was a harmonization of masculine and feminine values, with the former controlling the latter.[20]

Euripides' women: a new song

Streams of holy rivers run backward, and universal custom is overturned. Men have deceitful thoughts; no longer are their oaths steadfast. My reputation shall change, my manner of life have good report. Esteem shall come to the female sex. No longer will malicious rumour fasten upon women. The Muses of ancient poets will cease to sing of my unfaithfulness. Apollo, god of song, did not grant us the divine power of the lyre. Otherwise I would have sung an answer to the male sex.[21]

Thus sang the female chorus of Euripides' *Medea* in 431 BC. Were they directly reflecting the attitude of the poet? Noting the absence of female tragedians, did Euripides turn his gift of poetry to compositions in behalf of women? Of all the images of women in Classical literature, those created by Euripides pose the greatest dilemma to the modern commentator.

Among ancient critics, Euripides was the only tragedian to acquire a reputation for misogyny. In the comedy *Thesmophoriazusae*, by his contemporary Aristophanes, an assembly of women accuse Euripides of slandering the sex by characterizing women as whores and adultresses:

By the gods, it's not out of any self-seeking
That I rise to address you, O women. It's that
I've been disturbed and annoyed for quite some time now
When I see our reputations getting dirtied
By Euripides, son of a produce-salesgirl.
And our ears filled with all sorts of disgusting things!
With what disgusting charges has he *not* smeared us?
Where hasn't he defamed us? Any place you find
Audiences, or tragedies, or choruses
We're called sex fiends, pushovers for a handsome male,
Heavy drinkers, betrayers, babbling-mouthed gossips,
Rotten to the core, the bane of men's existence.
And so they come straight home from these performances
Eyeing us suspiciously, and go search at once
For lovers we might hide about the premises.
We can't do anything we used to do before.
This guy's put terrible ideas in the heads of
Our menfolk. If any woman should start weaving
A wreath – this proves she's got a lover. If she drops
Anything while meandering about the house,
It's *Cherchez l'homme!* 'For whom did the pitcher crack up?
It must have been for that Corinthian stranger!'
If a girl's tired out, then her brother remarks:
'I don't like the colour of that girl's complexion.'
If a woman just wants to procure a baby
Since she lacks one of her own, no deals in secret!

For now the men hover at the edge of our beds.
And to all the old men who used to wed young girls
He's told slanderous tales, so that no old man wants
To try matrimony. You remember that line:
'An old bridegroom marries a tyrant, not a wife.'

(383–413)

If he cuts up Phaedra.
Why should *we* worry? He's neglected to tell how
A woman flung her stole in front of her husband
For scrutiny under the light, while dispatching
The lover she's hidden – not a word about that!
And a woman I know claimed that her delivery
Lasted ten whole days – till she'd purchased a baby!
While her husband raced to buy labour-speeding drugs
An old crone brought her an infant, stuffed in a pot.
Its mouth stuffed with honeycomb so it wouldn't cry.
When this baby-carrier gave the signal, she yelled,
'Out, husband, out I say! I think the little one's
Coming' (the baby was kicking the *pot's* belly)!
So he runs out, delighted; she in turn pulls out
What had plugged up the infant's mouth – and he hollers!
The dirty old woman who'd brought in the baby
Dashes out to the husband, all smiles, and announces,
'You've fathered a lion – he's your spitting image
In all of his features including his small prick
Which looks just like yours, puckered as a honeycomb.'
Why, don't we do such naughty things? By Artemis
We do. Then why get angry at Euripides?
We're accused of far less than what we've really done!

(497–519)[22]

Since the borderline between levity and seriousness in Aristophanes'
comedies is ambiguous, and the world is often topsy-turvy, in antiquity,
as now, it has been difficult to decide whether he truly thought
Euripides was a misogynist or the opposite. Influenced by Aristophanes,
many biographical sketches written about Euripides after his death
presented him as a misogynist and repeated the insulting charge that
his mother was a vegetable-monger. According to Aulus Gellius, writing
in the mid-second century AD:

Euripides is said to have had a strong antipathy toward nearly all
women, either shunning their society due to his natural inclination,
or because he had two wives simultaneously – since that was legal

according to an Athenian decree – and they had made marriage abominable to him.[23]

The ancient biographies of Euripides are unreliable, since they do not hesitate to cull material from the author's creations and apply it indiscriminately to his life. Therefore inconsistent with Gellius is the anecdote reported by Athenaeus at the end of the second century AD:

> The poet Euripides was fond of women. Hieronymus, at any rate, in *Historical Commentaries*, says, 'When someone said to Sophocles that Euripides was a woman-hater in his tragedies, Sophocles said. "When he is in bed, certainly he is a woman-lover." '[24]

In addition to the pronouncements of ancient critics, the plays themselves provide evidence of misogyny, although one ought not attribute to a playwright the remarks of his characters. Apparently obvious sources are the anti-female pronouncements scattered through the tragedies. In Euripidean tragedy, misogynists like Hippolytus and Orestes (in *Orestes*), masochists like Andromache, aggressive women like Medea and Phaedra, and sympathetic female choruses are equally capable of misogynistic remarks. In these statements women are usually lumped together as a nameless group, defined simply as the 'female sex', in a manner rarely applied to males. These statements are platitudes, familiar to women even today, but are so arresting by their stark hostility that it is easy to overlook how few they are in the context of Euripides' extant work.

Some of the abbreviated platitudes are: 'Women are the best devisers of evil.'[25] 'Women are a source of sorrow.'[26] Others point out that if their sex life is satisfactory, women are completely happy;[27] clever women are dangerous;[28] stepmothers are always malicious;[29] upper-class women were the first to practise adultery;[30] and women use magical charms and potions with evil intentions.[31] The longest and best-known tirade against women was delivered by Hippolytus:

> O Zeus, why, as a fraudulent evil for men,
> Have you brought women into the light of the sun?
> For if you wished to engender the mortal race,
> There was no need for women as source of supply,
> But in your shrines mortal men could have offered up
> Either gold or iron or heavy weight of bronze
> To purchase their breed of offspring, each paid in sons
> According to his own gift's worth, and in their homes
> They could live without women, entirely free.

Yet now to our homes we bring this primal evil,
And – without a choice – drain the wealth from our households.
Woman is a great evil, and this makes it clear:
The father who sires her and rears her must give her
A dowry, to ship off and discard this evil.
Then he who takes in his home this baneful creature
Revels in heaping upon his most vile delight
Lovely adornment, and struggles to buy her clothes.
Poor, poor fellow, siphoning wealth from his household.
He cannot escape his fate: gaining good in-laws
Brings joy to him – and preserves a bitter marriage:
But an excellent wife with worthless male kinfolk
Weights him down with good luck *and* misfortune alike.
A nobody's simplest to marry, though worthless,
A woman of guilelessness set up in the house.
I hate clever women. May my home never house
A woman more discerning than one ought to be.
For Cypris more often produces wrongdoing
In clever females. An untalented woman
Through lack of intelligence stays clear of folly.
No servant should have to come close to a woman.
Instead they should live among dumb, savage creatures,
So they would have no humans whom they could talk to
And no one who'd respond to the things that they say.
But now evil women sit at home and plan evils –
Plots their servants execute when they go outside.
And so, evil woman, you've come, to propose that
I sleep with her whom my father alone may touch.
I'll wipe out your words with streams of running water,
Drenching my ears. How, tell me, might I be evil
When I feel impure from even hearing such things?
Be certain my piety protects me, woman.
If my oaths to the gods hadn't caught me off guard,
I would not have refrained from telling my father.
But now, while Theseus is out of the country,
I'll depart from this house – and keep my mouth silent.
Returning when my father does, I shall witness
How you and your mistress manage to confront him.
I'll have firsthand knowledge of your effrontery.
Go to hell, I'll never have my fill of hating
Women, not if I'm said to talk without ceasing.
For women are also unceasingly wicked.
Either someone should teach them to be sensible.
Or let me trample them underfoot forever.[32]

I can scarcely believe that so subtle a dramatist as Euripides, who called into question traditional Athenian beliefs and prejudices surrounding foreigners, war, and the Olympian gods, would have intended his audience simply to accept the misogynistic maxims. Rather, he uses the extreme vantage point of misogyny as a means of examining popular beliefs about women. On the other hand, Euripides does not present a brief for women's rights. Not only is Greek tragedy not a convenient vehicle for propaganda, but the playwright saw too many contradictions in life to be able to espouse a single cause. Euripides is questioning rather than dogmatic. Judgments about his presentation of heroines vary, some critics believing he is sympathetic, some antipathetic.

My subjective estimate of Euripides is favourable. I do not think it misogynistic to present women as strong, assertive, successful, and sexually demanding even if they are also selfish or villainous. Other feminists share my opinion, and British suffragists used to recite speeches from Euripides at their meetings. Yet, it is fair to add that conventional critics – who far outnumber feminists – judge that Medea and Phaedra disgrace the entire female sex, and label Euripides a misogynist for drawing our attention to these murderesses. The controversy that the doctrines of women's liberation invariably arouse among women is analogous to the dilemma posed by subjective judgments of Euripides. For every feminist who insists that women have the same capabilities (whether for good or for evil) as men, but that they have been socialized into their present passivity, there have been countless conservatives denying that women are what the feminists claim they are.

Many women perpetrate villainous deeds in Euripidean tragedy. However, old myths are paraded not to illustrate that the female sex is evil, but rather to induce the audience to question the traditional judgment on these women. Euripides counters the ideas expressed in the misogynistic platitudes by portraying individual women and their reason for their actions. The crime of Clytemnestra had tainted the entire female sex ever since Agamemnon's judgment of her in the *Odyssey*.[33] Euripides reiterates the accusations but adds a strong defence for Clytemnestra in her speech to her daughter Electra:

Tyndareus placed me in your father's care.
So that neither I nor my offspring would perish.
Yet he promised my child marriage to Achilles
And left our household, taking her off to Aulis,
Where the ships anchored, stretched her out above the flames,
Then slit the white throat of my Iphigenia.
Had it been to save our state from being captured,

> Preserve our homes, or protect our other children,
> One death averting many, I'd be forgiving.
> But because Helen proved lustful, and her husband
> Didn't know how to punish his wife's seducer,
> For the sake of these people he destroyed my child.
> In this I was wronged, but for this I would never
> Have behaved like a savage, nor slain my husband,
> But he returned to me with a crazed, god-filled girl,
> And took her into our bed – so the two of us,
> Both of us brides, were lodged in the very same house.[34]

Elsewhere, Phaedra ponders the moral impotence of humanity, not specifically of the 'weaker sex', noting that people may know what virtue is, but not achieve it.[35]

Helen was reviled in every Classical tragedy where her name was mentioned, including those by Euripides.[36] Yet Euripides also wrote an entire play, *Helen*, using the myth that she was not at Troy at all but imprisoned in Egypt, remaining chaste throughout the Trojan War.

Self-sacrifice or martyrdom is the standard way for a woman to achieve renown among men; self-assertion earns a woman an evil reputation. But in Euripides this formula is not so simple. Medea and Hecuba are lavishly provoked. They refuse to be passive, and take a terrible revenge on their tormentors. Medea murders her own children and destroys her husband's new bride and father-in-law with a magic potion Hecuba kills the two children of her son's murderer and blinds their father. The desire for revenge is unfeminine,[37] as had been noted for Sophociles' Antigone; Hecuba is often referred to with masculine adjectives.[38] Her vengeance is considered so ghastly that she ends up metamorphosed into a barking bitch. Medea escapes, but since she clearly had loved her children, one can imagine her perpetual anguish. When I compare Euripidean to Sophoclean heroines, I prefer Euripides' Medea and Hecuba, for they are successful. Deianira, in Sophocles' *Trachinian Women*, naïvely mixes a potion intended to restore her husband's affection for her; instead, the potion tortures and kills him. Antigone courageously and singlemindedly defends her ideals, and is willing to die for them, but her last words dwell not upon her achievements but lament that she dies unwed. Medea and Hecuba are too strong to regret their decisions.

Euripides shows us a number of self-sacrificing heroines who win praise from the traditionally minded. But it seems to me that the playwright does not totally approve of them. Among self-denying young women, Iphigenia is willing to submit to the sacrificial knife, arguing that in wartime 'it is better that one man live to see the light of day than ten thousand women'.[39] Similarly, Polyxena wins the praise of soldiers for the noble way she endures being sacrificed to the ghost of Achilles.[40] Evadne kills herself because she cannot live without her husband,[41] and Helen is expected to do the same if she learned of her husband's death.[42] Alcestis died to prove her love for her husband, and thereby won honour for all women, but her father-in-law suggests that she is foolish.[43] Euripides structures these plays so as to leave us doubtful whether the men for whom the women sacrificed themselves were worth it.

The double standard in sexual morality is implicit in many of the myths Euripides chose as the basis of his plots. He is the first author we know of to look at this topic from both the woman's and the man's point of view. Many husbands are adulterous. Enslaved after the fall of Troy, Andromache laments:

Dearest Hector, I, for your sake, even joined with you in loving, if Aphrodite made you stumble. I often offered my breast to your bastards so as not to exhibit any bitterness to you.[44]

Some wives, notably Medea and Clytemnestra, reacted with overt hostility to their rivals and husbands. Hermione, on the other hand, reasoned that the legitimate wife was in a better position regarding money, the household, and the status of her children and that it was better to have an unfaithful husband than to be unwed.[45] Euripides appears to question the patriarchal axiom that husbands may be polygamous, while wives must remain monogamous, when he shows us Phaedra committing suicide because she merely thought about adultery and points out that women suspected of sexual irregularities are gossiped about, while men are not.[46] Euripides does not advocate that women should have the same sexual freedom as men, but rather suggests that it is better for all concerned if the husband is as monogamous as the wife.

Even when they are not essential to the plot, the horrors of patriarchy compose a background of unremitting female misery. Grotesque marriages or illicit liaisons humiliating or unbearable to women abound in Euripides. Andromache is forced to share the bed of her husband's murderer. Cassandra becomes the concubine of Agamemnon, destroyer of her family and city. Hermione marries Orestes, who had threatened to kill her. Clytemnestra marries Agamemnon, the murderer of her son and first husband. Phaedra is married to the hero who seduced her sister and conquered her country. Alcestis returns from the dead to 'remarry' the husband who let her die in his stead.[47]

Euripides shows us women victimized by patriarchy in almost every possible way. A girl needs both her virginity and a dowry to attract a husband.[48] Women are raped and bear illegitimate children whom they must discard. The women are blamed, while the men who raped them are not.[49] When marriages prove unfruitful, wives are inevitably guilty.[50] Despite the grimness of marriage, spinsterhood is worse.[51]

Women as mothers always arouse sympathy in Euripides. All his women love their children and fight fiercely in their behalf.[52] Even Medea never stopped loving her children, although she murdered them to spite Jason. Women glory especially in being the mothers of sons, and the lamentation of mothers over sons killed in war is a standard feature in Euripides' antiwar plays.[53] Yet in patriarchal society the father is the more precious parent. The suffering of the children of Heracles in the absence of a father is the basic plot of the *Heracleidae*. Mothers whose husbands are dead refer to their children as 'orphans'.[54] Alcestis, when she chooses death, includes in her calculations that her children need a father more than a mother, but expresses some doubt whether he loves them as much as she does.[55]

In subtle ways Euripides reveals an intimacy with women's daily lives remarkable among Classical Greek authors. He knows that upon returning from a party a husband quickly falls asleep, but a wife needs time to prepare for bed. The chorus of Trojan women relates that, on the night Troy was taken. 'My husband lay asleep. . . . But I was arranging my hair in a net looking into the bottomless gleam of the golden mirror, preparing for bed.'[56] Euripides recognizes that childbirth is a painful ordeal, that daughters are best helped by their mothers on these occasions, and that after giving birth women are dishevelled and haggard.[57]

Although the dramatic date is the Bronze Age, the comments of various characters on questions of female etiquette in Euripidean tragedy anachronistically agree with the conventions of Classical Athens: women, especially unmarried ones, should remain indoors;[58] they should not adorn themselves nor go outdoors while their husbands are away, nor should they converse with men in public;[59] out of doors a woman should wear a veil;[60] she should not look at a man in the face, not even her husband.[61]

In the post-Classical period Euripides enjoyed greater popularity than the other tragic poets. His influence can perhaps be detected even among the early Christians who idealized the dying virgin as the most valuable of martyrs, and among whom – in a manner not dissimilar to Euripides' Bacchantes – women spread the worship of a revolutionary cult which challenged established religion.

The women of Sophocles and Aeschylus have a heroic dimension which says little about women in Classical Athens. The women of Euripides are scaled down closer to real life, and in this respect the tragic poetry of Euripides approaches comedy.

Notes

1. Gomme, *op. cit.*; Hadas, *op. cit.*; Kitto, *op. cit.*, pp. 219–36; Seltman, *Women in Antiquity*, pp. 110–11, and 'Status of Women'; and Donald C. Richter, *op. cit.*
2. Soph. *Antigone* 61–62.
3. Candaules' wife: Hdt. 1. 10–13; Artemisia: 8. 87; Amestris: 9. 112. Cf. the vengeance of Tomyris on the corpse of Cyrus: 1. 214.
4. Slater, *op. cit.*
5. Ar. *Birds* 130–32 and *Clouds* 1382–90, 863–64. Ehrenberg, *op. cit.*, p. 197. MARIE-THÉRÈSE CHARLIER and GEORGES RAEPSET, 'Etude d'un comportement social: Les relations entre parents et enfants dans la société athénienne à l'époque classique.'
6. Arist. *Poetics* 15. 4.
7. A. ADLER, *Understanding Human Nature*, pp. 124–5. For an analysis of Clytemnestra as a masculine personality whose motive for murder was jealousy of Agamemnon's power, see R. P. WINNINGTON-INGRAM, 'Clytemnestra and the Vote of Athena.'
8. Eur. *Or.* 553–57.
9. SIMONE DE BEAUVOIR, *The Second Sex*, p. 73 note 8.
10. Hdt. 8. 88, 93.
11. R. JEBB, ed., *Sophocles: Antigone*, p. 91 note 464, p. 124 note 651. Cf. R. KÜHNER and B. GERTH, *Ausführliche Grammatik der Griechischen Sprache*, 2, part I, p. 83.
12. Hdt. 3. 119. Cf. Octavia's refusal to choose between brother and husband in SHAKESPEARE, *Antony and Cleopatra*, III, vi, 15–20.
13. JEBB, *Sophocles: Antigone*, p. 164. See C. M. BOWRA, *Sophoclean Tragedy*, pp. 93–96; A. J. A. WALDOCK, *Sophocles the Dramatist*, pp. 133–42.
14. Deutsch, *op. cit.*, pp. 285–6, 289–92.
15. In the light of the heroine's cruel treatment of the female members of her family, it is surprising to read sentimental judgments of her 'womanly nature,' her absolute valuation of the bonds of blood and affection,' and that she represents 'the all-embracing motherly love' (C. SEGAL, 'Sophocles' Praise of Man and the Conflicts of the *Antigone*,' p. 70). Cf. E. FROMM, *The Forgotten Language*, p. 224.
16. Cf. Eur. *Hipp.* 525–63.
17. A. R. W. HARRISON, *op. cit.*, p. 22; Soph. *Oed. Col.* 830–33.
18. SIGMUND FREUD, *Civilization and Its Discontents*, p. 73.
19. Aesch. *PV* 436–71, 476–506; but cf. Soph. *Oed. Col.* 668–719, where olive culture is included.
20. I owe these suggestions to Froma Zeitlin.
21. Eur. *Med.* 410–29.
22. Translated by Judith Peller Hallett.
23. Aul. Gell. 15. 20.
24. Ath. 13. 557e; cf. 13. 603e.
25. Eur. *Med.* 408–9.
26. Eur. *Or.* 605.
27. Eur. *Med.* 569–73.
28. Eur. *Med.* 285, 319–20.
29. Eur. *Ion* 1025, 1330; *Alc.* 304–19, 463–65.
30. Eur. *Hipp.* 409–10.
31. Eur. *Ion* 617, 844, 1003; *Andr.* 33, 157.
32. Eur. *Hipp.* 616–68. Translated by Judith Peller Hallett.

33. Hom. *Od.* 24. 196–202.
34. Eur. *El.* 1018–34. Translated by Judith Peller Hallett.
35. Eur. *Hipp.* 378–84.
36. E.g., Eur. *Hec.* 941 and *Tro.* 773; *Iph. Taur.* 326, 524; *Rhes.* 261.
37. Eur. *Heracl.* 979.
38. Eur. *Hec.* 237, 511, 1252–53.
39. Eur. *Iph. Aul.* 139.
40. Eur. *Hec.* 545–83.
41. Eur. *Supp.* 990–1071.
42. Eur. *Hel.* 352–56; *Tro.* 1012–14.
43. Eur. *Alc.* 623–24, 728.
44. Eur. *Andr.* 222–25; cf. 465–85, 911; *El.* 945–46, 1033; *Med.* 155–56. The wife of the elder Cato often suckled her slaves' children, so that, by being nursed together, they might feel affection for her own son (Plut. *Cato the Elder* 20. 3).
45. Eur. *Andr.* 1350.
46. Eur. *El.* 1039–40.
47. Eur. *Andr.; Tro.; Or.; Iph. Aul.,* 1148–56; *Hipp.; Alc.*
48. Eur. *Med.* 232–35; *Andr.* 675, 940.
49. The mother of Rhesus in Eur. *Rhes.;* Creusa in *Ion;* Melanippe in the lost *Melanippe the Wise.*
50. Hermione in Eur. *Andr.;* Creusa in *Ion.*
51. Eur. *Iph. Taur.* 219; *Supp.* 790–92; *Heracl.* 523, 579–80, 592–93; *Med.* 233–34.
52. Eur. *Phoen.* 355; *Iph. Aul.* 918; *Andr., passim; Hec., passim.*
53. Eur. *Tro.* 84, 792–85; *Med.* 1090–1115; *Andr.* 720–79; *Hec.* 650–56; *Hel.* 367.
54. Eur. *Supp.* 1132–35.
55. Eur. *Alc.* 303.
56. Eur. *Hec.* 924–26.
57. Eur. *Med.* 250–51; *Phoen.* 355; *Hipp.* 161–69; *Alc.* 315–19; *El.* 1107–8.
58. Eur. *Or.* 107; *Tro.* 646; *Heracl.* 476; *Iph. Aul.* 996.
59. Eur. *El.* 343–44, 1072–75; *Iph. Aul.* 830–34.
60. Eur. *Phoen.* 1485–86.
61. Eur. *Hec.* 975; *Tro.* 654.

The Rope and the Sword*

NICOLE LORAUX

A woman's suicide for a man's death

> For a woman it is already a distressing evil to remain at
> home, abandoned, without a husband. And when suddenly
> one messenger arrives, and then another, always bringing worse
> news, and all proclaiming disaster for the house . . . ! If this man
> had received as many wounds [*traumatōn*] as were reported to his
> home through various channels, his body would now have more
> cuts [*tetrōtai*] than a net has meshes . . . Those were the cruel
> rumours which made me more than once hang my neck in a
> noose, from which I was wrenched only by force.
>
> (Aeschylus, *Agamemnon*, 861–76)

Beyond the lie that the queen handles with consummate skill, there
is a truth, or at least an apparent truth, proper to tragedy, which is
expressed in these words of Clytemnestra as she welcomes Agamemnon
on his return to his palace. The death of a man inevitably calls for the
suicide of a woman, his wife. Why should a woman's death
counterbalance a man's? Because of the heroic code of honour that
tragedy loves to recall, the death of a man could only be that of a
warrior on the field of battle. Thus the children of Agamemnon in the
Choephoroe dream for a moment of what might have been their father's
glorious death under the walls of Troy; and, on merely being told of
her husband's death, his wife, immured in her home, would kill herself
with a noose round her neck. It was as part of this tragic pattern that
Hecuba in the *Troades* (1012–14) was bitterly to rebuke Helen because
nobody had ever 'surprised her in the act of hanging up a noose or
sharpening a dagger as a noble-hearted woman [*gennaia gynē*] would
have done in mourning her first husband'.

* Reprinted from *Tragic Ways of Killing a Woman*, trans. ANTHONY FORSTER
(Cambridge, Mass., and London: Harvard University Press, 1987).

Of course Clytemnestra did not kill herself, any more than her sister Helen did. Not only was the queen no Penelope (even though in her lying speech she speaks of her eyes burning with tears as she lay sleepless, crying for her absent husband), but she was also no ordinary tragic wife. Clytemnestra did not kill herself, and it was Agamemnon who was to die, ensnared in her veil and his body pierced with wounds. She turned death away from herself and brought it upon the king, just as Medea, instead of killing herself, was to kill Jason indirectly through his children and his newly-wed wife.[1] In Clytemnestra, the mother of Iphigenia and the mistress of Aegisthus triumphed over the king's wife. The murdering queen denied the law of femininity, that in the extreme of misery a knotted rope should provide the way out.[2]

A death devoid of male courage

Finding a way out in suicide was a tragic solution, one that was morally disapproved in the normal run of everyday life. But, most important, it was a woman's solution and not, as has sometimes been claimed, a heroic act.[3] That the hero Ajax, both in Sophocles and in the epic tradition, killed himself was one thing; that he killed himself in a virile manner was another, and I shall come back to this. But to infer from this example that in the Greek imagination all suicide was inspired by *andreia* (the Greek word for courage as a male characteristic) is a step we should not take. Heracles in Euripides without doubt conforms much more to the traditional ethic when, from the depths of his disasters, he agrees to go on living.[4] In the case of mere citizens, things are even clearer. Nothing was further from suicide than the hoplites' imperative of a 'fine death', which must be accepted and not sought.[5] We know that after the battle of Plataea the Spartan Aristodamus was deprived by his fellow citizens of the posthumous glory of appearing on the roll of valour because he had sought death too openly in action. Whether he were a Spartan or not, a warrior committed suicide only when struck by dishonour, as Othryadas did in book I of Herodotus and Pantites in book VII. Plato in the *Laws* echoes these practices; he is prescribing laws but is loyal to civic conventions when he lays down that the suicide should be formally punished, 'for total lack of manliness', by being buried in a solitary and unmarked grave on the edge of the city, in the darkness of anonymity (IX.873c–d). I would add (and it is relevant) that the Greek language, in the absence of a special word for suicide, describes the act by resorting to the same words as are used for the murder of parents, that ultimate ignominy.[6]

Suicide, then, could be the tragic death chosen under the weight of necessity by those on whom fell 'the intolerable pain of a misfortune from which there is no way out'.[7] But in tragedy itself it was mainly a woman's death. There was one form of suicide – an already despised form of death – that was more disgraceful and associated more than any other with irremediable dishonour. This was hanging, a hideous death, or more exactly a 'formless' death (*aschēmōn*), the extreme of defilement that one inflicted on oneself only in the utmost shame.[8] It also turns out – but is it just chance? – that hanging is a woman's way of death: Jocasta, Phaedra, Leda, Antigone ended in this way, while outside tragedy there were deaths of innumerable young girls who hanged themselves, to give rise to a special cult or to illustrate the mysteries of female physiology.[9]

Hanging was a woman's death. As practised by women, it could lead to endless variations, because women and young girls contrived to substitute for the customary rope those adornments with which they decked themselves and which were also the emblems of their sex, as Antigone strangled herself with her knotted veil. Veils, belts, head-bands – all these instruments of seduction were death traps for those who wore them, as the suppliant Danaids explained to King Pelasgus.[10] To borrow Aeschylus' powerful expression, there was here a fine trick, *mēchanē kalē*, by which erotic *peithō* (persuasion) became the agent of the most sinister threat.

I am not going to dwell here on women's relation to *mētis*, that very Greek concept of cunning intelligence. Yet this is a good moment to recall that, even when a woman was armed with a sword to kill herself or another, every action of hers was likely to be covered by the vocabulary of cunning. Thus, in the *Agamemnon*, in order to suggest the murderous designs of Clytemnestra as she sharpened her sword for use against her husband, Cassandra quite unexpectedly resorts to the imagery of poison mixed in a cup. But the text of the *Oresteia* will soon substitute a very real snare, the garment that will imprison Agamemnon as in a net – a bold materialization of every metaphor concerning *mētis*. The same logic is at work in the *Trachiniae*. Without meaning to, Deianira has caught Heracles in the poisoned trap of Nessus' shirt. She straightway turns to the sword for a quick death and her release, but even so her suicide can still be construed, if only momentarily, as the product of cunning intelligence.[11]

Against this ensnaring *mētis*, which works in the words and actions of women and weaves the meshes of death or busily tightens knots, tragedy sets up in contrast the weapons that cut and tear, those that draw blood. This brings us back to the Suppliants of Aeschylus and their drive toward hanging. As a last resort in their headlong flight from the sons of Aegyptus, the deadly rope would protect the Danaids against the violent desire of the male, just as hurling themselves from the top of a steep rock (something they dreamed for a moment of doing) would have kept them safe from marriage, that prison where the husband is only a master. But it is significant that they give this master the name of *daiktor*, which does not mean 'ravisher' (as an influential translation has it) but, very precisely, 'tearer'.[12] From this tearing – which clearly refers to rape or deflowering – there are only two ways of escape: either the death of the Danaids by the rope, resulting in defilement of the city, or their survival at the cost of a war that would spill the blood of men 'on behalf of women' (*Supplices* 476–7). The Danaids did not hang themselves. We know the result – marriage arranged in the end, a wedding night ending in bloodshed, fatal for the husbands, and later punishment in Hades. But that is another story.

The gash in the man's body

If we are to believe Euripides, Thanatos (Death) was armed with a sword. This was certainly not pure chance. If death, the same for all, makes no distinction between its victims and cuts the hair of men and women alike, it was for Thanatos, the male incarnation of death, to carry the sword, the emblem of a man's demise.[13]

A man worthy of the name could die only by the sword or the spear of another, on the field of battle. The Menelaus of Euripides was an inglorious character, being the only warrior to come back from Troy without even a trace of a wound suffered in close combat, the only wound that made a man complete.[14] Even in human sacrifice, an act that was corrupt from every point of view, the executioner had to be a man, especially when the victim was a male. There is proof of this in *Iphigenia in Tauris*, where Orestes questions the sister whom he has not yet recognized: 'Would you, a woman, strike men with a sword?' and Iphigenia assures him in reply that there is a male killer (*sphageus*) in the sanctuary to carry out the task.[15]

Even suicide in tragedy obeys this firm rule, that a man must die at a man's hand, by the sword and with blood spilt. In Sophocles, as in Pindar, Ajax kills himself by the sword, faithful till the end to his status as a hero who lives and dies in war, where wounds are given and received in an exchange that, on the whole, is subject to rules. So Ajax kills himself, but in the manner of a warrior.[16] Pierced by the blade with which he identifies himself (*Ajax* 650–1), he tears open his side on the sword that, in staging his own death, he makes into an actor: 'the killer [*sphageus*] is there,' he says, 'standing upright so that he can slice as cleanly as possible.'[17] Ajax's sword is a basic signifier in Sophocles' play, recurring at each step in the metaphorical texture of the tragedy and serving to bind it together. If it is the warrior's sword itself that becomes the healing blade that Ajax invokes in his prayers, there are also in a figurative sense many other swords in the *Ajax*, such as the words that have been sharpened like steel and 'cut the living flesh'. No wonder then that, at the sight of the hero's corpse, the sharp blade of grief pierced Tecmessa 'to the liver'.[18]

I shall say no more about Ajax's sword. Others before me have discussed it ably, sometimes brilliantly like Jean Starobinski.[19] Nor shall I dwell on the theme of spilt blood, even though it is central to the *Ajax*, for there is another of Sophocles' heroes to make the point that a man's suicide is inevitably bloody. This is the betrothed of Antigone, whose death is announced punningly in words that cannot adequately be translated: 'Haemon is dead; his own hand has drenched him in blood.'[20] It is enough to recall that the name Haemon is only too like the word for blood (*haima*). In this way the son of Creon, pierced by his own sword, fulfills the prophecy of his own name and dies like a man.

Hanging or *sphagē*

There is a word that must now be mentioned, because it is obsessively present in Greek tragedy and is insistently opposed to the language of hanging. This word is *sphagē*, which means sacrificial throat-cutting, and also the gash and the blood that flows from it. Together with the verb *sphazō* and its derivatives, it is of course used to indicate sacrifices – the sacrifice of Iphigenia in Aeschylus and Euripides, but also in Euripides that of Macaria in the *Heraclidae*, of Polyxena in the *Hecuba* and the *Troades*, of Menoeceus in the *Phoenissae*, and finally of the daughters of Erechtheus offered to their country by way of *sphagia* (*Ion* 278). Up to this point there is nothing abnormal to note, or scarcely so. But, from Aeschylus through Sophocles to Euripides, *sphazō* and *sphagē* are also used to denote murder within the family of the Atreides. Moreover, the same words are used to describe a suicide when it is stained with blood, such as the suicides of Ajax, Deianira, and Eurydice. In order to justify this slight deviation from the usual meaning, can one call on some principle of semantic looseness in the character of tragic speech? Is *sphazō* to be lumped together with words that are more neutral or descriptive like *schizō* and *daizō*, which imply tearing of the body?[21] This would be a misunderstanding of the verbal rigour of Greek tragedy, which twists language only for a very definite purpose, such as to upset the normal categories. It is better to trust in the strong sacrificial sense of these words and to notice that *sphazō*, *sphagē*, and *sphagion*, terms laden with religious values, do not signify in tragedy just any throat-cutting murder or suicide, but the long series of 'murders that result from the application of the blood law' in the family of the Atreides, or the self-inflicted death of Eurydice at the foot of the altar of Zeus Herkeios.[22] More generally, *sphagē* is used to characterize death by the sword as a 'pure' death in opposition to hanging.[23]

No sooner have we recalled this difference between two modes of death, one male and the other female, than we are forced to admit that the distinction is in fact violated in the 'virile' deaths of Deianira and Eurydice, who plunge swords into their bodies. And in Euripides there is no lack of heroines who, as they contemplate death, prefer the sword to the rope. Thus Electra, as she mounts guard at the door of the house where Clytemnestra is being murdered, brandishes a sword, ready to turn it on herself if the enterprise should fail (*Electra* 688, 695–6). (Conversely, in Euripides there are men who die fatally strangled, in the manner of women. Thus Hippolytus, entangled in the reins of his horses, was smashed against the rocks by the roadside.[24] However, as far as men were concerned, it must be said that this irregular form of death was evidently less frequent.)

The confusion in tragedy that consists in giving a man's death to a woman is not a matter of chance. Let us take the death of Jocasta in the *Phoenissae*. In Sophocles, as we all know, as soon as Jocasta came to see the truth about Oedipus, she hanged herself, as a woman overwhelmed by a crushing misfortune. The Jocasta of Euripides did not hang herself. She survived the revelation of her incest and it was the death of her sons that killed her, as she turned on herself the sword that had killed them.[25] This was a remarkable departure from a tradition that had been well established since Homer and the hanging of Epicaste (Jocasta). Should one attribute this innovation, as some do, to a change in outlook that had become increasingly hostile to death by hanging?[26] There is really nothing to support this hypothesis: ever since the *Odyssey* (XXII.462–4), the rope dealt the impurest of deaths, and one cannot see how attitudes could have developed on this point. But above all one should read the text of Euripides beside that of Sophocles, and one will see that the *Phoenissae* brings a whole new interpretation of the character of Jocasta. She is no longer, as she is in Sophocles, above all a wife; she is exclusively a mother,[27] and her manly death should be seen as a consequence of this critical reshaping of the tradition.

Starting from this example and several others, I offered in an earlier publication a generalization about women's deaths in tragedy, to the effect that hanging was associated with marriage – or rather, with an excessive valuation of the status of bride (*nymphē*) – while a suicide that shed blood was associated with maternity, through which a wife, in her 'heroic' pains of childbirth, found complete fulfilment.[28] I still abide by that reading. However, I shall not return to it, for it is simply the confusion as such that interests me here, and more particularly the many statements in Euripides that seem to assume that the rope and the sword come to the same thing.

The rope or the sword – in brief, death at any price, whatever the method. That is the way manlike women, who would in general prefer the sword, reason in a desperate situation. It is also the way women who are overfeminine boast when, like Hermione, they will not dare even to hang themselves. But, in either case, the way the text runs makes it perfectly clear what would be the real choice for the particular woman in despair – the sword or the rope. It is this choice that the chorus leaves to Admetus, in face of the imminent death of Alcestis, saying that 'a misfortune of this kind justifies cutting one's throat [*sphagē*] or slipping a noose round one's neck' – a simple way of indicating that, having avoided death, a womanish man would not be able to escape the distress that breaks women's spirits.[29]

Paradoxically, as these few examples have already suggested, the confusion even at its very height aims only to reinforce the standard opposition. So it is with Helen in the play that bears her name, summoning death in her prayers: 'I shall put my neck in a deadly, dangling noose, or in a mighty effort I shall sink the whole blade of a sword in my flesh, and its murderous thrust will open up a stream of blood from my throat, and I will sacrifice myself to the three goddesses' (353–7). As the final outcome indicates, the only possibility that Helen sees as truly worthy of her is *sphagē*; but, on closer inspection, the choice was already revealed through the very words in which Helen spoke of hanging herself, and especially in the expression *phonion aiōrēma* (353), the untranslatable and contradictory 'gory suspension' that translators cover up as best they can, because in their view the distinctive feature of hanging is that no blood flows.[30] But it is precisely in this oxymoron that one can and must guess what the heroine's choice will be. For her no death can be considered that does not shed blood, and her words reject hanging at the very moment that she mentions its possibility. *Phonion aiōrēma*: proclaiming in advance the blood of the *sphagē*, Helen's language runs ahead of her thought.

At the end of this inquiry, therefore, the contrast between the rope and the sword stands more strongly than ever. But certain facts must be clearly understood. A man never hangs himself, even when he has thought of doing so;[31] a man who kills himself does it in a manly way. For a woman, however, there is an alternative. She can seek a womanly way of ending her life, by the noose, or she can steal a man's death by seizing a sword. Is this a matter of identification, of personal coherence in her character within the play? Perhaps. The imbalance is nonetheless obvious, proving, if proof were needed, that the genre of tragedy can easily create and control a confusion of categories, and also knows the limits it cannot cross. To put it another way, the woman in tragedy is more entitled to play the man in her death than the man is to assume any aspect of woman's conduct, even in his manner of death. For women there is liberty in tragedy – liberty in death.

The wife in flight

As there is an alternative open to women, and as some of them choose the ways of femininity to the very end, the question of hanging and of the values associated with it deserves a little more attention.

Beyond the vocabulary of *mētis* and the judgment that it inevitably involves a death where the victim is trapped in her own snare, there is another word that deserves our attention because it describes and suggests rather than judges. The word *aiōra* (or *eōra*) evokes a double image, of a corpse hanging in the air, and of its movement, a gentle swaying.[32] *Aiōra* was in fact the name of a festival at Athens in which representations of hanging were associated with a game on a swing. This religious Aiora is not itself in question here, but rather the visual image induced by the use of the word in tragedy. *Aiōra* of Jocasta and *aiorēma* of Helen: Oedipus has forced open the door that Jocasta had carefully closed on herself, and now everyone can see the woman hanging, 'caught in the noose that swings' (*plektais eōrais empeplegmenēn*). For Helen, equally, who did not hang herself, hanging was summed up in the term *aiorēma*. It is at this point that the reader of tragedies recalls the word from another context, of the woman who throws herself to her death. In the *Suppliant Women* of Euripides, as Evadne prepares to hurl herself into the fire from the top of an airy rock (*aitheria petra*) that dominates the funeral pyre of her husband, Capaneus, she cries: 'Here I am on this rock, like a bird, above the pyre of Capaneus, I rise lightly, upward on a deadly swing [*aiorēma*]' (1045–7).

Aiorēma signifies both the swaying of the hanged woman and the soaring flight of Evadne, and we should pause at this: in the language of tragedy there is a thematic relationship between hanging and throwing oneself to one's death. This may seem surprising. The woman who has hanged herself has certainly thrown herself into the void, but her body has left the ground – it is supported, now, by the roof. To throw oneself down, on the other hand, is to fall into the depths (*bathy ptōma*). The same word, *aeirō*, which means elevation and suspension, applies to these two flights in opposite directions, upward and downward, as though height had its own depth: as though the place below – whether it be the ground, or the world under that – could be reached only by first rising up.[33] Strange as it may seem, this is the logic that alone makes sense of the association between these two ways of rising, an association that recurs in the 'escape odes', those lyrical pieces in which often the chorus and sometimes that tragic heroine, overwhelmed by events, voice their desire for a merciful flight into death. The *Supplices* of Aeschylus may be mentioned here, and the *Hippolytus* of Euripides, and there are many other texts as well. The vital point is that for both movements the same image returns – that of winged flight and, explicitly, the flight of a bird. If Evadne is a bird, so is Phaedra – recently a bird of ill omen, and now a pathetic bird escaped from the hands of Theseus. Falling from the heights of a rock or held in the noose, it makes no difference: Evadne and Phaedra have taken flight, forever. There are women, too, who go no further than dreaming of flight, such as Hermione, who in her desire for death wishes she were a bird; or the Danaids, distraught at the approach of men; or again the women of the chorus in *Iphigenia in Tauris* or *Helen*, wingless halcyons burning with regret for their far-off country.[34]

The bird is in tragedy an operator that stands for escape, and because it presents a concrete image of flight, it provides several suggestions on what is said about women in connection with hanging.[35] These wives (who were properly represented in everyday life as sedentary) show in their propensity for flight a kind of natural rapport with the beyond: there they are, throwing themselves into the air and hanging between earth and sky. Again, a misfortune was enough to make them escape from a man, abandoning his life, and their own, as abruptly as they left the stage. Identified as he was with the hoplite model, a man had to hold his ground and face death head on, as Ajax at his end rejoins the earth, fastened to it by his sword, which is at once fixed in the ground and plunged to its hilt in his body.

For women, death is an exit. *Bebēke*, 'she is gone', is said of a woman who dies or has killed herself. It is said of Alcestis, and of Evadne, who with a leap (*bebēke pēdēsasa*) left her father's house to reach the rock from which she was to throw herself, with another leap, the last (*pēdēsasa*). Theseus, too, as he mourns the death of Phaedra, who 'like a bird escaped from one's hands has disappeared', cries out: 'A sudden leap [*pēdēma*] has carried you off to Hades.'[36] But one must remember about these heroines that, although for a woman death is always a movement, the only ones to take flight are those who are too feminine. In fact the announcement of the death of Deianira, who preferred the sword to the rope, starts as one might expect, but ends on an unusual note: 'She has gone, Deianira, on her last journey, her very last, on motionless foot [*Bebēke . . . ex akinētou podos*]' (*Trachiniae* 874–5).

The motionless foot of Deianira may be (as Jebb has suggested) something like a proverbial euphemism for death, a way of indicating that the journey and the road are purely metaphorical . . . I myself would prefer to see the phrase, in its opposition to the flight implied in *aiōra*, as a way of suggesting, even before the chorus speculates on how she died, that Heracles' wife has not fled by hanging herself, and that she has died like a soldier. But, conversely, we must come back to the martial suicide of Ajax: Sophocles, in his treatment of this death, still manages to remind us that for a man suicide is a deviation. The hero's death was indeed a manly one, with this difference, that it was the sword that stood (*hestēken*) in the hoplite's place: Ajax transfixed himself on it, hurling himself with a swift leap, and it is no surprise that this leap is called a *pēdēma*.[37]

This is a good place to notice again that, if in tragedy male and female behaviour can disregard the division of humanity into men and women, this shift is not an accident, since it serves to show how each character – whether by conformity or by deviation – lives out a destiny as an individual man or woman. There are dimensions of both reality and imagination to these lives, while the city would like to make them fundamentally a matter of social reality.

In any case, whether they are womanly or manlike, women have at their disposal a way of dying in which they remain entirely feminine. It is the way they have of acting out their suicide, offstage. It is meticulously prepared, it is hidden from the spectators' view, and it is in its main details recounted orally. The staging in Sophocles even follows a standard sequence – a silent exit, a choral chant, and then the announcement by a messenger that, out of sight, the woman has killed herself.

Silence and secrecy

Silence is the adornment of women. Sophocles said so, and Aristotle repeated it. In Euripides, Macaria, as she prepares to take an active role, makes a point of showing her awareness of this sentiment, remarking that the best thing for a woman is not to leave the closed interior of her house.[38] But women in tragedy have become involved in men's world of action and have suffered for it. So, silently, the heroines of Sophocles return to die in the home that they had left behind. Silence of Deianira under the accusations of Hyllos; heavy silence of Eurydice, in which the chorus correctly divines a hidden threat; half-silence of Jocasta, with ambiguous words and a voice that finally dies away.[39]

These silences, which are heard as expressions of anguish, precede an action that the woman wants to hide from view. Phaedra has made herself invisible (*aphantos*) and Deianira has disappeared (*dieistōsen*): she has organized, one might say, her final disappearance, which takes her far from mortal view to the invisible world of Hades, away from all eyes, even those in the palace where she has taken refuge.[40] In the same way Jocasta and Phaedra hide behind closed doors, which are hermetically sealed on death – an obstacle that puts the body, in hanging, into a double prison. Oedipus has to throw himself against the door, Theseus has to storm and beg that the bolts be drawn back,[41] so that at last they can see their wives – dead. The spectators did not see Jocasta's body, but they do see Phaedra's, and that of Eurydice, revealed to them and Creon at the same time. It was for the messenger to emphasize the effect: 'You can see her; for she is no longer in her retreat [*en mychois*].'[42]

An astonishing interplay of the seen and the hidden, by which we do not see a woman's death, but do see the dead woman. Then, as though the last ban had been lifted on staring at this mournful scene, the dramatic action could continue – even, as it does in the *Hippolytus*, centre itself on the corpse of the dead woman and her silent presence. Phaedra had disappeared, but her corpse was there, released from the fatal noose to be laid out on the ground as was seemly – the corpse which she had wanted to make into evidence against Hippolytus and which, though silent forever, yet bore the message of the absent woman.[43] That was, without the shadow of a doubt, a very feminine way of exploiting one's own death. In the case of Ajax, whose dead body was at least as important a dramatic element as that of Phaedra, things are very different, and what is seen and what is hidden do not bear at all the same relation to one another. As Ajax is the model of the manly suicide, it follows that he has the right to kill himself in front of the spectators;[44] but because his death is only a poor imitation of a warrior's noble death, there is a ban on seeing his body. Indeed, before the leaders of the Greek army start to discuss whether the dead body would be appropriately hidden in a tomb, Tecmessa and then Teucer have each taken good care to cover up a sight that was as painful as it was improper.[45]

Finally, there is the very special oscillation between revelation and concealment that occurs in the case of Alcestis, who dies in place of a man. Alcestis dies onstage, and her body, first carried inside the palace and then brought back, is displayed onstage again for a long *prothesis* (exposure) before the funeral cortège (*ekphora*) takes it out of sight – for good, the chorus supposes; and it is true that, without the intervention of Heracles, Alcestis would certainly have disappeared forever.[46] But she was an exception, the only woman not to reach Hades. We will confine ourselves to the host of women in tragedy who go away and never return.

In the *Thalamos*: death and marriage

Let us come back to the door of that closed place where a woman takes
refuge to die, far out of sight. With its solid bolts that have to be forced
back for the dead woman to be reached – or rather the dead body from
which the woman has already fled – this room reveals the narrow space
that tragedy grants to women for the exercise of their freedom. They
are free enough to kill themselves, but they are not free enough to
escape from the space to which they belong, and the remote sanctum
where they meet their death is equally the symbol of their life – a life
that finds its meaning outside the self and is fulfilled only in the
institutions of marriage and maternity, which tie women to the world
and lives of men. It is by men that women meet their death, and it is
for men, usually, that they kill themselves.[47] By a man, for a man: not
all texts make the distinction, but Sophocles is particularly careful to
mark it – in the *Antigone*, where Eurydice dies *for* her sons but *because*
of Creon, and in the *Trachiniae*, where Deianira dies *because* of Hyllos
but *for* love of Heracles. So the death of women confirms or
reestablishes their connection with marriage and maternity.

The place where women kill themselves, to give it its name, is the
marriage chamber, the *thalamos*. Deianira plunges into it, as does
Jocasta. Alcestis sheds her last tears there before facing Thanatos; and
when she leaves the palace to die, it is toward this place that she turns
her thoughts and her regrets. As for the funeral pyre of Capaneus, on to
which Evadne hurls herself to renew her union in the flesh with her
husband, it is described as *thalamai* (funeral chamber), a word that
encapsulates the many connections of her death with marriage.[48]

If the *thalamos* is in the depths of the house, there is also within the
thalamos the bed (*lechos*), scene of the pleasure that the institution of
marriage tolerates if it is not excessive and, above all, the place of
procreation. No death of a woman takes place without involving the
bed. It is there, and there alone, that Deianira and Jocasta are able,
before suicide, to affirm their identity to themselves.[49] It is there that
Deianira even dies, on that couch that she had too much associated
with the pleasures of the *nymphē*. Even when a woman kills herself like
a man, she nevertheless dies in her bed, like a woman.

Finally, by fastening the rope to the ceiling of the marriage chamber,
Jocasta and Phaedra call attention to the symbolic framework of the
house. The rooftree, which the *Odyssey* called *melathron*, Euripides
calls *teramna*. By metonymy it can mean the palace considered in its
dimension of verticality; but it goes even further. From Sappho's
epithalamium ('Come, carpenters, lift up the rooftree [*melathron*],
Hymenaeus, for here enters the house a bridegroom the equal of Ares')

to Euripides, the roof seems to have been much connected with the husband, whose tall stature it dominates and protects.[50] One might perhaps recall that Clytemnestra, in her irreproachable speech that is also a total lie, called Agamemnon 'the column sustaining the high roof' (*Agamemnon* 897–8). Just before a woman leaps into the void, it is the missing presence of the man that she feels for the last time, in every corner of the *thalamos*.

To die with . . .

It is no wonder, then, if many of these solitary deaths were thought of as ways of dying with one's husband. To die with: a form in death of *synokein*, 'to live with', which was one of the commonest expressions in Greek to mean marriage.[51]

To die with . . . It was certainly not the fate that Clytemnestra sought, for she much preferred to live with Aegisthus than to die. However, it was the lot that Orestes, with cutting irony, singled out for Clytemnestra when, just before striking her, he told her to go and sleep in death with the man she loved and preferred to her own husband. A just turn of events in the logic of the *Oresteia*, a just retribution for the death of Cassandra at Agamemnon's side, a death that a short while back Clytemnestra had presented as the fate deserved by a mistress.[52] To die with . . . The fate that, in the *Oresteia*, is imposed on women by the logic of murder becomes, in the case of female suicides, the object of a will that seems at once like love and like despair. The moment Deianira knows that disaster is on its way, she announces to her confidantes, the women of Trachis, her intention of joining Heracles in death: 'I have decided that, if misfortune befalls him, I too shall die with him, in the same impulse, the same moment' (*Trachiniae* 719–20). This is a firm intention, expressed four times within the same line, and she will carry it out in every respect, except that the word 'with' will have meaning only for herself. Because she robs Heracles of a man's death, the hero when he is laid low will deny her, condemning her beyond death to the solitude that was her lot in life. Euripides' Helen, too, should be mentioned, who does not die but talks much of dying. Like the virtuous Helen of Stesichorus in her Egyptian exile[53] she swears that, if Menelaus dies, she will kill herself with the same sword and rest at her husband's side. Finally, as any conduct has its extremes, Evadne deserves a special mention, who, in a bacchantic ecstasy of conjugal love, turned the funeral pyre of Capaneus into a shared tomb. Not content with aspiring to die with the man who was dear to her, she dreamed of annihilation in an erotic union of their two bodies: 'In the burning flame I shall mingle my corpse with my husband's, resting close against him. flesh to flesh.'[54]

To die with . . . A tragic way for a woman to go to the extreme limit of marriage, by, it must be said, drastically reordering events, since it is in death that 'living with' her husband will be achieved. Yet there is one woman, a mother rather than a wife – or, more precisely, a mother to excess – who displaces 'dying with' in the direction of maternity. I mean the Jocasta of Euripides, who, in keeping with her destiny as an incestuous mother, dies with the death of her sons and, 'dead, rests on her well-loved ones, embracing them both in her arms'.[55] This is how in the *Phoenissae* Euripides reconstructs the story of Jocasta, who, by marrying her son, mingled marriage with motherhood and so could die only as a mother. Moreover the men to whom women offer up their deaths can represent either of two relationships, as we have seen; and when it comes to dying, a Eurydice may prefer death for her sons' sake to life with her husband. Jocasta is original because she 'dies with' those whom she brought into the world, killing herself on their bodies, at the very place where they died in battle.

The glory of women

The time has come to bring out what tragedy's treatment of the death of women borrows from socially accepted norms in classical Athens, and what separates it from them. What is at stake is the thorny question of the 'glory of women' (*kleos gynaikōn*); even the most routine formulation of this is not entirely covered by Pericles' terse declaration.

The funerary epitaphs, which represent a traditional ethic, are not so uncompromising, where women's glory is concerned, as the radicalism of Pericles in his funeral speech. The idea is not completely strange to them, but this glory, which is always subordinated to a career as a 'good wife', often merges into feminine 'worth' (*aretē*). This means that the glory of women is often mentioned in a tentative, not to say reticent, manner. Female worth is never confused with real worth, which belongs to men and in their case needs no further specification. There is no male worth, there is simply *aretē* itself.

Listen to the words of mourning in their orthodox form:

Supposing that feminine virtue still exists in the human race, she partook of it

cautiously says an epitaph from Amorgos; and an inscription from the Piraeus goes further:

Glykera was found to have a double gift, which is rare in women's nature – virtue allied to chastity.

In the praise and admiration of mankind that are sometimes accorded to a wife, her death, that final accident, counts for nothing and the life she led for everything. This is the sentiment in another epitaph from the Piraeus:

What is in the world the highest praise for a woman Chairippe received in the fullest measure, when she died.

Still more explicit is the epitaph engraved on the tomb of an Athenian woman:

It was you, Anthippe, who in the world had the most acclaim open to women. Now that you are dead, you have it still.

So much for the daily glory of women. This may have been, for Athens, substantial, but it is also very little. It is true that 'good' wives are not material for tragedy.

This does not mean that women in tragedy are not wives. But they are wives in their deaths – and apparently only in their deaths, because only their deaths belong to them, and in them they bring their marriages to fulfilment. It follows that we can take two views of their deaths, contradictory but at the same time complementary. The first, which is attuned to traditional values, holds that in fulfilling themselves as spouses in their deaths the heroines of tragedy are confirming tradition at the very moment that they are innovating. The second view, which is anxious to lay hold of anything in tragedy that tends to support the 'women's side',[56] takes the point that wives in death win a renown that goes far beyond the praise traditionally granted to their sex. It is not necessary to choose one view over the other: each has its truth, and in fact it is impossible not to accept, in each case, both at once. This is what is meant by ambiguity, and there must have been an ambiguous thrill to the *katharsis* when, during a tragic performance, male citizens watched with emotion the suffering of these heroic women, represented onstage by other male citizens dressed in women's clothes. Women's glory in tragedy was an ambiguous glory.

Take the case of Alcestis, an exemplary figure in this interpretation of marriage through death. The chorus readily says of her that 'of all women she behaved the best towards her husband'. Her last word is to say to her husband 'farewell' (*chaire*), just like those fair effigies on the stelae in Athenian cemeteries. And yet this irreproachable figure of Alcestis strikingly shows the way in which the glory of women is always twisted. Alcestis was devoted, loving, and virtuous, but she

earned her 'glorious death' only through the male qualities of courage
and endurance. Since a fine death is essentially virile and the loyal wife
has taken the man's place, this *tolma* has the recoil effect of feminizing
the well-loved husband. He is driven to become the mother as well as
the father of their children, and condemned to live henceforward
cloistered like a virgin or chaste as a bride inside the palace, which
his wife has left to join in death the open spaces of manly heroism.[57]

The glory of Evadne is also very ambiguous. She wants to die as both
wife and warrior. To honour her marriage the wife of Capaneus seeks
death like some equivocal hoplite who has strayed from the scene of
battle. She stands on the steep rock, longing for a tomb to share with
her husband and anxious that all Argos should know of her fate, yet
decked like a woman who wants to seduce – like a *nymphē* perhaps.
As a result, the victory that she claims as her due takes her far beyond
the limits of her sex, which usually makes its mark at the loom or by a
prudent reserve. When Evadne maintains that her victory is one of *aretē*,
neither the woman nor the warrior in her seems to get much from it.
For the chorus, made up of mothers in mourning, does not really
believe either in her virtue as a woman, which is tainted by excess,
or in her courage, whose 'virility' is unseemly in the good wife she
professes to be.[58]

There is also the belated glory of Deianira, who waits until she has
committed the irreparable act before proclaiming her wish for a good
reputation (*Trachiniae* 721–2). Above all, there is the strange paradox of
Phaedra's glory. As infatuated with glory as she was with Hippolytus,
Pheadra dies for having lost her reputation as the wife of Theseus. But
her death, which she stages in the noble manner, is still an act of *mētis*:
the noose she ties round her neck is to prove a trap for Hippolytus, the
written note she leaves is to proclaim a false story. Yet her name will
achieve renown, because of this love, which she thought would ruin
her honour, and because of this disastrous death. This is the height of
contradiction. Of course Aphrodite had a hand in all this, but Phaedra
herself was to a great extent responsible.[59]

In the matter of femininity, tragedy is two-faced . . . Although they are
'out of place', the glories of these women give food for thought; they
are to be listened to and seen. Yet, whether excessive or inadequate as
wives, Phaedra, Deianira, Alcestis, and Evadne still die within the orbit
of marriage. We should accept that tragedy constantly disturbs the
norm in the interest of the deviant, but at the same time we must be
aware that under the deviant the norm is often silently present. So we
have tried out two possible readings at once. One of them draws up a
list of all the distortions that, in a system of values, can be applied to
those values; the other lends an ear to the occasional dissenting voice in
the unison of Greek *logoi* about women.

Notes

1. Compare EURIPIDES, *Medea* 39–40 and 379.
2. The knot of the rope (*brochos*) makes real the metaphorical knot of misfortune. Compare *Hipploytus* 671 and 781.
3. A. KATSOURIS ('The Suicide Motive in Ancient Drama', *Dioniso*, 47 [1956]: 5–36) asserts this, although he cannot avoid admitting (p. 9) that in tragedy the majority of suicides were committed by women.
4. It is worth remembering that traditionally Ajax is the only male hero to carry a suicide through to the end. The interpretation of Heracles' choice proposed here contradicts that of JACQUELINE DE ROMILLY ('Le refus du suicide dans l'Héraclès d'Euripide', *Arkhaiognosia*, 1 [1980]: 1–10.
5. This shows all the difference between a wish of reason (*ethelō*) and an inclination (*boulomai*). See NICOLE LORAUX, *The Invention of Athens* (Cambridge, Mass.: Harvard University Press, 1986), pp. 102–4, and, on Aristodamus (Herodotus IX.71), 'La belle mort spartiate', *Ktema*, 2 (1977): 105–20. It should be noted that, in *Le suicide* (new edn., Paris: Presses Universitaires de France, 1981, p. 374), EMILE DURKHEIM interprets Aristodamus' death as a suicide. Othryadas: Herodotus 1.82; Pantites: Herodotus VII.232.
6. For example, *autophons* and *autocheir*. The overdetermination suicide/death in combat/family murder is particularly clear in the single combat between the sons of Oedipus. See AESCHYLUS, *Seven against Thebes* 850; SOPHOCLES, *Antigone* 172; EUIPIDES, *Phoenissae* 880. Other examples are AESCHYLUS, *Agamemnon* 1091; EURIPIDES, *Orestes* 947; and SOPHOCLES, *Antigone* 1175. See also the commentary of L. GERNET on book IX of Plato's *Laws* (Paris: Ernest Leroux, 1917), p. 162 (873c5–6).
7. This is one of the extenuating circumstances envisaged by PLATO in his condemnation of suicide (*Laws* IX.873c5–6).
8. Shame: PLATO, *Laws* IX.873e6; ugliness of hanging: EURIPIDES, *Helen* 298–302; defilement: SOPHOCLES, *Antigone* 54 (*lōbē*), also AESCHYLUS *Supplices* 473 (*miasma* in a system of suicide as revenge); dishonour: EURIPIDES, *Helen* 134–6, 200–2, 686–7 (death of Leda).
9. As it closes forever the too open bodies of women, hanging is almost latent in feminine physiology. See NICOLE LORAUX, 'Le corps étranglé', in *Le châtiment dans la cité*, ed. Y. THOMAS (Rome and Paris: Ecole Française de Rome, 1984), pp. 195–218.
10. SOPHOCLES, *Antigone* 1220–2; AESCHYLUS, *Supplices* 455–66.
11. Poison: *Agamemnon* 1260–3. The veil as net: ibid., 1382–3, 1492, 1580, 1611; *Choephoroe* 981–2, 998–1004; *Eumenides* 460, 634–5. Deianira: SOPHOCLES, *Trachiniae* 883–4 (*emēsato*), 928 (*technomenēs*). The mixing of the 'straight path' of the sword and of *mētis* is at its height in *Medea* 384–409 and 1278 (where the sword is a net).
12. Hanging rather than the male: AESCHYLUS, *Supplices* 787–790; precipitation rather than the *daiktōr*: 794–9. Compare *daiktōr* with *gōos daiktēr*, *Seven against Thebes* 917: a tearing sob, a doleful mourning in which one tears one's body in imitation of the torn bodies of the dead, in this case the sons of Oedipus, themselves *autodaiktoi*, 735. Finally, note that at line 680 of the *Supplices*, the verb *daizō* (tear) has made its first appearance, to characterize civil war as the tearer of the city. So there is no reason to turn 'tearer' euphemistically into 'ravisher'.
13. EURIPIDES, *Alcestis* 74–6. Other metaphors of death as cutting or bloody: 118 and 225. On Thanatos as the masculine form of death, see J.-P. VERNANT,

Feminism and Tragedy

'Figures féminines de la mort', forthcoming in a collective work *Masculin/ Féminin en Grèce ancienne* (ed. NICOLE LORAUX).

14. EURIPIDES, *Andromache* 616: *oude trōtheis*. It is the scholiast who is right (as opposed to L. MÉRIDIER, the translator of the Belles Lettres edition). Menelaus in book IV of the *Iliad* was certainly wounded from afar by an arrow from Pandarus, but no wound was inflicted on him at close quarters, by a sword or a lance; and this was the sign of his dubious courage.

15. EURIPIDES, *Iphigenia in Tauris* 621–2. On the place given to the slaughterer at the heart of feminine sacrifice, see M. DETIENNE, 'Violentes Eugénies', in *La cuisine du sacrifice en pays grec*, ed. M. DETIENNE and J.-P. VERNANT (Paris: Gallimard, 1979), p. 208.

16. On this exchange, on which I have commented in 'Blessures de virilité' (*Le Genre Humain*, 10 [1984]: 38–56), see PINDAR, *Nemean* VIII.40 (also *Nemean* VII.35 and *Isthmian* IV.35). We must remember that in the tragedy of Sophocles, Hector's sword is a gift from the enemy. As for Ajax, he dies as a warrior 'falls' (*piptō: Ajax* 828, 841, 1033).

17. *Ajax* 815, with the translation and commentary of J. CASABONA, *Recherches sur le vocabulaire des sacrifices en Grèce* (Aix-en-Provence: Annales Fac. Lettres, 1966), p. 179. One will note that the sword is set upright (*hestēken*) as is usually a hoplite at his post. In 1026 Teucer speaks of his sword as a *phoneus*, a killer.

18. The blade: *Ajax* 581–2, in a context at once medical and sacrificial (cf. *Trachiniae* 1032–3 and *Antigone* 1308–9); the sharpened tongue: 584; the flesh cut by words: 786; the misfortune that pierces the liver: 938.

19. JEAN STAROBINSKI, 'L'épée d'Ajax', in *Trois fureurs* (Paris: Gallimard, 1974), particularly pp. 27–9 and 61. See also D. COHEN, 'The Imagery of Sophocles: A Study of Ajax' Suicide', *Greece and Rome*, 25 (1978): 24–36, and CHARLES SEGAL, 'Visual Symbolism and Visual Effects in Sophocles', *Classical World*, 74 (1981): 125–42.

20. Haemon: *Antigone* 1175 (see also 1239). On *haima* as a word for effusion of blood, see H. KOLLER, 'Haima', *Glotta*, 15 (1967): 149–55.

21. *Schismos*: AESCHYLUS, *Agamemnon* 1149 (Cassandra), *schizō*: SOPHOCLES, *Electra* 99 (murder of Agamemnon). *Daizō*: AESCHYLUS, *Agamemnon* 207–8 (sacrifice of Iphigenia), *Choephoroe* 860, 1071 (murder).

22. The blood law: CASABONA, *Vocabulaire*, p. 160. Compare in Euripides' *Electra* the presence of sacrificial equipment (*kanoun, sphagis*) in the description of Clytemnestra's murder (1142; cf. 1222: *katarchomai*, commented on by P. STENGEL, *Opferbraüche der Griechen*, Leipzig and Berlin: Teubner, 1910, p. 42). Eurydice is a *sphagion: Antigone* 1291, with the commentary of CASABONA, *Vocabulaire*, p. 187. See also the remarks in the text commentary by R. C. JEBB (Cambridge: Cambridge University Press, 1900) on *bōmia* (suicide at the foot of the altar) and the suicide's sword as sacrificial knife (1301).

23. See, for example, EURIPIDES, *Helen* 353–9.

24. *Hippolytus* 1236–7, 1244–5. In his agony of pain, the dying Hippolytus, caught in a snare like Heracles, will ask for a flesh-cutting sword that will deliver him (1357; cf. Sophocles, *Trachiniae* 1031–3).

25. I deliberately use this phrase, which is logically impossible, for the text of the *Phoenissae* not only does not specify which of the two swords she uses, but even suggests in a general way that the common sword of the sons is involved (see 1456 and 1578).

26. R. HIRZEL, 'Der Selbstmord', *Archiv für Religionswissenschaft*, 11 (1908), especially pp. 256–8.

27. One can compare *Oedipus Tyrannus*, where Jocasta is *pantelēs damar* (accomplished wife), and the *Phoenissae*, where Jocasta dies 'with' her

250

The Rope and the Sword

sons and will be buried with them (1282, 1483, 1553–4, 1635). In the same way Eurydice is *pammētor*, entirely given to maternity (*Antigone* 1282).

28. 'Le lit, la guerre', *L'Homme*, 21 (1981): 37–67. See also '*Ponos*. Sur quelques difficultés de la peine comme nom du travail', *Annali dell' Instituto Orientale di Napoli*, 4 (1982): 171–92.

29. Rope or sword: for Helen, if she had been a *gennaia gynē* (*Troades* 1012–14); for Creusa, if her death plan should fail (*Ion* 1063–5); for the manlike Electra (*Orestes*, 953), who would prefer the sword (1041), 1052); for the boastful Hermione (*Andromache* 811–13, 841–4), whose nurse dreads above all her hanging herself (815–16); for Admetus (*Alcestis* 227–9). See again *Andromache* 412, as well as *Hercules Furens* 319–20 and 1147–51.

30. I differ here from the interpretation of CASABONA, *Vocabulaire*, p. 161. One should add that the verb *oregomai* used by the heroine is more suited to the act of wounding (frequent in the *Iliad*) than to that of knotting.

31. Hanging is mentioned by Orestes (AESCHYLUS, *Eumenides* 746; EURIPIDES, *Orestes* 1062–3) and by Oedipus (SOPHOCLES, *Oedipus Tyrannus* 1374; Euripides, *Phoenissae* 331–4).

32. See P. CHANTRAINE, *Dictionnaire étymologique de la langue grecque*, s.v. *aeirō* (I, 23, on the derivative *aiōra*). Jocasta's *eōra*: SCPHOCLES, *Oedipus Tyrannus* 1264. A controversy rages among historians of religion about the Athenian *aiōra*, the festival of suspension and balancing during which young girls play on swings while dolls hang in the branches of trees. Is it a rural fertility rite? Or an expiatory rite? I do not intend to examine the difficult question here. See, for example, R. MARTIN and H. METZGER, *La religion grecque* (Paris: Presses Universitaires de France, 1976), pp. 127–8. I will simply recall that this feast finds its *aition* in the suicide of Erigone and the hanging of a young girl.

33. *Bathy ptōma*: AESCHYLUS, *Supplices* 796–7. *Aeirō*: for example, *Hippolytus* 735 (escape ode) and 779 (*ērtēmenē*, from *artaō*, derivative of *aeirō*), *Andromache* 848, 861–2. The depth of the ether: *Medea* 1295.

34. Wings, flight: *Medea* 1297, *Hercules Furens* 1158, *Hecuba* 1110, *Ion* 796–7 and 1239, *Helen* 1516. The bird: *Hippolytus* 733 (the chorus), 759, 828 (Phaedra); *Andromache* 861–2 (Hermione); *Iphigenia in Tauris* 1089, 1095–6 (*apteros ornis pothousa*); *Helen* 1478–94. On the bird caught in the snare and the hanged woman, see LORAUX, 'Le corps étranglé'.

35. And, in another mode, womanly men, e.g., Jason; or Heracles, who, after committing feminine crime of murdering children, dreams of flying away (before giving up suicide and recovering his manhood); or Polymestor, mutilated by women and slaves. Flight: AESCHYLUS, *Supplices* 806; EURIPIDES, *Ion* 1239.

36. EURIPIDES, *Alcestis* 262–3 (image of the journey), 392, 394; *Suppliant Women* 1039, 1043, and 1017; *Hippolytus* 828–9.

37. SOPHOCLES, *Ajax* 815 and 833. Lycophron (*Alexandra* 466) will also talk of *pēdēma*.

38. ARISTOTLE, *Politics* I.13.1260a30, after SOPHOCLES, *Ajax* 293 (it is the 'eternal refrain' with which Ajax answers Tecmessa's questions); EURIPIDES, *Heraclidae* 474–7.

39. SOPHOCLES, *Trachiniae, Antigone, Oedipus Tyrannus* 1073–5 (with the remarks of Jebb on *siōpē* and its difference from *sigē*).

40. *Hippolytus* 828, *Trachiniae* 881 (*dieistōsen* is derived from *aistos*, invisible). Much could be made of the play between seeing and looking in the account of Deianira's death.

41. On the bolted interior and the opening of the doors, see *Oedipus Tyrannus* 1261–2 and *Hippolytus* 782, 793, 808, and 825 (note the use of the verb *chalan*

in connection with the opening of the bolts, a verb that in *Oedipus Tyrannus* 1266 describes the unknotting of Jocasta's rope).

42. *Antigone* 1293 (and 1295, 1299). On *mychos*, the innermost cavity of the house, and the word's relation to femininity, see J.-P. VERNANT, 'Hestia-Hermes', in *Mythe et pensée chez les grecs*, I (Paris: François Maspéro, 1971), 152. In this connection one will note with EMILY VERMEULE (*Aspects of Death in Early Greek Art and Poetry*, Berkeley and London: University of California Press, 1979, pp. 167–9) that the death of women, being always implicitly eroticized, is drawn to the hollow and the deep.

43. Note that Phaedra is no longer named. When they talk of her corpse, Theseus and Hippolytus talk of 'that woman' (958) or use the word *sōma* (1009).

44. It is not certain that this was in fact the case, and a controversy rages on this death, as on many deaths in tragedy. See, for example, A. M. DALE, 'Seen and Unseen on the Greek Stage', in *Collected Papers*, ed. T. B. L. WEBSTER and E. G. TURNER (Cambridge: Cambridge University Press, 1969), pp. 120–1; and C. P. GARDINER, 'The Staging of the Death of Ajax', *Classical Journal*, 75 (1979): 10–14.

45. The body of the hero: *Ajax* 915–19, 992–3, 1001, 1003–4. The body of the warrior fallen in battle is on the contrary, 'noble': cf. J.-P. VERNANT, 'La belle mort et le cadavre outragé', in *La mort, les morts dans les sociétés anciennes*, ed. G. GNOLI and J.-P. VERNANT (Cambridge and Paris: Cambridge University Press, 1982), pp. 45–76.

46. Alcestis dies onstage: 397–8. From 606 the funeral convoy is ready, but the intervention of the old father of Admetus leads to the setting up of a *prothesis* (between 608 and 740; see also 1012).

47. The most obvious case is that of Alcestis, who pursues conjugal devotion to the point of dying in her husband's place. Euripides' text uses many prepositions (*pro, hyper, peri* or *anti*) to express this exaggerated version of marital exchange: *Alcestis* 18, 37, 155, 178, 282–3, 284, 433–4, 460–3, 620, 682, 698, 1002. In this assemblage of women who die for men, Leda, who died for her daughter, is an exception, which one should perhaps link up with the theme of Demeter and Kore in the *Helen*.

48. SOPHOCLES, *Trachiniae* 913; EURIPIDES, *Alcestis* 175, 187, and 248–9; *Suppliant Women* 980 (see 1022: the *thalamos* of Persephone). *Thalamos* and marriage: see, for example, V. MAGNIEN, 'Le mariage chez les grecs anciens. L'initiation nuptiale', *L'Antiquité Classique*, 5 (1936): 115–17.

49. See SOPHOCLES, *Trachiniae* 918–22, *Oedipus Tyrannus* 1242–3, 1249; also EURIPIDES, *Alcestis* 175, 177, 183, 186–8, 249.

50. *Odyssey* XI.278: Epicaste attaches the rope *aph' hypsēloio melathrou*; EURIPIDES, *Hippolytus* 769–70: *teramnon apo nymphidiōn*. *Melathron*, rooftree: R. MARTIN, 'Le palais d'Ulysse et les inscriptions de Delos', in *Recueil Plassart* (Paris, 1976), pp. 126–9 (with references); *melathron* as metonymy of the palace: *Iliad* II 414, *Odyssey* XVII.150; *melathron* as metonymy of the nuptial abode: EURIPIDES, *Iphigenia in Tauris* 375–6. *Melathron* and the husband: Sappho, fr. 111 Campbell (with the translation of D. A. CAMPBELL in *Greek Lyric*, Cambridge, Mass., and London: Harvard University Press, 1982).

51. Thus Admetus invites Alcestis to wait for him in Hades to 'live with him there': EURIPIDES, *Alcestis* 364. Furthermore, he at the same tiome expresses the normally feminine wish to lie at Alcestis' side (366, 897–902).

52. AESCHYLUS, *Choephoroe* 905–7, also 894–5 and 979 (Clytemnestra); *Agamemnon* 1441–7 (Cassandra, who indeed accepted this 'dying with': *Agamemnon* 1139 and 1313–14).

53. I am alluding to the *Palinodia* by which the poet Stesichorus, after having like Homer 'spoken ill' of Helen, substituted a phantom for the adulterous woman, which followed Paris to Troy. Meanwhile the real Helen, a model of virtue, spent the duration of the Trojan War in Egypt. Pledge to die: EURIPIDES, *Helen* 837, a declaration echoed by Menelaus in 985–6.

54. Joint tomb: EURIPIDES, *Suppliant Women* 1002–3; *synthanein*: 1007, 1040, 1063 (1071); union of bodies: 1019–21.

55. *Phoenissae* 1458–9 (*en toisi philtatois*); in 1578 she falls *amphi teknoisi* ('among' or 'around' her sons).

56. I borrow this expression from an article by C. NANCY, 'Euripide et le parti des femmes', in *La femme dans les sociétés antiques*, ed. E. LÉVY (Strasbourg: Université des Sciences Humaines de Strasbourg, 1983).

57. The best (*aristē, esthlē,* philtātē) of women: EURIPIDES, *Alcestis* 83–5, 151–2, 200, 231, 235–6, 241–2, etc.; the last word: 391; death accepted: 17 (*thelein,* verb of the hoplite imperative; cf. 155); glorious death: 150 (see 157 and 453–4); boldness: 462, 623–4 and 741; nobility: 742, 994.

58. Virility, glory, and boldness: EURIPIDES, *Suppliant Women* 987, 1013, 1014–16, 1055 (*kleinon*), 1059, 1067; the nuptial/funeral adornment of Evadne: 1055; beyond femininity: 1062–3; this side of virility: 1075. Other examples of feminine glory in EURIPIDES: *Helen* 302, *Hecuba* 1282–3.

59. I have expanded on this in 'La gloire et la mort d'une femme', *Sorcières*, 18 (1979): 51–7.

7 Ritual and Tragedy

From its inception as a dramatic form, tragedy has been grounded in ritual, by which term we may understand a relation to specific organisational structures whereby cultures assign meaning to their existence. In that sense, ritual is closely aligned with religion and myth, but also with the very forms, ideologies and ethical paradigms that cultures construct in order both to understand themselves and to recreate themselves. Thus ritual operates in a reciprocal relation to political concerns in so far as ritual inscribes the *principles* of particular political structures while political structures express the ritual underpinnings of cultural myths – the stories cultures tell about themselves. By 'ritual', then, we may understand not only a specific set of actions whose reiterations occur at set intervals of time but also the political and ethical narratives informed by religious belief and performed in those actions. As the expression of foundational cultural narratives, ritual underpins tragedy as the active expression of the tragedy's *raison d'être*.

Along these lines, René Girard discusses what he calls 'sacred violence' as the foundational act upon which Western civilisation is built. In his view, the inevitable 'slippage' that disturbs or pollutes an important status quo by an act or a threat of violence – the moment of 'sacrificial crisis' – is redressed by the destruction of a victim whose removal is required to restore or ensure that status quo. This 'sacred' violence is distinct from 'impure' violence, which is merely slaughter, a violence beyond the constraint of ritual, and thus itself complicit in continuing rather than removing the dangerous pollution. Sacred violence is a necessary act of purification within and for the social body; the fate of the entire represented community is at stake. For Girard, the central matter of dramatic tragedy is the 'opposition of symmetrical elements' – the enacted dilemma of dialogue that occurs when necessary distinctions are blurred. What is performed in tragedy is the redifferentiation of indistinction, what Victor Turner (following Arnold van Gennep) called the 'ritual process', the passage through liminality to a new structure and hierarchy. In Girard's terms this redifferentiation occurs by the removal of the scapegoat or doubling substitute (often, but not always, one of a pair of brothers) by violent means and is required to prevent further and more socially contagious violence. For Girard, dramatic tragedy from that of the ancient Greeks through to that of Shakespeare and his contemporaries provides a vast body of performance of these sacrificial crises and their respondent acts of sacred violence. In tragedy, however, as distinct from actual ritual, the socially dangerous collapse of necessary distinctions (the sacrificial crisis) and its redressive violence remain immanent and continually threaten to recur.

Jan Kott's focus is on Greek tragedy as the enactment of a sacrificial ritual, but for him the significance of the scapegoat inheres less in its broad social symbolism than in the expression of a Dionysian divine frenzy, *sparagmos* (tearing flesh) and *omophagia* (eating raw flesh), in the human. According to this view, tragedy is the representation of extremity, pushing the human beyond recognisable limits in an expression of its divine alter ego. As the agents of these *sparagmos* and *omophagia* rites are usually women, and young males (human or animal) are the sacrificial victims, Kott sees these performances as representations of both incest and its structural reverse, the negation of generational succession, which accounts for the insistently sexual emphases of these myths and their performances in tragedy. For Kott as for Girard, tragedy's representation of ritual sacrifice aims at the restoration of both the social and the sacred principles of culture. The physicality of the enactment, its somatic and sexual intensity, is closely aligned with Artaud's description of the 'Theater of Cruelty', a theatre which rejects *logos* and finds instead its proper expression in gesture and dance, the languages of the body. Greek theatre, says Kott, like that of the Eastern world, is a theatre 'of symbolic sign' wherein myth and rite 'not only are *topos* and plot but reach deep into the structure of performance' and operate on two levels – the sacred and the profane – simultaneously.

The Nigerian playwright Wole Soyinka is also concerned with the relation between tragedy and ritual, although for him, tragedy as a genre already represents a perhaps inevitable dilution of traditional cultural practice: 'I shall begin by commemorating the gods for their self-sacrifice on the altar of literature' (p. 298). Soyinka questions whether traditional African ritual performances of the rites of passage of hero-gods can be 'translated' into commerical theatre in Africa and the African Americas, in the first instance, and at a further remove, into the progressive theatrical experiments of the 1960s and 1970s by European and American directors. He makes an important distinction between ritual and its representation in tragedy, whose symbolical form sometimes misses the 'emotional and spiritual over-tones' of actual rite, but in other instances successfully syncretises African and Christian elements in both narrative and iconic modes. For Soyinka, ritual echoes still inhere in tragedy even in post-colonial times; it is the audience's and with greater difficulty the critic's recep-tion of these echoes that is problematic. For Soyinka, it may fairly be said that interpretive and theoretical interventions occlude mean-ingful reception of tragedy's resonance, and make of it, especially in the West, as he says elsewhere,

> a form of esoteric enterprise spied upon by fee-paying strangers, as contrasted with a communal evolution of the dramatic mode of expression, this latter being the African [which, unlike Western dramatic criticism, retains] a belief in culture as defined within man's knowledge of fundamental, unchanging relationships between himself and society and within the larger context of the observable universe.
> (*Myth, Literature, and the African World*,
> (Cambridge: Cambridge University Press, 1976), p. 38)

Susanne K. Langer returns our attention to an Aristotelian empha-sis on plot-structure, which Northrop Frye called the *mythos*, as ex-pressive of part of the natural order itself. In tragedy, the hero is only a mediator between the audience and this mythos, the 'conductor' through whom the great power of the tragedy is transmitted. For Langer, it is the hero's action – expressing 'the consciousness of life and death' – which moves the drama, and tragedy, representing that heroic action, 'must make life seem worth while, rich, beautiful, to make death awesome'. The 'vital rhythm' of tragedy, she says, is that of self-consummation, as distinct from the 'self-preservation' of the comic mode. It always turns 'toward an absolute close', its cadences of human potentiality moving to completion or fulfilment.

The Eating of the Gods, or
*The Bacchae**

Jan Kott

I

The corpse of Pentheus, torn to pieces on Mount Cithaeron by his
mother, Agave, her sisters and the women of Thebes, is gathered
together and placed on the stage by his grandfather Cadmus, the
former king of Thebes. Only the head is missing. A short while before,
Agave had danced with it in her hands. At last the head is put against
the body. The *disiecta membra* are joined together. Dionysus, wearing a
mask with a fixed smile, is lifted by machine high above the stage roof:
'Long ago my father Zeus ordained these things' (1349).[1] Cadmus and
Agave go into exile. The bacchants recite the closing moral: 'But god
has found his way for what no man expected' (1391). They depart
without dancing, their heads down. In the empty arena only the corpse
remains.

The principal actors in Euripides' tragedy *The Bacchae* are Dionysus
and Pentheus, the god and the man, the King and the Stranger.

> I am Dionysus, the son of Zeus,
> come back to Thebes, this land where I was born.
> ... And here I stand, a god incognito,
> disguised as man ...
>
> (1–2, 5–6)

In the shape of a youth, and looking like a girl with his long fair
hair falling to his shoulders, Dionysus comes to Thebes from Asia
with a train of women beating drums, dancing and singing. They
wear loosely sewn fawn skins and brandish the sacred thyrsi, long
sticks twined with ivy branches and tipped with pine cones. The
tomb of Semele, Dionysus' mother, is represented on the stage: in the
courtyard in front of the royal palace white smoke rises from it day and

---

* Reprinted from *The Eating of the Gods: An Interpretation of Greek Tragedy*, trans.
Boleslaw Taborski and Edward J. Czerwinski (New York: Random House, 1973).

night. No one in the royal family believes that Semele was taken by god the father and bore him a child. They suspect her of having an earthly lover. For this, Dionysus has stricken the women of Thebes with madness. They have left the city and fled to the mountains to celebrate the Dionysian ritual – all of them, even Semele's sisters Ino, Autonoë and Agave, Pentheus' mother.

The middle part of the tragedy contains two symmetric agones; twice the King meets the Stranger. Pentheus tells the soldiers to find the disturber of the peace and bring him in chains before him.

> PENTHEUS:
> > First of all.
> I shall cut off your girlish curls.
> > DIONYSUS:
> > > My hair is holy.
> My curls belong to god.
>
> (492)

Pentheus does not know of a god for whom long hair is holy and who orders women to dance in the mountains. There has been no such god in Thebes.

> . . . a foreigner has come to Thebes
> from Lydia, one of those charlatan magicians,
> with long yellow curls smelling of perfumes,
> with flushed cheeks and the spells of Aphrodite
> in his eyes. His days and nights he spends
> with women and girls, dangling before them the joys
> of initiation in his mysteries.
>
> (233 ff.)

Pentheus looks at the Stranger the way a sheriff in Arizona would at a bearded guru who has invaded the town with a gang of tattered girls. He counters the arrogance of mysticism with the arrogance of pragmatic reason, cuts off the Stranger's tresses and orders him to be locked in a stable. The god has been offended. Sacrilege has been committed. The Chorus cries to the heavens for revenge.

No sooner have the Bacchants completed their threnody than the earth shakes, flames burst from Semele's tomb and a wing of the royal palace falls down. The god has emerged from darkness into light. He has returned to his women. They touch his hands from which the fetters have fallen. He is alive.

In the second agon Pentheus has lost all his self-confidence. The Stranger has trapped him even before he leads him to the place of execution. Pentheus wants to see the women on Mount Cithaeron. He, too, has been liberated by Dionysus. 'Your mind was once unsound, but now you think as sane men do' (947). Pentheus is now ready for anything.

> DIONYSUS:
> I shall go inside with you
> and help you dress.
> PENTHEUS:
> Dress? In a *woman's* dress,
> you mean? I would die of shame.
>
> (827 ff.)

But this shame gives him a strange delight. He puts on a gaudy dress made of fawn skin which comes down to his ankles. On his head he wears a wig of long fair tresses. He sings, dances convulsively and sways his head from side to side. When the Stranger adjusts his wig for him, he shivers with excitement: 'Arrange it. I am in your hands completely' (932).

Dionysus leads Pentheus out of Thebes, just as he led out the women. Since Pentheus cannot see the women when they reach the slopes of Cithaeron, he suggests climbing a tree for a better view. Dionysus bends a tall fir tree until its top touches the ground and puts Pentheus on it, then lets it go with Pentheus huddling in the top. The sexual symbolism of this image is striking. But Pentheus will not enjoy the view for long. The frenzied women have already noticed him. He will not be a spectator but the victim of the sacrament. 'And let the dance begin' (114). The dance of these women on the mountain clearing, to the ceaseless beat of the drums and the shrill wailing of the Phrygian pipes, drives them to ecstasy.

> He delights in the raw flesh. . . .
> He is Bromius who leads us!
>
> (139, 141)

The climax of the Dionysian rite in Euripides' *Bacchae* is the *sparagmos* and the *omophagia*, tearing wild animals to pieces and consuming their raw flesh, still warm with blood.[2]

> Unarmed, they swooped down upon the herds of cattle
> grazing there on the green of the meadow. And then
> you could have seen a single woman with bare hands
> tear a fat calf, still bellowing with fright,
> in two, while others clawed the heifers to pieces.

There were ribs and cloven hooves scattered everywhere,
and scraps smeared with blood hung from the fir trees.

(735 ff.)

In the dramatic structure of *The Bacchae* this is a forecast, a preparation
and a dress rehearsal for the tragic *sparagmos*, in which Pentheus himself
is the scapegoat. The women, in their godsent frenzy, take him for an
animal hiding among the pines. They try to get him down by throwing
stones, then uproot the tree, tearing at the branches. Even when
Pentheus takes off his wig of fair tresses. Agave does not recognize her
son. 'First his mother started the slaughter as priestess and falls upon
him . . .' (1114).[3]

This account by the Messenger, who has rushed in from the
mountains, is made visual when Cadmus brings the torn fragments
of Pentheus' body onstage: what follows is the cruellest recognition
scene in all Greek drama. Agave enters the stage with a severed head
impaled on a thyrsus. All the characters are present. On the roof stands
Dionysus – a smiling bull. The Chorus of *The Bacchae*, which a little
while before was leaping ecstatically and wallowing in the *orchestra*, in
praise of Dionysus' victory, is now motionless. Only Agave continues
to dance. The holy trance has not yet left her. She is proud of her prey.
In her blindness she believes she has killed a lion and brought back its
severed head. She wants the Chorus to fulfill the ritual of *omophagia* and
consume the fresh meat.

AGAVE:
Then share my glory,
share the feast.
CHORUS:
Share, unhappy woman?

(1184 f.)[4]

The ritual has meant filicide. Agave recognizes that the lion's head
is the head of Pentheus. Why lion's? There were no lions on Mount
Cithaeron. To answer this question is to begin the interpretation of both
the ritual and the tragedy. Next to the bull and the snake, the lion was
one of the three emblems of Dionysus. But why, in the hour of his
agony, was Pentheus given an emblem of the god?

The parallelism of the two agones in *The Bacchae* corresponds to the
structural symmetry of the first and second halves of the play, but it is
a peculiar parallelism and a peculiar symmetry, shaping a central
symbolic reversal of situation, role and sign between the protagonists,
Dionysus and Pentheus.[5]

They are both the same age. Their mothers are sisters. They have a
common grandfather, Cadmus.[6] Before the youth in armour, proud of

his newly acquired manhood, stands the girl-like Stranger. Dionysus
has always been a bisexual deity. In the fragment of a lost tragedy
by Aeschylus he causes astonishment by his appearance: 'Where do
you come from, man-woman, and where is your home? What is the
meaning of your dress?' In Ovid, and later in Seneca, he has the face
of a virgin. Pentheus calls the visitor an 'effeminate stranger', but in
the second half he himself puts on the dress of a bacchant. He learns
from the Stranger how a woman moves; he wiggles like a female
impersonator. In this very moment the Stranger undergoes a change.
He is no longer a gentle, defenceless boy-girl.

> PENTHEUS:
> . . . And you – you are a bull
> who walks before me there. Horns have sprouted
> from your head. Have you always been a beast?
> But now I see a bull.
> DIONYSUS:
> It is the god you see. . . .
>
> (920 ff.)

Pentheus sees in the Stranger the divine bull. The Chorus, too.
observes the metamorphosis: 'He dressed in woman's dress . . . led by
a bull to Hades' (1156, 1159). The Bacchae now demand an apotheosis.
The time of the visible god has come, visible in all his attributes. The
epiphany is foretold: 'Appear as a bull or a many-headed snake or a
fire-blazing lion to behold!' (1016 f., Kirk's translation).

Dionysus comes to Thebes as a stranger; Pentheus leaves Thebes as a
stranger. He wanted to be a spectator at a holy orgy, but it is Dionysus
who turns out to be the great voyeur. The godlike King had thrown the
Stranger into the palace stable; now the Stranger, transformed into a
god, looks in his glory from the tall stage roof at the royal body. The
persecutor becomes the persecuted, the hunted becomes the executioner,
and these switches in roles are parallel. Pentheus sends his soldiers like
a pack of hounds to track down the Stranger. 'We captured the quarry
you sent us out to catch. But our prey here was tame . . .' (435 f.). But
it is Pentheus who is hunted down and torn like a beast by a pack of
women – 'Happy was the hunting' (1171). The hunter has become the
beast.

Pentheus is made the scapegoat. The scapegoat is a surrogate who
must be made to resemble the One whom he has replaced; in an
ancient ritual a ram led to sacrifice had his horns gilded and a wreath
hung around his neck. The scapegoat is the image of the One to whom
he is sacrificed. The ritual is a repetition of divine sacrifice. Pentheus is
torn to pieces because the Other had also been torn to pieces. Pentheus'

body is put together from the torn fragments, because the dismembered fragments of the Other had also been joined together. 'Long ago my father Zeus ordained these things.'

II

Accounts of Dionysian myths, no matter what their source, character and date of recording, show an amazing similarity. It is as if on every occasion the same event has been described. Only the names of antagonists and places vary.

Zeus, or Persephone at his command, sent the newly born Dionysus to be brought up by Athamas, king of Orchomenus, and his wife Ino, the sister of Semele, Autonoë and Agave. Hera punished the royal couple with madness: they killed their own son, mistaking him for a deer. When Dionysus came to Thrace after a long trip which took him from the mythical mountain Nysa ('tree') through Crete, Egypt and India, King Lycurgus resisted him. Dionysus made him lose his reason: in one version, Lycurgus mistook his own son for a vine bush and cut him down with an ax. For this Lycurgus was taken to the mountains and torn apart by wild horses. Also in Orchomenus, when Dionysus returned, the king's three daughters refused to take part in the mysteries. Dionysus, in the shape of a girl, had invited them himself. Angered, he turned in front of them into a lion, a bull and a panther. The sisters fell into madness: the oldest tore her son to pieces, then all three of them ate him. Toward the end of his trip, in Argos, when the king refused to believe in his divine origin, Dionysus drove all the women in the city to madness: they tore their children to pieces and ate them raw.[7]

If we put these accounts one on top of the other, like cutout drawings, certain common elements in them emerge. These are: madness, the divine frenzy, sent most commonly by Dionysus; the murder of a child, most commonly a son; murder effected by tearing to pieces (*sparagmos*); murder connected with eating of raw flesh ('the joy of eating raw flesh', praised by the Chorus in *The Bacchae* [138]); the son torn apart and eaten by the mother. This pattern in its bare structure is not a myth, nor is it – as has been frequently asserted – grouped legends from the period when the invasion of the Dionysian cult was being resisted. It is an image of the same ritual, a ritual which repeats and commemorates events that happened, in Mircea Eliade's words, 'at the beginning of time, *in illo tempore*'. As Dodds has stated: 'History no doubt repeats itself; but it is only ritual that repeats itself *exactly.*'[8] The sacral offering is the repetition of the first sacrifice. It is told in the ur-myth, the original Dionysian myth, with which two 'indirect' myths are connected: perhaps they are variations of the basic myth. They will take us a step further in the interpretation of *The Bacchae*.

The first is the story of Actaeon. He had watched Artemis bathing in a mountain brook. The offended goddess turned him into a stag and set his own dogs on him. Actaeon climbed a tree, but the dogs got at him and tore him to pieces. The fifty hounds who – baited by the goddess – failed to recognize their own master are like the mad women of Thebes who tore their king to pieces. Euripides recalls the history of Actaeon three times in *The Bacchae*. The wild dogs, writes G. S. Kirk in his commentary, 'are described as "carnivorous" or "eaters of raw food", reminding one of the "joy of eating raw flesh".'[9] Actaeon was the son of Autonoë, the sister of Semele and Agave, so he was Dionysus' and Pentheus' first cousin. Everything is still happening in the same family; all three were grandsons of Cadmus, and, like Pentheus, Actaeon was a king. Actaeon's slaughter occurred on the same spot, on Mount Cithaeron. Like Pentheus, he was a scapegoat. And in that *sparagmos* too, the ritual victim was a youth and the body was torn by a woman.[10]

AGAVE:
But where did [Pentheus] die?
At home? Or whereabouts?
CADMUS:
. . . where previously the hounds
divided out Acteon.

(1290 ff., Kirk's translation)

Orpheus too is recalled in *The Bacchae*. In all the accounts he is connected with Dionysus, as his prophet, originator of the cult, initiator of the mysteries. He is one of the figures of Dionysus and his alter ego, as John the Baptist is of Christ. 'Orpheus,' Proclus wrote, 'because he was the principal in the Dionysian rites, is said to have suffered the same fate as the god.'[11] Orpheus, at Dionysus' instigation, was torn to pieces by the Maenads. The gods saved only his head and his lyre.[12] Thus Orpheus, too, was a scapegoat, the Surrogate made to resemble the One whom he stands for; his *sparagmos*, too, was only a repetition of the first sacrifice, *in illo tempore*. 'Later Orphic priests, who wore Egyptian costume,' observes Graves, 'called the demi-god whose raw bull's flesh they ate "Dionysus".' In this cult as well, the ritual communion, the eating of the living god, is connected with *sparagmos*.

The basic Dionysian myth, present most strongly in the Orphic tradition, tells about the passion, death and resurrection of the divine child. The newly born son of Zeus, called Dionysus, or in other records Zagreus, was kidnapped by the Titans. He tried to escape or confuse his captors by taking in turn the shape of a goat, lion, snake, tiger and bull. While he was in this last disguise, the Titans tore him to pieces and consumed his raw flesh. Zeus killed the Titans with a flash of

lightning, and of the soot that remained of the fire that had burned
them, men were created. Dionysus' head was saved by Athene or Rhea;
his dismembered fragments, the *disiecta membra*, were miraculously
joined together; Dionysus was resurrected. In a fragment of his lost
tragedy, *Cretans*, Euripides writes: 'We lead pure lives since we were
initiated in the mysteries of Zeus and Ida; we pour libations in honour
of Zagreus, who enjoys nocturnal rites, we take part in the feasts of
omophagia lighting torches in the mountains in homage to the Great
Mother'.[13]

The Dionysus myth is genetic and cosmic at the same time. The first
human beings grew out of the earth, like plants. Titans were the image
of subterranean forces (*chthonic*). In the Platonic and Neo-Platonic
interpretation, the myth spoke about the double nature of man. Men
rose from the Titans' ashes. But Titans had eaten Dionysus before they
turned to ashes. Hence the proverbial expressions: 'Titans in us', 'the
Titanic nature of man'. The soul imprisoned in the body, in the Orphic
doctrine and for the mystically inclined Neo-Platonists, was a Dionysian
substance, which survived in the ashes of the Titans.

The resurrected Dionysus descended into Hades in order to free his
dead mother, Semele. Then he ascended to Olympus with her and
was admitted to the company of the immortal ones. Semele became
Persephone, who, at the advent of winter, descends to the underworld,
leaving it toward the close of the season to rejoin the spring Dionysus.
The dismembering and reunification of Dionysus is the cosmic myth
of eternal renewal, death and rebirth, chaos and cosmos. Plutarch, in
his famous treatise *De E Delphico*, considers the opposites contained
in this myth and their significance, almost like a modern structural
anthropologist:

We hear from the mythographers, both prose writers and poets, that
the god is by nature indestructible and eternal, but yet, under the
impulsion of some predestined plan and purpose, he undergoes
transformation in his beings. At one time he sets fire to nature and
reduces all things to one likeness; at another, entering upon a state of
infinite diversity (such as prevails at present), with varied shapes,
sufferings, and powers, he is called Cosmos (to use the name which
is best known). The wiser folk, in their secret doctrines which they
conceal from the world, call the transformation into fire by the name
of Apollo because of the oneness of that state, or by the name of
Phoebus because of its purity and lack of defilement. But when the
god is changed and distributed into winds, water, earth, stars, plants,
and animals, they describe this experience and transformation
allegorically by the terms 'rending' and 'dismemberment'. They apply
to him the names Dionysus, Zagreus, Nyetelius, Isodaites, and they

construct allegorical myths in which the transformations that have been described are represented as death and destruction followed by restoration to life and rebirth.[14]

To Plutarch's list of Dionysian gods we can add many new names today. The myth, in which the beginning of nature's fertility and its annual renewal are connected with the coming of god's son on earth, his murder and resurrection, is one of the most common and persistent; it is present in civilizations as remote from one another as the Mediterranean and the Polynesian, or those of the Mayas and the Uitoto cannibals. 'Creation cannot take place except from a *living being who is immolated*,' writes Eliade in a way very similar to Plutarch's. 'A single being transforms itself into a Cosmos, or takes multiple rebirth in a whole vegetable species or race of mankind. A living "whole" bursts into fragments and disperses itself in myriads of animated forms. In other terms, here again we find the well-known cosmogonic pattern of the primordial "wholeness" broken into fragments by the act of creation.'

In the anthropological perspective, especially since the studies of Jensen and Eliade, the structure of this myth and its common elements are very clearly delineated. After the creation, fertility comes only from a new union of heaven and earth. Out of this is born a son or sons of god the father. Mother is either Earth or a mortal woman, who will later become the Great Mother. The son of god is killed, torn to pieces, and his body becomes food. His scattered fragments are reunited and he is resurrected; he visits the realm of the dead and with his mother enters the heavens. The repetition of the passion and sacrifice of the son of god and of the murder, dismembering and eating of the Deputy's body is the guarantee of abundance, fertility and renewal, and in more spiritual religions, a form of participation in the sacred history of the world and a guarantee of salvation.[15]

> The edible plant is not given by Nature: it is the product of an assassination, because that is how it was created at the beginning of time ... Cannibalism is not a 'natural' depravity of primitive man ... but a kind of cultural behaviour based upon a religious vision of life. So that the vegetable world may continue, man must kill and be killed; he must, moreover, assume sexuality, even to its extreme limits – the orgy. An Abyssinian song proclaims this: 'She who has not yet given birth, let her give birth; he who has not yet killed, let him kill!' It is a way of saying that the two sexes are condemned each to accept its destiny.[16]

In such myths and *sparagmos* rites, women are the priestesses. They tear bodies to pieces and partake of the raw flesh. The sacrificial victim is always male: a child of the male sex, or a young man, or a ram, he-goat, or bull.

> CHORUS:
> Who struck the blow?
> > AGAVE:
> > > Mine was the privilege first.
> > CHORUS:
> Happy Agave . . .
> > AGAVE:
> > . . . is what I am called in the sacred bands!
> > > (1179 ff., Kirk's translation)

Sacral cannibalism found in the Dionysian myths its most cruel and dramatic expression. In archaic Greek culture the finality of later tragedy is already present: mother kills, tears apart and consumes her own son; the son's body is the tormented body of a god, earthly nourishment and communion.

Anthropologists and psychoanalysts have not as yet devoted sufficient attention to this darkest of rituals. *Omophagia* of the son by the mother is similar to incest, and at the same time its structural reversal. In an incestuous relationship with the mother, the son is the father's surrogate, thus the sacral killing of king the father is linked with sacral incest. In the symbols of Dionysian rite, it is not god the father who is torn to shreds, but god the son; *genesis* annihilated, moved back to its origins. The eating of the son by the mother is the reversal of giving birth and feeding; the negation of succession, since it is king the son who has been eaten; and the negation of time, because it is a return to the point where it all began. This simultaneous fili-, regi-, and dei-cide is the ultimate completion of the cycle. Cosmos has become chaos again so that everything can begin anew. 'The symbolic return to Chaos,' writes Eliade, 'is indispensable to any new creation.'[17] Fertility is mortally wounded in order that it may be renewed.

> —Blessèd, blessèd are those who know the mysteries of god.
> —Blessèd is he who hallows his life in the worship of god.
>   he whom the spirit of god possesseth, who is one
>   with those who belong to the holy body of god.
> > (73 ff.)

III

The sacral *sparagmos* and agony of Pentheus in *The Bacchae* takes place offstage, and the audience learns about it from messengers. But the Chorus of bacchants is present on the stage from the first to the last scene. The Chorus, as in Aeschylus, not only witnesses events but

267

participates in them. It is a Chorus of believers, not unlike a
congregation assembled to take part in the sacrifice. It is touched by the
hand of the living god who in the epiphany will appear in his animal
shape. The Chorus calls for his coming, praises his glory, bewails his
imprisonment and triumphs when his adversary has been beaten down.
The name of the god is repeated until the voices grow hoarse and choke.
The chants are religious songs, extraordinarily close in their fervent
appeals for the coming of the saviour to the prophecies of Isaiah and
the medieval hymns sung in Christian churches during Holy Week.

The Chorus sings in the first *stasimon*:

> —O Thebes, nurse of Semele,
> crown your hair with ivy!
> Grow green with bryony!
> Redden with berries! O city,
> with boughs of oak and fir,
> come dance the dance of god!

(105 ff.)

Compare Isaiah (lii.1):

> Awake, awake, put on your strength, O Zion;
> put on your beautiful garments,
>   O Jerusalem, the holy city;
> for there shall no more come into you
>   the uncircumcised and the unclean.

Bacchants:

> —Blessèd are the dancers and those who are purified,
> who dance on the hill in the holy dance of god.
> —Blessèd are they who keep the rite of Cybele the Mother.
> —Blessèd are the thyrsus-bearers, those who wield in their hands
>   the holy wand of god.
> Blessèd are those who wear the crown of the ivy of god.
> —Blessèd, blessèd are they: Dionysus is their god!

(76 ff.)

The song becomes a dance. 'Why should I take part in the sacred
dance?' cries the leader of the Chorus in *Oedipus* when it seems for a
while that man can be stronger than the curse of the gods. 'My heart
is a dance of fear,' sing the women in the *Libation-bearers*, when the
Stranger pours a libation on the tomb of Agamemnon. 'What dance
shall I dance for death?' calls the Chorus of Theban elders when
Heracles murders his wife and sons. Dionysus is a god who enters the

body through dance. 'Be favourable, O Insewn, Inspirer of frenzied woman!' are the words of the Homeric Hymn to Dionysus. 'We singers sing of you as we begin and as we end a strain, and none forgetting you may call holy song to mind.'[18]

The Chorus of bacchants from Lydia dances the madness sent by Dionysus on the women of Thebes. Dionysus is a deity to be drunk down.[19] To be possessed means to be possessed by god. The sacral dance and the sacred Eros are prayers of the body. 'A bacchant, through his orgiastic rites, imitates the drama of the suffering Dionysus; an Orphic, through his initiation ceremonial, repeats the original gestures of Orpheus ... A dance always imitates an archetypal gesture or commemorates a mythical moment.'[20]

In Negro spirituals, God is praised in rhythms that are the sign and symbol of sex. Singers in coloured surplices praise the Lord with deep voices. They wave their arms, jump, clap their hands, shout a hundred, a thousand times, as if they still could not believe that God has been born, that he will lead the chosen out of captivity, that he is a living God; that he can be touched, that he is food and drink. The joy at the good tidings shakes the body. Legs, hands, belly and breasts all begin to dance. The mysticism of Negro spirituals, like that of the bacchants, is physical. Lucian wrote in *Saltatio:*'whosoever beholds dancing must be able "to understand the mute and hear the silent".' Further on, in the same treatise, he tells how a certain barbaric prince, invited to the theatre by Nero, said to the first dancer after the performance: 'I did not realise, my friend, that though you have this one body, you have many souls.'[21]

The Dionysian rite in *The Bacchae* takes place offstage. The medium is the body of the Chorus. The sacred also has its technology. 'Among primitives as well as among the civilized,' writes Eliade, 'religious life brings about, in one way or another, the religious use of sensibility. Broadly speaking, there can be no religious experience without the intervention of the senses ...'[22] Artaud transformed Rimbaud's *'long, immense, et raisonné dérèglement de tous le sens'* into a method: 'It is through the skin that metaphysics must be made to reenter our minds.'

The dance to the beat of drums, punctuated by the wailing of flutes and high tones of pipes, leads into a holy trance. When, at the climax of the tragedy, the Messenger speaks about Pentheus' torn body, the dance becomes a spasm. The dances of the Uitoto tribe, described by Eliade, 'consist of repetitions of all the mythical events, including therefore the first assassination, followed by anthropophagy'. The Chorus in *The Bacchae*, as in an initiation rite, discovers the *tremendum* – the 'almost simultaneous revelation of the sacred, of death and of sexuality'.[23]

No other extant Greek tragedy is as permeated by religious imagery as *The Bacchae*. Just before the *sparagmos*, the slopes of Cithaeron flow with milk and wine, water runs from the rocks, streams of honey trickle from laurel-adorned wands. The cult of Dionysus blended with old agrarian rites of the nature deities' death and resurrection. The Roman Bacchus was almost exclusively the god of wine; the Greek Dionysus incarnated all vital fluids; water, milk, wine and sperm. 'The wine miracle at Cana was the same as the miracle in the temple of Dionysus, and it is profoundly significant that, on the Damascus Chalice, Christ is enthroned among vine tendrils like Dionysus himself.'[24] The Dionysian miracle of Cana on the slopes of Cithaeron occurs offstage, but *The Bacchae* is one of very few tragedies in which a miracle is part of the action onstage. The earth shakes, a wing of the royal palace collapses, shackles fall off Dionysus' hands. Verrall and the rationalists took the view that the miracle is an illusion of the Chorus. Later interpreters thought that the Greek stage had been equipped with theatre machinery which made spectacular effects possible; these 'irrationalists', brought up on nineteenth-century naturalistic theatre, believed that a visible and 'real' miracle could be made only by such means. It seems that Verrall with all his positivist narrow-mindedness was closer to the truth. On a bare stage, Greek as well as modern, the shaking of the earth is confirmed by the shaking of bodies. The miracles of the mysteries do not need pyrotechnics.[25]

It is not only the mythological apparatus that is put in motion in *The Bacchae*. In no other tragedy, perhaps excepting Aeschylus' *Prometheus*, are the images evoked so close to basic religious archetypes. When Semele was about to go into labour, Zeus visited her in a pillar of fire. Semele was consumed by flames, but Dionysus was saved by Zeus in his thigh. 'My mother was Cadmus' daughter, Semele by name, midwived by fire, delivered by the lightning's blast' (3 ff.). In the anthropology of religious signs, to be struck by thunder means to be counted among the chosen ones by the god, through a mystic death and the promise of resurrection.[26] The last supernatural event evoked in *The Bacchae* is the bending of a tall pine tree by Dionysus:

> And now the stranger worked a miracle.
> Reaching for the highest branch of a great fir,
> he bent it down ...
>   ... No mortal could have done it.
> Then he seated Pentheus at the highest tip
> and with his hands let the trunk rise straightly up,
> slowly and gently, lest it throw its rider.
> And the tree rose, towering to heaven, with my master
> huddled at the top.

(1063–5, 1069–74)

Before the ultimate fulfilment of the sacrifice, the solemn liturgical
gestus of elevation occurs. Pentheus' flight toward the heavens is
ecstatic levitation, known from shamans' accounts as well as from the
experience of Christian mystics. The imprisonment of Dionysus in the
darkness, his symbolic death, is a forecast of Pentheus' real death.
Pentheus' flight to heaven in turn prefigures Dionysus' final ascension.

Pentheus' fragmented body is put together, as the members of
Dionysus' torn body were reassembled. Agave, the priestess, is still
holding the head.

> I am overjoyed,
> great things have I achieved,
> great and manifest for this land.
>
> (1198 ff., Kirk's translation)

In the Greek theatre, the mask is the person; the ritual emblem
denotes the god. Agave rushes onto the stage with a mask impaled on
a thyrsus. Experience of Oriental theatres – the Japanese Nō dramas,
the Chinese opera and the sacred Hindu theatre – may be just as
important for the understanding of Greek theatre as archaeological
records and vase drawings. They are all theatres of symbolic sign.

> bring from the mountains
> a freshly cut tendril to these halls.
>
> (1169 f., Kirk's translation)[27]

Agave has removed the mask from the thyrsus. Still dazed, she
continues to see in it the head of a slaughtered beast. She strokes the
crest of the soft hair. What sort of mask was it? The *tendril*, fastened to
the thyrsus, looking like a curling shot of ivy, is not a lion's head, but a
wig of long tresses.

In the first agon, Pentheus tore a wig from the Stranger's head. When
Pentheus is dressed as a bacchant, he wears the same wig of long fair
hair. The Stranger himself adjusts a misplaced lock. When the frenzied
Maenads drag him off the tree, he tries in vain to get his mother to
recognize him by taking off the wig. Agave then enters with his wig
attached to the thyrsus instead of laurel leaves. When god-man is
transformed in the final epiphany into an animal god, his emblem, the
'hair of Dionysus', covers the body of his Surrogate in place of the
head. 'My hair is holy. My curls belong to god.' The travels of the
wig of long fair tresses must be the most brilliant use of a stage prop
in the entire history of drama.

In *The Bacchae*, the signs of ritual not only appear in metaphors and
on the verbal level of the drama but are visible theatrical signs. The

myth and the rite in *The Bacchae* not only are *topos* and plot but reach
deep into the structure of performance. Man and God, King and
Stranger, the Surrogate and the One exchange their parts in turn; as in a
pattern of theory of combinations, all signs are reversed one after the
other and all permutations are exhausted. The symbolic signs of *The
Bacchae* can, however, be understood in two ways, as if they belonged
to two different systems, two different languages, two separate codes,
and meant something different in each. The ritual icons, the 'significant',
have two separate 'significations', the sacred and the profane. Such
signs, which operate on two different levels, are the 'divine' wig of fair
tresses and the tree with Pentheus on it, which have a double – mystical
and sexual – symbolism. In *The Bacchae*, two separate and contradictory
structures coexist. The eating of the god, the rite of death and renewal,
becomes in the end a cruel killing of son by mother. The ritual turns
into a ritual murder. Brecht wrote in his 'Little Organon': 'Theater may
be said to be derived from ritual, but that is only to say that it becomes
theater once the two have separated.'[28]

Notes

1. All quotations from *The Bacchae*, unless otherwise indicated, are given in
   the translation by WILLIAM ARROWSMITH from *The Complete Greek Tragedies,
   Euripides V* (Chicago, University of Chicago Press, 1959).
2. E. R. DODDS, in the introduction to the edition of *The Bacchae* (Oxford,
   Clarendon Press, 1944; 2nd ed., 1957), which became a milestone in the new
   understanding of Euripides, was the first to demonstrate decisively the
   importance of the Dionysian myth, particularly of the *sparagmos* and the
   omophagia, for the interpretation of *The Bacchae* and the bacchants' place in
   Greek culture. However, for all his sensitivity, intellectual insight, knowledge
   of Freudianism and new anthropology, Dodds remained a positivist to the
   end. *The Bacchae* was to him a historical and sociological representation of
   genuine ritual and mass psychosis. Because the Chorus in *The Bacchae* talks
   about the festival which takes place 'each second year', and there is evidence
   that Dionysian festivals of an orgiastic nature took place every two years in
   midwinter, Dodds assumes that the rite in the tragedy is a winter one and
   therefore distinct from the fertility rites of the dying and reviving god which
   used to take place in the spring ('Maenadism' in his *The Greeks and the
   Irrational* [Berkeley, University of California Press, 1951], pp. 272–9). In spite
   of his impressive use of all available material, Dodds's thesis does not seem
   convincing. The Dionysian rite in *The Bacchae* is shown syncretically and is
   subject to the rigours of artistic construction. In Greek tragedy there are no
   seasons; time is syncretic too. 'The Bacchae', Arrowsmith writes in the
   introduction to his translation (p. 143), 'is neither a study of Dionysiac *cultus*
   nor a cautionary essay on the effects of religious hysteria; nor, for that
   matter, however faithfully it may present the *hieros logos* or sacred myth of

Dionysiac ritual, is it best read as an anthropological passion-play of the mystical scapegoat or the Year-Daimon.'

3. As translated by Geoffrey S. Kirk, *The Bacchae* (Englewood Cliffs, NJ, Prentice-Hall, 1970).

4. This is one of the key lines for the interpretation of the tragedy. Kenneth Cavander translates it in a most brutal manner: 'Come with me now ... to the meal ...' (unpublished manuscript). *The Bacchae* was produced in Cavander's translation at the Yale Repertory Theatre in 1969.

5. Kirk, *The Bacchae*, in the introduction to his translation, points to the reversal of roles and situations: 'Pentheus' temporal authority is progressively revealed as impotence in relation to the unfolding power of the god; and since king and god are in direct conflict it follows that the victim will become the aggressor, the hunted the hunter and vice versa.' But although Kirk stresses the fact that both protagonists are contemporaries and cousins, and demonstrates with great precision the transformation of the hunter into the hunted, he is quick to withdraw from attributing any essential meaning to these. 'Let us take note of these correspondences, but not exaggerate their significance. They do not of themselves imply that Pentheus was an aspect or perverted double of the god ...' And a few lines further on: 'There is great subtlety and complexity, as well as great irony, in Euripides' description of the two opponents and their relationship: but although Pentheus may be thought of as dedicated to Dionysus as his victim by being dressed in the ritual apparel of Dionysus' worshippers, *there is little real evidence that he is a kind of aberrant incarnation of the power and personality* of the god himself' (my italics; pp. 14–15).

6. Pentheus, observes Arrowsmith is beardless at the time of his death, so he cannot be more than sixteen or seventeen (Introduction to *The Complete Greek Tragedies*, p. 147).

7. Basic sources for the story of Lycurgus are Homer, *Iliad*, VI, 130 ff., [Apollodorus] 3, 5, 7; for the three daughters of Minyas in Orchomenus: Plutarch, *Quaestiones Graecae*, 38; for the frenzy of the women in Argos [Apollodorus] 2, 2, 2. See Dodds, *The Bacchae*, Introduction, p. xxiii, and Robert Graves, *Greek Myths*, Vol. I (Baltimore, Penguin Books, 1955), pp. 105 ff. Cf. J. G. Frazer, *The New Golden Bough*, edited by Theodore G. Gaster (New York, Mentor Books, 1964), p. 298: 'The suspicion that this barbarous custom by no means fell into disuse even in later days is strengthened by a case of human sacrifice which occurred in Plutarch's time at Orchomenus, a very ancient city of Boeotia, distant only a few miles across the plain from the historian's birthplace. ... Every year at the festival of the Agrigonia, the priest of Dionysus pursued these women with a drawn sword, and if he overtook one of them he had a right to slay her. In Plutarch's lifetime the right was actually exercised by a priest, Zoilus. Now, the family thus liable to furnish at least one human victim every year was of royal descent, for they traced their lineage to Minyas, the famous old king of Orchomenus ... Tradition ran that the king's three dagughters long despised the other women of the country for yielding to the Bacchic frenzy and sat at home in the king's house scornfully plying the distaff and the loom, while the rest, wreathed with flowers, their dishevelled locks streaming to the wind, roamed in ecstasy the barren mountains that rise above Orchomenus, making the solitude of the hills to echo to the wild music of cymbals and tambourines. But in time the divine fury infected even the royal damsels in their quiet chamber; they were seized with a fierce longing to partake of human flesh,

and cast lots among themselves which should give up her child to furnish a cannibal feast.'

8. DODDS seems to have been the first to question the so-called resistance theory which saw in those accounts a reflection of the historic invasion of Greece by the Dionysian cult. He writes: '... always it is the king's daughters who go mad; always there are three of them ... regularly they murder their children, or the child of one of them ...' (Introduction, p. xxiv).

9. KIRK, *The Bacchae*, p. 54, commentary to 1, 340.

10. GRAVES, *Greek Myths*, Vol. I, p. 85, compares the Artemis of this myth to the Cretan 'Lady of the Wild Things', whose cult was orgiastic. But he must be mistaken when he writes: 'The Nymph properly took her bath after, not before, the murder.' One should rather trust the myth. The ritual bath was a purification of the priestess *before* the sacrificial ceremony. Euripides' bacchants begin the sacred rites with 'reverent purifications' (77). In the *Odyssey* (III, 439 ff.), '... Aretus came out from the store-room, carrying in his right hand a flowered bowl of lustral water, and in the other a basket with the barley corns ... The old charioteer Nestor now started the ritual with the lustral water and the scattered grain, and offered up his earnest prayers to Athene as he began the sacrifice by throwing a lock from the victim's head on the fire.' In Euripides' *Electra* the Messenger tells about the sacrifice offered by Aegisthus. He was a murderer and an adulterer, but he offered his sacrifices in a ritual manner: first he washed his hands in spring water, then he slaughtered a bull (800 ff.). In *Iphigenia in Aulis*, Achilles, who ultimately came to believe in the necessity of Iphigenia's murder, grasped the prepared bowl of spring water and rushed around the altar with it, sprinkling the warriors (1568 ff.).

11. PROCLUS, *Commentary on Plato's Politics*, quoted from GRAVES, *Greek Myths*, Vol. I, p. 114.

12. The symbol of a saved head in the Orpheus and Dionysus myths merits a closer examination. The head of Orpheus, hurled by the Maenads into a river, did not sink but continued to sing until it drifted to the sea and waves took it to Lesbos, along with his lyre: '... his talking head voyaged on the lyre' (LUCIAN, *The Dance*, 51). According to another record, the head of Orpheus was deposited in the temple of Dionysus at Antyssa, where it talked day and night, forecasting the future, until Apollo silenced it, angered by the competition to other oracles. The lyre, through the intercession of the Muses, was later placed in the sky as a constellation by Apollo. The opposition of Dionysian head and Apolline lyre seems a very late interpretation.

For Graves, this myth tells of the sacral murder of a king. 'A sacred king necessarily suffered dismemberment, and the Thracians may well have had the same custom as the Iban Dayaks of modern Sarawak. When the men come home from a successful head-hunting expedition the Iban women use the trophy as a means of fertilizing the rice crop by invocation. The head is made to sing, mourn, and answer questions, and nursed tenderly in every lap until it finally consents to enter an oracular shrine, where it gives advice on all important occasions ...' (*Greek Myths*, Vol. I, p. 115).

The 'severed head' belongs, it seems, to two different rites: to ensure harvest and fertility, and to forecast the future. C. G. JUNG writes in 'Transformation Symbolism in the Mass' (*Psyche and Symbol*, edited by VIOLET S. DE LASZLO [Garden City, NY, Doubleday, 1958]): 'Skull worship is widespread among primitives. In Melanesia and Polynesia it is chiefly the skulls of the ancestors that are worshipped, because they establish connections with the spirits or serve as tutelary deities, like the head of

Osiris in Egypt. Skulls also play a considerable role as sacred relics. . . .
Equally, the head or its parts (brain, etc.) can act as magical food or as a
means for increasing the fertility of the land' (p. 193). Jung should have
recalled the myth of Osiris, whom Greeks often identified with Dionysus
and who also rose from the dead, having been torn to pieces. Like Dionysus,
Osiris, the god of harvest and fertility, is connected with wine, trees and
water (Nile floods).

Also interesting is the presence of the severed-head symbol in Jewish
tradition. Jung quotes the twelfth-century legend, published by Bin Gorion
in *Die Sagen der Juden*: 'The teraphim were idols, and they were made in
the following way. The head of a man, who had to be a first-born, was
cut off and the hair plucked out. The head was then sprinkled with salt
and anointed with oil. Afterwards a little plaque, of copper or gold, was
inscribed with the name of an idol and placed under the tongue of the
decapitated head. The head was set up in a room, candles were lit before
it, and the people made obeisance. And if any man fell down before it, the
head began to speak, and answered all questions that were addressed to it'
(p. 190).

In this wide anthropological perspective, the severed head of St. John the
Baptist suddenly resembles the head of Orpheus. They were both prophets
and 'doubles' of a god-man.

One other, modern interpretation of the severed head merits attention.
'Onians' [*The Origins of European Thought*, (New York, Cambridge University
Press, 1951)], writes JUNG, 'rightly emphasises the fact that the psyche, whose
seat was in the head, corresponds to the modern "unconscious", and that at
that stage of development consciousness was identified with *thumos* (heart)
and *phrenes* (lungs), and was localised in the chest or heart region. Hence
Pindar's expression for the soul – *eiōnos eidōlon* (image of Aion) – is
extraordinarily apt, for the collective unconscious not only imparts "oracles"
but forever represents the microcosm (i.e., the form of a physical man
mirroring the Cosmos)' (p. 193). We are now back with the symbol of the
cosmos, which perishes and dissolves in order to regenerate itself once more.

13. The basic sources for Dionysus-Zagreus *sparagmos* are Diodorus i. 96;
Firmicus Maternus, *De err. prof. rel.* 6; Clemens Alexandrinus *Protrepticus*,
ii. 18. A review and critical commentary of all accounts of the myth: IVAN
M. LINFORTH, *The Arts of Orpheus* (Berkeley, University of California Press,
1941), particularly the chapter 'Myth of the Dismemberment of Dionysus',
pp. 307 ff. For Euripides, see A. NAUCK, *Tragicorum Graecorum Fragmenta*,
2nd edn (Hildesheim: G. Olms, 1964), p. 475.

14. *De E Delphico* 9, 388 E. I quote LINFORTH, pp. 317–8. E. ROHDE, in *Psyche*,
(Leipzig, 1898) takes the view that it was a myth about the unity and
multigeneity of the cosmos (Vol. II, p. 119).

15. FRAZER, *New Golden Bough*, p. 543: 'It is now easy to understand why a savage
should desire to partake of the flesh of an animal or man whom he regards
as divine. By eating the body of the god he shares the god's attributes and
powers. . . . Thus the drinking of wine in the rites of a vine-god like
Dionysus is not an act of revelry, it is a solemn sacrament.'

16. MIRCEA ELIADE, *Myths, Dreams, and Mysteries*, translated by PHILIP MAIRET
(New York, Harper, 1960), pp. 46 and 183–84. In the same study Eliade
describes the bloody rite of the Khonds in India, which is similar to the
Dionysian *sparagmos*: 'The *meriah* was a voluntary victim, bought by the
community: he was allowed to live for years, he could marry and have
children. A few days before the sacrifice, the *meriah* was consecrated, that

is, he was identified with the divinity to be sacrificed; the people danced around and worshipped him. After this, they prayed to the Earth: "O Goddess, we offer thee this sacrifice; give us good harvests, good seasons and good health." And they added, turning to the victim: "We have bought thee and have not seized thee by force: now we sacrifice thee, and may no sin be accounted to us." The ceremony also included an orgy lasting several days. Finally the *meriah* was drugged with opium, and, after they had strangled him, they cut him into pieces. Each of the villages received a fragment of his body which they buried in the fields. The remainder of the body was burnt, and the ashes strewn over the land. This bloody rite evidently corresponds to the myth of the dismemberment of a primordial divinity' (pp. 187–8).

JUNG (*Origins of European Thought*) quotes the description by Bernardino de Sahagún, a Spanish missionary to the Aztecs six years after Mexico's conquest by Cortéz, of the 'eating of the god' – *teoqualo*. In this rite, a statue of the god Huitzilopochtli is moulded from the paste of the seed of prickly poppy.

And upon the next day the body of Huitzilopochtli died.

And he who slew him was the priest known as Quetzalcoatl. And that with which he slew him was a dart, pointed with flint, which he shot into his heart.

And he had died, thereupon they broke up his body of . . . dough. His heart was apportioned to Moctesuma.

And as for the rest of his members, which were made, as it were, to be his bones, they were distributed and divided up among all. . . . Each year . . . they ate it. . . . And they divided among themselves his body made of . . . dough, it was broken up exceeding small, very fine, as small seeds. The youths ate it.

And of this which they ate, it was said: 'The god is eaten.' And of those who ate it, it was said: 'They guard the god.'

(p. 170)

ALFRED MÉTRAUX describes in *Tupinamba: War and Cannibalism* (New York, 1955) the ritual of cannibalism among American Indians: 'Tupinamba restricted their cannibalism to prisoners specially captured for this purpose. Once captured and brought back to the captor's community, the prisoner was allowed to roam around in relative freedom during the weeks or months preceding his sacrifice. . . . During his stay he was alternately teased, flattered, insulted, honored. He in turn reciprocated by being as nasty toward his captors as he could, throwing nuts, fruits, and stones at them when they danced, foretelling their doom, boasting about his own bravery. The festivities surrounding his sacrifice would last from three to five days. He was eventually put to death by his executioner, often the man who'd touched him first at the time of his capture, which was a gruesome affair, since this was done by clubbing him to death . . . When he finally collapsed, dead from a cracked skull, his body was immediately quartered and barbecued, and the tasty morsels were distributed to the happy company. The prisoner's wife shed some tears over him, and then joined in the banquet. . . . As for the executioner, he ran away from the scene of the sacrifice . . . The flesh of the prisoner he was absolutely forbidden to eat. For a period of time, he was forbidden from full participation in the community's affairs, had a restricted diet, and had to keep to himself. His return to the tribe after the designated period was celebrated by a big drinking bout, during which he tattooed his body by slashing it. He came out of such an experience with his prestige in the community substantially enhanced' (pp. 151–5). (The author is grateful to Dr Sasha Weitman for having drawn his attention to this text.)

17. ELIADE, *Myths*, p. 80.
18. *Hesiod, The Homeric Hymns and Homerica*, translated by HUGH G. EVELYN-WHITE (Loeb Classical Library; Cambridge, Mass., Harvard University Press, 1967), p. 289.
19. DODDS, *The Bacchae*, Introduction, p. xi: 'Thus wine acquired religious value: he who drinks it becomes *ev θeos* – he has drunk deity.'
20. MIRCEA ELIADE, *Cosmos and History: The Myth of the Eternal Return*, translated by WILLARD R. TRASK (New York, Harper, 1959), pp. 22 and 28.
21. *The Works of Lucian*, Vol. V, translated by A. M. HARMON and M. D. MACLEOD (Loeb Classical Library; Cambridge, Mass., Harvard University Press, 1953), pp. 265, 269.
22. ELIADE, *Myths*, p. 74.
23. ELIADE, *ibid.*, pp. 47 and 196. On rites of initiation in Dionysian ceremonies, see H. JEANMAIRE, *Dionysus* (Paris, 1951). See also KIRK's commentary (*The Bacchae*) to 11. 857–60, p. 93.
24. JUNG, *Origins of European Thought*, p. 203. See also R. EISLER, *Orpheus – the Fisher* (London, 1923), pp. 280 ff.
25. ARNOTT writes in *Greek Scenic Conventions* about three scenes of earthquake, in *Prometheus*, in *Heracles* and in *The Bacchae*: 'These three earthquake scenes use the same method and the same formula – promise, elaboration and anticipation, statement. The effect is threatened, its result forecast and dwelt on in detail, and then finally announced as happening. In *Heracles Furens* the emphasis is on Heracles' madness and on the earthquake as a natural phenomenon, but the technique is the same. Given a theatre without a realistic scenery, there is no other way in which the effect can be obtained. The *skene* cannot crumble, for it is a permanent part of the theatre, but when the chorus say that it does, then by all the rules of conventional drama, the audience must accept that it does. Accompanied by an evocative dance-movement, this would be enough. Jean-Louis Barrault once produced Pompey's galley scene in *Antony and Cleopatra* with a row of oarsmen at the back of the stage rocking rhythmically from side to side; this, with the characters' words, gave a perfect impression of movement on the water, although there was no other scenery. We must imagine a similar effect here; the chorus reel and swirl to illustrate their wild words, a balletic accompaniment to the action' (pp. 124 f.; Oxford, Clarendon Press, 1962).
26. On thunder as a mystic sign, see ELIADE, *Myths*, pp. 81 ff.; on the symbolism of flight to the skies, *ibid.*, pp. 105 ff.
27. KIRK, *The Bacchae*, writes in his commentary (p. 120): '*tendril*: the Greek word means anything shaped like a spiral – here, presumably, a curling shot of ivy. The "lion's head" that Agave carries on her thyrsus-point (1141 f.), with its "crest of soft hair" (1186), is described as though it were ivy that was ordinarily fastened to the thyrsus-tip. Whether this is metaphor or delusion remains ambiguous.'
28. *Brecht on Theatre: The Development of an Aesthetic*, edited and translated by JOHN WILLETT (New York, Hill & Wang, 1964), p. 181.

The Sacrificial Crisis*

René Girard

As we have seen, the proper functioning of the sacrificial process requires not only the complete separation of the sacrificed victim from those beings for whom the victim is a substitute but also a similarity between both parties. This dual requirement can be fulfilled only through a delicately balanced mechanism of associations.

Any change, however slight, in the hierarchical classification of living creatures risks undermining the whole sacrificial structure. The sheer repetition of the sacrificial act – the repeated slaughter of the same type of victim – inevitably brings about such change. But the inability to adapt to new conditions is a trait characteristic of religion in general. If, as is often the case, we encounter the institution of sacrifice either in an advanced state of decay or reduced to relative insignificance, it is because it has already undergone a good deal of wear and tear.

Whether the slippage in the mechanism is due to 'too little' or 'too much' contact between the victim and those whom the victim represents, the results are the same. The elimination of violence is no longer effected; on the contrary, conflicts within the community multiply, and the menace of chain reactions looms ever larger.

If the gap between the victim and the community is allowed to grow too wide, all similarity will be destroyed. The victim will no longer be capable of attracting the violent impulses to itself; the sacrifice will cease to serve as a 'good conductor', in the sense that metal is a good conductor of electricity. On the other hand, if there is *too much* continuity the violence will overflow its channels. 'Impure' violence will mingle with the 'sacred' violence of the rites, turning the latter into a scandalous accomplice in the process of pollution, even a kind of catalyst in the propagation of further impurity.

These are postulates that seem to take form a priori from our earlier conclusions. They can also be discerned in literature – in the adaptations

---

* Reprinted from *Violence and the Sacred*, trans. Patrick Gregory (Baltimore and London: The Johns Hopkins University Press, 1977).

of certain myths in classical Greek tragedy, in particular in Euripides' version of the legend of Heracles.

Euripides' *Heracles* contains no tragic conflict, no debate between declared adversaries. The real subject of the play is the failure of a sacrifice, the act of sacrificial violence that suddenly *goes wrong*. Heracles, returning home after the completion of his labours, finds his wife and children in the power of a usurper named Lycus, who is preparing to offer them as sacrificial victims. Heracles kills Lycus. After this most recent act of violence, committed in the heart of the city, the hero's need to purify himself is greater than ever, and he sets about preparing a sacrifice of his own. His wife and children are with him when Heracles, suddenly seized by madness, mistakes them for his enemies and *sacrifices* them.

Heracles' misidentification of his family is attributed to Lyssa, goddess of madness, who is operating as an emissary of two other goddesses, Iris and Hera, who bear Heracles ill will. The preparations for the sacrifice provide an imposing setting for the homicidal outburst; it is unlikely that their dramatic significance passed unnoticed by the author. In fact, it is Euripides himself who directs our attention to the ritualistic origins of the onslaught. After the massacre, Heracles' father, Amphitryon, asks his son: 'My child, what happened to you? How could this horror have taken place? Was it perhaps the spilt blood that turned your head?' Heracles, who is just returning to consciousness and remembers nothing, inquires in turn: 'Where did the madness overtake me? Where did it strike me down?' Amphitryon replies: 'Near the altar, where you were purifying your hands over the sacred flames.'

The sacrifice contemplated by the hero succeeded only too well in polarizing the forces of violence. Indeed, it produced a superabundance of violence of a particularly virulent kind. As Amphitryon suggested, the blood shed in the course of the terrible labours and in the city itself finally turned the hero's head. Instead of drawing off the violence and allowing it to ebb away, the rites brought a veritable flood of violence down on the victim. The sacrificial rites were no longer able to accomplish their task; they swelled the surging tide of impure violence instead of channelling it. The mechanism of substitutions had gone astray, and those whom the sacrifice was designed to protect became its victims.

The difference between sacrificial and nonsacrificial violence is anything but exact; it is even arbitrary. At times the difference threatens to disappear entirely. There is no such thing as truly 'pure' violence. Nevertheless, sacrificial violence can, in the proper circumstances, serve as an agent of purification. That is why those who perform the rites are obliged to purify themselves at the conclusion of the sacrifice. The procedure followed is reminiscent of atomic power plants; when the expert has finished decontaminating the installation, he must himself be decontaminated. And accidents can always happen.

The catastrophic inversion of the sacrificial act would appear to be an essential element in the Heracles myth. The motif reappears, thinly concealed behind secondary themes, in another episode of his story, in Sophocles' *The Women of Trachis*.

Heracles had mortally wounded the centaur Nessus, who had assaulted Heracles' wife, Deianira. Before dying, the centaur gave the young woman a shirt smeared with his sperm – or, in Sophocles' version, smeared with his blood mixed with the blood of a Hydra. (Once again, as in the *Ion*, we encounter the theme of the two kinds of blood mingling to form one.)

The subject of the tragedy, as in Euripides' *Heracles*, is the return of the hero. In this instance Heracles is bringing with him a pretty young captive, of whom Deianira is jealous. Deianira sends a servant to her husband with a welcoming gift, the shirt of Nessus. With his dying breath the centaur had told her that the shirt would assure the wearer's eternal fidelity to her; but he cautioned her to keep it well out of the way of any flame or source of heat.

Heracles puts on the shirt, and soon afterward lights a fire for the rites of sacrificial purification. The flames activate the poison in the shirt; it is the rite itself that unlooses the evil. Heracles, contorted with pain, presently ends his life on the pyre he has begged his son to prepare. Before dying, Heracles kills the servant who delivered the shirt to him; this death, along with his own and the subsequent suicide of his wife, contributes to the cycle of violence heralded by Heracles' return and the failure of the sacrifice. Once again, violence has struck the beings who sought the protection of sacrificial rites.

A number of sacrifice motifs intermingle in these two plays. A special sort of impurity clings to the warrior returning to his homeland, still tainted with the slaughter of war. In the case of Heracles, his sanguinary labours render him particularly impure.

The returning warrior risks carrying the seed of violence into the very heart of his city. The myth of Horatius, as explicated by Georges Dumézil, illustrates this theme: Horatius kills his sister before any ritual purification has been performed. In the case of Heracles the impurity triumphs over the rite itself.

If we examine the mechanism of violence in these two tragedies, we notice that when the sacrifice goes wrong it sets off a chain reaction of the sort defined in the first chapter. The murder of Lycus is presented in the Euripides play as a last 'labour' of the hero, a still-rational prelude to the insane outburst that follows. Seen from the perspective of the ritualist, it might well constitute a first link of impure violence. With this incident, as we have noted, violence invades the heart of the city. This initial murder corresponds to the death of the old servant in *The Women of Trachis*.

Supernatural intervention plays no part in these episodes, except perhaps to cast a thin veil over the true subject: the sacrificial celebration that has gone wrong. The goddess Lyssa, Nessus' shirt – these add nothing to the meaning of the two stories; rather, they act as a veil, and as soon as the veil is drawn aside we encounter the same theme of 'good' violence turning into 'bad'. The mythological accompaniments of the stories can be seen as redundant. Lyssa, the goddess of madness, sounds more like a refugee from an allegorical tale than a real goddess, and Nessus' shirt joins company with all the acts of violence that Heracles carries on his back.

The theme of the Warrior's Return is not, strictly speaking, mythological, and readily lends itself to sociological or psychological interpretations. The conquering hero who threatens to destroy the liberty of his homeland belongs to history, not myth. Certainly that is the way Corneille seems to approach the subject in *Horace*, although in his version of the tale the ideology is somewhat reversed – the returning warrior is rightly shocked by his sister's lack of patriotism. We could easily translate the 'case histories' of Heracles and Horatius into psychological or psychoanalytical terms and come up with numerous working theories, each at variance with the other. But we should avoid this temptation, for in debating the relative merits of each theory we would lose sight of the role played by ritual – a subject that has nothing to do with such debates, even though it may, as we shall see, open the way to them. Being more *primitive*, ritualistic action is hospitable to all ideological interpretations and dependent on none. It has only one axiom: the contagious nature of the violence encountered by the warrior in battle – and only one prescription: the proper performance of ritual purification. Its sole purpose is to prevent the resurgence of violence and its spread throughout the community.

The two tragedies we have been discussing present in anecdotal form, as if dealing exclusively with exceptional individuals, events that are significant because they affect the community as a whole. Sacrifice is a social act, and when it goes amiss the consequences are not limited to some 'exceptional' individual singled out by Destiny.

Historians seem to agree that Greek tragedy belonged to a period of transition between the dominance of an archaic theocracy and the emergence of a new, 'modern' order based on statism and laws. Before its decline the archaic order must have enjoyed a certain stability; and this stability must have reposed on its religious element – that is, on the sacrificial rites.

Although they predate the tragedians, the pre-Socratics are often regarded as the philosophers of classical tragedy. In their writings we can find echoes of the religious crisis we are attempting to define. The fifth fragment of Heraclitus quite clearly deals with the decay of sacrificial rites, with their inability to purify what is impure. Religious beliefs are compromised by the decadent state of the ritual: 'In vain do they strive for purification by besmirching themselves with blood, as the man who has bathed in the mire seeks to cleanse himself with mud. Such antics can only strike the beholder as utter folly! In addressing their prayers to images of the gods, they might just as well be speaking to the walls, without seeking to know the true nature of gods or heroes.'

The difference between blood spilt for ritual and for criminal purposes no longer holds. The Heraclitus fragment appears in even sharper relief when compared to analogous passages in the Old Testament. The preexilian prophets Amos, Isaiah, and Micah denounce in vehement terms the impotence of the sacrificial process and ritual in general. In the most explicit manner they link the decay of religious practices to the deterioration of contemporary behaviour. Inevitably, the eroding of the sacrificial system seems to result in the emergence of reciprocal violence. Neighbours who had previously discharged their mutual aggressions on a third party, joining together in the sacrifice of an 'outside' victim, now turn to sacrificing one another. Empedocles' *Purifications* brings us even closer to the problem:

> 136. When will the sinister noise of this carnage cease? Can you not see that you are devouring one another with your callous hearts?
> 137. The father seizes hold of the son, who has changed form; in his mad delusion he kills him, murmuring prayers. The son cries out, imploring his insane executioner to spare him. But the father hears him not, and cuts his throat, and spreads a great feast in his palace. In the same way the son takes hold of the father, the children their mother, one slaughtering the other and devouring their own flesh and blood.

The concept of a 'sacrificial crisis' may be useful in clarifying certain aspects of Greek tragedy. To a real extent it is sacrificial religion that provides the language for these dramas; the criminal in the plays sees himself not so much as a righter-of-wrongs as a performer-of-sacrifices. We always view the 'tragic flaw' from the perspective of the new, emergent order; never from that of the old order in the final stages of decay. The reason for this approach is clear: modern thought has never been able to attribute any real function to the practice of sacrifice, and because the nature of the practice eludes us, we naturally find it difficult to determine when and if this practice is in the process of disintegration. In the case of Greek tragedy it is not enough merely to believe in the existence of the old order; we must look deeper if we hope to discover the religious problems of the era. Unlike the Jewish prophets, whose viewpoint was historical, the Greek tragedians evoked their own sacrificial crisis in terms of legendary figures whose forms were fixed by tradition.

All the bloody events that serve as background to the plays – the plagues and pestilences, civil and foreign wars – undoubtedly reflect the contemporary scene, but the images are unclear, as if viewed through a glass darkly. Each time, for example, a play of Euripides deals with the collapse of a royal house (as in *Heracles, Iphigenia in Aulis*, or *The Bacchae*), we are convinced that the poet is suggesting that the scene before our eyes is only the tip of the iceberg, that the real issue is the fate of the entire community. At the moment when Heracles is slaughtering his family offstage, the chorus cries out: 'Look, look! The tempest is shaking the house; the roof is falling in.'

If the tragic crisis is indeed to be described in terms of the sacrificial crisis, its relationship to sacrifice should be apparent in all aspects of tragedy – either conveyed directly through explicit reference or perceived indirectly, in broad outline, underlying the texture of the drama.

If the art of tragedy is to be defined in a single phrase, we might do worse than call attention to one of its most characteristic traits: the opposition of symmetrical elements. There is no aspect of the plot, form, or language of a tragedy in which this symmetrical pattern does not recur. The third actor, for instance, hardly constitutes the innovation that critics have claimed. Third actor or no third actor, the core of the drama remains the tragic dialogue; that is, the fateful confrontation during which the two protagonists exchange insults and accusations with increasing earnestness and rapidity. The Greek public brought to these verbal contests the same educated sense of appreciation that French audiences many centuries later evinced for their own classic drama – for Théramène's famous speech from the last act of *Phèdre*, for example, or for almost any passage from *Le Cid*.

The symmetry of the tragic dialogue is perfectly mirrored by the stichomythia, in which the two protagonists address one another in alternating lines. In tragic dialogue hot words are substituted for cold steel. But whether the violence is physical or verbal, the suspense remains the same. The adversaries match blow for blow, and they seem so evenly matched that it is impossible to predict the outcome of the battle. The structural similarity between the two forms of violence is illustrated by the description of the duel between the brothers Eteocles and Polyneices in Euripides' *Phoenician Women*. There is nothing in this account that does not apply equally to both brothers: their parries, thrusts, and feints, their gestures and postures, are identical: 'If either saw the other's eye peer over the rim of his shield, He raised his spear.'

Polyneices loses his spear in the fight, and so does Eteocles. Both are wounded. Each blow upsets the equilibrium, threatening to decide the outcome then and there. It is immediately followed by a new blow that not only redresses the balance but creates a symmetrical disequilibrium that is itself, naturally enough, of short duration. The tragic suspense follows the rhythm of these rapid exchanges, each one of which promises to bring matters to a head – but never quite does so. 'They struggle now on even terms, each having spent his spear. Swords are unsheathed, and the two brothers are locked in close combat. Shield clashes with shield, and a great clamour engulfs them both.' Even death fails to tip the balance. 'They hit the dust and lay together side by side: and their heritage was still unclaimed.'

The death of the brothers resolves nothing; it simply perpetuates the symmetry of the battle. Each had been his army's champion, and the two armies now resume the struggle, reestablish the symmetry. Oddly enough, however, the conflict is now transferred to a purely verbal plane, transforming itself into a true tragic dialogue. Tragedy now assumes its proper function as a verbal extension of physical combat, an interminable debate set off by the chronically indecisive character of an act of violence committed previously:

The soldiers then leapt to their feet, and the argument began. We claimed that our king had won; they claimed the victory for Polyneices. The captains quarrelled, too. Some said that Polyneices had struck the first blow; others replied that death had snatched the palm of victory from both claimants.

The indecisiveness of the first combat spreads quite naturally to the second, which then sows it abroad. The tragic dialogue is a debate without resolution. Each side resolutely continues to deploy the same arguments, emphases, goals; *Gleichgewicht* is Hölderlin's word for it, Tragedy is the balancing of the scale, not of justice but of violence. No sooner is something added to one side of the scale than its equivalent is contributed to the other. The same insults and accusations fly from one combatant to the other, as a ball flies from one player to another in tennis. The conflict stretches on interminably because between the two adversaries there is no difference whatsoever.

The equilibrium in the struggle has often been attributed to a so-called tragic impartiality; Hölderlin's word is *Impartialität*. I do not find this interpretation quite satisfactory. Impartiality implies a deliberate refusal to take sides, a firm commitment to treat both contestants equally. The impartial party is not eager to resolve the issue, does not want to know if there is a resolution; nor does he maintain that resolution is impossible. His impartiality-at-any-price is not unfrequently simply an unsubstantiated assertion of superiority. One of the adversaries is right, the other wrong, and the onlooker is obliged to take sides; either that, or the rights and wrongs are so evenly distributed between the two factions that taking sides is impossible. The self-proclaimed advocate of impartiality does not want to commit himself to either course of action. If pushed toward one camp, he seeks refuge in the other. Men always find it distasteful to admit that the 'reasons' on both sides of a dispute are equally valid – which is to say that *violence operates without reason.*

Tragedy begins at that point where the illusion of impartiality, as well as the illusions of the adversaries, collapses. For example, in *Oedipus the King*, Oedipus, Creon, and Tiresias are each in turn drawn into a conflict that each had thought to resolve in the role of impartial mediator.

It is not clear to what extent the tragedians themselves managed to remain impartial. For example, Euripides in *The Phoenician Women* barely conceals his preference for Eteocles – or perhaps we should say his preference for the Athenian public's approval. In any case, his partiality is superficial. The preferences registered for one side or another never prevent the authors from constantly underlining the symmetrical relationship between the adversaries.

At the very moment when they appear to be abandoning impartiality, the tragedians do their utmost to deprive the audience of any means of taking sides. Aeschylus, Sophocles, and Euripides all utilize the same procedures and almost identical phraseology to convey symmetry, identity, reciprocity. We encounter here an aspect of tragic art that has been largely overlooked by contemporary criticism. Nowadays critics tend to assess a work of art on the basis of its *originality*. To the extent that an author cannot claim exclusive rights to his themes, his style, and his aesthetic effects, his work is deemed deficient. In the domain of aesthetics, singularity reigns supreme.

Such criteria cannot apply, of course, to Greek tragedy, whose authors were not committed to the doctrine of originality at any price. Nevertheless, our frustrated individualism still exerts a deleterious effect on modern interpretations of Greek tragedy.

It is readily apparent that Aeschylus, Sophocles, and Euripides shared certain literary traits and that the characters in their plays have certain characteristics in common. Yet there is no reason to label these resemblances mere stereotypes. It is my belief that these 'stereotypes' contain the very essence of Greek tragedy. And if the tragic element in these plays still eludes us, it is because we have obstinately averted our attention from these similarities.

The tragedians portray men and women caught up in a form of violence too impersonal in its workings, too brutal in its results, to allow any sort of value judgement, any sort of distinction, subtle or simplistic, to be drawn between 'good' and 'wicked' characters. That is why most modern interpretations go astray; we have still not extricated ourselves entirely from the 'Manichean' frame of reference that gained sway in the Romantic era and still exerts its influence today.

In Greek tragedy violence invariably effaces the differences between antagonists. The sheer impossibility of asserting their differences fuels the rage of Eteocles and Polyneices. In Euripides' *Heracles* the hero kills Lycus to keep him from sacrificing his family, and next he does what he wanted to prevent his enemy from doing, thereby falling victim to the ironic humour of a Destiny that seems to work hand in glove with violence. In the end it is Heracles who carries out the crime meditated by his counterpart. The more a tragic conflict is prolonged, the more likely it is to culminate in a violent mimesis; the resemblance between the combatants grows ever stronger until each presents a mirror image of the other. There is a scientific corollary: modern research suggests that individuals of quite different make-up and background respond to violence in essentially the same way.

It is the act of reprisal, the repetition of imitative acts of violence, that characterizes tragic plotting. The destruction of differences is particularly spectacular when the hierarchichal distance between the characters, the amount of respect due from one to the other, is great – between father and son, for instance. This scandalous effacement of distinctions is apparent in Euripides' *Alcestis*. Father and son are engaged in a tragic dialogue; each accuses the other of fleeing from death and leaving the heroine to die. The symmetry is perfect, emphasized by the symmetrical interventions of the members of the Chorus, who first castigate the son ('Young man, remember to whom you are speaking; do not insult your father'), and then rebuke the father ('Enough has been said on this subject; cease, we pray you, to abuse your own son').

In *Oedipus the King* Sophocles frequently puts in Oedipus's mouth words that emphasize his resemblance to his father: resemblance in desires, suspicions, and course of action. If the hero throws himself impetuously into the investigation that causes his downfall, it is because he is reacting just as Laius did in seeking out the potential assassin who, according to the oracles, would replace him on the throne of Thebes and in the bed of the queen.

Oedipus finally kills Laius, but it is Laius who, at the crossroads, first raised his hand against his son. The patricide thus takes part in a reciprocal exchange of murderous gestures. It is an act of reprisal in a universe based on reprisals.

At the core of the Oedipus myth, as Sophocles presents it, is the proposition that all masculine relationships are based on reciprocal acts of violence. Laius, taking his cue from the oracle, violently rejects

286

Oedipus out of fear that his son will seize his throne and invade his
conjugal bed. Oedipus, taking his cue from the oracle, does away with
Laius, violently rebuffs the sphinx, then takes their places – as king and
'scourge of the city', respectively. Again, Oedipus, taking his cue from
the oracle, plots the death of that unknown figure who may be seeking
to usurp his own position. Oedipus, Creon, and Tiresias, each taking his
cue from the oracle, seek one another's downfall.

All these acts of violence gradually wear away the differences that
exist not only in the same family but throughout the community. The
tragic combat between Oedipus and Tiresias pits the community's chief
spiritual leaders against one another. The enraged Oedipus seeks to
strip the aura of 'mystery' from his rival, to prove that he is a false
prophet, nothing more:

> Come tell us: have you truly shown yourself a prophet? When the
> terrible sphinx held sway over our countrymen, did you ever whisper
> the words that would have delivered them? That riddle was not to be
> answered by anyone; the gift of prophecy was called for. Yet that gift
> was clearly not yours to give; nor was it ever granted to you, either
> by the birds or by the gods.

Confronted by the king's frustration and rage at being unable to
uncover the truth, Tiresias launches his own challenge. The terms are
much the same: 'If you are so clever at solving enigmas, why are you
powerless to solve this one?' Both parties in this tragic dialogue have
recourse to the same tactics, use the same weapons, and strive for the
same goal: destruction of the adversary. Tiresias poses as the champion
of tradition, taking up the cudgels on behalf of the oracles flouted by
Oedipus. However, in so doing he shows himself insolent to royal
authority. Although the targets are individuals, it is the institutions
that receive the blows. Legitimate authority trembles on its pedestal,
and the combatants finally assist in the downfall of the very order they
strove to maintain. The impiety referred to by the chorus – the neglect
of the oracles, the general decadence that pervades the religion of
the community – are surely part of the same phenomenon that works
away at the undermining of family relationships, as well as of religious
and social hierarchies.

The *sacrificial crisis*, that is, the disappearance of the sacrificial rites,
coincides with the disappearance of the difference between impure
violence and purifying violence. When this difference has been effaced,
purification is no longer possible and impure, contagious, reciprocal
violence spreads throughout the community.

The sacrificial distinction, the distinction between the pure and the
impure, cannot be obliterated without obliterating all other differences

as well. One and the same process of violent reciprocity engulfs the whole. The sacrificial crisis can be defined, therefore, as a crisis of distinctions – that is, a crisis affecting the cultural order. This cultural order is nothing more than a regulated system of distinctions in which the differences among individuals are used to establish their 'identity' and their mutual relationships.

In the first chapter [of *Violence and the Sacred*] the danger threatening the community with the decay of sacrificial practices was portrayed in terms of physical violence, of cyclical vengeance set off by a chain reaction. We now discover more insidious forms of the same evil. When the religious framework of a society starts to totter, it is not exclusively or immediately the physical security of the society that is threatened; rather, the whole cultural foundation of the society is put in jeopardy. The institutions lose their vitality; the protective façade of the society gives way; social values are rapidly eroded, and the whole cultural structure seems on the verge of collapse.

The hidden violence of the sacrificial crisis eventually succeeds in destroying distinctions, and this destruction in turn fuels the renewed violence. In short, it seems that anything that adversely affects the institution of sacrifice will ultimately pose a threat to the very basis of the community, to the principles on which its social harmony and equilibrium depend.

A single principle is at work in primitive religion and classical tragedy alike, a principle implicit but fundamental. Order, peace, and fecundity depend on cultural distinctions; it is not these distinctions but the loss of them that gives birth to fierce rivalries and sets members of the same family or social group at one another's throats.

Modern society aspires to equality among men and tends instinctively to regard all differences, even those unrelated to the economic or social status of men, as obstacles in the path of human happiness. This modern ideal exerts an obvious influence on ethnological approaches, although more often on the level of technical procedure than that of explicit principle. The permutations of this ideal are complex, rich in potential contradictions, and difficult to characterize briefly. Suffice it to say that an 'antidifferential' prejudice often falsifies the ethnological outlook not only on the origins of discord and conflict but also on all religious modes. Although usually implicit, its principles are explicitly set forth in Victor Turner's *The Ritual Process*: 'Structural differentiation, both vertical and horizontal, is the foundation of strife and factionalism, and of struggles in dyadic relations between incumbents of positions or rivals for positions.'[1] When differences come unhinged they are generally identified as the cause of those rivalries for which they also furnish the stakes. This has not always been their role. As in the case of sacrificial rites, when they no longer serve as a dam against violence, they serve to swell the flood.

In order to rid ourselves of some fashionable intellectual attitudes – useful enough in their place, but not always relevant in dealing with the past – we might turn to Shakespeare, who in the course of the famous speech of Ulysses in *Troilus and Cressida* makes some interesting observations on the interaction of violence and 'differences'. The point of view of primitive religion and Greek tragedy could not be better summarized than by this speech.

The Greek army has been besieging Troy for a long time and is growing demoralized through want of action. In commenting on their position, Ulysses strays from the particular to a general reflection on the role of 'Degree', or distinctions, in human endeavours. 'Degree', or *gradus*, is the underlying principle of all order, natural and cultural. It permits individuals to find a place for themselves in society; it lends a meaning to things, arranging them in proper sequence within a hierarchy; it defines the objects and moral standards that men alter, manipulate, and transform. The musical metaphor describes that order as a 'structure', in the modern sense of the word, a system of chords thrown into disharmony by the sudden intervention of reciprocal violence:

> . . . O when Degree is shaked
> Which is the ladder to all high designs,
> The enterprise is sick! How could communities,
> Degrees in schools, and brotherhoods in cities,
> Peaceful commerce from dividable shores,
> The primogenitive and due of birth,
> Prerogative of age, crowns, sceptres, laurels,
> But by degree, stand in authentic place?
> Take but degree away, untune that string,
> And, hark, what discord follows! Each thing meets
> In mere oppugnancy: the bounded waters
> Should lift their bosoms higher than the shores,
> And make a sop of all this solid globe:
> Strength should be lord of imbecility,
> And the rude son should strike his father dead:
> Force should be right; or rather, right and wrong
> Between whose endless jar justice resides,
> Should lose their names, and so should justice too.

As in Greek tragedy and primitive religion, it is not the differences but the loss of them that gives rise to violence and chaos, that inspires Ulysses' plaint. This loss forces men into a perpetual confrontation, one that strips them of all their distinctive characteristics – in short, of their 'identities'. Language itself is put in jeopardy. 'Each thing meets/In mere oppugnancy': the adversaries are reduced to indefinite objects, 'things' that wantonly collide with each other like loose cargo on the decks of a storm-tossed ship. The metaphor of the floodtide that transforms the earth's surface to a muddy mass is frequently employed by Shakespeare to designate the undifferentiated state of the world that is also portrayed in Genesis and that we have attributed to the sacrificial crisis.

In this situation no one and nothing is spared; coherent thinking collapses and rational activities are abandoned. All associative forms are dissolved or become antagonistic; all values, spiritual or material, perish. Of course, formal education, as represented by academic 'degrees', is rendered useless, because its value derives from the now inoperative principle of universal differentiation. To say that this speech merely reflects a Renaissance commonplace, the great chain of being, is unsatisfactory. Who has ever seen a great chain of being collapse?

Ulysses is a career soldier, authoritarian in temper and conservative in inclination. Nevertheless, the order he is committed to defend is secretly acknowledged as arbitrary. The end of distinctions means the triumph of the strong over the weak, the pitting of father against son – the end of all human justice, which is here unexpectedly defined in terms of 'differences' among individuals. If perfect equilibrium invariably leads to violence, as in Greek tragedy, it follows that the relative nonviolence guaranteed by human justice must be defined as a sort of imbalance, a difference between 'good' and 'evil' parallel to the sacrificial difference between 'pure' and 'impure'. The idea of justice as a balanced scale, an exercise in exquisite impartiality, is utterly foreign to this theory, which sees the roots of justice in differences among men and the demise of justice in the elimination of these differences. Whenever the terrible equilibrium of tragedy prevails, all talk of right and wrong is futile. At that point in the conflict one can only say to the combatants: Make friends or pursue your own ruin.

If the two-in-one crisis that we have described is indeed a fundamental reality – if the collapse of the cultural structure of a society leads to reciprocal violence and if this collapse encourages the spread of violence everywhere – then we ought to see signs of this reality outside the restricted realms of Greek tragedy or Shakespearean drama. The closer our contact with primitive societies, the more rapidly these societies tend to lose their distinctive qualities; but this loss is in some cases effected through a *sacrificial crisis*. And in some cases these crises have been directly observed by ethnologists. Scholarly literature on the subject is rather extensive; rarely, however, does a coherent picture emerge. More often than not the accounts are fragmentary, mingled with commentary relating to purely structural matters. A remarkable exception, well worth our attention here, is Jules Henry's *Jungle People*, which deals with the Kaingang Indians of Santa Katarina in Brazil.[2] The author came to live with the Indians shortly after they had been transferred to a reservation, when the consequences of that last and radical change had not yet completely taken hold. He was thus able to observe at first hand, or through the testimony of witnesses, the process I call the sacrificial crisis.

The extreme poverty of the Kaingang culture on a religious as well as a technological level made a strong impression on Henry, who attributed it to the blood feuds (that is, the cyclical vengeance) carried on among close relatives. To describe the effects of this reciprocal violence he instinctively turned to the hyperbolic imagery of the great myths, in particular to the image of plague: 'Feuds spread, cleaving the society asunder like a deadly axe, blighting its life like the plague.'[3]

These are the very symptoms that we have made bold to identify with the sacrificial crisis, or crisis of distinctions. The Kaingang seem to have abandoned all their old mythology in favour of stories of actual acts of revenge. When discussing internecine murders, 'they seem to be fitting together the parts of a machine, the intricate workings of which they know precisely. Their absorbed interest in the history of their own destruction has impressed on their minds with flawless clarity the multitudinous cross-workings of feuds.'[4]

Although the Kaingang blood feuds represent the decadence of a system that once enjoyed relative stability, the feuds still retain some remnant of their original 'sacrificial' nature. They constitute, in fact, a more forceful, more violent – and therefore less effective – effort to keep a grip on the 'good' violence, with all its protective and constraining powers. Indeed, the 'bad' violence does not yet penetrate the defences of those Indians who are said to 'travel together'; that is, go out together on hunting expeditions. However, this group is always small in number, and the relative peace that reigns within it is in sharp contrast to the violence that rages triumphantly outside – *between* the different groups.

Within the group there is a spirit of conciliation. The most inflammatory challenges pass unacknowledged; adultery, which provokes an instant and bloody reprisal among members of rival groups, is openly tolerated. As long as violence does not cross a certain threshold of intensity, it remains sacrificial and defines an inner circle of nonviolence essential to the accomplishment of basic social functions – that is, to the survival of the society. Nonetheless, the moment arrives when the inner group is contaminated. As soon as they are installed on a reservation, members of a group tend to turn against one another.

291

They can no longer polarize their aggressions against outside enemies, the 'others', the 'different men'.[5]

The chain of killings finally reaches the heart of the individual group. At this point, the very basis of the social life of the group is challenged. In the case of the Kaingang, outside factors – primarily the Brazilian authorities – intervened assuring the physical survival of the last remnants of the Kaingang while guaranteeing the extinction of their culture.

In acknowledging the existence of an internal process of self-destruction among the Kaingang, we are not attempting to diminish or dismiss the part played by the white man in this tragedy. The problem of Brazilian responsibility would not be resolved even if the new settlers had refrained from using hired assassins to speed up the process of destruction. Indeed, it is worth asking whether the impetus behind the Kaingang's dismemberment of their culture and the inexorable character of their self-destruction were not ultimately due to the pressure of a foreign culture. Even if this were the case, cyclical violence still presents a threat to any society, whether or not it is under pressure from a foreign culture or from any other external interference. The process is basically internal.

Such is Henry's conclusion after contemplating the terrible plight of the Kaingang. He uses the phrase 'social suicide', and we must admit that the potentiality for such self-destruction always exists. In the course of history a number of communities doubtless succumbed to their own violent impulses and disappeared without a trace. Even if we have certain reservations about his interpretation of the case under discussion, Henry's conclusions have direct pertinence to numberless groups of human beings whose histories remain unknown. 'This group, excellently suited in their physical and psychological endowments to cope with the rigours of their natural environment, were yet unable to withstand the internal forces that were disrupting their society, and having no culturally standardized devices to deal with them, were committing social suicide.'[6]

The fear generated by the kill-or-be-killed syndrome, the tendency to 'anticipate' violence by lashing out first (akin to our contemporary concept of 'preventive war') cannot be explained in purely psychological terms. The notion of a *sacrificial crisis* is designed to dissipate the psychological illusion; even in those instances when Henry borrows the language of psychology, it is clear that he does not share the illusion. In a universe both deprived of any transcendental code of justice and exposed to violence, everybody has reason to fear the worst. The difference between a projection of one's own paranoia and an objective evaluation of circumstances has been worn away.[7]

Once that crucial distinction has vanished, both psychology and sociology falter. The professional observer who distributes good or bad marks to individuals and cultures on the basis of their 'normality' and 'abnormality' is obliged to make his observations from the particular perspective of someone *who does not run the risk of being killed.* Psychologists and other social scientists ordinarily suppose a peaceable substructure for their subjects; indeed, they tend to take this pacific quality for granted. Yet nothing in their mode of reasoning, which they like to regard as radically 'enlightened', solidly based, and free of idealistic nonsense, justifies such an assumption – as Henry's study makes clear: 'With a single murder the murderer enters a locked system. He must kill and kill again, he must plan whole massacres lest a single survivor remain to avenge his kin.'[8]

Henry encountered some particularly bloodthirsty specimens among the Kaingang, but he also fell in with individual members of the tribe who were peaceable and perspicacious and who sought in vain to free themselves from the machinery of destruction. *'Kaingang murderers are like characters of a Greek tragedy in the grip of a natural law whose processes once started can never be stayed.'*

Although they approached the subject more obliquely, the Greek tragedians were concerned, like Jules Henry, with the destruction of a cultural order. The violent reciprocity that engulfs their characters is a manifestation of this destructive process. Our own concern with sacrificial matters shows the vital role the ritualistic crisis – the abolition of all distinctions – plays in the formation of tragedy. In turn, a study of tragedy can clarify the nature of this crisis and those aspects of primitive religion that are inseparably linked to it. For in the final analysis, the sole purpose of religion is to prevent the recurrence of reciprocal violence.

I am inclined, then, to assert that tragedy opens a royal way to the great dilemmas of religious ethnology. Such a stand will no doubt elicit the scorn of 'scientific' researchers as well as fervent Hellenophiles, from the defenders of traditional humanism to the disciples of Nietzsche and Heidegger. The scientifically inclined have a tendency to regard literary folk as dubious company, whose society grows increasingly dangerous as their own efforts remain obstinately theoretical. As for the Hellenophiles, they are quick to see blasphemy in any parallel drawn between classical Greece and primitive societies.

It is essential to make it clear, once and for all, that to draw on tragic literature does not mean to relinquish scholarly standards of research; nor does it constitute a purely 'aesthetic' approach to the subject. At the same time we must manage to appease the men of letters who tremble at the thought of applying scientific methods of any kind to literature, convinced as they are that such methods can only lead to facile 'reductionism' of the works of art, to sterile analyses that disregard the spirit of the literature. The conflict between the 'two cultures', science and literature, rests on a common failure, a negative complicity shared by literary critics and religious specialists. Neither group perceives the underlying principle on which their objects are based. The tragedians seem to have laboured in vain to make this principle manifest. They never achieve more than partial success, and their efforts are perpetually undone by the differentiations imposed on their work by literary critics and social scientists.

Ethnologists are not unaware that ritual impurity is linked to the dissolution of distinctions between individuals and institutions.[10] However, they fail to recognize the dangers inherent in this dissolution. As we have noted, the modern mind has difficulty conceiving of violence in terms of a loss of distinctions, or of a loss of distinctions in terms of violence. Tragedy can help to resolve this difficulty if we agree to view the plays from a radical perspective. Tragic drama addresses itself to a burning issue – in fact, to *the* burning issue. The issue is never directly alluded to in the plays, and for good reason, since it has to do with the dissolution by reciprocal violence of those very values and distinctions around which the conflict of the plays supposedly revolves. Because this subject is taboo – and even more than taboo, almost unspeakable in the language devoted to distinctions – literary critics proceed to obscure with their own meticulously differentiated categories the relative lack of difference between antagonists that characterizes a tragic confrontation in classical drama.

The primitive mind, in contrast, has no difficulty imagining an affiliation between violence and nondifferentiation and, indeed, is often obsessed by the possible consequences of such a union. Natural differences are conceived in terms of cultural differences, and vice versa. Where we would view the loss of a distinctive quality as a wholly natural phenomenon having no bearing on human relationships, the primitive man might well view this occurrence with deep dread. Because there is no real difference between the various modes of differentiation, there is in consequence no difference between the manner in which things fail to differ; the disappearance of natural differences can thus bring to mind the dissolution of regulations pertaining to the individual's proper place in society – that is, can instigate a sacrificial crisis.

Once we have grasped this fact, certain religious phenomena never explained by traditional approaches suddenly become intelligible. A brief glance at one of the more spectacular of these phenomena will,

I think, serve to demonstrate the usefulness of applying the tragic tradition to religious ethnology.

In some primitive societies twins inspire a particular terror. It is not unusual for one of the twins, and often both, to be put to death. The origin of this terror has long puzzled ethnologists.

Today the enigma is presented as a problem of classification. Two individuals suddenly appear, where only one had been expected; in those societies that permit them to survive, twins often display a single social personality. The problem of classification as defined by structuralism does not justify the death of the twins. The reasons that prompt men to do away with certain of their children are undoubtedly bad reasons, but they are not frivolous ones. Culture is not merely a jigsaw puzzle where the extra pieces are discarded once the picture has been completed. If the problem of classification becomes crucial, that is because its implications are crucial.

Twins invariably share a cultural identity, and they often have a striking physical resemblance to each other. Wherever differences are lacking, violence threatens. Between the biological twins and the sociological twins there arises a confusion that grows more troubled as the question of differences reaches a crisis. It is only natural that twins should awaken fear, for they are harbingers of indiscriminate violence, the greatest menace to primitive societies. As soon as the twins of violence appear they multiply prodigiously, by scissiparity, as it were, and produce a sacrificial crisis. It is essential to prevent the spread of this highly contagious disease. When faced with biological twins the normal reaction of the culture is simply to avoid contagion. The way primitive societies attempt to accomplish this offers a graphic demonstration of the kind of danger they associate with twins. In societies where their very existence is considered dangerous, the infants are 'exposed'; that is, abandoned outside the community under conditions that make their death inevitable. Any act of *direct* physical violence against the anathema is scrupulously avoided. Any such act would only serve to entrap the perpetrators in a vicious circle of violence – the trap 'bad' violence sets for the community and baits with the birth of twins.

An inventory of the customs, prescriptions, and interdictions relating to twins in those societies where they are regarded with dread reveals one common concern: the fear of pollution. The divergences from one culture to the next are easily explained in terms of the religious attitudes defined above, which pertain to the strictly empirical – that is, terrorstricken – character of the precautions taken against 'bad' violence. In the case of twins, the precautions are misdirected; nevertheless, they become quite intelligible once we recognize the terror that inspires them.

Although the menace is somewhat differently perceived from society to society, it is fundamentally the same everywhere, and a challenge with which all religious institutions are obliged to cope.

The Nyakyusa maintain that the parents of twins are contaminated by 'bad' violence, and there is a certain logic about that notion, since the parents are, after all, responsible for engendering the twins. In reference to the twins the parents are designated by a term that is applied to all threatening individuals, all monstrous or terrifying creatures. In order to prevent the spread of pollution the parents are required to isolate themselves and submit to rites of purification; only then are they allowed to rejoin the community.[11]

It is not unreasonable to believe that the relatives and close friends of the twins' parents, as well as their immediate neighbours, are those most directly exposed to the infection. 'Bad' violence is by definition a force that works on various levels – physical, familial, social – and spreads from one to the other.

Twins are impure in the same way that a warrior steeped in carnage is impure, or an incestuous couple, or a menstruating woman. All forms of violence lead back to violence. We overlook this fact because the primitive concept of a link between the loss of distinctions and violence is strange to us; but we need only consider the calamities primitive people associate with twins to perceive the logic of this concept. Deadly epidemics can result from contact with twins, as can mysterious illnesses that cause sterility in women and animals. Even more significant to us is the role of twins in provoking discord among neighbours, a fatal collapse of ritual, the transgression of interdictions – in short, their part in instigating a sacrificial crisis.

As we have seen, the sacred embraces all those forces that threaten to harm man or trouble his peace. Natural forces and sickness are not distinguished from the threat of a violent disintegration of the community. Although man-made violence plays a dominant role in the dialectics of the sacred and is never completely omitted from the warnings issued by religion, it tends to be relegated to the background and treated as if it emanated from outside man. One might say that it has been deliberately hidden away almost out of sight behind forces that are genuinely exterior to man.

Behind the image of twins lurks the baleful aspect of the sacred, perceived as a disparate but formidably unified force. The sacrificial crisis can be viewed as a general offensive of violence directed against the community, and there is reason to fear that the birth of twins might herald this crisis.

In the primitive societies where twins are not killed they often enjoy a privileged position. This reversal corresponds to the attitudes we have noted in regard to menstrual blood. Any phenomenon linked to impure violence is capable of being inverted and rendered beneficent; but this can take place only within the immutable and rigorous framework of ritual practice. The purifying and pacifying aspects of violence take precedence over its destructive aspects. The apparition of twins, then, if properly handled, may in certain societies be seen to presage good events, not bad ones.

Notes

1. VICTOR TURNER, *The Ritual Process* (Chicago, 1969), p. 179.
2. JULES HENRY, *Jungle People* (New York, 1964).
3. Ibid., p. 50.
4. Ibid., p. 51.
5. The Kaingang use one and the same term to refer to (1) differences of all kinds; (2) men of rival groups, who are always close relatives; (3) Brazilians, the traditional enemy; and (4) the dead and all mythological figures, demonic and divine, generally spoken of as 'different things'.
6. Henry, *Jungle People*, p. 7.
7. 'When Yakwa says to me, "My cousin wants to kill me," I know he wants to kill his cousin, who slaughtered his pigs for rooting up his corn; and when he says, "Eduardo (the Agent) is angry with me," I realize that he is angry with the Agent for not having given him a shirt. Yakwa's state of mind is a pale reflection of the Kaingang habit of projecting their own hate and fear into the minds of those whom they hate and fear. Yet one cannot always be sure that it is just a projection, for in these feuds currents of danger may radiate from any number of points of conflict, and there is often good and sufficient cause for any fear' (ibid., p. 54).
8. Ibid., p. 53.
9. Ibid.
10. Cf. Mary Douglas, *Purity and Danger* (London, 1966).
11. MONICA WILSON, *Rituals of Kinship among the Nyakyusa* (Oxford, 1957).

Morality and Aesthetics in the Ritual Archetype*

WOLE SOYINKA

I shall begin by commemorating the gods for their self-sacrifice on the altar of literature, and in so doing press them into further service on behalf of human society, and its quest for the explication of being. I have selected three paradigms. The number is purely fortuitous; there is no intent to create a literary trinity, holy or unholy – their choice is governed by the nature of their attributes which, in addition to their manipulable histories, have made them the favourites of poets and dramatists, modern and traditional. In addition (and this of course is true for many of their companion deities), they appear to travel well. The African world of the Americas testifies to this both in its socio-religious reality and in the secular arts and literature. Symbols of Yemaja (Yemoja), Oxosi (Ososi), Exu (Esu) and Xango (Sango) not only lead a promiscuous existence with Roman Catholic saints but are fused with the twentieth-century technological and revolutionary expressionism of the mural arts or Cuba, Brazil and much of the Caribbean.

The three deities that concern us here are Ogun, Obatala and Sango. They are represented in drama by the passage-rites of hero-gods, a projection of man's conflict with forces which challenge his efforts to harmonise with his environment, physical, social and psychic. The drama of the hero-god is a convenient expression; gods they are unquestionably, but their symbolic roles are identified by man as the role of an intermediary quester, an explorer into territories of 'essence-ideal' around whose edges man fearfully skirts. Finally, as a prefiguration of conscious being which is nevertheless a product of the conscious creativity of man, they enhance man's existence within the cyclic consciousness of time. These emerge as the principal features of the drama of the gods; it is within their framework that traditional society poses its social questions or formulates its moralities. They

* Reprinted from *Myth, Literature and the African World* (Cambridge: Cambridge University Press, 1976).

control the aesthetic considerations of ritual enactment and give to
every performance a multi-level experience of the mystical and the
mundane.

The setting of Ritual, of the drama of the gods, is the cosmic entirety,
and our approach to this drama might usefully be made through the
comparable example of the Epic which represents also, on a different
level, another access to the Rites of Passage. The epic celebrates the
victory of the human spirit over forces inimical to self-extension. It
concretises in the form of action the arduous birth of the individual or
communal entity, creates a new being through utilising and stressing
the language of self-glorification to which human nature is healthily
prone. The dramatic or tragic rites of the gods are, however, engaged
with the more profound, more elusive phenomenon of being and non-
being. Man can shelve and even overwhelm metaphysical uncertainties
by epic feats, and prolong such a state of social euphoria by their
constant recital, but this exercise in itself proves a mere surrogate to the
bewildering phenomenon of the cosmic location of his being. The
fundamental visceral questioning intrudes, prompted by the patient,
immovable and eternal immensity that surrounds him. We may
speculate that it is the reality of this undented vastness which created
the need to challenge, confront and at least initiate a rapport with the
realm of infinity. It was – there being no other conceivable place – the
natural home of the unseen deities, a resting-place for the departed, and
a staging-house for the unborn. Intuitions, sudden psychic emanations
could come, logically, only from such an incomparable immensity. A
chthonic realm, a storehouse for creative and destructive essences, it
required a challenger, a human representative to breach it periodically
on behalf of the well-being of the community. The stage, the ritual
arena of confrontation, came to represent the symbolic chthonic space
and the presence of the challenger within it is the earliest physical
expression of man's fearful awareness of the cosmic context of his
existence. Its magic microcosm is created by the communal presence,
and in this charged space the chthonic inhabitants are challenged.

This context however is the cosmic *totality*, in speaking of which
it must be constantly recalled that we do not excise that portion of
it which, because so readily and physically apprehended, tends to
occupy a separate (mundane) category in modern European
imagination. This was not always so. This gradual erosion of Earth
in European metaphysic scope is probably due to the growth and
influence of the Platonic-Christian tradition. After all, the pagan Greek
did not neglect this all-important dimension. Persephone, Dionysos and
Demeter were terrestrial deities. Pluto not merely ruled but inhabited
the netherworld. Neptune was a very watery god who conducted his
travels on water-spouts. Those archetypal protagonists of the chthonic

realm, Orpheus, Gilgamesh, Ulysses, did penetrate this netherworld in concrete and elemental terms. And before that oriental twin-brother of Christianity – Buddhism – attenuated and circumscribed Asiatic thought, Lord Shiva drove his passionate course through earth, uniting all the elements with his powerful erection which burst through to the earth's surface, split in three and spurted sperm in upper cosmos. In Asian and European antiquity, therefore, man did, like the African, exist within a cosmic totality, did possess a consciousness in which his own earth being, his gravity-bound apprehension of self, was inseparable from the entire cosmic phenomenon. (For let it always be recalled that myths arise from man's attempt to externalise and communicate his inner intuitions.) A profound transformation has therefore taken place within the human psyche if, to hypothesise, the same *homo sapiens* mythologises at one period that an advanturous deity has penetrated earth, rocks and underground streams with his phallus, going right through into the outer atmosphere, and, at another period, that a new god walks on water without getting his feet wet. The latter hints already at cosmic Manichaeism, evidence of which we shall encounter in the aesthetic structure of the drama of African deities in their new syncretic abode across the Atlantic. The seed of anti-terrestrialism sowed by Buddhism and Judeo-Christianity had to end with such excesses as the transference of the underworld to a new locale up in the sky, a purgatorial suburb under the direct supervision of the sky deities. The multiple epiphanous deities have become for the European a thing of distant memory, and heroes who once dared the divine monopoly of the chthonic realm fade into dubious legend. The ultimate consequence of this – in terms of man's cosmic condition – is that the cosmos recedes further and further until, while retaining something of the grandeur of the infinite, it loses the essence of the tangible, the immediate, the appeasable. It moves from that which can be tangibly metaphorphosed into realms of the fantasied; commencing *somewhere else*, where formerly it began, co-existed with, and was completed within the reality of man's physical being and environment. Thus, where formerly the rites of the exploration of the chthonic realm, of birth and re-birth, the rites of regress and entry, were possible from any one of the various realms of existence into any other, for and on behalf of any being – ancestor, living, or unborn – living man now restricted his vision of existence to the hierarchic circuits immediately above earth. Ritual drama, that is drama as a cleansing, binding, communal, re-creative force, disappears or is vitiated during such periods or within such cultures which survive only by the narrowing of the cosmic whole. It is instructive to observe the commencement of this process in the drama of the gods in contemporary Christian-influenced societies of the African world.

To speak of space, music, poetry or material paraphernalia in the drama of the gods is to move directly from the apparent to deeper effects within the community whose drama (that is history, morality, affirmation, supplication, thanksgiving or simple calendrification) it also is. This is not to suggest that such drama *always* operates on this level. Casual secular entertainment may also involve the gods – the gods are quite amenable to fustian, nowhere more so than in their most sacred *oriki* (praise-chants) – but such pieces do not concern themselves with creating the emotional and spiritual overtones that would pervade, as a matter of course, the consecrated spot where the divine presence must be invoked and borne within the actor-surrogate.

This brings us briefly to the question of art. The difficulty of today's agent of a would-be ritual communication (call him the producer) is that, where the drama of the gods is involved, his sensibility is more often than not that of an enthusiastic promoter, very rarely that of a truly communicant medium in what is essentially a 'rite of passage'. To move from its natural habitat in the shrine of the deity, or a historic spot in the drama of a people's origin, or a symbolic patch of earth amidst grain stalks on the eve of harvest; to move from such charged spaces to a fenced arena at a Festival of Arts, or even to an authentic shelter of the god only lately adapted for tourists and anthropologists alike; this constitutes an unfair strain on the most even-tempered deity, and also on the artistic temperament he shares with humanity. This is not simply a question of truncation, such as the removal of the more sacred events from profane eyes. The essential problem is that the emotive progression which leads to a communal ecstacy or catharsis has been destroyed in the process of re-staging. So this leads us intentionally to the perennial question of whether ritual can be called drama, at what moment a religious or mythic celebration can be considered transformed into drama, and whether the ultimate test of these questions does not lie in their capacity to transfer from habitual to alien environments.

These questions are as frequently posed as they are largely artificial. The anguish over what is ritual and what drama has indeed been rendered even more abstract by the recent reversion of European and American progressive theatre to ritualism in its 'purest' attainable form. This is especially true of the black theatre in America but is also true of the current white avant-garde in Europe and America. How, except as a grouping towards the ritual experience (alas, only too often comically misguided) could we describe the theatrical manifestations of the so-called 'Liquid Theatre' or the more consciously anthropological 'Environmental Theatre' in America? Or the intense explorations of Grotowski into the human psyche? What more concise expression could capture the spirit of the spectacle mounted by the French director Mnouchkine in her *1789* other than a 'ritual of revolution'? Peter Brook's experiments which took his company to Persepolis for a production of *Orghast*, a play in a wholly invented non-language, are propelled by this same need to re-discover the origin, the root experience of what Western European man later reduced to specialist terminologies through his chronic habit of compartmentalisation. (It is by the way a very catching habit; we have all caught it to some extent.) Their modern forerunner (European that is) was of course Jean Genêt, but his drama only revealed a potential for the eventual distillation of a heavily literary theatre into pure ritualistic essence. It is no surprise that towards the close of the sixties, the company which created a New York version of Euripides' *Bacchae* should draw, among other sources, upon an Asmat New Guinea ritual in its search for the tragic soul of twentieth-century white bourgeois-hippie American culture. The question therefore of the supposed dividing line between ritual and theatre should not concern us much in Africa, the line being one that was largely drawn by the European analyst. Groups such as the Ori-Olokun Theatre in Ife, and Duro Ladipo's company, also of Nigeria, have demonstrated the capability of the drama (or ritual) of the gods to travel as aesthetically and passionately as the gods themselves have, across the Atlantic. So indeed have groups in black America, such as Barbara Ann Teer's Harlem Theatre. If civil servants (beginning with the colonial administrators) and even university entrepreneurs who are most often responsible for bringing our Cultural Heritage out of its wraps to regale foreign delegations, Institute of African Studies conferences etc., retain the basic attitude that traditional drama is some kind of village craft which can be plonked down on any stall just like artifacts in any international airport boutique, it should not surprise us that the spectator sums up his experience as having been entertained or bored by some 'quaint ritual'. Such presentations have been largely responsible for the multitude of false concepts surrounding the drama of the gods; that, and their subjection to anthropological punditry where they are reduced, *in extremis*, to behavioural manifestations in primitive society. The burden on a producer is one of knowledge, understanding, and of sympathetic imagination. Whatever deity is involved demands an intelligent communication of what is, indeed, pure essence.

Now let us speak of the gods and of their fates – both in myth and at the hands of their creative exploiters.

Sango interests us in respect of his essentiality, which enables us to relate him to a cosmic functionalist framework, in company with several deities. This description 'functionalist' does not imply that other deities such as Ogun and Obatala with whom he is later contrasted do not also fulfil functionalist roles in the Yoruba man–cosmos organisation. The distinction is largely one of degree, or emphasis: in what primary sense a deity is thought upon in a community of his worshippers, the affective ends towards which he is most readily invoked. In Sango's case, it is as the agency of lightning, lightning in turn being the cosmic instrument of a swift, retributive justice.

Sango is anthropomorphic in origin, but it is necessary, in attempting to enter fully into the matrix of a society's conceptions of becoming, to distinguish between the primary and secondary paradigms of origin – the primal becoming of man, and his racial or social origination. Sango is cast in the latter frame, and his tragic rites are consequently a deadly conflict on the human and historic plane, charged nonetheless with the passion and terror of superhuman, uncontrollable forces. Duro Ladipo's play *Oba Koso* will be discussed more fully in another context, but some apposite lines from the Brazilian Zora Zeljan's play on Oxala (Orisa-nla) in which Sango features prominently will convey some of the awesome passion of the man. After dearth, famine and plagues, caused by a crime of injustice against a disguised deity committed within his kingdom but without his knowledge. Sango at last discovers the identity of the long-suffering god. In rage, he challenges Olodumare, the Supreme Deity:

> Blow, winds, and efface the memory of this crime! Swell seas, and wash my kingdom clean of this guilt! And you, lord of destiny, how can I respect you from now on? You wrote my life in the eternal books. You are to blame for it! Thunders that I control, explode with all your might! Attack the heavens! I want to fight with Olodumare. I challenge that power which made me cover myself with so much shame! More! More! More! Set fire to the skies![1]

He is brought under control only by Oxala, the victim of the original injustice, who rebukes Sango's blasphemy. Yet Sango's rage is wholly understandable and reinforces a clever philosophical issue deployed by Zora Zeljan to reinforce the essence of Sango as the principle of justice. Since the crime against the disguised deity was committed in his own land, Sango has to bear responsibility for it; yet he is innocent of the crime. Zora Zeljan's dramatic shrewdness lay in basing the motivation for Sango's passion, not on the unfairness of the long curse on his land, but on the egotistical realisation that he, Sango, principle of justice itself, had been unwittingly made to commit an unjust act. His reaction, terrible and blasphemous as it is, raises him to truly superhuman, superdaemonic levels. It is doubtful if any philosopher would want to raise, confronted with this spectacle of passion, the finer points of the principles of culpability. Sango embodies in his person, in that culminating moment, the awesome essence of justice; nor is it disputable that the achievement of this is in large measure due to the ritualist

mould of the play, where all action and all personae reach deeply
through reserves of the collective memory of human rites of passage –
ordeal, survival, social and individual purgation – into an end result
which is the moral code of society.

Sometimes, in the historic pattern of Sango's rites, there appears to be
a temporal dislocation. I have stressed that Sango's history is not the
history of primal becoming but of racial origin, which is historically
dated. Yet he leaps straight after his suicide (or non-suicide, to be
liturgically correct) into an identification (by implication) with the
source of lightning. This seeming cosmic anachronism is in fact a very
handy clue to temporal concepts in the Yoruba world-view. Traditional
thought operates, not a linear conception of time but a cyclic reality.
One does not suggest for a moment that this is peculiar to the Yoruba
or to the African world-view. Kerenyi elicits parallel verities from Greek
mythology in his essay 'The primordial child in primordial times'.[2] But
the degree of integrated acceptance of this temporal sense in the life-
rhythm, mores and social organisation of Yoruba society is certainly
worth emphasising, being a reflection of that same reality which denies
periodicity to the existences of the dead, the living and the unborn. The
expression 'the child is father of the man' becomes, within the context
of this time-structure, not merely a metaphor of development, one that
is rooted in a system of representative individuation, but a proverb of
human continuity which is not uni-directional. Neither 'child' nor
'father' is a closed or chronological concept. The world of the unborn,
in the Yoruba world-view, is as evidently older than the world of the
living as the world of the living is older than the ancestor-world. And,
of course, the other way around: we can insist that the world of the
unborn is older than the world of the ancestor in the same breath as we
declare that the deities preceded humanity into the universe. But there
again we come up against the Yoruba proverb: *Bi o s'enia, imale o si* (if
humanity were not, the gods would not be). Hardly a companionable
idea to the Judeo-Christian theology of 'In the beginning, God *was*', and
of course its implications go beyond the mere question of sequential
time. Whatever semantic evasion we employ – the godness, the
beingness of god, the otherness of, or assimilate oneness with god –
they remain abstractions of man-emanating concepts or experiences
which presuppose the human medium. No philosophy or ontological
fanaticism can wish that away, and it is formulative of Yoruba
cosmogonic wisdom. It is also an affective social principle which
intertwines multiple existences so absolutely that, to take a common
enough example, an elderly man would refer to a child as *Baba* (father,
or elder) if the circumstances of his birth made his actual entry into the
living world retrospective. His conduct towards the child would be so
deferential that he might never call him by his real name. If he held a

family feast, the elder's place of honour would go to the child-guest. It is a balancing principle, one which prevents total inflexibility in the age-hierarchies which normally govern traditional society.

The deities exist in the same relation with humanity as these multiple worlds and are an expression of its cyclic nature. Sango's fusion with a primal phenomenon is an operation of the same concept, and the drama on a human plane that precedes his apotheosis is a further affirmation of the principle of continuity inherent in myths of origin, secular or cosmic. Sango's 'tragic fall' is the result of a hubristic act: the powerful king throws himself in conflict not simply with subjects or peers but with the racial found of his own being. Weak, vacillating, treacherous and disloyal, the human unit that constitutes the chorus of his downfall is, in Sango's drama, the total context of racial beginning; the ritual metaphor communicates this and the poetry is woven into its affirmation. Yet side by side with acceptance of the need to destroy this disruptive, uncontrollable factor in the mortal community, the need to assert the communal will for a harmonious existence, is recognition of the superhuman energies of an exceptional man. Apotheosis, the joining of energies in cosmic continuity, follows logically; and Sango is set to work at his new functions with a wide safety zone of ether between him and lesser mortals.

Of course we may also, like Paul Radin, be justified in seeing this act of apotheosis in the opportunistic light of the self-entrenching priesthood.[3] Duro Ladipo's play *Oba Koso*[4] indicates quite clearly that Sango did commit suicide, that it was the priests who got quickly together, hushed the wailing of the women and rebuked them for revealing that Sango took his own life. The body conveniently disappears and his elevation is attested: The king is dead; long live the god! And why not indeed? Economics and power have always played a large part in the championing of new deities throughout human history. The struggle for authority in early human society with its prize of material advantages, social prestige and the establishment of an elite has been nowhere so intensely marked as in the function of religion, perpetuating itself in repressive orthodoxies, countered by equally determined schisms. In the exploration of man's images of essence-ideal, fashioned in the shape of gods, we cannot afford to jettison our cynical faculties altogether. Adapting *The Bacchae* of Euripides quite recently for a production – *The Bacchae* is of course the finest extant drama of the social coming-into-being of a semi-European deity – I found it necessary to emphasise this impure aspect of the priesthood. There is a confrontation between King Pentheus who is properly opposed to the presence and activities of the god Dionysus in his kingdom, and the seer Tiresias who is already an enthusiastic promoter of the god. Here are a few lines from King Pentheus' denunciation:

This is your doing Tiresias; I know
You talked him into it, and I know why.
Another god revealed is a new way opened
Into men's pockets, profits from offerings,
Power over private lives – and state affairs –
Don't deny it! I've known your busy priesthood
Manipulations.

It seemed only fair to give Pentheus a persuasive dissenting view, the view of state authority in conflict with an imagined theocratic conspiracy since, as he is to learn so tragically, he happens to be wrong. Of course it is quite possible to re-create the Sango myth from this basic viewpoint; indeed, Duro Ladipo's play would provide a good beginning. The result would hardly be ritual, however. The narration of a moment in the history of the Oyo, even a tragic conflict involving their first king, might result from it, but not the drama of the gods as a medium of communal recollection and cohesion, not the consolation which comes from participating in the process of bringing to birth a new medium in the cosmic extension of man's physical existence.

We now turn to Obatala, a gentler sector of the arc of the human psyche (to keep within that cyclic image of Yoruba existential concepts). Within his crescent is stored those virtues of social and individual accommodation: patience, suffering, peaceableness, all the imperatives of harmony in the universe, the essence of quietude and forbearance; in short the aesthetics of the saint. On the very far side of such an arc we find the protagonist assertiveness of Ogun, our third deity. Common to all these gods, it may be remarked at this point, is that even when, like Obatala, they bear the essence of purity, their history is always marked by some act of excess, hubris or other human weakness. The consequences are, significantly, measured in human terms and such gods are placed under an eternal obligation of some practical form of penance which compensates humanity. Since the resemblance of the Greek pantheon to the Yoruba is often remarked, leading even in some instances of strong scholarly nerve to 'conclusive evidence' for the thesis that the Yoruba religion is derived from the Greek, it is instructive to point out a fundamental contrast. Like the Yoruba deities, but to a thousandfold degree, the Greek gods also commit serious infractions against mortal well-being. The Greek catalogue is one of lust, greed, sadism, megalomania and sheer cussedness. But the morality of reparation appears totally alien to the ethical concepts of the ancient Greeks. Punishments, when they occur among the Olympians, invariably take place only when the offence happens to encroach on the moral preserves of another deity and that deity is stronger or successfully appeals to Father Zeus, the greatest reprobate of all. And of course it was commonly accepted that the rape, mutilation, or death of a mortal minion of the offending deity could go some way towards settling the score to the satisfaction of all. This is the ethical basis of Greek tragedy, not as it began in the ritual *tragodia* but as it developed through the pessimistic line of Aeschylus to Shakespeare's

> As flies to wanton boys, are we to the gods;
> They kill us for their sport.
>
> *(King Lear)*

The psychological base – the 'tragic flaw' in the hero – was a later refinement; Oedipus the Innocent remained the ethical archetype of Greek tragedy.

That Greek religion shows persuasive parallels with, to stick to our example, the Yoruba is by no means denied; the Delphic Oracle and the Ifa Corpus of the Yoruba are a fascinating instance of one such structural parallel. But the essential differences in the actual autochthonous myths of the gods themselves provide clues to differences in the moral bias of the two world-views. The penalties which societies exact from their deities in reparation for real or symbolic injuries are an index of the extent to which the principles of *natural* restitution for social disharmony may be said to govern the moral structure of that society and influence its social laws – a *natural* restitution, because the relationship between man and god (embodiment of nature and cosmic principles (cannot be seen in any other terms but those of naturalness. This relationship represents the deductions and applications of cosmic and natural ordering, and it is not only ethical but technical (for instance, economic) norms which they provide for such a society. By making the gods responsible to judgements so based, a passive reliance on the whims of external forces is eschewed, their regenerative aspects are catalysed into operation through a ritual recourse to the gods' error-ridden rites of passage. Even in the corpus of Ifa curative verse we encounter constant references to such antecedents in divine moral history. Divine memory is not permitted to rest and prayers are uttered as reminders of natural responsibilities. Of course, it must be admitted that the actualities of the continent today reveal no such awareness to the observer. The saying *orisa l'oba* (the king is a god), embraced at a superficial self-gratifying level, fails to recall today's power-holders to the moral nature of the African deity. The leaders' mentality is decidedly Olympian, their gods are Greek. Yet it is from their lips that is most often heard the boast of indigenous authenticity. The African deities must be chuckling in their abodes – except perhaps Obatala the saint.

Ritual and Tragedy

The uncancelled error of Obatala, god of soul purity, was his
weakness for drink. To him belongs the function of moulding human
beings, into whose forms life is breathed by the supreme deity himself,
Olodumare. One day, however, Obatala allowed himself to take a little
too much of that potent draught, palm wine. His craftsman's fingers
slipped badly and he moulded cripples, albinos and the blind. As a
result of this error, Obatala rigidly forbids palm wine to his followers.
(Part of the compensating principle of the Yoruba world-view is
revealed in the fact that by contrast, Ogun, who was yet another victim
of the draught, makes palm wine a mandatory ingredient of his
worship. The Yoruba can be reassuringly pragmatic. Unless one is in
the unfortunate position of being actually marked for priesthood in the
worship of Obatala it is possible still to be a sincere follower of that
deity, stay ecstatically sober at his outing, then wind up the festival of
the gods by getting beatifically drunk on Ogun's day.) Obatala's day of
error is occasionally but not consistently given as a contributory factor
to the necessity of his rites of passage. It emerges as a drama of his
spiritual essence through capture, ordeal, ransoming, and triumphal
return – a passion play which is linked to the dearth-and-plenty cycle of
nature.

Two plays are of particular interest in the drama of this god; one by
Obotunde Ijimere is titled *The Imprisonment of Obatala.*[5] The other is by
the Brazilian Zora Zeljan. Entitled *The Story of Oxala* and subtitled *The
Feast of Bomfin*, on which Brazilian feast it is based, the play testifies
directly to the vitality of African religions in Latin America and the
Caribbean.[6] Oxala is the Brazilian corruption of the name Orisa-nla,
which is another name by which Obatala is known among the Yoruba.
In the prologue to her play, Zora Zeljan writes:

The Feast of Bomfin, in Bahia, is one of the best examples of religious
syncretism in our times. It is a compound of Catholic saints and
African orisas, which testifies to the conciliatory spirit of mixed
civilizations. That is why the Feast of Bomfin is also the story of
Oxala. The play originates in one of the legends of Oxala, the god
that the candomble believers have syncretised with our Lord of
Bomfin. In the process of being catechised, the slaves embodied the
new idea of Christ's Passion with their ancestral memory of Oxala's
captivity. He was the father of all the other gods in their theogony.
In a sort of penance, and echoing customs whose origins were buried
in time, the uncomplicated piety of the Brazilian Negroes induced in
them a desire to expiate a racial burden. It was as if they wanted to
relive the sorrow of their main deity, a sort of compensation and
restitution of his figure to its former majesty and dignity.

(*Oxala*, p. 33)

There are, of course, a few points to quarrel with in that the concept of
expiating a racial burden is something which has been taken over from
Judeo-Christianity. Compensation and restitution are natural enough
goals for an enslaved race in those circumstances, but expiation of a
racial burden is pure racial transposition by the guilty. Nothing,
especially in the rebellious history of the slaves in Brazil, can uphold
this interpretation which is a reflection of the European conscience.

A determination to replant the displaced racial psyche was one
reason for the ease and permanence with which the African gods
were syncretised with Roman Catholic saints. The process was so
complete that these deities became part of the spiritual lives of the
white Roman Catholics themselves who, in Brazil or Cuba, became
regular worshippers in the *candomble* or *bembe* (the respective Brazilian
and Cuban terms) adopting the Yoruba orisa in their full essence as
their patron gods. One interesting point I ought to mention, as it is
related to the actual course of action in Zeljan's play: she remarks in
her introduction that while she obtained the story of Oxala's tragic
wanderings from Pierre Verger's *Dieux d'Afrique*, she found in that
book no reference to the motives which made Oxala face Destiny in
that form. These motives were later gradually clarified for her through
legends with which she came into contact in Rio or Bahia, and they had
to be re-assembled as they had become appended to several other
legends to which they did not belong. And the remote causes which
Zeljan uncovered in Brazil and assigns to Oxala's journey not only
differ from those of Obotunde Ijimere and Yoruba traditional lore, but
offer us, by contrast, a significant piece in the fabric of Yoruba
metaphysics. Zora Zeljan makes Sango journey in pursuit of his wife
Nana Buruku, who has deserted him. And in the reasons for her
desertion and Oxala's defence we find where Christian god-attributes
differ from the Yoruba. We learn from the Brazilian that Oxala made a
son for himself called 'Omolu', lord of the Earth. Since he was to be the
curative god, with power over illness and health, life and death, Oxala
made him ugly and sick in his own flesh. So disgusted was Nana
Buruku who gave birth to him that she threw him into an abyss where,
in addition to the deformities from which he was already suffering, he
also developed a club foot. When, to add insult to injury, Oxala gave
her a second son, Exu, who was created indifferent to the principles
of good and evil, she fled him and took refuge in Sango's kingdom,
swearing never to return.

We see how, in contrast to the Yoruba assertion of moments of
weakness and general shortcomings in the god in the performance of
his functions, Christian syncretism in Bahia rationalises the existence
of the malformed in human society within the overall framework of
farsightedness and supra-human understanding of the creator god. The

Yoruba assert straightforwardly that the god was tipsy and his hand slipped, bringing the god firmly within the human attribute of fallibility. Since human fallibility is known to entail certain disharmonious consequences for society, it also requires a search for remedial activities, and it is this cycle which ensures the constant regenerative process of the universe. By bringing the gods within this cycle, a continuity of cosmic regulation involving the worlds of the ancestor and the unborn is also guaranteed. The act of hubris or its opposite – weakness, excessive passivity or inertia – leads to a disruption of balances within nature and this in turn triggers off compensating energies.

The action in both versions – Zora Zeljan's and Ijimere's – follows a near-identical pattern, apart from the motivation. Oxala undertakes the journey into Xango's kingdom, is molested on the way by Esu the trickster god and subjected to a hundred humiliations. He bears all patiently. He is imprisoned (once again through Esu's machinations) on a false charge of stealing the king's favourite horse. But he must not reveal himself or else he forfeits the rewards of patience and humility which alone can make him attain his objective. This was the warning of his Babalorisa, the priest of the Oracle. But now a plague descends on humanity, for Oxala *is* the god of creation. Rains cease, children die in their mothers' wombs. In Ijimere's play:

A curse has fallen on Oyo
The corn on its stalk is worm-eaten
And hollow like an old honeycomb;
The yam in the earth is dry and
Stringy like palm fibre . . . Creation comes to a standstill
When he who turns blood into children
Is lingering in jail.

(*The Imprisonment of Obatala*, p. 31)

Complementarity is lost and balance is destroyed. Obatala (or Oxala) is the god who turns blood into children; Ogun is the the god who turns children into blood. With the former immobilised, Ogun comes into his own and enjoys full ascendancy. There is distortion in the processes of the universe:

The Bringer of Peace, the Father of Laughter
Is locked in jail
You have unleashed Ogun, who bathes in blood
Even now does his reign begin.
He kills suddenly in the house and suddenly in the field
He kills the child with iron with which it plays.

Ogun kills the slave-owner and the slaves as well
He kills the owner of the house and paints the hearth with his blood!

(p. 27)

It rains blood, earthquakes disrupt the city, beasts collapse and die in
the forests, the rivers dry and the land turns barren. In prison Obatala
sits, instilling in all the virtues of patience and fortitude, obedient to the
injunctions of the Ifa priest, Babalorisa. In Ijimere's version, it is Esu who
decides the nature of Obatala's punishment and then torments him on
the way. It is a trial of the spirit.

In both the Yoruba and the Brazilian versions, Obatala's journey
is presented as a parable of confrontation with Destiny. The initial
motivation in Ijimere's play soon becomes secondary: Obatala longs for
the warm contact of friendship. The new yam, he says, soft and creamy
as it is, has turned stringy in his mouth, the succulent meat of the
grass-cutter tastes gristly, and all because his friend Sango is not there
to share it with him. But even if this craving were not present in
Obatala, some other cause would still have to be found, for the god of
creation has a date with Destiny at which his only weapon must be
patience. The Babalawo expounds his fortune and reminds him of his
crime:

You drank the milky wine of the palm
Cool and sizzling it was in the morning,
Fermenting in the calabash
Its sweet foam overflowed
Like the eyes of a woman in love.
You refreshed yourself in the morning
But by evening time your hands were unsteady,
Your senses were dull, your fingertips numbed.

(p. 10)

He lists all the human deformities which resulted from Obatala's mortal
slip and pronounces judgement: 'You must pay for your sins'.

Contrast this with the crime of the same deity in the Brazilian play.
Yes, he does mould a deformed being but it is a deliberate act. Not only
that, but the immediate victims of his aesthetic twist are not mortal
beings but other deities – one a physical, the other a moral deformity.
That this thereupon leads to a confrontation with Destiny is then
attributed to the vanity and lack of understanding in a rather ill-
tempered wife who would sooner have a son of external beauty than an
ugly genius. Nowhere is Oxala held to have done wrong or committed
any act that demands expiation. There results from this an abstract,
disinterested quality about his sacrifice, one which suggests influences
of the Christian passion play.

311

Sango's conduct in Ijimere's play compounds the criminality of
the deities. Zora Zeljan ensures that in her version, Sango remains
completely ignorant of the identity of the innocent sufferer. Not so in
the Yoruba version. It is not merely the principle of justice which is
abused in Sango's summary assumption of Obatala's guilt but, more
eloquently, the demands of friendship and hospitality. Obatala's longing
for the company of his fiery friend has been answered by a
megalomaniac contempt:

> Is it possible that the wisest of all
> Should have become the most foolish?
> And the purest, the most foul?
> Oh horror, the father of laughter,
> Who rides the hunchback, has turned
> A common thief.

(p. 22)

It is commonplace knowledge that hospitality is one of the most
treasured laws of the African social existence. Sango's wife Oya is
horrified by Sango's unthinking repudiation of friendship and seeks
to assuage his anger by recalling to him Obatala's sumptuous reception
of Sango on a previous occasion; the praise-singing, the yam-pounding,
the wine, the venison, the feasting. Sango places himself beyond
reciprocation. With every plea, his hubris mounts. Every law of
traditional social relationship is broken by the fiery god who is now
beyond recall even to the demands of honourable or generous conduct.
But the supreme act of hubris, the cosmic affront, lies in the fact that
Obatala is the god of creation and may not be treated like an irrelevant
factor in cosmic harmony. Oya is quick to remind her husband of the
dangers of a disruption in the cosmic principle of complementarity, but
Sango is beyond caring. Ogun now appears as the unchallenged half of
the destructive–creative principle, for the destruction is not simply the
physical havoc wreaked by Sango but a havoc done to Nature herself:

> Some women die in childbirth; they bleed
> Until their body is drained and dry.
> Or else the fruit rots in their womb
> Before it sees the light of day.

(pp. 30–1)

'I fear', says Oya, who remains throughout the voice of reason and
foresight, 'I fear that we are paying now for the king's injustice.'
 Two gods, both guilty of anti-social behaviour. The consequences of
their actions are experienced by their mortal subjects. The victims in

Zora Zeljan's play are also mortals but both gods here are innocent of evil. Ironically, since we cannot but observe that the structural basis of Zora Zeljan's rites is the elicitation of 'essence', it should be remarked that it is in her version that Oxala is permitted a reduction of the 'pure stoic essence'. A beatific expression of godhead, yes; but although his physical sufferings appear to be greater than in *The Imprisonment*, he does not experience that level of rejection in Zeljan's play which he does in Ijimere's. Sango's rejection of him in Ijimere leaves Obatala with no further recourse, no hope and no prospects of restitution. Moreover, since he is conscious of his own causative infraction, his situation must be one of guilt-laden spiritual dejection. Oxala in the other play is constantly reassured by knowledge of his complete innocence and goodness and therefore of the certainty of vindication. It is doubtful whether he could have reached the definitive level of rejection which fell to Obatala in *The Imprisonment*, seeing that Obatala's primary objective for that journey had deliberately made himself the instrument of his humiliation. This, however, is by the way. What Zeljan seems more concerned to establish is the exact opposite of Ijimere – the conception of Sango as a principle of Justice. And not Sango alone but all the deities as principles, abstractions, essences. Transcendental emanations rather than flesh-and-blood creations. Consider the following lines from *The Imprisonment*:

> So the new yam has come again
> Whiter than teeth, whiter than salt,
> Whiter than eyeballs,
> Whiter than the beads in my crown.
> Yam:
> You have the power to turn a wise man into a fool
> You cause the newly wedded wife to lose her manners
> The modest man unbuttons his shirt, his eyes grow wide
> The new yam knows no difference between beggar and king
> Between the thief and the rich man, between man and God;
> You turn them all greedy alike
>
> *(The Imprisonment of Obatala, p. 3)*

Or these, from Sango's verbal laceration of the hapless Obatala:

> What madness to steal a horse he cannot ride
> Like an impotent old chief
> Who marries a moist young wife
> And hides the shrivelled fruit
> Between his legs.
> Oh, had he tried to mount

This quivering black flame
He would have shook him off
Even quicker than the frustrated wife
Got rid of her limp husband
Who lacked the tool
To make her bleed and sweat.

(pp. 24–5)

Such language will not be encountered in the Brazilian play. The Yoruba gods in the Brazilian version do not sweat or copulate. A scene such as takes place in Ijimere's play where Obatala not only argues with a clod of a farmer but is actually insulted and beaten to the ground by the mortal would be out of place in the Zeljan play. What we encounter in their place is the transcendentalist essence, the commencement of the attenuation of terrestrialism that I spoke of earlier, brought upon by the encounter of the gods with Christian saints.

Zeljan's kingdom of Sango is very much an Olympian setting. Even the boudoirs where the women of the gods meet, gossip and organise the day's domestic business is a bastion of divine remoteness. At the end of his ordeal, Oxala's reward to his wife for her faithfulness is a crown made of melted sun and precious stars. The effect of this aesthetic foundation is that even the ethical order and balances which are implicit in the play belong to a different order of existence, quite unlike the drama of Obatala where the pithiness of metaphor and the passions of the deities are brought to a terrestrial level, and the resolution – the moral elicited from the complementarity principle – is stated in terms of the well-being of the race. There is an allegorical distance about *The Feast of Bomfin*: the creatures who people it are unquestionably, and quite naturally, rarefied by the incorporeality of those saints with whom the Yoruba gods have become syncretised. Even in a forest setting:

Iassan is happy and gay. She dances away with the light breezes from the woods! She dresses with gentle dry leaves and golden drops of morning dew!

(*Oxala*, p. 22)

We will not find such ethereal imagery employed in the original homeland of these deities. Or again:

What else do you want, exquisite one? Your face is as soft as dawn, your body moves with the elegance of sea waves. When you go to the spring for water the butterflies follow you and the trees bend down to touch you with their foliage.

(p. 23)

In plays from the original source the gods are conceived more in the imagery of peat, chalk, oil, kernels, blood, heartwood and tuber, and active metaphors of human social preoccupations. (An incidental consideration is that in creating Omolu, Oxala stepped outside the elysian matrix of aesthetics and created a healer with the face of a yam tuber. A deplorable lapse into atavism perhaps, but hardly a sufficiently profound cause, were his wife Nana Buruku not culturally alienated, to generate a need in Nature for 'rites of passage'.) More seriously, however, the structural weakening of the dramatic moralities implicit in all such confrontations with Destiny is the logical result of this aesthetics of estrangement that defines, in the Brazilian play, the gods' reality. When ritual archetypes acquire new aesthetic characteristics, we may expect re-adjustments of the moral imperatives that brought them into existence in the first place, at the centre of man's efforts to order the universe.

There is far less of the essence of forbearance in the composition of Ogun, the last of our three representative deities. In an earlier essay of mine – 'The Fourth Stage'[7] – I attempted to illustrate the essential Ogun using Hellenic concepts as a combination of the Dionysian, Apollonian and Promethean principles. In Yoruba metaphysics, no other deity in the pantheon correlates so absolutely, through his own history and nature, with the numinous temper of the fourth area of existence which we have labelled the abyss of transition. Commonly recognised in most African metaphysics are the three worlds we have already discussed: the world of the ancestor, the living and the unborn. Less understood or explored is the fourth space, the dark continuum of transition where occurs the inter-transmutation of essence-ideal and materiality. It houses the ultimate expression of cosmic will.

Ogun's history is the story of the completion of Yoruba cosmogony; he encapsulates that cosmogony's coming-into-being in his own rites of passage. In our encounter with Obatala we came across some rather sanguinary lines which contrasted the nature of Ogun with that of Obatala. So perhaps we ought to begin by redressing this with other lines from Ogun's praise-chants, lines which give a more balanced perspective of his truthful nature. He is known as 'protector of orphans', 'roof over the homeless', 'terrible guardian of the sacred oath'. He stands for a transcendental, humane, but rigidly restorative justice:

Rich-laden is his home, yet, decked in palm fronds
He ventures forth, refuge of the down-trodden.
To rescue slaves he unleashed the judgement of war
Because of the blind, plunged into the forest

Of curative herbs, Bountiful One
Who stands bulwark to offsprings of the dead in heaven
Salutations O lone being, who bathes in rivers of blood.

Yes, the blood is never completely absent, but at least we know that
this is not simply due to bloodthirstiness.

And Ogun is also the master craftsman and artist, farmer and warrior,
essence of destruction and creativity, a recluse and a gregarious imbiber,
a reluctant leader of men and deities. He is 'Lord of the road' of Ifa; that
is, he opens the way to the heart of Ifa's wisdom, thus representing
the knowledge-seeking instinct, an attribute which sets him apart as
the only deity who 'sought the way', and harnessed the resources of
science to hack a passage through primordial chaos for the gods' reunion
with man. The journey and its direction are at the heart of Ogun's being
and the relationship of the gods and man. Its direction and motivation
are also an indication of the geocentric bias of the Yoruba, for it was
the gods who needed to come to man, anguished by a continuing sense
of incompleteness, needing to recover their long-lost essence of totality.
Ogun it was who led them, his was the first rite of passage through the
chthonic realm.

The cause of the gods' spiritual unrest dated from their own origin.
Once, there was only the solitary being, the primogenitor of god and
man, attended only by his salve, Atunda. We do not know where
Atunda came from – myth is always careless about detail – perhaps
the original one moulded him from earth to assist him with domestic
chores. However, the slave rebelled. For reasons best known to himself
he rolled a huge boulder on to the god as he tended his garden on a
hillside, sent him hurtling into the abyss in a thousand and one
fragments. Again the figure varies. The fragmentation of the original
godhead may be seen, however, as fundamental to man's resolution of
the experience of birth and the disintegration of consciousness in death.
Ritualism itself is allied to these axial constants; in the gods' tragic
drama the gods serve as media for this central experience, the conflicts
and events are active contrivances for ease of entry into the experience,
dramatic motifs whose aesthetic formalism dissolves the barrier of
individual distance.

The creation of the multiple godhead began a transference of social
functions, the division of labour and professions among the deities
whose departments they were thereafter to become. The shard of
original Oneness which contained the creative flint appears to have
passed into the being of Ogun, who manifests a temperament for artistic
creativity matched by technological proficiency. His world is the world
of craft, song and poetry. The practitioners of *Ijala*, the supreme lyrical
form of Yoruba poetic art, are followers of Ogun the hunter. Ijala

celebrates not only the deity but animal and plant life, seeks to capture the essence and relationships of growing things and the insights of man into the secrets of the universe. With creativity, however, went its complementary aspect, and Ogun came to symbolise the creative–destructive principle. This does not in any way usurp the province of Obatala whose task is to create the lifeless form of man. Nor is Obatala ever moved to destroy. Obatala is a functionalist of creation, not, like Ogun, the essence of creativity itself.

Yet none of them, not even Ogun, was complete in himself. There had to be a journey across the void to drink at the fount of mortality though, some myths suggest, it was really to inspect humanity and see if the world peopled by the mortal shards from the common ancestor was indeed thriving. But the void had become impenetrable. A long isolation from the world of men had created an impassable barrier which they tried, but failed, to demolish. Ogun finally took over. Armed with the first technical instrument which he had forged from the ore of mountain-wombs, he cleared the primordial jungle, plunged through the abyss and called on the others to follow. For this feat the gods offered him a crown, inviting him to be king over them. Ogun refused. Human society was to commit the same error, and to prove sufficiently persistent to sway him from his wisely considered refusal. On arrival on earth, the various deities went their way, observing and inspecting. Ogun in his wanderings came to the town of Ire where he was well received, later returning its hospitality when he came to its aid against an enemy. In gratitude he was offered the crown of Ire. He declined and retired into the mountains where he lived in solitude, hunting and farming. Again and again he was importuned by the elders of Ire until he finally consented.

When he first descended among them, the people took to their heels. Ogun presented a face of himself which he hoped would put an end to their persistence. He came down in his leather war-kit, smeared in blood from head to foot. When they had fled he returned to his mountain-lair, satisfied that the lesson had been implanted. Alas, back they came again. They implored him, if he would only come in less terrifying attire, they would welcome him as king and leader. Ogun finally consented. He came down decked in palm fronds and was crowned king. In war after war he led his men to victory. Then, finally, came the day when, during a lull in the battle, our old friend Esu the trickster god left a gourd of palm wine for the thirsty deity. Ogun found it exceptionally delicious and drained the gourd to the dregs. In that battle the enemy was routed even faster than usual, the carnage was greater than ever before. But by now, to the drunken god, friend and foe had become confused; he turned on his men and slaughtered them. This was the possibility that had haunted him from the beginning and made him shrink from the role of king over men. Such, however, is the wilful nature of Ogun that he does not, unlike Obatala, forbid the use of palm wine in his worship – on the contrary. Ogun is the embodiment of challenge, the Promethean instinct in man, constantly at the service of society for its full self-realisation. Hence his role of explorer through primordial chaos, which he conquered, then bridged, with the aid of the artifacts of his science. The other deities following through the realm of transition could only share vicariously in the original experience. Only Ogun experienced the process of being literally torn asunder in cosmic winds, of rescuing himself from the precarious edge of total dissolution by harnessing the untouched part of himself, the will, This is the unique essentiality of Ogun in Yoruba metaphysics: as embodiment of the social, communal will invested in a protagonist of its choice. It is as a paradigm of this experience of dissolution and re-integration that the actor in the ritual of archetypes can be understood.

Ogun's action did not take place in a vacuum. His venture was, necessarily a drama of individual stress, yet even his moment of individuation was communicant, one which enabled the other gods to share, whose end-in-view was no less than a strengthening of the communal psyche. This is a different dimension from Obatala's internalised saintly passage or Sango's destructive egotism. The action has been undertaken both on the practical and on the symbolic level of protagonist for the community. The actor in ritual drama operates in the same way. He prepares mentally and physically for his disintegration and re-assembly within the universal womb of origin, experiences the transitional yet inchoate matrix of death and being. Such an actor in the role of the protagonist becomes the unresisting mouthpiece of the god, uttering sounds which he barely comprehends but which are reflections of the awesome glimpse of that transitional gulf, the seething cauldron of the dark world-will and psyche. Tragic feeling in Yoruba drama stems from sympathetic knowledge of the protagonist's foray into this psychic abyss of the re-creative energies.

It is because of the reality of this gulf, this abyss, so crucial to Yoruba cosmic ordering, that Ogun becomes a key figure in understanding the Yoruba metaphysical world. The gulf is what must constantly be diminished (or rendered less threateningly remote) by sacrifices, rituals, ceremonies of appeasement to the cosmic powers which lie guardian to the gulf. Ogun, by incorporating within himself so many seemingly contradictory attributes, represents the closest conception to the original oneness of Orisa-nla. Significantly, his festival is climaxed by the symbolic sacrifice of his favourite animal. A dog, now a surrogate for the god, is cut clean through the neck. After this, a symbolic mock-struggle takes place between the priest and his acolytes for the possession of the body, that is, the god. Earlier, the staff of Ogun, represented by long willowy poles topped by lumps of ore bound in palm frond, is borne by men through the town. The heavy ore at the top and the suppleness of the wood strain the stave in vibrant curves, forcing the men to move about among the revellers who constantly yield them room as they seek to keep the pole balanced. They then go up to the grove of Ogun in the mountain-tops where more revellers are decked in palm fronds and bear palm branches in their hands.

The dynamic fusion in the wilful nature of Ogun, represented in the dance of lumps of ore, is complemented by the peaceful symbolism of the palm in which the ore is bound; the men's manic leaps up the hillside by the beatific recessional of the women who meet them at the foothills and accompany them home with song. Through it all – in the association of the palm frond with the wine of Ogun's error, yet the symbol of his peaceful nature; the aggressive ore and its restraining fronds, a balletic tension of balance in the men with the leaded poles; in the fusion of image and fertility invocations in the straining phallus-heads framed against the sky and the thudding feet of sweat-covered men on the earth; in the resonant rhythms of Ogun's iron gongs and the peaceful resolution of the indigo figures and voices of women on the plain – a dynamic marriage unfolds of the aesthetics of ritualism and the moralities of control, balance, sacrifice, the protagonist spirit and the imperatives of cohesion, diffusing a spiritual tonality that enriches the individual being and the community.

George Thomson in his *Aeschylus and Athens* (Lawrence & Wishart, 1941) comes very close to giving a perceptive description of the process by which the office of the protagonist actor transcends the actual conflict of the ritual and conveys the deeper experience of a challenger of the transitional abyss. But he shies away finally from the fullness of his obvious illumination, and retracts in mid-word the observable reality of the protagonist–audience relation. This is an interesting example of what results when scholars subvert their intelligent deductions to imperatives of alien and jealous gods, in his case, Marxism:

> Myth was created out of ritual. The latter term must be understood in a wide sense, because in primitive society everything is sacred, nothing profane. Every action – eating, drinking, tilling, fighting – has its proper procedure, which being prescribed, is holy.
>
> (pp. 63–4)

This, of course, is what Jonathan Swift would call 'enthusiasm', a pardonable exaggeration common to the more positive among foreign sociologists. Herskovits was another notable sinner in this respect in his efforts to understand traditional African theatre. However, Thomson continues:

In the song and dance of the mimetic rite, each performer withdrew, under the hypnotic effect of rhythm, from the consciousness of reality, which was peculiar to himself, individual, into the subconscious world of fantasy, which was common to all, collective, and from that inner world they returned *charged with new strength for action*. Poetry and dancing, which grew out of the mimetic rite, are speech and gesture raised to a magical level of intensity. For a long time, in virtue of their common origin and function, they were inseparable. The divergence of poetry from dancing, of myth from ritual, only began with the rise of the ruling class whose culture was divorced from the labour of production.

(p. 64)

We shall leave the latter Marxist speculations alone, as being outside the scope of this subject. The points which concern us here are (1) the recognition of the integral nature of poetry and dancing in the mimetic rite, and (2) the withdrawal of the individual into an inner world from which he returns, communicating a new strength for action. The definition of this inner world as 'fantasy' betrays a Eurocentric conditioning or alienation. We describe it as the primal reality, the hinterland of transition. The community emerges from ritual experience 'charged with new strength for action' because of the protagonist's Promethean raid on the durable resources of the transitional realm; immersed within it, he is enabled empathically to transmit its essence to the choric participants of the rites – the community. Nor would we consider that such a communicant withdraws from conscious reality, but rather that his consciousness is stretched to embrace another and primal reality. The communicant effect on the audience which is the choric vessel and earthing mechanism for the venturer is not a regression into 'the subconscious world of fantasy'. Except through mass hypnotism, which is not suggested by Thomson, fantasy is individual and incommunicable – at least, not until after the event, and only by graphic or verbal means. To describe a *collective* inner world as fantasy is not intelligible, for the nature of an inner world in a cohesive society is the essentialisation of a rational world-view, one which is elicited from the reality of social and natural experience and from the integrated reality of racial myths into a living morality. The electronic (or is it simply telepathic?) transmission of ideograms of a collective fantasy is a fantasy of its claimants only. What is transmitted in ritual is essence and response, the residual energies from the protagonist's excursion into the realm of cosmic will which, in Thomson's expressive phrase, charges the community with new strength for action.

But perhaps Thomson's understanding derives from Jung's theories. Jung, begetter of so many racist distortions of the structure of the human psyche, interchangably employs ritual archetypes and images of psychotic fantasy. While the intrusion of archetypal images into the psychotic condition (or fevered, drunken deliriums for that matter) is an acknowledged occurrence, Jung's perception becomes narrowed in his indifferently hierarchic relation of such products of the disturbed mind to the immanent quality of the ritual archetype. The one is a de-contextualised, unharmonised homologue (at best!) of the other, deprived of meaning and relatedness (or wrenched out of normal relations into abnormal ones). Image shorn of, cut off from, symbolic relations with apprehended reality. The profession of the psycho-analyst lies in the sorting out of the new discrete images from their hostile environment; he has no equipment (as an outsider) for the equation of such images themselves with the essence–reality of their origin. Where illusion besets the analyst is when new patterns of discrete components, because they attain a consistent direction of their own, are taken to simulate or reflect the cohesive archetypal motifs of a primal inner world.

'Primitive mentality' declared Jung (and his assumptions are based on *living* examples, not on a retrospective projection into human development), 'differs from civilized chiefly in that the conscious mind is far less developed in extent and intensity. Functions such as thinking, willing etc. are not yet differentiated . . . [the primitive] is incapable of any conscious effort of will . . . owing to the chronic twilight state of his conscious, it is often next to impossible to find out whether he merely dreamed something or whether he really experienced it . . .'.[8] And so, on the authority of European ethnologists who lack the *language* to penetrate the Australian and other natives' own significations of 'dreaming', 'experiencing', 'thinking' and so on, Jung proceeds to identify the territories of dream, fantasy, psychotic exhalations etc., with the historic–empirical–ethical–psychic structure in which the ritual archetype is housed. What *we* call the mythic inner world is both the psychic substructure and temporal subsidence, the cumulative history and empirical observations of the community. It is nonetheless primal in that time, in its cyclic reality, is fundamental to it. The inner world is not static, being constantly enriched by the moral and historic experience of man. Jung, by contrast declares that 'the archetype does not proceed from physical facts'. So it is primordially autogenous? The contradictions suggested by other observations, such as 'the archetype . . . mediates between the unconscious substratum and the conscious mind . . .', 'throws a bridge between the consciousness of the present . . . and the natural, unconscious, instinctive wholeness of primeval times' is explainable by this simple observation: that Jung differentiates the nature of the archetype in the 'primitive' mind from that of the 'civilised' mind even as he pays lip-service to the universality of a collective unconscious, and to the archetype as the inhabitant of that hinterland.

The means to our inner world of transition, the vortex of archetypes and kiln of primal images is the ritualised experience of the gods themselves and of Ogun most especially. Nor is Ogun's identification with the innate mythopoeia of music fortuitous. Music is the intensive language of transition and its communicant means, the catalyst and solvent of its regenerative hoard. The actor dares not venture into this world unprepared, without symbolic sacrifices and the invocation of eudaemonic guardians of the abyss. In the symbolic disintegration and retrieval of the protagonist ego is reflected the destiny of being. This is ritual's legacy to later tragic art, that the tragic hero stands to his contemporary reality as the ritual protagonist on the edge of transitional gulf; alas, the evolution of tragic art in the direction of the specific event has shrunk its cosmic scope, however closely the hero approaches the archetypal. And its morality has become a mere extraction of the intellect, separated from the total processes of being and human continuity.

Notes

1. Zora Zeljan, *Oxala, Transition*, 47 (1974): 31.
2. In C. G. Jung and C. Kerenyi. *Introduction to a Science of Mythology*, trans. R. F. C. Hull (London: Routledge & Kegan Paul, 1970).
3. Paul Radin, *Primitive Religion. its Nature and Origin* (New York: Dover, 1957).
4. Duro Ladipo, *Three Yoruba Plays* (London: Heinemann, 1973).
5. Obotunde Ijimere, *The Imprisonment of Obatala and other plays* (London: Heinemann, 1966).
6. *Transition*, 47 (1974).
7. In *The Morality of Art*, ed. D. W. Jefferson.
8. Jung and Kerenyi, *Introduction to a Science of Mythology*, p. 101.

The Great Dramatic Forms:
The Tragic Rhythm*

Susanne K. Langer

As comedy presents the vital rhythm of self-preservation, tragedy exhibits that of self-consummation.

The lilting advance of the eternal life process, indefinitely maintained or temporarily lost and restored, is the great general vital pattern that we exemplify from day to day. But creatures that are destined, sooner or later, to die – that is, all individuals that do not pass alive into new generations, like jellyfish and algae – hold the balance of life only precariously, in the frame of a total movement that is quite different; the movement from birth to death. Unlike the simple metabolic process, the deathward advance of their individual lives has a series of stations that are not repeated; growth, maturity, decline. That is the tragic rhythm.

Tragedy is a cadential form. Its crisis is always the turn toward an absolute close. This form reflects the basic structure of personal life, and therewith of feeling when life is viewed as a whole. It is that attitude – 'the tragic sense of life', as Unamuno called it – that is objectified and brought before our eyes in tragedy. But in drama it is not presented as Unamuno presents it, namely by an intellectual realization of impending death which we are constitutionally unable to accept and therefore counter with an irrational belief in our personal immortality, in 'immortalizing' rites and supernatural grace.[1] Irrationalism is not insight, but despair, a direct recognition of instincts, needs, and therewithal of one's mental impotence. A 'belief' that defies intellectual convictions is a frantically defended lie. That defence may constitute a great tragic theme, but it is not itself a poetic expression of 'the tragic sense of life'; it is actual, pathetic expression, springing from an emotional conflict.

Tragedy dramatizes human life as potentiality and fulfilment. Its virtual future, or Destiny, is therefore quite different from that created

* Reprinted from *Feeling and Form: A Theory of Art* (New York: Charles Scribner's Sons, 1953).

in comedy. Comic Destiny is Fortune – what the world will bring, and
the man will take or miss, encounter or escape; tragic Destiny is what
the man brings, and the world will demand of him. That is his Fate.

What he brings is his potentiality: his mental, moral and even
physical powers, his powers to act and suffer. Tragic action is the
realization of all his possibilities, which he unfolds and exhausts in the
course of the drama. His human nature is his Fate. Destiny conceived
as Fate is, therefore, not capricious, like Fortune, but is predetermined.
Outward events are merely the occasions for its realization.

'His human nature', however, does not refer to his *generally* human
character; I do not mean to say that a tragic hero is to be regarded as
primarily a symbol for mankind. What the poet creates is a personality;
and the more individual and powerful that personality is, the more
extraordinary and overwhelming will be the action. Since the
protagonist is the chief agent, his relation to the action is obvious; and
since the course of the action is the 'fable' or 'plot' of the play, it is also
obvious that creating the characters is not something apart from
building the plot, but is an integral portion of it. The agents are prime
elements in the action; but the action is the play itself, and artistic
elements are always for the sake of the whole. That was, I think, what
prompted Aristotle to say: 'Tragedy is essentially an imitation[2] not of
persons but of action and life, of happiness and misery. All human
happiness or misery takes the form of action; the end for which we live
is a certain kind of activity, not a quality. Character gives us qualities,
but it is in our actions – what we do – that we are happy or the
reverse. In a play accordingly they do not act in order to portray
the Characters; they include the Characters for the sake of the action.
So that it is the action in it, i.e. its Fable or Plot, that is the end and
purpose of the tragedy; and the end is everywhere the chief thing.'[3] This
'end' is the work as such. The protagonist and all characters that support
him are introduced that we may see the fulfillment of his Fate, which is
simply the complete realization of his individual 'human nature'.

The idea of personal Fate was mythically conceived long before
the relation of life history to character was discursively understood.
The mythical tradition of Greece treated the fate of its 'heroes' – the
personalities springing from certain great, highly individualized families
– as a mysterious power inherent in the world rather than in the man
and his ancestry; it was conceived as a private incubus bestowed on
him at birth by a vengeful deity, or even through a curse pronounced
by a human being. Sometimes no such specific cause of his peculiar
destiny is given at all; but an oracle foretells what he is bound to do. It
is interesting to note that this conception of Fate usually centers in the
mysterious predictability of *acts* someone is to perform. The occasions
of the acts are not foretold; the world will provide them.

For the development of tragedy, such determination of the overt acts without circumstances and motives furnished an ideal starting point, for it constrained the poets to invent characters whose actions would issue naturally in the required fateful deeds. The oracular prophecy, then, became an intensifying symbol of the necessity that was really given with the agent's personality; the 'fable' being just one possible way the world might elicit his complete self-realization in endeavour and error and discovery, passion and punishment, to the limit of his powers. The prime example of this passage from the mythical idea of Fate to the dramatic creation of Fate as the protagonist's natural, personal destiny is, of course, the *Oedipus Tyrannus* of Sophocles. With that tremendous piece of self-assertion, self-divination and self-exhaustion, the 'Great Tradition' of tragedy was born in Europe.

There is another mythical conception of Fate that is not a forerunner of tragedy, but possibly of some kinds of comedy: that is the idea of Fate as the will of supernatural powers, perhaps long decreed, perhaps spontaneous and arbitrary. It is the 'Fate' of the true fatalist, who takes no great care of his life because he deems it entirely in the hand of Allah (or some other God), who will slay or spare at his pleasure no matter what one does. That is quite a different notion from the 'oracular' Fate of Greek mythology; the will of a god who gives and takes away, casts down or raises up, for inscrutable reasons of his own, is Kismet, and that is really a myth of Fortune.[4] Kismet is what a person encounters, not what he is. Both conceptions often exist side by side. The Scotsman who has to 'dree his weird' believes nonetheless that his fortunes from moment to moment are in the hands of Providence. Macbeth's Weird Sisters were perfectly acceptable to a Christian audience. Even in the ancient lore of our fairy tales, the Sleeping Beauty is destined to prick herself – that is, she has a personal destiny. In Greek tradition, on the other hand, where the notion of 'oracular Fate' was so generally entertained that the Oracle was a public institution, Fate as the momentary decree of a ruling Power is represented in the myth of the Norns, who spin the threads of human lives and cut them where they list; the Three Fates are as despotic and capricious as Allah, and what they spin is, really, Kismet.

Tragedy can arise and flourish only where people are aware of individual life as an end in itself, and as a measure of other things. In tribal cultures where the individual is still so closely linked with his family that not only society but even he himself regards his existence as a communal value, which may be sacrificed at any time for communal ends, the development of personality is not a consciously appreciated life pattern. Similarly, where men believe that Karma, or the tally of their deeds, may be held over for recompense or expiation in another earthly life, their current incarnation cannot be seen as a self-sufficient whole in which their entire potentialities are to be realized. Therefore genuine tragedy – drama exhibiting 'the tragic rhythm of action', as Professor Fergusson has called it[5] – is a specialized form of art, with problems and devices of its own.

The word 'rhythm', which I have used freely with respect to drama, may seem a question-begging word, borrowed from the realm of physiology – where indeed the basic vital functions are generally rhythmic – and carried over somewhat glibly to the realm of conscious acts, which, for the most part – and certainly the most interesting part – are not repetitive. But it is precisely the *rhythm* of dramatic action that makes drama 'a poetry of the theatre', and not an imitation (in the usual, not the Aristotelian sense) or make-believe of practical life. As Hebbel said, 'In the hand of the poet, Becoming must always be a passage from *form* to *form* [von *Gestalt* zu *Gestalt*], it must never appear, like amorphous clay, chaotic and confused in our sight, but must seem somehow like a perfected thing.'[6] The analysis and definition of rhythmic structure may be applied without distortion or strain to the organization of elements in any play that achieves 'living' form.

A dramatic act is a commitment. It creates a situation in which the agent or agents must necessarily make a further move; that is, it motivates a subsequent act (or acts). The situation, which is the completion of a given act, is already the impetus to another – as, in running, the footfall that catches our weight at the end of one bound already sends us forward to land on the other foot. The bounds need not be alike, but proportional, which means that the impetus of any specially great leap must have been prepared and gathered somewhere, and any sudden diminution be balanced by some motion that carries off the driving force. Dramatic acts are analogously connected with each other so that each one directly or indirectly motivates what follows it.[7] In this way a genuine rhythm of action is set up, which is not simple like that of a physical repetitive process (e.g. running, breathing), but more often intricate, even deceptive, and, of course, not given primarily to one particular sense, but to the imagination through whatever sense we employ to perceive and evaluate action; the same general rhythm of action appears in a play whether we read it or hear it read, enact it ourselves or see it performed. That rhythm is the 'commanding form' of the play; it springs from the poet's original conception of the 'fable', and dictates the major divisions of the work, the light or heavy style of its presentation, the intensity of the highest feeling and most violent act, the great or small number of characters, and the degrees of their development. The total action is a cumulative form; and because it is constructed by a rhythmic treatment of its elements, it appears to *grow* from its beginnings. That is the playwright's creation of 'organic form'.

The tragic rhythm, which is the pattern of a life that grows, flourishes, and declines, is abstracted by being transferred from that natural activity to the sphere of a characteristically human action, where it is exemplified in mental and emotional growth, maturation, and the final relinquishment of power. In that relinquishment lies the hero's true 'heroism' – the vision of life as accomplished, that is, life in its entirety, the sense of fulfilment that lifts him above his defeat.

A remarkable expression of this idea of tragedy may be found in the same book from which I borrowed, a few paragraphs above, the phrase, 'the tragic rhythm of action'. Speaking of Hamlet, Professor Fergusson observes:

> In Act V . . . he feels that his role, all but the very last episode, has been played. . . . He is content, now, to let the fated end come as it will. . . . One could say that he feels the poetic rightness of his own death. . . .
>
> However one may interpret it, when his death comes it 'feels right,' the only possible end for the play. . . . We are certainly intended to feel that Hamlet, however darkly and uncertainly he worked, had discerned the way to be obedient to his deepest values, and accomplished some sort of purgatorial progress for himself and Denmark.[8]

'The second scene of Act V,' the critique continues, 'with the duel between Hamlet and Laertes, shows the denouements of all the intrigues in the play. . . . But these events, which literally end the narratives in the play, and bring Claudius' regime to its temporal end, tell us nothing new but the fact: that the sentence, which fate or providence pronounced long since, has now been executed. It is the pageantry, the ceremonial mummery, in short the virtual character of this last scene which makes us feel it as the final epiphany. . . .'[9]

Tragic drama is so designed that the protagonist grows mentally, emotionally, or morally, by the demand of the action, which he himself initiated, to the complete exhaustion of his powers, that limit of his possible development. He spends himself in the course of the one dramatic action. This is, of course, a tremendous foreshortening of life; instead of undergoing the physical and psychical, many-sided, long process of an actual biography, the tragic hero lives and matures in some particular respect; his entire being is concentrated in one aim, one passion, one conflict and ultimate defeat. For this reason the prime agent of tragedy is heroic; his character, the unfolding situation, the scene, even though ostensibly familiar and humble, are all exaggerated, charged with more feeling than comparable actualities would possess.[10] This intensification is necessary to achieve and sustain the 'form in suspense' that is even more important in tragic drama than in comic, because the comic denouement, not marking an absolute close, needs only to restore a balance, but the tragic ending must recapitulate the whole action to be a visible fulfilment of a destiny that was implicit in the beginning. This device, which may be called 'dramatic exaggeration', is reminiscent of 'epic exaggeration', and may have been adopted quite unconsciously with the epic themes of ancient tragedy. But that does not mean that it is an accidental factor, a purely historical legacy from an older poetic tradition; inherited conventions do not maintain themselves long in any art unless they serve its own purposes. They may have their old *raison d'être* in new art forms, or take on entirely new functions, but as sheer trappings – traditional requirements – they would be discarded by the first genius who found no use for them.

Drama is not psychology, nor (though the critical literature tends to make it seem so) is it moral philosophy. It offers no discourse on the hero's or heroine's native endowments, to let us estimate at any stage in the action how near they must be to exhaustion. The action itself must reveal the limit of the protagonist's powers and mark the end of his self-realization. And so, indeed, it does: the turning point of the play is the situation he cannot resolve, where he makes his 'tragic error' or exhibits his 'tragic weakness'. He is led by his own action and its repercussions in the world to respond with more and more competence, more and more daring to a constantly gathering challenge; so his character 'grows', i.e. he unfolds his will and knowledge and passion, as the situation grows. His career is not change of personality, but maturation. When he reaches his limit of mental and emotional development, the crisis occurs; then comes the defeat, either by death or, as in many modern tragedies, by hopelessness that is the equivalent of death, a 'death of the soul', that ends the career.

It has been reiterated so often that the hero of tragedy is a strong man with one weakness, a good man with one fault, that a whole ethics of tragedy has grown up around the significance of that single flaw. Chapters upon chapters – even books – have been written on the required mixture of good and evil in his character, to make him command pity and yet make his downfall not repugnant to 'our moral sense'. Critics and philosophers, from Aristotle to Croce, have written about the spectator's acceptance of the hero's fate as a recognition of the moral order he has defied or ignored, the triumph of justice the hero himself is supposed to accept in his final 'conciliation' or 'epiphany'. The restoration of the great moral order through suffering is looked upon as the Fate he has to fulfil. He must be imperfect to break the moral law, but fundamentally good, i.e. striving for perfection, in order to achieve his moral salvation in sacrifice, renunciation, death.

All this concern with the philosophical and ethical significance of the hero's sufferings, however, leads away from the *artistic* significance of the play, to discursive ideas about life, character, and the world. At once we are faced with the usual dilemma of the critic who sees art as a representation of actual life, and an art form as a *Weltanschauung*: not every work of the genre can really be said to express the *Weltanschauung* that is supposed to characterize it, nor to give us the same general picture of the world, such as the 'moral order' in which justice is inevitably done or the amoral 'cosmic order' in which man is a plaything of forces beyond his control. Then the critic may come to the despairing conclusion that the genre cannot be defined, but is really just a name that changes its essential meaning from age to age. No less an authority than Ashley Thorndike decided that tragedy is really indefinable; one can trace the historical evolution of each conception, but not the defining attribute that runs through them all and brings them justly under one name. The only features that he found common to all tragedies were representation of 'painful and destructive actions', and 'criticism of life'.[11] Either of these could, of course, occur in other art forms, too. A. C. Bradley, in his excellent *Shakespearean Tragedy*, points out that Shakespeare did not, like the Greek tragedians, postulate a superhuman power determining men's actions and accidents, nor a special Nemesis, invoked by past crimes, belonging to certain families or persons; he claims, in fact, to find no representation of Fate in Shakespeare.[12] Even justice, he holds, is not illustrated there, because the disasters men bring upon themselves are not proportioned to their sins; but something one might call a 'moral order', an order not of right and wrong, but at least of good and evil. Accident plays its part, but in the main the agents ride for the fall they take.[13] Edgar Stoll, exactly to the contrary, maintains that the action in Shakespeare's tragedies 'does not at bottom develop out of character'.[14] One could go on almost indefinitely in citing examples of contradiction or exception to the various standards of tragic action, especially the fatalistic standard.

The fallacy which leads to this crisscross of interpretations and opinions is the familiar one of confusing what the poet creates with what he represents. It is the fallacy of looking, not for the artistic function of everything he represents and the way he represents it, but for something that his representations are supposed to illustrate or suggest – something that belongs to life, not the play. If, then, tragedy is called an image of Fate, it is expected to illustrate the workings of Fate. But that is not necessary; it may just as well illustrate the workings of villainy, neurosis, faith, social justice, or anything else the poet finds usable to motivate a large, integral action. The myth of Fate often used in Greek tragedies was an obvious motif, as in later plays romantic love defying circumstance, or the vast consequences of a transgression. But one should not expect a major art form to be bound to a single motif, no matter in how many variations or even disguises; to reduce the many themes that may be found in tragedy, from Aeschylus to O'Neill, all to 'the workings of Fate', and the many *Weltanschauungen* that may be read out of (or into) it to so many recognitions of a supernatural order, a moral order, or a pure causal order, leads only to endless sleuthing after deeper meanings, symbolic substitutions, and far-reaching implications that no playgoer could possibly infer, so they would be useless in the theatre.

Fate in tragedy is the created form, the virtual future as an accomplished whole. It is not the expression of a belief at all. Macbeth's fate is the structure of his tragedy, not an instance of how things happen in the world. That virtual future has the form of a completely individualized, and therefore mortal, life – a measured life, to be exhausted in a small span of time. But growth, efflorescence, and exhaustion – the prototype of Fate – is not what the play is about; it is only what the movement of the action is like. The play is about somebody's desires, acts, conflict, and defeat; however his acts are motivated, however his deeds undo him, the total action is his dramatic fate. Tragic action has the rhythm of natural life and death, but it does not refer to or illustrate them; it abstracts their dynamic form, and imprints it on entirely different matters, in a different time span – the whole self-realization may take place in days or hours instead of the decades of biological consummation – so the 'tragic rhythm' stands clear of any natural occasion, and becomes a perceptible form.

The kind of art theory that measures the value of drama by the way it represents life, or by the poet's implied beliefs about life, not only leads criticism away from poetry into philosophy, religion, or social science, but also causes people to think of the protagonist as an ordinary fellow man whom they are to approve or condemn and, in either case, pity. This attitude, which is undoubtedly derived – whether rightly or mistakenly – from Aristotle, has given rise to the many moral demands on the hero's character: he must be admirable but not perfect, must command the spectators' sympathy even if he incurs their censure; they must feel his fate as their own, etc.[15]

In truth, I believe, the hero of tragedy must *interest* us all the time, but not as a person of our own acquaintance. His tragic error, crime, or other flaw is not introduced for moral reasons, but for structural purposes: it marks his limit of power. His potentialities appear on stage only as successful acts; as soon as his avowed or otherwise obvious intentions fail, or his acts recoil on him and bring him pain, his power has reached its height, he is at the end of his career. In this, of course, drama is utterly different from life. The moral failure in drama is not a normal incident, something to be lived down, presumably neither the

doer's first transgression nor his last; the act that constitutes the
protagonist's tragic error or guilt is the high-water mark of his life, and
now the tide recedes. His 'imperfection' is an artistic element: that is
why a single flaw will do.

All persistent practices in art have a creative function. They may
serve several ends, but the chief one is the shaping of the work. This
holds not only for character traits which make a dramatic personage
credible or sympathetic, but also for another much-discussed device in
drama – so-called 'comic relief', the introduction of trivial or humorous
interludes in midst of serious, ominous, tragic action. The term 'comic
relief' indicates the supposed purpose of that practice: to give the
audience a respite from too much emotional tension, let them have
entertainment as well as 'pity and fear'. Here again traditional criticism
rests too confidently, I think, on Aristotle's observations, which – after
all – were not the insights of a playwright, but the reflections of a
scientifically inclined man interested in psychology. Aristotle considered
the comic interlude as a concession to human weakness; and 'comic
relief' has been its name ever since.

The humorous interludes in tragedy are merely moments when the
comic spirit rises to the point of hilarity. Such moments may result from
all sorts of poetic exigencies; the famous drunken porter in *Macbeth*
makes a macabre contrast to the situation behind the door he beats
upon, and is obviously introduced to heighten rather than relieve the
tense secrecy of the murder.

But the most important fact about these famous touches of 'comic
relief' is that they always occur in plays which have a vein of comedy
throughout, kept for the most part below the level of laughter. This vein
may be tapped for special effects, even for a whole scene, to slow and
subdue the action or to heighten it with grotesque reflection. In those
heroic tragedies that are lowered by the incursion of farce, and not
structurally affected by its omission, there is no integral, implicit
comedy – no everyday life – in the 'world' of the play, to which
the clowning naturally belongs and from which it may be derived
without disorganization of the whole.[16] In *Macbeth* (and, indeed, all
Shakespearean plays) there is a large, social, everyday life of soldiers,
grooms, gossips, courtiers and commoners, that provides an essentially
comic substructure for the heroic action. Most of the time this lower
stratum is subdued, giving an impression of realism without any
obvious byplay; but this realism carries the fundamental comic rhythm
from which grotesque interludes may arise with perfect dramatic logic.

The fact that the two great rhythms, comic and tragic, are radically
distinct does not mean that they are each other's opposites, or even
incompatible forms. Tragedy can rest squarely on a comic substructure,

and yet be pure tragedy.[17] This is natural enough, for life – from which all felt rhythms spring – contains both, in every mortal organism. Society is continuous though its members, even the strongest and fairest, live out their lives and die; and even while each individual fulfils the tragic pattern it participates also in the comic continuity.[18] The poet's task is, of course, not to copy life, but to organize and articulate a symbol for the 'sense of life'; and in the symbol one rhythm always governs the dynamic form, though another may go through the whole piece in a contrapuntal fashion. The master of this practice is Shakespeare.

Did the stark individual Fate of the purest Greek tragedy rule out, by its intense deathward movement, the comic feeling of the eternally full and undulating stream of life? Or was the richness that the comic-tragic counterpoint creates in other poetic traditions supplied to Aeschylus and Sophocles by the choric dance which framed and embellished the play? The satyr play at the end of the long, tragic presentation may well have been necessary, to assure its truth to the structure of subjective reality by an exuberant celebration of life.

There is yet another factor in drama that is commonly, and I think mistakenly, treated as a concession to popular taste: the use of spectacle, pageantry, brilliant show. Many critics apparently believe that a playwright makes provision for spectacular effects quite apart from his own poetic judgment and intent, simply to lure the audience into the theatre. Thorndike, in fact, asserts that the use of spectacle bespeaks 'the double purpose, hardly separable from the drama and particularly manifest in the Elizabethan dramatists, the two desires, to please their audiences and to create literature'.[19] Brander Matthews said bluntly that not only theatre, but all art whatever is 'show business', whatever it may be besides.[20]

Art, and especially dramatic art, is full of compromises, for one possible effect is usually bought at the expense of another; not all ideas and devices that occur to the poet are co-possible. Every decision involves a rejection. And furthermore, the stage, the available funds, the capabilities of the actors, may all have to be considered. But no artist can make concessions to what he considers bad taste without ruining his work. He simply cannot think as an artist and accept inexpressive forms or admit an element that has no organic function in the whole. If, therefore, he wishes to present spectacular scenes, he must start with an idea that demands spectacular presentation.

Every play has its intended audience, and in that audience there is one pre-eminent member: the author. If the play is intended for, say, an Elizabethan audience, that honorary member will be an Elizabethan theatre-goer, sharing the best Elizabethan taste, and sometimes setting its fashion. Our dramatic critics write as though the poets of the past were all present-day people making concessions to interests that have long spent themselves. But the poets who provided stage spectacles had spectacular ideas, and worked with them until their expressive possibilities were exhausted.

The element of pure show has an important function in dramatic art, for it tends to raise feeling, whatever the feeling is. It does this even in actual life: a splendid hall, an ornate table arrangement, a company in full dress, make a feast seem bigger and the gathering more illustrious than a plain table in a cafeteria, refectory, or gymnasium, with the guests in street dress. A splendid funeral, passing in procession behind chanting priests, is more solemn than a drab one, though perhaps no one at the spectacular service feels more sad than at the colourless one. In the theatre, the element of show is a means of heightening the atmosphere, whether of gaiety of terror or woe; so it is, first of all, a ready auxiliary.

But in tragedy it has a more specialized and essential function, too. Tragedy, which expresses the consciousness of life and death, must make life seem worth while, rich, beautiful, to make death awesome. The splendid exaggerations of the stage serve tragic feeling by heightening the lure of the world. The beautiful world, as well as the emotional tone of the action, is magnified by the element of spectacle – by lighting and colour, setting and grouping, music, dance, 'excursions and alarums'. Some playwrights avail themselves freely of this help; others dispense with it almost entirely (never quite; the theatre is spectacular at any time), because they have other poetic means of giving virtual life the glory that death takes away, or despair – the 'death of the soul' – corrupts.

Spectacle is a powerful ingredient in several arts. Consider what playing fountains can do for a courtyard or a square, and how a ceremonial procession brings the interior of a cathedral to visible life! Architectural design may be marvelously altered by a supplement of fortuitous spectacle. The Galata bridge over the Golden Horn in the middle of Istanbul, with thousands of people and vehicles passing over it, coming from steep hillsides on either hand, looks as though it were hung from the mosque-crowned heights above; without the pageantry of its teeming cosmopolitan traffic it shrinks to a flat thoroughfare across the river, between its actual bridgeheads. An esplanade without the movement of water below it would be utterly unimpressive; flooded with moonlight, which picks out the surface movement of the water, or standing immovable against a towering surf, it may become veritably an architect's dream.

But pure show, not assimilated to any art, does not constitute a 'work'. Acrobatics, tennis playing, some beautiful occupational rhythms such as hauling nets, swinging hammers, or the evolutions of boats in a race, are fascinating, aesthetically thrilling, so they hold the spectator in a joyful trance; but they are not art. For a work of art, this trance is only one requisite. Spectacle, however beautiful, is always an *element* in art. It may well be a major element, as it was in Noverre's ballets, and in the court masques, but even these largely spectacular products are rated as 'works' because they had something else that motivated the display: an imaginative core, a 'commanding form'. A circus could be a work of art if it had some central feeling and some primary, unfailing illusion. As it is, the circus sometimes contains genuine little 'works' – a riding act that is really an equestrian dance, a piece of clowning that rises to genuine comedy. But on the whole the circus is a 'show', not a work of art, though it is a work of skill, planning and fitting, and sometimes copes with problems that arise also in the arts. What it lacks is the first requisite for art – a conception of feeling, something to express.

Because a dramatic work has such a core, everything in it is poesis. It is, therefore, neither a hybrid product pieced together at the demand of many interests, nor a synthesis of all the arts – not even of a more modest 'several'. It may have use for paint and plaster, wood and brick, but not for painting, sculpture, or architecture; it has use for music, but not for even a fragment of a concert programme; it may require dancing, but such dancing is not self-contained – it intensifies a scene, often abstracts a quintessence of its feeling, the image of sheer powers arising as a secondary illusion in the midst of the virtual history.

Drama is a great form, which not only invites expression of elemental human feeling, but also permits a degree of articulation, complexity, detail within detail, in short: organic development, that smaller poetic forms cannot exhibit without confusion. To say that such works express 'a concept of feeling' is misleading unless one bears in mind that it is the whole life of feeling – call it 'felt life', 'subjectivity', 'direct experience', or what you will – which finds its articulate expression in art, and, I believe, only in art. So great and fully elaborated a form as (say) a Shakespearean tragedy may formulate the characteristic mode of perception and response, sensibility and emotion and their sympathetic overtones, that constitutes a whole personality. Here we see the process of art expression 'writ large', as Plato would say; for the smallest work does the same thing as the greatest, on its own scale: it reveals the patterns of possible sentience, vitality, and mentality objectifying our subjective being – the most intimate 'Reality' that we know. This function, and not the recording of contemporary scenes, politics, or even moral attitudes, is what relates art to life; and the big unfolding of feeling in the organic, personal pattern of a human life, rising, growing, accomplishing destiny and meeting doom – that is tragedy.

Notes

1. See his *The Tragic Sense of Life*, trans. J. E. C. FLITCH (London: Macmillan & Co., 1921), *passim*. Unamuno's feelings are strong and natural; his aphorisms are often poetic and memorable. With his philosophical assertions, however, one cannot take issue, because he prides himself on being inconsistent, on the ground that 'life is irrational', 'truth is not logical', etc. Consistency of statements he regards as a mark of their falsity. Like some exasperating ladies, who claim 'a woman's right to be inconsistent', he cannot, therefore, be worsted in argument, but – also like them – he cannot be taken seriously.

2. 'Imitation' is used by Aristotle in much the same sense in which I use 'semblance'. I have avoided his word because it stresses similitude to actuality rather than abstraction from actuality.

3. *De Poetica*, chap. 6, II (1450a), translation by W. R. ROBERTS.

4. Cf. N. N. MARTINOVITCH, *The Turkish Theatre* (New York: Theatre Arts, Inc., 1933), p. 36: 'According to Islamic speculation, man has almost no influence on the development of his own fate. Allah is sovereign, doing as he likes and accounting to no one. And the screen of the haial [the comic shadow theatre] is the dramatization of this speculative concept of the world.'

5. In *The Idea of a Theater* (Princeton: Princeton University Press, 1949), especially p. 18.

6. FRIEDRICH HEBBEL, *Tagebücher*, collected in BERNHARD MÜNZ's *Hebbel als Denker* (Munich, 1913).

7. An act may be said to motivate further acts indirectly if it does so through a total situation it helps to create; the small acts of psychological import that merely create personality are of this sort.

8. FERGUSSON, *The Idea of a Theater*, pp. 132–133. 'To be obedient to his deepest values' is nothing else than to realize his own potentialities, fulfil his true destiny.

9. Ibid., p. 138.

10. As ROBERT EDMOND JONES has put it: 'Great drama does not deal with cautious people. Its heroes are tyrants, outcasts, wanderers. From Prometheus, the first of them all, the thief who stole the divine fire from heaven, these protagonists are all passionate, excessive, violent, terrible. "Doom eager," the Icelandic sage calls them.' *The Dramatic Imagination* (New York: Duell, Sloan & Pearce, 1941), p. 42.

11. 'Any precise and exact definition is sure to lack in comprehensiveness and veracity. . . . We seem forced to reject the possibility of any exact limitation for the dramatic species, to include as tragedies all plays presenting painful or destructive actions, to accept the leading elements of a literary tradition derived from the Greeks as indicating the common bonds between such plays in the past, but to admit that this tradition, while still powerful, is variable, uncertain, and unauthoritative' (*Tragedy* (Boston: Houghton, Mifflin & Co., 1908), p. 12.) At the end of the book he sets up, as the only common standard, 'an unselfish, a social, a moral inquiry into life' (p. 376).

12. In a footnote on p. 30 he writes: 'I have raised no objection to the use of the idea of fate, because it occurs so often both in conversation and in books about Shakespeare's tragedies that I must suppose it to be natural to many readers. Yet I doubt whether it would be so if Greek tragedy had never been written; and I must in candour confess that to me it does not often occur while I am reading, or when I have just read, a tragedy of Shakespeare' (London: Macmillan & Co., 1932).

13. The discussion of justice (Lecture I, 'The Substance of Tragedy', p. 5) is noteworthy especially for his recognition of the *irrelevance of the concept* to dramatic art.

14. *Shakespeare and Other Masters* (Cambridge, Mass.: Harvard University Press, 1940), p. 31.

15. THORNDIKE regarded tragedy as the highest art form, because, as he put it, 'it brings home to us the images of our own sorrows, and chastens the spirit through the outpouring of our sympathies, even our horror and despair, for the misfortune of our fellows' (*Tragedy*, p. 19). Shortly before, he conceded that it might also give us – among other pleasures – 'aesthetic delight in a masterpiece' (p. 17).

16. THORNDIKE points out that *Tamburlaine* is of this genre: 'Originally,' he says, 'the play contained comic scenes, omitted in the published form and evidently of no value in structure or conception' (*Tragedy*, p. 90).

    See also J. B. MOORE, *The Comic and the Realistic in English Drama* (Chicago: University of Chicago Press, 1925).

17. A striking example is J. M. BARRIE's little tragedy dating from the first World War, *The Old Lady Shows her Medals*. Despite the consistently comic treatment one expects the inevitable (and wordless) last scene.

18. There is also a genre known as 'tragicomedy' (the Germans call it *Schauspiel*, distinguishing it from both *Lustspiel* and *Trauerspiel*), which is a comic pattern playing with the tragic; its plot-structure is *averted tragedy*, temporizing with the sense of fate, which usually inspires a tragic diction, little or no exuberance (humour), and often falls into melodrama. A study of its few artistic successes, and their precise relations to pure comedy and pure tragedy, might raise interesting problems.

19. *Tragedy*, p. 98.

20. *A Book About the Theater* (New York: Charles Scribner's Sons, 1916), pp. 8–9.

8 Deconstruction and Tragedy

Throughout this selection it is evident that tragedy is deeply concerned with questions of knowledge, of 'reality', of the ritual elements in communal life, and of the various ways in which these topics achieve representation. These materialist accounts of tragedy do much to disturb the traditional philosophical foundations upon which the form has been grounded, and the challenges from psychoanalysis and feminism particularly served to problematise this tradition even further. In a manner which subsumes many of the concerns articulated in the various categories of this selection, Derrida's 'Plato's pharmacy' seeks to focus on writing itself as the site upon which a drama of *difference* is played out. For Derrida, the *pharmakos* is a composite figure, a wizard, magician and poisoner who is a kind of scapegoat involved in a ritual which is structurally similar to the operation of tragedy itself. What he calls 'the ceremony of the *pharmakos*' is enacted on a boundary-line between the inside and the outside of the community/body, and as such serves to define the conditions of possibility of tragedy. If in the writing of someone such as Georg Lukács, tragedy discloses the operation of a metaphysics, for Derrida, all metaphysically sanctioned order is put in question by probing the conditions under which it achieves both its legitimacy and its authority. Derrida is concerned in this essay not only with the kind of ritualistic account of violence that we found in Girard, but at least as much with the conflict between a metaphysically sanctioned order and those material historical forces which pose a challenge to hierarchical structures. Derrida's reliance upon the structuring mechanism of *difference* allows him to chart not just the *production* of order, but also its 'other', which serves as a challenge to its imperatives. The identification of that otherness also offers a possibility for resistance, and allows the possibility of a radical reading of tragic form. It is fitting that deconstruction, the radical questioning of the conditions under which definitions achieve their authority, should come at the end.

Plato's Pharmacy*

JACQUES DERRIDA

The use Socrates makes of the *pharmakon* does not have as its goal the guaranteeing of the *pharmakeus'* power. The technique of infiltration or paralysis can even eventually be turned against its user although one must always, in the symptomatological manner of Nietzsche, be careful to diagnose the *economy*, the investment and deferred benefit behind the sign of pure renunciation or the *bidding* of disinterested sacrifice.

The nakedness of the *pharmakon*, the blunt bare voice (*psilos logos*), carries with it a certain mastery in the dialogue, on the condition that Socrates overtly renounce its benefits: knowledge as power, passion, pleasure. On the condition, in a word, that he consent to die. The death of the body, at least: that is the price that must be paid for *alētheia* and the epistēmē, which are also powers.

The fear of death is what gives all witchcraft, all occult medicine, a hold. The *pharmakeus* is banking on that fear. Hence the Socratic pharmacy, in working to free us from it, corresponds to an operation of *exorcism*, in a form that could be envisaged and conducted from the side and viewpoint of God. After wondering whether some God had given men a drug to induce fear (*phobou pharmakon*), the Athenian of the *Laws* dismisses the idea: 'Let's repeat the point we were making to the legislator: "Agreed then: there is probably no such thing as a drug (*pharmakon*) to produce fear, either by gift or human contrivance (I leave quacks (*goētas*) out of account: they're beyond the pale). But is there a drink that will produce a lack of fear (*aphobias*) and stimulate overconfidence about the wrong thing at the wrong moment? What do we say to this?"' (649*a*).

It is the child in us that is afraid. The charlatans will all disappear when the 'little boy within us' no longer fears death as he fears a *mormolukeion*, a scarecrow set up to frighten children, a bogeyman. And incantations must be redoubled daily in order to free the child from

* Reprinted from *Dissemination*, trans. with an introduction and additional notes BARBARA JOHNSON (Chicago: The University of Chicago Press, 1981).

this fantasy: '*Cebes*: Probably even in us there is a little boy who has these childish terrors. Try to persuade him not to be afraid of death as though it where a bogey. – What you should do, said Socrates, is to say a magic spell over him every day until you have charmed his fears away. – But, Socrates, said Simmias, where shall we find a magician (*epōdon*) who understands these spells now that you are leaving us?' (*Phaedo, 77e*). In the *Crito*, too, Socrates refuses to give in to the people who 'conjure up fresh hordes of bogeys to terrify our childish minds, by subjecting us to chains and executions and confiscations of our property' (46c).

The counterspell, the exorcism, the antidote, is dialectics. In answer to Cebes, Socrates recommends seeking not only a magician but also – the surest incantation – training in dialectics: 'Seek for him among all peoples, far and wide, sparing neither pains nor money; for there is no better way of spending your money. And you must seek among yourselves, too; for you will not find others better suited for the task' (*Phaedo, 78a–b*).

To seek 'among yourselves' by mutual questioning and self-examination, to seek to know oneself through the detour of the language of the other, such is the undertaking presented by Socrates, who recalls the Delphic inscription (*tou Delphikou grammatos*), to Alcibiades as the antidote (*alexipharmakon*), the counterpotion. In the text of the *Laws* which we left off quoting earlier, when the necessity of the letter has been firmly laid down, the introjection or internalization of the *grammata* into the judge's soul – their most secure dwelling-place – is then prescribed as an antidote. Let us pick up the thread of the text again.:

He that would show himself a righteously equal judge must keep these matters before his eyes; he must procure books on the subject, and must make them his study. There is, in truth, no study whatsoever so potent as this of law, if the law be what it should be, to make a better man of its student – else 'twould be for nothing that the law which so stirs our worship and wonder bears a name so cognate with that of understanding [*nomos/nous*]. Furthermore, consider all other discourse, poesy with its eulogies and its satires, or utterances in prose, whether in literature or in the common converse of daily life, with their contentious disagreements and their too often unmeaning admissions. The one certain touchstone of all is the writings of the legislator (*ta tou nomothetou grammata*). *The good judge will possess those writings within his own soul (ha dei kektēmenon en hautōi) as antidotes (alexipharmaka) against other discourse,* and thus he will be the state's preserver as well as his own. He will secure in the good the retention and increase of their rectitude, and in the evil, or those of them whose vicious principles admit remedy, will promote, so far as he can, conversion from folly, from profligacy, from cowardice, in a word, from all forms of wrong. As for those who are fatally attached to such principles, if our judges and their superiors prescribe death as a cure (*iama*) for a soul in that state, they will, as has been more than once said already, deserve the praise of the community for their conduct.

(XII, 957*c*–958*a*; emphasis mine)

Anamnesic dialectics, as the repetition of the *eidos*, cannot be distinguished from self-knowledge and self-mastery. Those are the best forms of exorcism that can be applied against the terrors of the child faced with death and the quackery of the bogeyman. Philosophy consists of offering reassurance to children. That is, if one prefers, of taking them out of childhood, of forgetting about the child, or, inversely, but by the same token, of speaking first and foremost *for* that little boy within us, of teaching him to speak – to dialogue – by displacing his fear or his desire.

One could play at classifying, within the weave of the *Statesman* (280*a* ff), that species of protection (*amuntērion*) that is called dialectics and apprehended as a counter-poison. Among the things that can be called artificial (manufactured or acquired), the Stranger distinguishes those with the function of doing something (tending toward *poiein*) and those, called defences (*amuntēria*), with the function of preventing suffering (*tou me paskhein*). Among the latter, one can distinguish (1) *antidotes* (*alexipharmaka*), which can be either human or divine (and dialectics is from this perspective the very antidoteness of the antidote in general, before any possibility of dividing it up between the human and the divine. Dialectics is precisely the passage between the two) and (2) *problems* (*problēmata*): what stands before one – obstacles, shelters, armour, shields, defences. Leaving antidotes aside, the Stranger pursues the division of the *problēmata*, which can function either as armaments or as fences. The *fences* (*phragmata*) are screens or protections (*alexētēria*) against storm and heat; these *protections* can be housings or coverings; *coverings* can be spread below (like rugs) or wrapped around, etc. The process of division goes on through the different techniques for manufacturing these wraps until it reaches the woven garment and the art of weaving: the *problematic* space of protection. This art would thus rule out, if one follows the divisions literally, all recourse to antidotes, and consequently, to that species of antidote or inverted *pharmakon* constituted by dialectics. The text excludes dialectics. And yet, it will nevertheless be necessary later to distinguish between two sorts of texture, if one bears in mind that dialectics is also an art of weaving, a science of the *sumplokē*.

The dialectical inversion of the *pharmakon* or of the dangerous supplement makes death both acceptable and null. Acceptable because it is annulled. In making us welcome death, the immortality of the soul, which acts like an antibody, dissipates its terrifying fantasy. The inverted *pharmakon*, which scatters all the hobgoblins, is none other than the origin of the *epistēmē*, the opening to truth as the possibility of repetition and the submission of that 'greed for life' (*epithumein zēn*, *Crito*, 53e) to law (the good, the father, the king, the chief, the capital, the sun, all of which are invisible). It is the laws themselves that, in the *Crito*, urge one not to 'cling so greedily to life, at the price of violating the most stringent laws'.

What indeed does Socrates say when Cebes and Simmias ask him to provide them with a magician? He urges them to practice the philosophic dialogue and seek its most worthy object: the truth of the *eidos* as that which is identical to itself, always the same as itself and therefore simple, incomposite (*asuntheton*), undecomposable, invariable (78c,e). The *eidos* is that which can always be repeated as *the same*. The ideality and invisibility of the *eidos* are its power-to-be-repeated. Now, law is always a law of repetition, and repetition is always submission to a law. In the personification of the Laws in the *Crito*, Socrates is called upon to accept both death and law *at once*. He is asked to recognize himself as the offspring, the son or representative (*ekgonos*) or even the slave (*doulos*) of the law that, in uniting his father and mother, made possible his birth. Violence is thus even more sacrilegious when it offends the law of the mother/country than when it wounds the father and mother (51c). This is why, say the Laws, Socrates must die in conformity with the law and within the confines of the city – Socrates, who was (almost) always reluctant to go outside:

> Are you so wise as to have forgotten that compared with your mother and father and all the rest of your ancestors your country is something far more precious, more venerable, more sacred, and held in greater honour both among gods and among all reasonable men? . . . Violence is a sin even against your country. . . . Socrates, we have substantial evidence that you are satisfied with us and with the state (*polis*). You would not have been so exceptionally reluctant to cross the borders of your country (*polis*) if you had not been exceptionally attached to it. You have never left the city to attend a festival or for any other purpose, except on some military expedition. You have never travelled abroad as other people do, and you have never felt the impulse to acquaint yourself with another country or constitution. You have been content with us and with our city (*polis*). You have definitely chosen us, and undertaken to observe us in all your activities as a citizen.
>
> (51a,c–51b–e)

The Socratic word does not wander, stays at home, is closely watched: within autochthony, within the city, within the law, under the surveillance of its mother tongue. This will take on its full significance further on, when writing will be described as errancy as such, mute vulnerability to all aggression. In nothing does writing reside.

The *eidos*, truth, law, the *epistēmē*, dialectics, philosophy – all these are other names for that *pharmakon* that must be opposed to the *pharmakon* of the Sophists and to the bewitching fear of death. It is *pharmakeus* against *pharmakeus*, *pharmakon* against *pharmakon*. This is why Socrates heeds the Laws as though, through their voices, he were under the power of an initiatic spell, a sonorous spell, then, or rather, a phonic spell, one that penetrates and carries away the inner courts of the soul. 'That, my dear friend Crito, I do assure you, is what I seem to hear them saying, just as a Corybant seems to hear the strains of music, and the sound of their arguments (*hē ēkhē toutōn tōn logōn*) rings so loudly in my head that I cannot hear the other side' (54*d*). Those Corybants, that music, are evoked by Alcibiades in the *Symposium* in his efforts to describe the effects of the Socratic utterance: 'the moment I hear him speak I am smitten with a kind of sacred rage, worse than any Corybant, and my heart jumps into my mouth' (215*e*).

The philosophical, epistemic order of *logos* as an antidote, as a force *inscribed within the general alogical economy of the pharmakon* is not something we are proposing here as a daring interpretation of Platonism. Let us, rather, look at the prayer that opens the *Critias*: 'I call on the god to grant us that most effective medicine (*pharmakon teleōtaton*), that best of all medicines (*ariston pharmakōn*): knowledge (*epistēmēn*).' And one could also consider the astonishing dramatic staging of the first act of the *Charmides*. It should be followed moment by moment. Dazzled by the beauty of Charmides, Socrates wants above all to undress the soul of this young man who loves philosophy. Charmides is sent for so that he can be presented to a doctor (Socrates) who can relieve him of his headaches and his weakness. Socrates accepts to pass himself off as a man who knows a cure for headaches. There then ensues a 'cloak' scene similar to the one in the *Phaedrus*, involving a certain *pharmakon*:

> When Critias told him that I was the person who had the cure (*ho to pharmakon epistamenos*), he looked at me in an indescribable manner, and made as though to ask me a question. And all the people in the palaestra crowded about us, and at that moment, my good friend, I glanced through the opening of his garment, and was inflamed by his beauty. Then I could no longer contain myself. . . . But still when he asked me if I knew the cure for the headache (*to tēs kephalēs pharmakon*) . . . I replied that it was a kind of leaf, which required to

be accompanied by a charm (*epōdē de tis epi tōi pharmakōi*), and if a person would repeat the charm at the same time that he used the cure, he would be made whole, but that without the charm the leaf would be of no avail. – Then I will write out the charm from your dictation, he said.

(155*d*–156*a*. Cf. also 175–176)[1]

But the head cannot be cured separately. Good doctors take care of 'the whole', and it is by caring for the whole that they have been inspired by a Thracian physician, 'one of the physicians of the Thracian king Zalmoxis who are said to be able even to give immortality', Socrates shows that the whole of the body can only be cured at the source – the soul – of all its goods and evils. 'And the cure of the soul, my dear youth, has to be effected by the use of certain charms (*epōdais tisin*), and these charms are fair words, and by them temperance (*sōphrosunēn*) is implanted in the soul, and where temperance comes and stays, there health is speedily imparted, not only to the head, but to the whole body' (157*a*). And the discussion turns to the essence of temperance, the best *pharmakon*, the capital cure.

Philosophy thus opposes to its other this transmutation of the drug into a remedy, of the poison into a counterpoison. Such an operation would not be possible if the *pharmako-logos* did not already harbour within itself that complicity of contrary values, and if the *pharmakon* in general were not, prior to any distinction-making, that which, presenting itself as a poison, may turn out to be a cure, may retrospectively reveal itself in the truth of its curative power. The 'essence' of the *pharmakon* lies in the way in which, having no stable essence, no 'proper' characteristics, it is not, in any sense (metaphysical, physical, chemical, alchemical) of the word, a *substance*. The *pharmakon* has no ideal identity; it is aneidetic, firstly because it is not monoeidetic (in the sense in which the *Phaedo* speaks of the *eidos* as something simple, noncomposite: *monoeides*). This 'medicine' is not a simple thing. But neither is it a composite, a sensible or empirical *suntheton* partaking of several simple essences. It is rather the prior medium in which differentiation in general is produced, along with the opposition between the *eidos* and its other; this medium is *analogous* to the one that will, subsequent to and according to the decision of philosophy, be reserved for transcendental imagination, that 'art hidden in the depths of the soul', which belongs neither simply to the sensible nor simply to the intelligible, neither simply to passivity nor simply to activity. The element-medium will always be analogous to a mixed-medium. In a certain way, Plato thought about and even formulated this ambivalence. But he did so in passing, incidentally, discreetly: in connection with the union of opposites within virtue, not the union of virtue with its opposite:

> *Stranger*: But in those of noble nature from their earliest days whose
> nurture too has been all it should be, the laws can foster the growth
> of this common bond of conviction and only in these. This is the
> talisman (*pharmakon*) appointed for them by the design of pure
> intelligence. This most godlike bond alone can unite the elements
> of virtue which are diverse in nature and would else be opposing
> in tendency.
>
> (*Statesman*, 310a)

This pharmaceutical nonsubstance cannot be handled with complete
security, neither in its being, since it has none, nor in its effects, the
sense of which is always capable of changing. In this way, writing,
touted by Theuth as a remedy, a beneficial drug, is later overturned and
denounced by the king and then, in the king's place, by Socrates, as a
harmful substance, a philtre of forgetfulness. Inversely, and although in
a less immediately readable manner, the hemlock, that potion which in
the *Phaedo* is never called anything but a *pharmakon*,[2] is presented to
Socrates as a poison; yet it is transformed, through the effects of the
Socratic *logos* and of the philosophical demonstration in the *Phaedo*, into
a means of deliverance, a way toward salvation, a cathartic power. The
hemlock has an *ontological* effect: it initiates one into the contemplation
of the *eidos* and the immortality of the soul.[3] *That is how Socrates takes it.*
Is this crossed connection-making the result of mere artifice or play?
There is certainly *play* in such a movement, and this chiasmus is
authorized, even prescribed, by the ambivalence of the *pharmakon*. Not
only by the polarity good/evil, but by the double participation in the
distinct regions of the soul and the body, the invisible and the visible.
This double participation, once again, does not mix together two
previously separate elements; it refers back to a *same* that is not the
identical, to the common element or medium of any possible
dissociation. Thus, writing is *given* as the sensible, visible, spatial
surrogate of the *mnēmē*; it later turns out to be harmful and benumbing
to the invisible interior of the soul, memory and truth. Inversely, the
hemlock is given as a poison that harms and benumbs the body. But it
later turns out to be helpful to the soul, which it delivers from the body
and awakens to the truth of the *eidos*. If the *pharmakon* is 'ambivalent', it
is because it constitutes the medium in which opposites are opposed,
the movement and the play that links them among themselves, reverses
them or makes one side cross over into the other (soul/body, good/evil,
inside/outside, memory/forgetfulness, speech/writing, etc.). It is on the
basis of this play or movement that the opposites or differences are
stopped by Plato. The *pharmakon* is the movement, the locus, and the
play: (the production of) difference. It is the differance of difference. It
holds in reserve, in its undecided shadow and vigil, the opposites and

344

the differends that the process of discrimination will come to carve out. Contradictions and pairs of opposites are lifted from the bottom of this diacritical, differing, deferring, reserve. Already inhabited by difference, this reserve, even though it 'precedes' the opposition between different effects, even though it preexists differences as effects, does not have the punctual simplicity of a *coincidentia oppositorum*. It is from this fund that dialectics draws its philosophemes. The *pharmakon*, without being anything in itself, always exceeds them in constituting their bottomless fund [*fonds sans fond*]. It keeps itself forever in reserve even though it has no fundamental profundity nor ultimate locality. We will watch it infinitely promise itself and endlessly vanish through concealed doorways that shine like mirrors and open onto a labyrinth. It is also this store of deep background that we are calling the *pharmacy*.

The pharmakos

It is part of the rules of this game that the game should *seem to stop*. Then the *pharmakon*, which is older than either of the opposites, is 'caught' by philosophy, by 'Platonism' which is constituted by this apprehension, as a mixture of two pure, heterogeneous terms. And one could follow the word *pharmakon* as a guiding thread within the whole Platonic problematic of the mixture. Apprehended as a blend and an impurity, the *pharmakon* also acts like an aggressor or a housebreaker, threatening some internal purity and security. This definition is absolutely general and can be verified even in cases where such forced entries are valorized: the good remedy, Socratic irony, comes to disturb the intestinal organization of self-complacency. The purity of the inside can then only be restored if the *charges are brought home* against exteriority as a supplement, inessential yet harmful to the essence, a surplus that *ought* never to have come to be added to the untouched plenitude of the inside. The restoration of internal purity must thus reconstitute, *recite* – and this is myth as such, the *mythology* for example of a *logos* recounting its origin, going back to the eve of the pharmakographic aggression – that to which the *pharmakon* should not have had to be added and attached like a *literal parasite: a letter* installing itself inside a living organism to rob it of its *nourishment* and to *distort* [like static, = '*bruit parasite*'] the pure audibility of a voice. Such are the relations between the writing supplement and the *logos-zōon*. In order to cure the latter of the *pharmakon* and rid it of the parasite, it is thus necessary to put the outside back in its place. To keep the outside out. This is the inaugural gesture of 'logic' itself, of good 'sense' insofar as it accords with the self-identity of *that which is*: being is what it is, the outside is outside and the inside inside. Writing must thus return to

345

being what it *should never have ceased to be*: an accessory, an accident, an excess.

The cure by *logos*, exorcism, and catharsis will thus eliminate the excess. But this elimination, being therapeutic in nature, must call upon the very thing it is expelling, the very surplus it is *putting out*. The pharmaceutical operation must therefore *exclude itself from itself*.

What does this mean about what (it is) to write?

Plato does not make a show of the chain of significations we are trying progressively to dig up. If there were any sense in asking such a question, which we don't believe, it would be impossible to say to what extent he manipulates it voluntarily or consciously, and at what point he is subject to constraints weighing upon his discourse from 'language'. The word 'language', through all that binds it to everything we are putting in question here, is not of any pertinent assistance, and to follow the constraints of a language would not exclude the possibility that Plato is playing with them, even if his game is neither representative nor voluntary. It is in the back room, in the shadows of the pharmacy, prior to the oppositions between conscious and unconscious, freedom and constraint, voluntary and involuntary, speech and language, that these textual 'operations' occur.

Plato seems to place no emphasis on the word *pharmakon* at the point where writing's effects swerve from positive to negative, when poison, under the eyes of the king, appears as the truth of the remedy. It is not said that the *pharmakon is* the locus, the support, and the executor of this mutation. Later – we will come to this – while expressly comparing writing to painting, Plato will not explicitly put this judgment together with the fact that elsewhere he refers to painting as a *pharmakon*. For in Greek, *pharmakon* also means paint, not a natural colour but an artificial tint, a chemical dye that imitates the chromatic scale given in nature.

Yet all these significations nonetheless appear, and, more precisely, all these words appear in the text of 'Plato'. Only the chain is concealed, and, to an inappreciable extent, concealed from the author himself, if any such thing exists. One can say in any event that all the 'pharmaceutical' words we have been pointing out do actually make an 'act of presence', so to speak, in the text of the dialogues. Curiously, however, there is another of these words that, to our knowledge, is never used by Plato. If we line it up with the series *pharmakeia-pharmakon-pharmakeus*, we will no longer be able to content ourselves with reconstituting a chain that, for all its hiddenness, for all it might escape Plato's notice, is nevertheless something that passes through certain discoverable *points of presence* that can be seen in the text. The word to which we are now going to refer, which is present in the language and which points to an experience that was present in Greek culture even in Plato's day, seems strikingly absent from the 'Platonic text'.

But what does *absent* or *present* mean here? Like any text, the text of 'Plato' couldn't not be involved, at least in a virtual, dynamic, lateral manner, with all the words that composed the system of the Greek language. Certain forces of association unite – at diverse distances, with different strengths and according to disparate paths – the words 'actually present' in a discourse with all the other words in the lexical system, whether or not they appear as 'words', that is, as relative verbal units in such discourse. They communicate with the totality of the lexicon through their syntactic play and at least through the subunits that compose what we call a word. For example, 'pharmakon' is already in communication with all the words from the same family, with all the significations constructed out of the same root, and these communications do not stop there. The textual chain we must set back in place is thus no longer simply 'internal' to Plato's lexicon. But in going beyond the bounds of that lexicon, we are less interested in breaking through certain limits, with or without cause, than in putting in doubt the right to posit such limits in the first place. In a word, we do not believe that there exists, in all rigour, a Platonic text, closed upon itself, complete with its inside and its outside. Not that one must then consider that it is leaking on all sides and can be drowned confusedly in the undifferentiated generality of its element. Rather, provided the articulations are rigorously and prudently recognized, one should simply be able to untangle the hidden forces of attraction linking a present word with an absent word in the text of Plato. Some such force, given the *system* of the language, cannot *not* have acted upon the writing and the reading of this text. With respect to the weight of such a force, the so-called 'presence' of a quite relative verbal unit – the word – while not being a contingent accident worthy of no attention, nevertheless does not constitute the ultimate criterion and the utmost pertinence.

The circuit we are proposing is, moreover, all the more legitimate and easy since it leads to a word that can, on one of its faces, be considered the synonym, almost the homonym, of a word Plato 'actually' used. The word in question is *pharmakos* (wizard, magician, poisoner), a synonym of *pharmakeus* (which Plato uses), but with the unique feature of having been overdetermined, overlaid by Greek culture with another function. Another *role*, and a formidable one.

The character of the *pharmakos* has been compared to a scapegoat. The *evil* and the *outside*, the expulsion of the evil, its exclusion out of the body (and out) of the city – these are the two major senses of the character and of the ritual.

Harpocration, commenting on the word *pharmakos*, describes them thus: 'At Athens they led out two men to be purifications for the city; it was at the Thargelia, one was for the men and the other for the

women.'[4] In general, the *pharmakoi* were put to death. But that, it
seems,[5] was not the essential end of the operation. Death occurred most
often as a secondary effect of an energetic fustigation. Aimed first at the
genital organs.[6] Once the *pharmakoi* were cut off from the space of the
city, the blows[7] were designed to chase away or draw out the evil from
their bodies. Did they burn them, too, in order to achieve purification?
In his *Thousand Histories*, Tzetzes gives the following account, based
on certain fragments by the satirical poet Hipponax, of the ceremony:
'The (rite of the) *pharmakos* was a purification of this sort of old. If a
calamity overtook the city by the wrath of God, whether it were famine
or pestilence or any other mischief, they led forth as though to a
sacrifice the most unsightly of them all as a purification and a remedy
to the suffering city. They set the sacrifice in the appointed place, and
gave him cheese with their hands and a barley cake and figs, and seven
times they smote him with leeks and wild figs and other wild plants.
Finally they burnt him with fire with the wood of wild trees and
scattered the ashes into the sea and to the winds, for a purification,
as I said, of the suffering city.'

The city's body *proper* thus reconstitutes its unity, closes around the
security of its inner courts, gives back to itself the word that links it
with itself within the confines of the agora, by violently excluding from
its territory the representative of an external threat or aggression. That
representative represents the otherness of the evil that comes to affect or
infect the inside by unpredictably breaking into it. Yet the representative
of the outside is nonetheless *constituted*, regularly granted its place by
the community, chosen, kept, fed, etc., in the very heart of the inside.
These parasites were as a matter of course domesticated by the living
organism that housed them at its expense. 'The Athenians regularly
maintained a number of degraded and useless beings at the public
expense; and when any calamity, such as plague, drought, or famine,
befell the city, they sacrificed two of these outcasts as scapegoats.'[8]

The ceremony of the *pharmakos* is thus played out on the boundary
line between inside and outside, which it has as its function ceaselessly
to trace and retrace. *Intra muros/extra muros.* The origin of difference and
division, the *pharmakos* represents evil both introjected and projected.
Beneficial insofar as he cures – and for that, venerated and cared for –
harmful insofar as he incarnates the powers of evil – and for that, feared
and treated with caution. Alarming and calming. Sacred and accursed.
The conjunction, the *coincidentia oppositorum*, ceaselessly undoes itself in
the passage to decision or crisis. The expulsion of the evil or madness
restores *sōphrosunē*.

These exclusions took place at critical moments (drought, plague,
famine). *Decision* was then repeated. But the mastery of the critical
instance requires that surprise be prepared for: by rules, by law, by the

regularity of repetition, by fixing the date. This ritual practice, which took place in Abdera, in Thrace, in Marseilles, etc., was reproduced *every year* in Athens. And up through the fifth century. Aristophanes and Lysias clearly allude to it. Plato could not have been unaware of it.

The date of the ceremony is noteworthy: the sixth day of the Thargelia. That was the day of the birth of him whose death – and not only because a *pharmakon* was its direct cause – resembles that of a *pharmakos* from the inside: Socrates.

Socrates, affectionately called the *pharmakeus* in the dialogues of Plato; Socrates, who faced with the complaint (*graphē*) lodged against him, refused to defend himself, declined the logographic offer of Lysias, 'the ablest writer of our time', who had proposed to ghost-write a defence for him; Socrates was born on the sixth day of the Thargelia. Diogenes Laertius testifies to this: 'He was born on the sixth day of Thargelion, the day when the Athenians purify the city.'

The ingredients: phantasms, festivals, and paints

The rite of the *pharmakos*: evil and death, repetition and exclusion.

Socrates ties up into a system all the counts of indictment against the *pharmakon* of writing at the point at which he adopts as his own, in order to uphold it, interpret it, and make it explicit, the divine, royal, paternal, solar word, the capital sentence of Thamus. The worst effects of writing were only predicted by that word. The king's speech was not demonstrative; it did not pronounce knowledge – it pronounced itself. Announcing, presaging, cutting. It is a *manteia*, Socrates suggests (275c). The discourse of Socrates will hence apply itself to the task of translating that *manteia* into philosophy, cashing in on that capital, turning it to account, taking account of it, giving accounts and reasons, upholding the reasoning of that basileo-patro-helio-theological dictum. Transforming the *mythos* into *logos*.

What indeed would be the first thing a disdainful god would find to criticize in that which seems to lie outside his field of effectiveness? Its ineffectiveness, of course, its improductiveness, a productiveness that is only apparent, since it can only repeat what in truth is already there. This is why – Socrates' first argument – writing is not a good *tekhnē*, by which we should understand an art capable of engendering, producing, bringing forth: the clear, the sure, the secure (*saphes kai bebaion*). That is, the *alētheia* of the *eidos*, the truth of being in its figure, its 'idea', its nonsensible visibility, its intelligible invisibility. The truth of what is: writing literally hasn't a damn sight to do with it. It has rather a blindness to do with it. Whoever might think he has produced truth through a grapheme would only give proof of the greatest foolishness (*euētheia*). Whereas the sage Socrates knows that he knows nothing, that nitwit would not know that he already knows what he thinks he is learning through writing, and which he is only recalling to mind through the types. Not remembering, by anamnesis, the *eidos* contemplated before the fall of the soul into the body, but reminding himself, in a hypomnesic mode, of that of which he already has mnesic knowledge. Written *logos* is only a way for him who already knows (*ton eidota*) to remind himself (*hupomnēsai*) of the things writing is about (*ta gegrammena*) (275d). Writing thus only intervenes at a time when a subject of knowledge already possesses the signifieds, which are then only given to writing on consignment.

Socrates thus adopts the major, decisive opposition that cleaves the *manteia* of Thamus: *mnēmē/hupomnēsis*, the subtle difference between knowledge as memory and nonknowledge as rememoration, between two forms and two moments of repetition: a repetition of truth (*alētheia*) which presents and exposes the *eidos*; and a repetition of death and oblivion (*lēthē*) which veils and skews because it does not present the *eidos* but re-presents a presentation, repeats a repetition.[9]

Hupomnēsis, which is here what forecasts and shapes the thought about writing, not only does not coincide with memory, but can only be constructed as a thing dependent on memory. And consequently, on the presentation of truth. At the moment it is summoned to appear before the paternal instance, writing is determined within a problematic of knowing-remembering. It is thus from the start stripped of all its own attributes or path-breaking powers. Its path-breaking force is cut not by repetition but by the ills of repetition, by that which within repetition is doubled, redoubled, that which repeats repetition and in so doing, cut off from 'good' repetition (which presents and gathers being within living memory), can always, left to itself, stop repeating itself. Writing would be pure repetition, dead repetition that might always be repeating nothing, or be unable *spontaneously* to repeat itself, which also means unable to repeat anything *but* itself: a hollow, cast-off repetition.

This pure repetition, this 'bad' reissue, would thus be tautological. Written *logoi* 'seem to talk to you as though they were intelligent, but if you ask them anything about what they say, from a desire to be instructed, they go on telling you just the same thing forever (*hen ti sēmainei monon tauton aei*)' (275d). Pure repetition, absolute self-repetition, repetition of a self that is already reference and repetition, repetition of the signifier, repetition that is null or annulling, repetition of death – it's all one. Writing is not the living repetition of the living.

Which makes it similar to painting. And just as the *Republic*, in its condemnation of the imitative arts, links poetry and painting together; just as Aristotle's *Poetics* associates them under the single heading of *mimēsis*; so too Socrates here compares a piece of writing to a portrait, the *graphēma* to the *zōgraphēma*. 'You know, Phaedrus, that's the strange (*deinon*) thing about writing, which makes it truly analogous to painting (*homoion zōgraphiai*). The painter's products stand before us as though they were alive (*hōs zōnta*), but if you question them, they maintain a most majestic (*semnōs*) silence. It is the same with written words. . . .' (275*d*).

The impotence to answer for itself, the unresponsiveness and irresponsibility of writing, is decried again by Socrates in the *Protagoras*. Bad public speakers, those who cannot answer 'a supplementary question', are 'like books: they cannot either answer or ask a question on their own account' (329*a*). That is why, says the Seventh Letter, 'no intelligent man will ever be so bold as to put into language those things which his reason has contemplated, especially not into a form that is unalterable – which must be the case with what is expressed in written symbols' (343*a*; cf. also *Laws* XII, 968*d*).

What, in depth, are the resemblances underlying Socrates' statements that make writing homologous to painting? From out of what horizon arise their common silence, their stubborn muteness, their mask of solemn, forbidding majesty that so poorly hides an incurable aphasia, a stone deafness, a closedness irremediably inadequate to the demands of *logos*? If writing and painting are convoked together, summoned to appear with their hands tied, before the tribunal of *logos*, and to respond to it, this is quite simply because both are being *interrogated*: as the presumed representatives of a spoken word, as agents capable of speech, as depositaries or even fences for the words the court is trying to force out of them. If they should turn out not to be up to testifying in this hearing, if they turn out to be impotent to represent a live word properly, to act as its interpreter or spokesman, to sustain the conversation, to respond to oral questions, then bam! they are good for nothing. They are mere figurines, masks, simulacra.

Let us not forget that painting is here called *zōgraphia*, inscribed representation, a drawing *of the living*, a portrait of an animate model. The model for this type of paintings is representative painting, which conforms to a live model. The word *zōgraphēma* is indeed sometimes shortened to *gramma* (*Cratylus*, 430*e* and 431*c*). Similarly, writing was supposed to paint a living word. It thus resembles painting to the extent that it is conceived – in this whole Platonic problematic, this massive and fundamental determination can be stated in a word – on the basis of the particular model of phonetic writing, which reigned in Greek culture. The signs of writing functioned within a system where they were supposed to represent the signs of voice. They were signs of signs.

Thus, just as painting and writing have faithfulness to the model as their model, the resemblance between painting and writing is precisely *resemblance itself*: both operations must aim above all at resembling. They are both apprehended as mimetic techniques, art being first determined as mimesis.

Despite this resemblance of resemblance, writing's case is a good deal more serious. Like any imitative art, painting and poetry are of course far away from truth (*Republic* X, 603*b*). But these two both have mitigating circumstances. Poetry imitates, but it imitates voice by means of voice. Painting, like sculpture, is silent, but so in a sense is its model. Painting and sculpture are arts of silence, as Socrates, the son of a sculptor who at first wanted to follow in his father's footsteps, very well knows. He knows this and says it in the *Gorgias* (450*c–d*). The silence of the pictorial or sculptural space is, as it were, normal. But this is no longer the case in the scriptural order, since writing gives itself as the image of speech. Writing thus more seriously denatures what it claims to imitate. It does not even substitute an image for its model. It inscribes in the space of silence and in the silence of space the living time of voice. It displaces its model, provides no image of it, violently wrests out of its element the animate interiority of speech. In so doing, writing estranges itself immensely from the truth of the thing itself, from the truth of speech, from the truth that is open to speech.

And hence, from the king.

Let us recall the famous indictment of pictorial mimetics in the *Republic* (X, 597).[10] First, it is a question of banning poetry from the city, and this time, in contrast to what occurs in books II and III, for reasons linked essentially with its mimetic nature. The tragic poets, when they practice imitation, corrupt the minds of the listeners (*tēs tōn akouontōn dianoias*) if these do not possess an antidote (*pharmakon*, 595*a*). This counterpoison is 'knowledge of the real nature of things' (*to eidenai auta hoia tungkhanei onta*). If one considers that imitators and masters of illusion will later be presented as charlatans and thaumaturges (602*d*) – species of the genus *pharmakeus* – then once again ontological knowledge becomes a pharmaceutical force opposed to another pharmaceutical force. The order of knowledge is not the transparent order of forms and ideas, as one might be tempted retrospectively to interpret it; it is the antidote. Long before being divided up into occult violence and accurate knowledge, the element of the *pharmakon* is the combat zone between philosophy and its other. An element that is *in itself*, if one can still say so, *undecidable*.

Of course, in order to define the poetry of imitation, one has to know what imitation in general is. This is where that most *familiar* of examples comes in: the origin of the bed. Elsewhere, we will be able to take the time to inquire about the necessity governing the choice of this example and about the switch in the text that makes us slide insensibly from the table to the bed. The already made bed. In any case, God is the

true father of the bed, of the clinical *eidos*. The carpenter is its
'Demiurge'. The painter, who is again called a zoographer, is neither
its generator (*phutourgos*: author of the *phusis* – as truth – of the bed),
nor its demiurge. Only its imitator. It is thus by three degrees that he
is separated from the original truth, the *phusis* of the bed.

And hence, from the king.

'This, then, will apply to the maker of tragedies also, if he is an
imitator and is in his nature at three removes from the king and the
truth, as are all other imitators' (597*e*).

As for couching this *eidōlon* in written form, writing down the image
that poetic imitation has already made, that would be equivalent to
moving to a *fourth degree* of distance from the king, or rather, through a
change of order or of element, wandering into an excessive estrangement
from him, if Plato himself did not elsewhere assert, speaking of the
imitative poet in general, that 'he is always at an infinite remove from
truth' (*tou de alēthous porrō panu aphestōta*) (605*c*). For in contrast to
painting, writing doesn't even create a phantasm. The painter, of
course, does not produce the being-true but the appearance, the
phantasm (598*b*), that is, what is already a simulation of the copy
(*Sophist*, 236*b*). In general, *phantasma* (the copy of a copy) has been
translated as 'simulacrum'.[11] He who writes with the alphabet no longer
even imitates. No doubt because he also, in a sense, imitates perfectly.
He has a better chance of reproducing the voice, because phonetic
writing decomposes it better and transforms it into abstract, spatial
elements. This *de-composition* of the voice is here both what best
conserves it and what best corrupts it. What imitates it perfectly because
it no longer imitates it at all. For imitation affirms and sharpens its
essence in effacing itself. Its essence is its nonessence. And no dialectic
can encompass this self-inadequation. A perfect imitation is no longer
an imitation. If one eliminates the tiny difference that, in separating the
imitator from the imitated, by that very fact refers to it, one would
render the imitator absolutely different: the imitator would become
another being no longer referring to the imitated.[12] Imitation does not
correspond to its essence, is not what it is – imitation – unless it is in
some way at fault or rather in default. It is bad by nature. It is only
good insofar as it is bad. Since (de)fault is inscribed within it, it has no
nature; nothing is properly its own. Ambivalent, playing with itself by
hollowing itself out, good and evil at once – undecidably, *mimēsis* is
akin to the *pharmakon*. No 'logic', no 'dialectic', can consume its reserve
even though each must endlessly draw on it and seek reassurance
through it.

And as it happens, the technique of imitation, along with the
production of the simulacrum, has always been in Plato's eyes
manifestly magical, thaumaturgical:

And the same things appear bent and straight to those who view them
in water and out, or concave and convex, owing to similar errors of
vision about colours, and there is obviously every confusion of this
sort in our souls. And so scene painting (*skiagraphia*) in its exploitation
of this weakness of our nature falls nothing short of witchcraft
(*thaumatopoia*), and so do jugglery (*goēteia*) and many other such
contrivances.

(Republic X, 602c–d; cf. also 607c).[13]

The antidote is still the *epistēmē*. And since hybris is at bottom nothing
but that excessive momentum that (en)trains being in(to) the simulacrum,
the mask, the festival, there can be no antidote but that which enables
one to remain *measured*. The *alexipharmakon* will be the science of
measure, in every sense of the word. The text goes on:

But satisfactory remedies have been found for dispelling these
illusions by measuring (*metrein*), counting (*arithmein*), and weighing
(*histanai*). We are no longer at the mercy of an appearance
(*phainomenon*) of difference in size and quantity and weight; the
faculty which has done the counting and measuring or weighing
takes control instead. And this can only be the work of the calculating
or reasoning element (*tou logistikou ergon*) in the soul. (The word
translated as 'remedies' is the word used in the *Phaedrus* to qualify
the attendance, the assistance [*boētheia*] that the father of living speech
ought always to provide for writing, which is quite helpless in itself.)

The illusionist, the technician of sleight-of-hand, the painter, the
writer, the *pharmakeus*. This has not gone unnoticed: '. . . isn't the word
pharmakon, which means color, the very same word that applies to the
drugs of sorcerers or doctors? Don't the casters of spells resort to wax
figurines in pursuing their evil designs?'[14] Bewitchment [*l'envoûtement*]
is always the effect of a *representation*, pictorial or scriptural, capturing,
captivating the form of the other, par excellence his face, countenance,
word and look, mouth and eye, nose and ears: the *vultus*.

The word *pharmakon*, then, also designates pictorial colour, the
material in which the *zōgraphēma* is inscribed. Turn to the *Cratylus*:
in his exchange with Hermogenes, Socrates examines the hypothesis
according to which names imitate the essence of things. He compares,
in order to make a distinction between them, musical or pictorial
imitation, on the one hand, and nominal imitation, on the other. What
he does then is interesting to us not only because he refers to the
pharmakon but also because another necessity imposes itself on him, one
on which we will henceforth progressively attempt to shed some light:

at the moment he takes up the question of the differential elements of
nominal language, he is obliged, as is Saussure after him, to suspend
the insistence on voice as sonority imitative of sounds (imitative music).
If the voice names, it is through the differences and relations that are
introduced among the *stoikheia*, the elements or letters (*grammata*). The
same word (*stoikheia*) is used for both elements and letters. And one
ought to reflect upon what here appears to be a conventional or
pedagogical necessity: phonemes in general, vowels – *phōnēenta*[15] – and
consonants, are designated by the letters that inscribe them.

> *Socrates*: ... But how shall we further analyse them, and when does
> the imitator begin? Imitation of the essence is made by syllables
> and letters. Ought we not, therefore, first to separate the letters, just
> as those who are beginning rhythm first distinguish the powers
> of elementary sounds (*stoikheiōn*) and then of compound sounds,
> and when they have done so, but not before, proceed to the
> consideration of rhythms?
>
> *Hermogenes*: Yes.
>
> *Socrates*: Must we not begin in the same way with letters – first
> separating the vowels (*phōnēenta*), and then the consonants and
> mutes (*aphōna kai aphthonga*), into classes, according to the received
> distinctions of the learned, also the semivowels, which are neither
> vowels nor yet mutes, and distinguishing into classes the vowels
> themselves. And when we have perfected the classification of
> things, we shall give their names, and see whether, as in the case
> of letters, there are any classes to which they may all be referred,
> and hence we shall see their natures, and see, too, whether they
> have in them classes as there are in the letters. And when we have
> well considered all this, we shall know how to apply them to what
> they resemble, whether one letter is used to denote one thing, or
> whether there is to be an admixture of several of them, just as, in
> painting, the painter who wants to depict anything sometimes uses
> purple only, or any other colour (*allo tōn pharmakōn*), and sometimes
> mixes up several colours, as his method is when he has to paint
> flesh colour or anything of that kind – he uses a particular colour
> (*pharmakou*) as his figures appear to require it. And so, too, we
> shall apply letters to the expression of objects, either single letters
> when required, or several letters, and so we shall form syllables, as
> they are called, and from syllables make nouns and verbs, and
> thus, at last, from the combination of nouns and verbs arrive at
> language, large and fair and whole, just as the painter used his
> paint (*tēi graphikēi*) to reproduce a living creature (*zōon*).
>
> (424b–425a)

And further on:

> *Socrates*: Very good, but if the name is to be like the thing, the letters
> out of which the first names are composed must also be like things.
> Returning to the image of the picture, I would ask how anyone
> could ever compose a picture which would be like anything at all,
> if there were not pigments (*pharmakeia*) in nature which resembled
> the things imitated, and out of which the picture is composed.
>
> (434*a*–*b*)

The *Republic* also calls the painter's colours *pharmaka* (420*c*). The magic
of writing and painting is like a cosmetic concealing the dead under the
appearance of the living. The *pharmakon* introduces and harbours death.
It makes the corpse presentable, masks it, makes it up, perfumes it with
its essence, as it is said in Aeschylus. *Pharmakon* is also a word for
perfume. A perfume without essence, as we earlier called it a drug
without substance. It transforms order into ornament, the cosmos into
a cosmetic. Death, masks, makeup, all are part of the festival that
subverts the order of the city, its smooth regulation by the dialectician
and the science of being. Plato, as we shall see, is not long in identifying
writing with festivity. And play. A certain festival, a certain game.

Notes

1. The reader will have noted that this scene makes a strange, inverse and
   symmetrical pendant to the one in the *Phaedrus*. It is inverted in that the
   unit which, under the cloak, allowed a text and a *pharmakon* to (e)merge
   is *preinscribed* in the *Phaedrus* (the *pharmakon* is the text already written by
   'the ablest writer of our day'), and only *prescribed* in the *Charmides* (the
   prescription for the *pharmakon* Socrates recommends must be taken down
   under his dictation). The Socratic prescription here is oral, and speech
   accompanies the *pharmakon* as the condition of its effectiveness. Within the
   thickness and depth of this scene, one should reread, from the middle of the
   Statesman, the critique of the written medical prescription, the *'hypomnēmata
   graphein'* whose rigidity does not allow it to adapt to the specificity and the
   progress of the disease: this is an illustration of the political problem of
   written laws. Like the doctor who comes back to visit his patient, the
   legislator must be able to modify his initial prescriptions (294*a*–297*b*; see also
   298*d*–*e*).
2. The opening lines of the dialogue are: '*Echecrates*: Were you there with
   Socrates yourself, Phaedo, when he drank the poison (*pharmakon*) in his cell?'
   (57*a*).
   Near the end of the dialogue: '*Socrates*: . . . I prefer to have a bath before
   drinking the poison (*pharmakon*), rather than give the women the trouble of
   washing me when I am dead' (115*a*). Cf. also 117*a*.

3. One could therefore also consider the hemlock as a sort of *pharmakon* of immortality. Such an interpretation is invited by the ritual, ceremonial form with which the *Phaedo* closes (116*b*–*c*). In his *'Festin d'immortalité'* (*Esquisse d'une étude de mythologie comparée indo-européenne* 1924), G. Dumézil refers to certain 'traces, in Athens, of a cycle of Theseus correlated with the *Thargelia*' (we will later have occasion to speak of a certain relation between the Thargelia and the birth and death of Socrates), and notes: 'Neither Pherecydes nor Appollodorus has set down the rites that must have corresponded, in a certain district of Greece, to the story of the *pharmakon* of immortality desired by the *Giants*, and to that of the "artificial Goddess," *Athena*, who caused the Giants to lose their immortality' (p. 89).
4. The principal sources that enable us to describe the ritual of the *pharmakos* are collected in W. Mannhardt's *Mythologische Forschungen* (1884). These sources are themselves referred to in particular by J. G. Frazer in *The Golden Bough* (New York: S. G. Phillips, 1959), pp. 540 ff; by J. E. Harrison in *Prolegomena to the Study of Greek Religion* (New York: Meridian, 1903), pp. 95 ff, and in *Themis, a Study of the Social Origins of Greek Religion* (1912, p. 416); by Nilsson in *History of Greek Religion* (1925), p. 27; and by P. M. Schuhl in *Essai sur la formation de la pensée grecque* (1934), pp. 36–7. One can also consult the chapter Marie Delcourt devotes to Oedipus in her *Légendes et culte des héros en Grèce* (1942), p. 101; see also by the same author, *Pyrrhos et Pyrrha: Recherches sur les valeurs du feu dans les légendes helléniques* (1965), p. 29, and especially *Oedipe ou la légende du conquérant* (1944), pp. 29–65.

This is doubtless the moment to point out, in connection with the clear necessity of bringing together the figures of Oedipus and the *pharmakos*, that, despite certain appearances, the discourse we are holding here is not in a strict sense a psychoanalytical one. This is true at least to the extent that we are drawing upon the same textual stores (Greek culture, language, tragedy, philosophy, etc.) which Freud had to begin by tapping and to which he never ceased to refer. It is precisely these stores, this fund, that we propose to interrogate here. This does not, however, mean that the distance we have thus taken with respect to a psychoanalytical discourse which might evolve naïvely within an insufficiently deciphered Greek text is of the same order as that maintained for example by Delcourt, *Légendes*, pp. 109, 113, etc.; or J. P. Vernant, Oedipe sans complexe', in *Raison présente* (1967).

After the first publication of this text, there appeared the remarkable essay by J. P. Vernant, 'Ambiguité et renversement: sur la structure énigmatique d'Oedipe-Roi' in *Echanges et Communications, mélanges offerts à Claude Lévi-Strauss* (The Hague: Mouton, 1970) [translated by Page du Bois as 'Ambiguity and Reversal: On the Enigmatic Structure of *Oedipus Rex*', in *New Literary History* 10, no. 3 (1978)]. One can read, in particular, the following passage, which seems to confirm our hypothesis: 'How could the city admit into its heart one who, like Oedipus, "has shot his bolt beyond the others" and has become *isotheos?* When it establishes ostracism, it creates an institution whose role is symmetrical to and the inverse of the ritual of the Thargelia. In the person of the ostracized, the city expels what in it is too elevated, what incarnates the evil which can come to it from above. In the evil of the *pharmakos*, it expels what is the vilest in itself, what incarnates the evil that menaces it from below. By this double and complementary rejection it delimits itself in relation to what is not yet known and what transcends the known: it takes the proper measure of the human in opposition on one side to the divine and heroic, on the other to the bestial and monstrous' [Eng. trans. pp. 491–2]. See also (notably on the *poikilon* which we will mention

later) 'La metis d'Antiloque', *Revue des Etudes grecques*, January/December
1967, and 'La metis du renard et du poulpe', ibid. July/December 1969. An
additional confirmation can be found in the *Oeuvres* of MARCEL MAUSS,
which appeared in 1969. One can read the following:

'Moreover, all these ideas are double-faced. In other Indo-European
languages, it is the notion of poison which is not certain. Kluge and the
etymologists are right in comparing the *potio*, "Poison," series with *gift*, *gift*
["gift," which means "present" in English, means "poison" or "married" in
other Germanic languages. – Trans.]. One can also read with interest the
lively discussion by Aulus-Gellius (12) on the ambiguity of the Greek
pharmakon and the Latin *venenum*. Indeed, the *Lex Cornelia de Sicariis et
veneficis*, of which Cicero has fortunately preserved for us the actual
"recitation," still specifies *venenum malum* (13). The magic brew, the delectable
charm (14), can be either good or bad. The Greek *philtron* is not necessarily a
sinister word, either, and the potion of friendship or love is only dangerous
if the enchanter so desires.'

(12) 12, 9, with apt quotations from Homer.

(13) *Pro Cluentio*, 148. In the Digesta, it is still recommended that one
specify what sort of 'venenum', 'bonus sive malum', is intended.

(14) If the etymology linking *venenum* (see Walde, Lat. etym. Wört.)
with Venus and the skr. *van, vanati* is correct, which seems probable.

('*Gift-gift*' (1924), first published in *Mélanges offerts à Charles Andler par ses
amis et élèves*, Istra, Strasbourg; in *Oeuvres* III, 50 (Editions de Minuit, 1969).)

This brings us to *The Gift* [*L'Essai sur le don*], which refers to the above
article:

'(*Gift, gift: Mélanges. Ch. Andler*, Strasburg, 1924.) We asked why we do not
examine the etymology of *gift* as coming from the Latin *dosis*, Greek δόσις, a
dose (of poison). It would suppose that High and Low German had retained
a scientific word for a common event, and this is contrary to normal semantic
rules. Moreover, one would have to explain the choice of the word *Gift*.
Finally, the Latin and Greek *dosis*, meaning poison, shows that with the
Ancients as well there was association of ideas and moral rules of the kind
we are describing.

'We compare the uncertainty of the meaning of *Gift* with that of the Latin
venenum and the Greek φιλτρον and φάρμακον. Cf. also *venia, venus, venenum*
– *vanati* (Sanskrit, to give pleasure) and *gewinnen* and win.' [trans. Ian
Cunnison (Glencoe, Ill.: Free Press, 1954), p. 127.]

5. Cf. HARRISON, *Prolegomena*, p. 104.
6. 'Similarly, the object of beating the human scapegoat on the genital organs
with squills [a herbaceous, bulbous plant, sometimes grown for its
pharmaceutical, esp. diuretic, properties] must have been to release his
reproductive energies from any restraint or spell under which they might
be laid by demoniacal or other malignant agency . . .' Frazer, *Golden Bough*
(1954 edn), p. 541.
7. We recall the presumed etymology of *pharmakon/pharmakos*, detailed in E.
BOISACQ, *Dictionnaire étymologique de la langue grecque*. '*Pharmakon*: charm,
philtre, drug, remedy, poison. *Pharmakos*: magician, wizard, poisoner; the one
sacrificed in expiation for the sins of a city (cf. Hipponax; Aristophanes),
hence, rascal;* *pharmassō*: Attic, *-ttō*, work on or alter by means of a drug.

* Havers, *Indogermanische Forschungen* xxv, 375–92, on the basis of the
relation *parempharaktos: parakekommenos*, derives *pharmakon* from *pharma*: 'blow',
and the latter from R. *bher*: to strike, cf. Lith. *buriu*, so that *pharmakon* can be
said to signify: 'that which pertains to an attack of demonic possession or is

used as a curative against such an attack', given the common popular belief
that illnesses are caused by the doings of demons and cured in the same way.
Kretschmer Glotta III, 388 ff, objects that *pharmakon*, in epic, always designates
a substance, a herb, a lotion, a drink, or other matter, but not the act of
healing, charming, or poisoning; Havers' etymology adds only one possibility
among others, for example the derivation from *pherō, pherma, 'quod terra fert'.*
Cf. also HARRISON, p. 108: '. . . *pharmakos* means simply "magic-man." Its
Lithuanian cognate is *burin*, magic; in Latin it appears as *forma*, formula,
magical spell; our *formulary* retains some vestige of its primitive connotation.
Pharmakon in Greek means healing drug, poison, and dye, but all, for better
or worse, are magical.'

In his *Anatomy of Criticism* (New York: Atheneum, 1970), NORTHROP FRYE
sees in the figure of the *pharmakos* a permanent archetypal structure in
Western literature. The exclusion of the *pharmakos*, who is, says Frye, 'neither
innocent nor guilty' (p. 41), is repeated from Aristophanes to Shakespeare,
affecting Shylock as well as Falstaff, Tartuffe no less than Charlie Chaplin.
'We meet a *pharmakos* figure in Hawthorne's Hester Prynne, in Melville's
Billy Budd, in Hardy's Tess, in the Septimus of *Mrs Dalloway*, in stories of
persecuted Jews and Negroes, in stories of artists whose genius makes them
Ishmaels of a bourgeois society' (p. 41, cf. also pp. 45–8, pp. 148–9).

8. FRAZER, *Golden Bough* (1954 edn), pp. 540–1. Cf. also HARRISON, *Prolegomena*,
   p. 102.
9. It could be shown that all of Husserl's phenomenology is systematically
   organized around an analogous opposition between presentation and
   re-presentation (*Gegenwärtigung/Vergegenwärtigung*), and between primary
   memory (which is part of the originary 'in an extended sense') and
   secondary memory. Cf. *La Voix et le phénomène {Speech and Phenomena}.*
10. I shall study this passage from another viewpoint in a forthcoming text,
    'Entre deux coups de dés'.
11. On the place and evolution of the concept of *mimēsis* in Plato's thought, we
    refer the reader primarily to V. GOLDSCHMIDT's *Essai sur le Cratyle* (1940)
    (esp. pp. 165 ff). What is made clear there is the fact that Plato did not
    always and everywhere condemn *mimēsis*. But one can at any rate conclude
    this: whether or not Plato condemns imitation, he poses the question of
    poetry by determining it as *mimēsis*, thus opening the field in which
    Aristotle's *Poetics*, entirely subsumed under that category, will produce
    the concept of literature that reigned until the nineteenth century, up to
    but not including Kant and Hegel (not including them at least if *mimēsis*
    is translated as *imitation*).
    On the other hand, Plato condemns under the name *phantasm* or *simulacrum*
    what is being advanced today, in its most radical exigency, as writing. Or at
    any rate that is what one can call, *within* philosophy and 'mimetology', that
    which exceeds the conceptual oppositions within which Plato defines the
    phantasm. Beyond these oppositions, beyond the values of truth and
    nontruth, this excess (of) writing can no longer, as one might guess, be
    qualified simply as a simulacrum or phantasm. Nor can it indeed be named
    by the classical concept of writing.
12. 'Let us suppose the existence of two objects (*pragmata*). One of them shall be
    Cratylus, and the other the image of Cratylus, and we will suppose, further,
    that some god makes not only a representation such as a painter would
    make of your outward form and colour, but also creates an inward
    organization like yours, having the same warmth and softness, and into this
    infuses motion, and soul, and mind, such as you have, and in a word copies

all your qualities, and places them by you in another form. Would you say that this was Cratylus and the image of Cratylus, or that there were two Cratyluses? *Cratylus*: I should say that there were two Cratyluses' (432*b*–*c*).

13. On all these themes, see esp. P. M. SCHUHL, *Platon et l'Art de son temps*.
14. SCHUHL, *Platon*, p. 22. Cf. also *l'Essai sur la formation de la pensée grecque*, pp. 39 ff.
15. Cf. also Philebus, 18*a*–*b*.

Further Reading

ADORNO, THEODOR W., *Negative Dialectics*, trans. E. B. Ashton (London: Routledge, 1973).

ARTAUD, ANTONIN, *The Theater and Its Double*, trans. Mary Caroline Richards (New York: Glove Press, 1958).

BAKHTIN, MIKHAIL, *Toward a Philosophy of the Act*, ed. Vadim Liapunov and Michael Holquist (Austin, Tex.: University of Texas Press, 1993).

BAMBER, LINDA, *Comic Women, Tragic Men: A Study of Gender and Genre in Shakespeare* (Stanford, Calif.: Stanford University Press, 1982).

BENJAMIN, WALTER, *The Origins of German Tragic Drama*, trans. John Osborne (London: Verso, 1985).

BOAL, AUGUSTO, *Theater of the Oppressed*, trans. C. A. and M.-O. Leal McBride (London: Pluto Press, 1979).

BOOTH, STEPHEN, *King Lear, Macbeth, Indefinition, and Tragedy* (New Haven, Conn.: Yale University Press, 1983).

BRADLEY, A. C., *Shakespearean Tragedy* (London: Macmillan & Co., 1904).

BRECHT, BERTOLD, *Brecht on Theatre: The Development of an Aesthetic*, trans. J. Willett (New York and London: Hill & Wang, 1966).

BRONFEN, ELISABETH, 'Form Omphalos to Phallus: Cultural Representations of Femininity and Death', *Women: A Cultural Review* Vol. 3, no. 2 (Oxford, 1992), pp. 144–58.

DELEUZE, GILLES, *Nietzsche and Philosophy*, trans. Hugh Tomlinson (New York, 1983).

DERRIDA, JACQUES, 'The Theater of Cruelty and the Closure of Representation', in *Writing and Difference*, trans. Alan Bass (London, 1978).
—— 'Plato's Pharmacy', in *Dissemination*, trans. Barbara Johnson (Chicago: University of Chicago Press, 1981).

DOLLIMORE, JONATHAN, *Radical Tragedy: Religion, Ideology and Power in The Drama of Shakespeare and His Contemporaries*, 2nd edn (London and New York: Harvester Wheatsheaf, 1989).

DRAKAKIS, JOHN (ed.), *Shakespearean Tragedy* (London: Longman, 1994).

DOUGLAS, MARY, *Purity and Danger*, (Harmondsworth: Penguin books, 1966)

EAGLETON, TERRY, *Walter Benjamin or Towards a Revolutionary Criticism*, (London: Verso, 1981)

FIGES, EVA, *Tragedy and Social Evolution* (New York: Persea Books, 1990).

FREUD, SIGMUND, *Art and Literature*, The Pelican Freud Library, vol. 14, ed. Albert Dixon (Harmondsworth, 1985).

FRYE, NORTHROP, *Anatomy of Criticism* (Princeton: Princeton University Press, 1957).

Further Reading

VAN GENNEP, ARNOLD, *The Rites of Passage* (1909), trans. M. B. Vizedom and G. L. Caffee (Chicago: University of Chicago Press, 1960).

GIRARD, RENÉ, *Violence and the Sacred*, trans. Patrick Gregory (Baltimore: Johns Hopkins University Press, 1977).

GOLDMANN, LUCIEN, *The Hidden God: A Study of Tragic Vision in the 'Pensées' of Pascal and the Tragedies of Racine*, trans. Philip Thody (London: Routledge & Kegan Paul, 1976).

GREEN, ANDRÉ, *The Oedipus Complex in Tragedy*, trans. Alan Sheridan (Cambridge: Cambridge University Press, 1979).

KIERKEGAARD, SOREN, *Either/Or*, edited and translated Howard V. Hong and Edna H. Hong, 2 vols. (Princeton: Princeton University Press, 1987)

KOTT, JAN, *The Eating of the Gods: An Interpretation of Greek Tragedy*, trans. Boleslaw Taborski and Edward J. Czerwinski (New York: Random House, 1973).

LACAN, JACQUES, *The Ethics of Psychoanalysis 1959–1960*, ed. Jacques Alain-Miller and trans. Dennis Porter (London: Routledge, 1992).

LANGER, SUSANNE K., *Feeling and Form: A Theory of Art* (New York: Charles Scribner's Sons, 1953).

LEECH, CLIFFORD, *Tragedy* (London: Methuen, 1969).

LIEBLER, NAOMI CONN, *Shakespeare's Festive Tragedy: The Ritual Foundations of Genre* (London and New York: Routledge, 1995).

LORAUX, NICOLE, *Tragic Ways of Killing a Woman*, trans. Anthony Forster (Cambridge, Mass.: Harvard University Press, 1987).

LUKÁCS, GEORG, *Soul and Form*, trans. Ann Bostock, (London: Merlin Press, 1974)

MILLER, ARTHUR, *The Theatre Essays of Arthur Miller*, ed. Robert A. Martin (London: Methuen, 1994).

NIEBUHR, REINHOLD, *Beyond Tragedy: Essays on The Christian Interpretation of History* (New York, 1937).

NIETZSCHE, FRIEDRICH, *The Birth of Tragedy*, trans. Francis Golffing (New York: Anchor Doubleday, 1956).

NUTTALL, A. D. *Why Does Tragedy Give Pleasure?* (Oxford: Clarendon Press, 1996).

PAOLUCCI, ANNE and HENRY (eds) *Hegel on Tragedy* (New York and London: Harper Torchbooks, 1975).

POMEROY, SARAH, *Goddesses and Whores, Wives and Slaves: Women in Classical Antiquity*, (New York: Schocken Books, 1975).

RICHARDS, I. A. *Principles of Literary Criticism* (London: Routledge, 1934).

ROBBE-GRILLET, ALAIN, 'Nature, Humanism and Tragedy', *Snapshots and Towards an New Novel*, trans. Barbara Wright, (London: Calder and Boyars, 1965).

SCHOPENHAUER, ARTHUR, *The World as Will and Idea*, trans. J. B. Haldane, 3 vols. (London: Routledge & Kegan Paul, 1983).

SOYINKA, WOLE, *Myth, Literature and the African World* (Cambridge: Cambridge University Press, 1976).

STEINER, GEORGE, *The Death of Tragedy* (London: Faber & Faber, 1961).

STEINER, GEORGE, 'A Note on Absolute Tragedy', *Literature and Theology*, Vol. 4, no. 2, (July, 1990).

Thompson, George, *Aeschylus and Athens: A Study in The Social Origins of Drama*, 4th edition, (London: Lawrence and Wishart, 1980).

TURNER, VICTOR, *The Ritual Process: Structure and Anti-Structure* (Ithaca, NY: Cornell University Press, 1969).

UNAMUNO, MIGUEL, *The Tragic Sense of Life*, trans. J. E. Crawford-Flitch (New York, 1954).

WEIMANN, ROBERT, *Shakespeare and the Popular Tradition in the Theater: Studies in the Social Dimension of Dramatic Form and Function*, ed. Robert Schwartz (Baltimore: Johns Hopkins University Press, 1978).

WEISINGER, HERBERT, *Tragedy and the Paradox of the Unfortunate Fall* (London: Routledge & Kegan Paul, 1953).

WEITZ, MORRIS, 'Tragedy', *The Encyclopedia of Philosophy*, ed. Paul Edwards, 8 vols. (New York and London: Collier Macmillan, 1967).

WILLIAMS, RAYMOND, *Modern Tragedy* (Stanford, Calif.: Stanford University Press, 1966).

Index